Norbert Elias and Figurational Research: Processual Thinking in Sociology

The Sociological Review Monographs

Since 1958, *The Sociological Review* has established a tradition of publishing one or two Monographs a year on issues of general sociological interest. The Monograph is an edited book length collection of research papers which is published and distributed in association with Wiley-Blackwell. We are keen to receive innovative collections of work in sociology and related disciplines with a particular emphasis on exploring empirical materials and theoretical frameworks which are currently under-developed.

If you wish to discuss ideas for a Monograph then please contact the Monographs Editor, Chris Shilling, School of Social Policy, Sociology and Social Research, Cornwallis North East, University of Kent, Canterbury, Kent CT2 7NF, C.Shilling@kent.ac.uk

Our latest Monographs include:

Sociological Routes and Political Roots (edited by Michaela Benson and Rolland Munro)
Nature, Society and Environmental Crisis (edited by Bob Carter and Nickie Charles)
Space Travel & Culture: From Apollo to Space Tourism (edited by David Bell and Martin Parker)
Un/Knowing Bodies (edited by Joanna Latimer and Michael Schillmeier)
Remembering Elites (edited by Mike Savage and Karel Williams)
Market Devices (edited by Michel Callon, Yuval Millo and Fabian Muniesa)
Embodying Sociology: Retrospect, Progress and Prospects (edited by Chris Shilling)
Sports Mega-Events: Social Scientific Analyses of a Global Phenomenon (edited by John Horne and Wolfram Manzenreiter)
Against Automobility (edited by Steffen Böhm, Campbell Jones, Chris Land and Matthew Paterson)
A New Sociology of Work (edited by Lynne Pettinger, Jane Parry, Rebecca Taylor and Miriam Glucksmann)
Contemporary Organization Theory (edited by Campbell Jones and Rolland Munro)
Feminism after Bourdieu (edited by Lisa Adkins and Beverley Skeggs)
After Habermas: New Perspectives on the Public Sphere (edited by Nick Crossley and John Michael Roberts)

Other Monographs have been published on consumption; museums; culture and computing; death; gender and bureaucracy; sport plus many other areas. For further information on Monograph Series, please visit: http://www.wiley.com/WileyCDA/Section/id-324292.html

Norbert Elias and Figurational Research: Processual Thinking in Sociology

edited by Norman Gabriel and Stephen Mennell

Wiley-Blackwell/The Sociological Review

BLACKWELL PUBLISHING
350 Main Street, Malden, MA 02148–5020, USA
9600 Garsington Road, Oxford OX4 2DQ, UK
550 Swanston Street, Carlton, Victoria 3053, Australia

First published in 2011 by Blackwell Publishing Ltd

Library of Congress Cataloging-in-Publication Data

Norbert Elias and figurational research : processual thinking in sociology / edited by Norman Gabriel, Stephen Mennell.
    p. cm. – (Sociological review monographs ; 7)
    Includes bibliographical references and index.
    ISBN 978-1-4443-3957-4 (pbk.)
1. Elias, Norbert, 1897–1990. 2. Sociology–Philosophy. 3. Civilization–Philosophy. I. Gabriel, Norman. II. Mennell, Stephen.
    HM479.E38N655   2011
    301.092–dc23

                                                                2011016264

A catalogue record for this title is available from the British Library

Set by Toppan Best-set Premedia Limited

Printed and bound in the United Kingdom

by Page Brothers, Norwich

The publisher's policy is to use permanent paper from mills that operate a sustainable forestry policy, and which has been manufactured from pulp processed using acid-free and elementary chlorine-free practices. Furthermore, the publisher ensures that the text paper and cover board used have met acceptable environmental accreditation standards.

Contents

Series Editor's Introduction

Chris Shilling

The Sociological Review Monograph Series has for over half a century dedicated itself to the task of commissioning collections of original refereed articles that develop the discipline of sociology and enhance our understanding of the social and material worlds in which we live. It has pursued this project by encouraging established academics, often working with emerging figures within the profession, to engage with the widest range of themes, controversies and problems relevant to our understanding of sociological theory, methodology and research.

These published volumes vary enormously, but have historically constituted a key forum for discussion and debate in the social sciences: it is difficult to think of a topic or a theory that has not been illuminated by a Monograph, or a 'turn' a Monograph has not navigated. In the earlier stages of the Series, industrial societies, Hungarian and Japanese sociologies, mass communication, Latin America, economics and universities all made appearances, while computing, caste and museums were among the issues explored subsequently by these collections. Today, Monographs continue to welcome new perspectives and topics, while renewing our understanding of more established problems: animals, automobiles, genomes, global sport, utopias, Europe, organizations, work and new approaches to social class have all put in recent appearances; the Monographs have also sponsored ambitious attempts to revolutionize the discipline, through Actor Network Theory, for example, or by exploring the possibilities of embodying sociology.

The varied approaches undertaken by sociologists – but also by those anthropologists, economists, historians, feminists, geographers, literary specialists and others enlisted with a concern for *developing* sociology rather than fixing rigidly its disciplinary boundaries – do not lend themselves to easy categorization. Without, I hope, visiting upon them too much in the way of analytical distortion, I suggest that the Monographs in *The Sociological Review* series have drawn variously on three main strategies in pursuing their goals. First, they have engaged anew with both the dominant and the marginal traditions that constitute the sociological heritage, through an interrogation of important, fairly conventional disciplinary topics. Second, they have developed original perspectives – drawing on and reconfiguring themes and developments from elsewhere in the social sciences and humanities, and even from the biological and physical sciences – in attempting to develop and extend the discipline's boundaries in productive new directions. Third, they have defended the founding ambitions of sociology, elaborating upon them in a manner that maintains their strength, relevance and appeal by seeking to reenergize the discipline through the establishment of new methodologies and new ways of conceptualizing human and social existence.

This latest Monograph, *Norbert Elias and Figurational Research: Processual Thinking in Sociology*, demonstrates clearly the importance of *all three* strategies in the current era. First, in coordinating the development and assembly of this collection of original papers, Norman Gabriel and Stephen Mennell highlight how Elias engaged with the legacy of the discipline through an extensive critique of the abstract, neo-Kantian categories that threatened to restrict the scope of sociology, and embarked upon a mission which included among its planned achievements nothing less than the sociological resolution of all philosophical problems through theoretically informed analyses of human relationships. Second, while the figurational research promoted by Elias can no longer be described justifiably as 'new' – his *magnum opus*, *The Civilizing Process*, was published in Switzerland in 1939 – the papers in this Monograph demonstrate that Elias's legacy continues to stimulate a thriving programme of empirical work that introduces previously neglected processual perspectives into the study of a huge range of issues and subjects in the social science, arts and humanities. Third, while Elias's writings possess something of an ambivalent relationship with the major traditions in the sociological heritage, these articles reveal how figurational sociology attempts to provide a unifying framework for the analysis of humanity, society and history that aims to assist humans in achieving increasingly more adequate, or 'reality-congruent', knowledge of those processes that result in wars, conflicts and environmental degradation.

As noted by Stephen Dunne (2009) in a recent article in *The Sociological Review*, 'The Politics of Figurational Sociology', Elias's writings have sparked considerable controversy. His work has proved difficult for those dedicated to philosophical theorizing – that which takes cognitively constructed categories as its starting point rather than human actions – and unpopular to those committed to radical political perspectives predicated upon the absolute elevation of specific social factors over all others. They also continue to be ignored by many within the discipline whose view of the classics stops with the 'holy trinity' of Marx, Weber and Durkheim. The reception of his work has not always been helped, furthermore, by what could be seen as an over-zealous commitment on the part of certain of his advocates to defend an 'authorized interpretation' of his sociological thought over other readings.

Whatever one thinks about the scale of Elias's project and the growing corpus of work that continues to take inspiration from it, however, his robust defence and extension of sociology's ambitions remains timely. C. Wright Mills's

(1959) concerns about the proliferation of 'abstract empiricism' in his *The Sociological Imagination* are as relevant now as they ever were, given the restricted types of research being sponsored and validated in those universities and sociology departments that prioritize the pursuit of government/research council grants at the expense of the development of knowledge. In this context, Elias's analysis of the long-term development of humanity, and the webs of interdependence woven between people, and between individuals and the environments in which they live, stands as a prominent example of the potential of sociology to pursue many of the most important issues of our time rather than capitulating to the short-term political concerns and economic agendas that permeate so much current work.

This collection of papers is not intended to serve as an introduction to Elias's work. Readers in search of such a resource should turn to Stephen Mennell's extensive explication and analysis in his (1998) *Norbert Elias: An Introduction*, or Robert van Krieken's *Norbert Elias* contribution to the Routledge Key Sociologists series, while those interested in Elias's relationship with philosophy may wish to start with Richard Kilminster's *Norbert Elias: Post-Philosophical Sociology*. In this context, and given Norman Gabriel's and Stephen Mennell's concern to begin this collection by focusing on the important issue of the inter-generational transmission of Elias's ideas, it is useful here to outline in the briefest terms for those not yet familiar with his work some of the reasons that Elias has not yet received the recognition that accompanied other classical sociologists of his era, such as Talcott Parsons, and why there is the need for this present monograph.

Elias (1897–1990), a German sociologist, was a refugee from Nazi Germany. Before this, his early career was characterized by an engagement with, and a rejection, of philosophy, an intellectual move to historically oriented sociology, and a brief period of working with Karl Mannheim in Frankfurt. Exile began a lengthy period in which Elias was a largely unknown 'outsider' to the sociological establishment. Much of his work remained unpublished, or unnoticed, and it was only eight years before retirement age that Elias managed to obtain a university post in 1954 (at Leicester, in what became, for a period, one of the most influential sociology departments in England).

The republication of the original German *Über den Prozess der Zivilization* in 1969 did much to enhance his reputation, but while Elias's concern with long-term processes involving state formation and the monopolization of violence, the social division of labour, the development of personality and the search for distinction resonated with many of the discipline's founding themes, his thought was generally out of step with the radicalization, specialization and fragmentation of sociology that gained pace during the 1970s and 1980s, discussed in detail by myself and Philip A. Mellor in *The Sociological Ambition* (Shilling and Mellor, 2001). Elias's synthesizing ambitions were antithetical to the proliferation of '. . . isms' and paradigms during this time, and the scale of his writing only received anything approaching general recognition in the last years of his life. His work continued to be published after his death, and while the first two volumes of his Collected Works were published in 2006, the last of eighteen volumes is scheduled to appear in 2013.

In this context, and despite a proliferation of writings about Elias's work over the past decade, there remains a considerable need to assess and evaluate the legacy and continued relevance of his thought. While the writings of theorists like Bourdieu and Habermas remain more fashionable in contemporary sociology, and have also been the focus of recent Sociological Review Monographs, with those of Giddens and Bauman continuing to exert considerable influence, the articles that follow seek to make the case that future analyses of the canon and heritage of our discipline need to make room for an original thinker whose writings possess the capacity to steer sociological developments for decades to come. I am also particularly pleased that Norman Gabriel and Stephen Mennell agreed to edit this volume. Gabriel's work on processual psychology highlights the relevance of Elias's writings to this subject, while Stephen Mennell has for some years now been an extremely influential figure in introducing Elias's work to the English speaking world and in pushing forward the research agendas of figurational or processual sociology through such groundbreaking publications as his recent *The American Civilizing Process*.

References

Dunne, Stephen, (2009), 'The politics of figurational sociology', *The Sociological Review*, 57,1: 28–57.

Kilminster, Richard, (2007), *Norbert Elias: Post-philosophical Sociology*, London: Routledge.

van Krieken, Robert, (1998), *Norbert Elias*, London: Routledge.

Mennell, Stephen, (1998), *Norbert Elias: An Introduction*, Dublin: UCD Press.

Mennell, Stephen, (2007), *The American Civilizing Process*, Cambridge: Polity Press.

Mills, C. Wright, (1959), *The Sociological Imagination*, London: Oxford University Press.

Shilling, Chris and Philip A. Mellor, (2001), *The Sociological Ambition: Elementary Forms of Social and Moral Life*, London: Sage.

Handing over the torch: intergenerational processes in figurational sociology

Norman Gabriel and Stephen Mennell

Abstract: This collection of essays is designed to show how the various concepts of Norbert Elias's writings fit together in an overall vision for sociology, and how this has come to inspire the wide-ranging and interdisciplinary research tradition of 'figurational' sociology. In this introduction, we focus on a somewhat neglected aspect of Elias's work, the concept of generation. We explore his role as a teacher, passing the torch to a first generation of scholars, mainly in Europe, examining his generosity to younger colleagues as well as some of his well-known foibles. We then trace his influence in the emergence of a second generation that is more far-flung, both internationally and across disciplines.

For over four decades (1935–77) or almost half his life, Norbert Elias lived in Britain and strove to make his presence felt within British sociology, but with extremely limited success. Anecdotal evidence suggests that among his fellow sociologists in the post-war period he was commonly regarded as an eccentric voice or even as a Victorian throwback.[1] Professional sociologists at that time paid much more attention to the views of Talcott Parsons or of positivist philosophers such as Karl Popper, against both of whom Elias railed (2000 [1969], 2009a [1985], 2009b [1974]). At the time, very few people in Britain (or elsewhere) appreciated[2] that Elias was formulating and advocating a fundamental theoretical basis – a theoretical–empirical synthesis – for the social sciences that was quite as comprehensive as, but also in most respects antithetical to, the then-dominant structural functionalism propagated from Harvard. No sociological theorist has since attained the international dominance of the discipline that Parsons did, nor is it likely that anyone else will do so. Yet, in retrospect, it seems likely that the influence of Elias, that voice crying in the wilderness, will long outlast that of Parsons.[3] How could that have happened?

Norbert Elias himself was deeply ambivalent about those who would follow in his own footsteps and about the development of a 'school' of sociology based on processual thinking. A favourite image he used in his writings and conversations was the torch-race,[4] used to convey the intergenerational process in the creation and transmission of knowledge:

> Work in the human sciences, as in other sciences, is a torch race: we take over
> the torch from the preceding generations, carry it a distance further and hand it
> over to the following generation, so that it can go beyond us. (Elias, 2009c [1977]:
> 91)

Although this remark strongly suggests close and mutual co-operation between
each successive generation in passing on the existing stock of knowledge, Elias
identified another related aspect, just as important: the competition between
scientists who 'try to outstrip each other as lonely long-distance runners or as
torch-bearing teams' (2009d [1972]: 97). These participants are so involved in
their immediate efforts to make individual contributions that they are unable
to perceive the interdependent structure of the whole race, the long-term process
in which humanity has attempted to develop models that can be empirically
tested.

Apart from some comments in important texts about the life and work of Elias
(see, for example, van Krieken, 1998: 115–18), very little has been written about
the related aspects of competition and co-operation in the concept of 'generation',
inter-generational processes and the important part they played in the development
of Elias's work. A formative aspect of Elias's own intellectual development can
be traced to his experiences of competition within rival factions in the *Blau–Weiss*
movement,[5] one of the largest Zionist youth organizations in Germany, founded
before the First World War. Hackeschmidt (2004: 67) suggests that a 'strong
generational self-image' in the writings of Blau–Weiss led to 'painful conflicts'
with the previous generation of Zionists in the movement, who resented the new
emphasis on *bündisch* autonomy, a distinctive style associated with the goal of
establishing a Jewish nation-state based on the cultural values of the Italian
Renaissance. He argues that the 'handing on the torch' image conveyed the
central ethos of the *Blau–Weiss* movement: a deep commitment to the generational
process of promoting a Jewish national culture:

> These new teachings, which created distance and promised clear insights into deeper
> social-political interconnections and cultural historical mechanisms, served the major-
> ity of the young Blau–Weiss leaders in the 1920s as a protective mechanism and as a
> new style of thinking. (Hackeschmidt, 2004: 73)

As one of the leaders of the Breslau *Blau–Weiss*, Norbert Elias was involved in
the deep ideological divisions with the Frankfurt section of the *Blau–Weiss*[6]
movement about Jewish identity and the formation of a new Jewish culture.
Hackeschmidt argues that the development of themes within the *Blau–Weiss*
movement would later influence Elias's own views in several essays, including:
'The kitsch style and the age of kitsch' (2006b [1935]: 85–96), where Goethe and
Mozart are represented as men 'guided by the accustomed good taste'; *The
Germans* (1996 [1989]: 38–43, 251–67), in which he considers generational
conflict; and *The Established and the Outsiders* (2008 [1965]), a reflection of his
experiences as an 'outsider' with the more dominant East European Socialist-
Zionist movements. However, Hackeschmidt neglects to mention something
even more important in Elias's intellectual development – the significant influence

that these personal experiences of competitive ideological positions later had on his views about 'involvement and detachment' (Elias, 2007a [1987]). Kilminster (2007) argues that Elias's active participation in *Blau–Weiss* until its dissolution in 1926 played a role in shaping his rejection of the neo-Kantianism of the assimilated Jewish philosophers of the earlier generation and his strong commitment to establishing sociology in relation to rival academic disciplines, especially philosophy.

A good starting point to explain the formation of generational conflict are the comments made by Elias in *The Germans*. Although each younger generation strives for meaning and personal fulfilment, opportunities for power can widen or narrow, depending on particular historical periods:

> The narrowing and widening of life chances, and opportunities for meaning in general and career chances in particular, for the younger generations of a society at any one time are processes that undoubtedly most strongly affect the balance of power between the generations. One could say that these processes form the kernel of social conflict between the generations. (Elias, 1996 [1989]: 243–44)

These balances of power also play a significant role in the conflicts between older and younger generations at universities. Scientific establishments are collectively able to exercise monopolistic control over the production of scientific knowledge, excluding 'outsiders' from vital resources: locked together in a changing figuration of established–outsider relationships, scientists compete with one another over resources needed by others:

> In many cases they combine this activity with that of administering a fund of knowledge handed on to them, in their particular field, from previous generations, and with controlling the transmission of that fund (and whatever advances they themselves have contributed) to the following generations. (Elias, 2009e [1972]: 138)

This transmission of knowledge, from one generation to another, is also dependent on the distinctive aspects of human knowledge, a nexus of human-made symbols that act as a means of communication and orientation. In *The Symbol Theory*, Elias wanted to move beyond the highly individualised conception of the knowing subject which stems from traditional philosophical dualisms based upon subjective, objective distinctions. Rather than try to locate knowledge within the head of a person, he suggested that we should instead examine the communal growth processes that enabled our ancestors to survive and live with one another. We will now turn to how the formation of symbols over many generations has given human beings a 'survival' advantage over other species.

Symbols in intergenerational processes

In the very long evolutionary timescale of the human species, individual members of generations of humans have been 'able to orientate themselves and to steer their conduct not merely in the light of experiences and reflections accumulated within the short span of their own lives, but also with the help of symbols that embody experiences and reflections of a long line of ancestors' (Elias, 2009e [1972]: 139). 'Time' is a good example of a symbol that has been learnt and passed on from one generation to another: it allows human beings to connect and integrate events or different time periods in a high level of synthesis (Elias, 2007b [1992]). A key aspect of this long, intergenerational process of learning is memory. In several places in his book on time, he mentions how human beings are able to orientate themselves by connecting 'specific memory images, a particular meaning, with the perceptible form' (2007b [1992]: 13). The moon, for example, is a constantly changing form in the sky – Elias asks how our ancestors could achieve an integrating concept that would synthesize the different shapes in the sky? His answer is that, 'It could only have resulted from a long process of learning, of the growth of people's stock of experiences, some of which recurred again and again and, over the generations, were *remembered* as recurring (Elias, 2007b [1992]: 55).

The importance of memory similarly occurs in *The Symbol Theory* where (Elias, 2011 [1991]) addresses the problem of understanding the conceptual development of language by tracing the connections between thinking and speaking. In language communication, one of the functions of the term 'thinking' is to refer to the capacity of human beings to put through their paces symbols anticipating a sequence of possible future actions without their performance in reality. At this level, thought is not easily recognizable as a flow of voicelessly produced sound symbols, an abbreviated version of the audible use of language that can be converted into spoken language. These forms of abbreviated thinking are associated with the manipulation of stored memory images: according to him, these do not have to be set out step by step, but can be telescoped, recalled and used when occasion demands.

However, the recognition of these important intergenerational processes of concept formation are blocked by the human self-image of *homo clausus*. The individual seems like a 'completely self-reliant adult, forming no relationships and standing quite alone' (Elias, 1978 [1970]: 118). In his postscript to *The Civilizing Process* he writes

> The conception of the individual as *homo clausus*, a little world in himself who ulti-mately exists quite independently of the great world outside, determines the image of human beings in general. Every other human being is likewise seen as a *homo clausus*; his core, his being, his true self appears likewise as something divided within him by an invisible wall from everything outside, including every other human being. (Elias, 2000 [1969]: 472)

Because people see themselves as isolated individuals independent from others, they find it difficult to see their interdependence:

> Today it is still somewhat difficult to convey the depth of the dependence of people on each other. That the meaning of everything a person does lies in what she or he means to others, not only to those now alive but also to coming generations, that he

or she is dependent on the continuation of human society through generations, is certainly one of the most fundamental of human mutual dependences, those of future on past, of past on future, human beings. (Elias, 2010a [1985]: 28)

Teaching and learning – the first generation in Britain

We can begin to have an understanding of Elias's own role in passing on the baton to the new generations, 'as torch-bearers running a relay, who finally pass on to others the torch they have carried forward' (Elias, 2010a [1985]: 29), by looking at some of his own comments in autobiographical essays and in some of his essays recently published in the Collected Works.[7] There are also important remarks made by the first generation of Eliasian scholars who were taught by Elias, sociologists who knew Elias, or closely worked with him on some of his publications:

> For reasons unknown to me I very early on had the feeling of being a part of a chain of generations: I do my bit, take a few steps forward, in a chain of generations. That is what I can do: I have this gift and therefore the duty to make good use of it. I still feel the same today. I see something and have to put it down on paper as well as I can . . . How it goes on from there is a matter for later generations. (Elias, 1994: 38)[8]

Significantly, in his essay 'Fear of Death' (Elias, 2008 [1990]) – described by editors Kilminster and Mennell as an 'unusually personal document' (Elias, 2008 [1990]: xx) – Elias argues that the chain of generations has been 'broken'[9] by the growth of individualism, individual searches for meaning that can have a 'strange form of forgetfulness', because they encourage us to treat personal achievements as if they were not dependent on others, but existed in isolation. At the very end of the essay, Elias again refers, in very similar terms, to the fact that doing his bit as a scholar gives him fulfilment and satisfaction, 'only if it is continued critically by the following generations' (2008 [1990]: 264–5).

As he hoped, Elias's role as a teacher inspired a younger generation of sociologists. The following remarks by Miriam Glucksmann, who had known Elias since she was a child, are revealing:

> He engaged with their work, encouraged them, supported them in new or unfashionable avenues of research, and inspired many with a confidence they were otherwise lacking. Curiously, his conviction in the value of his own work was combined with a generosity towards the less worked out ideas of young scholars. (1999: 58–9)

Such generosity towards younger colleagues is evident in Eric Dunning's remarks in the preface to the new edition of *Quest for Excitement* (Elias and Dunning, 2008 [1986]), where he remembers how Elias supervised him in his MA dissertation on football (Elias and Dunning would later establish the sociology of sport as an important area for sociological research). Not only did Elias loan him the money for a new overcoat to conduct his fieldwork at Eton, but he would only allow him to submit his thesis after he had written five drafts: 'He went through

9

them meticulously word by word, as well as making numerous broader suggestions' (Dunning, in Elias and Dunning, 2008 [1986]: xii).

But Elias was equally able to attune to others in conversations. Stephen
Mennell (2006: 75) comments that with 'his usual perspicacity in interpersonal
relations', Elias soon picked up on his 'admiring ambivalence'. According to
(Waldhoff, 2007: 504), Elias had been sensitized to the reactions of his audience
and to the psychological significance of short silences. Before his death, he
mentioned the fruitfulness of his Group Analytic experiences for his scientific
seminars and lectures. Brown (1987: 538) makes similar claims about the
influence of group psychotherapy, commenting on his skills as an interviewer
and listener and a 'highly experienced and highly effective teacher of adult
students'.

Working with Norbert Elias – foibles and frustrations

So far, we have mentioned how Elias could be not only an inspirational teacher
but also a great supporter of colleagues in newly emerging areas of sociological
research. But he could equally be his own worst enemy, delaying the dissemination
and reception of his ideas, especially in his repeated obstructions of attempts to
publish an English translation of *The Civilizing Process* – the motivation of
which is unclear, but probably a matter of deep psychology. In a very frank and
personal review of the difficulties in working with Elias, Mennell (2006) recalls
how in 1981 he offered to shorten the very long draft of an intended introduction
to the second volume of *The Civilizing Process*, but Elias rejected the shortened
version. The reasons for Elias not being able to use it are recounted in the
following letter he wrote to Mennell, which reveal a great deal about his attitudes
to his own work and academic 'counter-ego':

> I was most grateful for the effort you have made to produce a shorter version of my
> introduction to Volume II and it reads much better than any introduction I can hope
> to produce on my own, but there are a number of things you have not included in
> your version of the introduction which my inescapable conscience tells me ought to
> be included. I have made a last ditch effort to find a compromise between your advice
> (which one part of myself knows is good advice) and my conscience (which has been
> a loyal advisor for 84 years or so). But that effort has been cut short by a very stern
> letter from David Martin [the then managing director of Blackwells, saying] . . . he
> will have to go ahead sans introduction if the MS is not forthcoming immediately.
> (Mennell, 2006: 84)

The second volume appeared without any introduction in 1982 – disastrously
four years after the first, the delay being substantially caused by Elias's work
on the abortive new introduction, which would have related the account of state
formation processes in medieval and early modern Europe to the entire
development of human society from the first cities in Mesopotamia. Cas Wouters
similarly recounts how, although Elias had treated him 'in a generous way' by
translating into English his article 'Has the civilizing process changed direction'

(1976), he had been completely taken by surprise when, after the publication of *Quest for Excitement* in 1986, Elias insisted that when using the striking expression 'an enjoyable and controlled decontrolling of emotions', Wouters should attribute it to him. Wouters pointed out that although Elias had first used the phrase in earlier publications, he had restricted its use and meaning to indicate an important function of sports and leisure. Wouters was beginning to use it much more extensively to refer to processes of informalization in society (Wouters, 2007: 231). Wouters stood his ground, arguing that Elias ought to have written a note acknowledging that he had fruitfully been using and developing this concept for many years. Elias said he would write this note, but it never appeared. Two years after Elias's death, Wouters was informed that such a note had indeed been written, but the draft in which it had been inserted had never been published.

But these difficulties were not just over translations and intellectual property. Goodwin and O'Connor (2006) explain some of the problems with Elias's leadership of the 'Young Worker Project', for which in 1962 he had been awarded what was by the standards of the time a large research grant by the UK Department of Scientific and Industrial Research (DSIR), a precursor of today's ESRC. In the grant application, the Principal Investigators were listed as Elias himself together with Dr (later Professor) Ilya Neustadt and Mrs S. Williams (later better known as Professor Sheila Allen). As 'Investigators' were listed Percy Cohen, Richard Brown and Anthony Giddens. But, at the time, Leicester was the biggest and, with the LSE, the leading department of sociology in Britain, and this was intended to be a collective departmental research project. So the next rung down in the project team included quite a large number of other and younger 'research officers', some of whom later became prominent sociologists and some of whom frankly had their careers impeded by their involvement in a failed project.

The central hypothesis was Elias's. Hitherto, the selection of occupation by school leavers had tended to be viewed as a matter of what would now be called 'rational choice'. Elias hypothesized rather that the transition from school to work was a 'shock' and psychologically traumatic. Misunderstandings over the direction of the research became an ongoing problem – hardly surprising in view of the fact that in the crucial period (1962–64) Elias went off to Africa as Professor of Sociology at the University of Ghana. Elias's suggestion that the researchers lacked even a basic understanding of what the research was about led the researchers to perceive that he had no real confidence in them or their ability. These disagreements led to the failure of the project and to the acrimonious break-up of the research team. It also led to the research being largely forgotten within British sociology until it was resurrected in the early 2000s by Goodwin and O'Connor.[10]

There were three main areas of disagreement between Elias and the research team. First there was an ongoing argument over the researchers' right to publish. Despite the research officers' eagerness to publish the results from the research, the research team felt that Elias had vetoed the publication of an article they had written, and Elias instructed that there should be no publications or interim reports based on the data. A second area for disagreement, and perhaps the main area of complication, was an ongoing argument between Elias and the research officers about the theoretical framework and the composition of the sample. From the outset of the research, Elias was keen to capture their initial work experiences, as he felt that the young people's experiences prior to work would not prepare them for employment. However, according to Elias, the research officers had interpreted the early discussions to mean that this research was to be a study of 'work' *per se*. Elias argued the study should not be about work but instead the 'work situation', as many of the problems faced by young people rarely sprang from work in isolation from other situations.

Third, the researchers and Elias also disagreed about the broader methodological debates representing a collision of two different traditions. The junior researchers came from the British tradition of empirical sociology with its emphasis on survey research, and were recruited for having previously worked on other large-scale quantitative research projects elsewhere. Elias came from a sociological tradition that was profoundly at odds with the abstract empiricism that was characteristic of social scientific research in Britain and America at that time. For Elias the value of the study did not ultimately reside in the ability to produce statistically significant quantitative results, but in the ability to explore the transition to work as the young people themselves experienced and accounted for it.

It is hard to say how far the failure of the Young Workers project was to blame, but certainly there was resentment at Elias among the diaspora of former Leicester sociologists who spread out through the rapidly proliferating departments of sociology established in British universities in the 1960s. The project itself was probably only one element within the wider theoretical, methodological and even epistemological quarrels that started early in Leicester and were eventually to engulf British sociology in the 'war of the schools' in the 1970s. Nevertheless, it has to be remembered that Elias also gained a devoted following among many former Leicester students and some former colleagues. It can be argued that he had a hidden influence within British academia through such distinguished scholars as the sociologist of religion Bryan Wilson and the ancient historian Keith Hopkins. In their work, Elias is rarely cited, but their mode of thought clearly resembles his – see, for instance, Wilson (1982) and Hopkins (1978, 1983). Much more visible an instance of Elias's influence is Eric Dunning, who arrived in Leicester as an undergraduate intending to read economics, but switched to sociology almost immediately, so impressed was he with Elias's introductory lecture course, and went on to collaborate with Elias, to all intents and purposes effectively establishing the field of the sociology of sport. Other students of Elias who then became Dunning's collaborators include Ivan Waddington, Patrick Murphy and Ken Sheard, while Richard Kilminster became the pre-eminent exponent of Elias's theory of knowledge and champion of his dismissive attitude to philosophy and philosophoidal sociology (1998, 2007, and his contribution to this monograph below). Stephen Mennell is unusual among the 'first generation', as he recounts (2006), in never having been Elias's student and in encountering his work through what can only be described as an accident.

The first generation internationally

In any case, this is to present a somewhat parochially British picture. The growth of an 'Eliasian', 'figurational' or 'process-sociological' research tradition cannot be understood without reference to the reception of his work in continental Europe. The key figure – much more important than any British sociologist – in the recognition of Elias's significance is Johan Goudsblom. As a first-year undergraduate reading social psychology at the University of Amsterdam in 1950, Goudsblom found a copy of the first edition of *Über den Prozess der Zivilization* in the university library, and immediately recognized its importance. He finally met Elias in person at the 1956 ISA World Congress in Amsterdam, and was in continuous contact with Elias thereafter. Goudsblom's book *Sociology in the Balance* (1977b), although not at all an explicit exposition of Elias's work, remains the most brilliant critique of conventional sociology from a 'figurational' point of view; unfortunately it was shoddily produced by Blackwells and did not receive the attention it deserved among English-speaking sociologists.

Goudsblom, however, has been a major figure in Dutch intellectual life at large and – even if his many Dutch books have been more influential than the few translated into English – his creation of the so-called 'Amsterdam School' of sociology was perhaps his greatest achievement. Appointed Professor at the University of Amsterdam in 1968, he invited Elias there as Visiting Professor for several periods starting in 1969.[11] Cometh the hour, cometh the man. Dutch society was undergoing a period of rapid change. Amsterdam became famous for its white bicycles and militant students. Elias fitted in.[12] There are memories of him sitting on the floor taking part in a student-organized seminar on 'Liberation: personal and political'. This helped Goudsblom to gather around him an impressive group of like-minded colleagues and a generation of doctoral students. Goudsblom's doctoral *promovendi* are too numerous to catalogue here, but they include (with examples of their publications in English): Maarten van Bottenburg (2001), Christien Brinkgreve, Jan-Willem Gerritsen (2000), Johan Heilbron (1995),[13] Paul Kapteyn (1996), Bram Kempers (1992), Giselinde Kuipers (2006), Ruud Stokvis, Wilbert van Vree (1999), Nico Wilterdink (1990), and Cas Wouters (2004, 2007). The list also includes Stephen Mennell – in whose career this is another quirk to place alongside that of never having been Elias's student. Although a distinctive 'Amsterdam School' was eclipsed after the retirement of Goudsblom in 1998 and Abram de Swaan in 2007, its influence diffused widely. The British 'Eliasians' such as Dunning, Kilminster and Mennell were in close touch with the Dutch group from the 1970s onwards, and received from them great sustenance in taking up what was (is?) still an unorthodox standpoint among sociologists at large. In January 1980 at Balliol College, Oxford, Mennell and Dunning organized a meeting of the BSA Theory Group devoted to Elias's ideas. It attracted more than a hundred participants from Britain, the Netherlands, Germany and several other countries. It also prompted the unannounced arrival of Tony Giddens and a consequent unscheduled but illuminating debate between him and Elias. It was at this conference that the various national groups really coalesced into something like a European research network.

Meanwhile, Elias had belatedly become an intellectual celebrity in his home country, Germany, following the republication of *Über den Prozess der Zivilization* and the first publication of (a revised and expanded version of) his pre-war Frankfurt *Habilitationsschrift, Die höfische Gesellschaft*, both in 1969.[14] Professors Peter Gleichmann (Hanover) and Hermann Korte (Bochum, later Hamburg), among others, championed his work there and, with Goudsblom, edited a Festschrift – with contributions from many countries – for Elias to mark his eightieth birthday in 1977.

In France too, where translations of *Über den Prozess der Zivilization* and *Die höfische Gesellschaft* appeared almost a decade before the English editions, his work was taken up by prominent scholars – including Pierre Bourdieu and the distinguished historians Emmanuel Le Roy Ladurie (for a time) and Roger Chartier.[15] France illustrates a characteristic of the reception of Elias that can be observed in other countries too: that the appeal of his work is by no means confined to the discipline of sociology. Besides the historians and sociologists, it has been championed by the political scientist Bernard Lacroix and his group at Nanterre. The French anthropological association held a conference in Metz in 2000 (Chevalier and Privat, 2004). The general British anthropological scepticism about Elias was represented on that occasion – as on many others – by Sir Jack Goody, who had met Elias in Ghana in the early 1960s,[16] but others were more sympathetic. Indeed Elias's interdisciplinary appeal had been evident elsewhere from the start. In the Netherlands, key friends of Elias and allies of Goudsblom included the political scientist Godfried van Benthem van den Bergh, Abram de Swaan who was originally a political scientist but became also both a sociologist and a psychoanalyst, and the anthropologist Anton Blok.[17] Stephen Mennell has indeed suggested that the appeal of Elias's work is strongest not within the heartland of conventional sociology but among scholars working in the interstices of history, the various social science disciplines, and the humanities.[18] This is apparent in the 'second generation' of those working under his influence, and it is reflected in the papers within this monograph.

The second generation

The 'second generation' may be defined as those who did not know or work with Elias himself, but came under his influence either through being students of the 'first generation', or simply by reading his work.[19] The latter route is much more common among the second generation than it was for the first. Members of the second generation, it is sometimes joked, are outsiders, at a power disadvantage *vis-à-vis* the first-generation establishment, because in disputes with them they cannot play the unanswerable card: 'Oh, well, I remember that Norbert said to me . . .'. On the other hand, as Korte (1994 [1974]: 174) pointed out, after Elias's death those who employed his ideas no longer ran the risk of being publicly corrected by their author.

Two general characteristics of professional sociology in the period marked by the rise of the second generation need to be mentioned.

First, although Elias aspired to formulate a 'central theory' (not a 'general theory' as Parsons termed his own conceptual Meccano set) for the social sciences, there is little sign of there any longer being any demand from most professional sociologists for any such thing. That was shown by the reaction to Quilley and Loyal's long essay (2005) making the case for Elias's sociology having precisely such a status in the orientation of the social sciences. In stark contrast to the Parsons era, American sociologists seem by and large to have given up any pretension to theoretical leadership in the discipline, and to be far gone in short-term empiricism. (Probe their unconscious, though, and one will often find a vestigial Parsonianism.) Both there and in Britain – maybe elsewhere too – 'theory' seems to have become a speciality in its own right, an autonomous sub-discipline, on a par with all the other specialisms. 'Theorists' form a sort of prestigious elite; among sociologists they are the members of the House of Lords, figuratively speaking (or, in the case of Tony Giddens, literally speaking). But their philosophoidal theory often plays little or no part in steering (nor is it tested and amended by) empirical sociological research. This abdication is indeed signalled by the fact that it is now often referred to as 'social theory' rather than 'sociological theory' (see Mouzelis, 1991), a terminological shift that precisely denotes the philosophoidal turn. This is all uncongenial to Elias and Eliasians.

Equally uncongenial is the second and related general characteristic. During recent decades, the discipline of sociology seems to have lost its recognizable intellectual common core, and fragmented into numerous areas of empirical specialization. One symptom is that many sociologists make their professional careers within other university departments – criminology, education, politics, business and management, medical schools – rather than in departments of sociology *per se*. People working in distinct empirical areas, even if it is within a sociology department, sometimes seem to have little to say to each other. Again this runs counter to the thrust of the thinking of Elias and his followers. Their interests, like his, always spread far beyond sociology as it was institutionalized in universities, even in the days when it did seem to have some common core. They have, for instance, maintained a keen interest in world history and indeed in the way the biological evolution and social development of human beings intertwined with each other – an interweaving that still seems not quite to have been grasped by palaeoanthropologists, but which is beautifully demonstrated in Goudsblom's *Fire and Civilization* (1992).

The fragmentation of sociology is unconsciously mirrored in sociologists' overuse of the word 'analysis', which means breaking something up into its component parts. Elias always stressed that the main intellectual tasks of the social scientist involve not analysis but *synthesis* – making connections, seeing how things hang together. His synthesis connects all the main elements of social scientific interest: power relations, the formation of habitus, of conscience and consciousness, self-identity and we-identity, knowledge both scientific and ideological, and concept formation – and all within the context of a *processual*, long-term developmental perspective that bypasses the old and sterile static conceptual polarities that so often waste sociologists' time (and *always* waste the time of philosophers).

These characteristics are evident in the work of what we have labelled the 'second generation', and we have attempted to compile contributions to the monograph that are reasonably representative of current thinking and research within what is loosely called the 'figurational research network'.[20] Because it shows the long-term perspective that is typical of the figurational approach, we have placed first Robert van Krieken's 2010 inaugural lecture at University College Dublin (revised for this monograph); it also flags the circumstance of the approach having accidentally established something of a base in Ireland. Next, to demonstrate the global scope of figurational or 'process' theory,[21] comes an essay by Andrew Linklater showing its relevance to the study of International Relations. Linklater is not the first scholar to apply Elias's ideas to International Relations. That honour belongs to Godfried van Benthem van den Bergh, who in the 1970s and 1980s wrote extensively about war, violence, the dynamics of the Cold War, and nuclear deterrence (1992), but Linklater is, in the course of his vast study of the problem of harm in world politics, making evident the very extensive scope and relevance of these ideas. Equally vast in its implications is Stephen Quilley's essay on – no less – the future of the planet, taking up Johan Goudsblom's (De Vries and Goudsblom, 2002) contextualizing of contemporary concerns with climate change and environmental degradation within the 'expanding anthroposphere' – the ever-growing domain of the human-made within the biosphere.

Richard Kilminster's contribution concerns the most fundamental theoretical bases of figurational sociology. Conventionally, one might say that Kilminster is concerned with the 'philosophical' foundations, were it not that his message is that we should forget philosophy and its claims to establish our foundations for us. Next comes what is perhaps the most surprising contribution to the monograph, by Nina Baur and Stefanie Ernst on processually-oriented research methods. At a time when many sociologists seem obsessed with their sophisticated research methods – perhaps by way of compensation for having abandoned anything much in the way of theoretical ideas – figurational sociologists have a reputation for being bored by methodological discussions. But Baur and Ernst, who are also advocates of the currently fashionable idea of 'mixed methods', show how that quintessentially Eliasian ingredient, *time*, needs to inform not just theory but also empirical research methods.

The final group of papers explores themes that were foreshadowed in Elias's own work. Cas Wouters has over four decades pursued the question that was first posed in the early 1970s after the republication of *Über den Prozess der Zivilization*: whether the less rigid and more permissive standards governing behaviour, feeling and emotion, especially since the 1960s, represent a *reversal* of the main trend of the European civilizing process traced by Elias. In his many books and essays, Wouters has steadily developed his empirically richly founded theory of 'informalization'. Roughly speaking, his answer is that the trend has *not* gone into reverse overall, and that the new, apparently less rigid standards actually require a *more* demanding standard of habitual self-constraint.

Katie Liston's paper broadly surveys the advance of figurational thinking and research in the sociology of sport, the now vast field that Elias and Dunning substantially founded. Steven Loyal applies the established–outsiders theory to the study of migration and ethnicity. He makes special reference to Ireland, a country that was for well over a century after the famine of the 1840s a country of heavy net emigration. Its encounter with newcomers from many parts of the world during the years of the 'Celtic Tiger' was thus more dramatic than in many other countries. Since the tiger was recently found lying on its back, stiff, silent, and with its legs in the air, the story may have many further instalments.

The papers by Norman Gabriel, John Pratt and Wilbert van Vree each show the appeal of figurational ideas at the interfaces between the social sciences.

In Gabriel's case, it is developmental psychology. No surprise there, because Elias always followed developments in psychology – indeed he taught psychology as well as sociology – and he was one of the founders with S. H. Foulkes of the Group Analysis school of psychotherapy. There has indeed been a great upsurge of interest in Elias among Group Analysts (see Dalal, 1998; Lavie, 2005). And in the final months of his life Elias was struggling to finish a long essay in which he evaluated Freud from a figurational point of view; these late typescripts have just been edited with sensational skill by Marc Joly (Elias, 2010b) and they do elucidate one of the unanswered questions that has often been raised: Elias's precise relationship with Freudian psychoanalysis.

John Pratt's essay on trends in penology in contemporary society is one sign of how central Elias's ideas have become in criminology, especially historical criminology, notably under the leadership of David Garland (for example 1990, 2001). Other criminologists in whose work Elias's influence can be detected include Tim Newburn, Manuel Eisner, Ian O'Donnell and Barry Vaughan.

Finally, although Wilbert van Vree does not himself work in a business school, his brilliant research on the origins and development of the modern 'meetings regime' is suggestive of how Elias's ideas have been applied in management and the study of organizations. His book on meetings (1999) has an affinity with the research by Willem Mastenbroek (1999) on the development of techniques of negotiation from historically often violent beginnings. In the field of management, others touched by Elias include Ralph Stacey, who makes Elias central to his unconventional course at the University of Hertfordshire, and Sue Dopson at Oxford.

The contributors to this monograph, it will be observed, come from the heartlands of figurational sociology: the Netherlands, Germany, Britain and (latterly) Ireland, with one outlier from New Zealand. But so-called figurational sociology has spread much more widely than that implies, and we regret that we have not been able to include contributions from Latin America – where it is now especially prosperous – Spain, Italy, Japan, Turkey, and elsewhere. Curiously, in spite of Stephen Mennell's attempt (2007) to demonstrate the relevance of the theory of civilizing processes to the history, development and contemporary character of the USA, America remains relatively barren ground for figurational ideas. Alan Sica, in an email to Chris Rojek, wittily summed up why:

> The reason Americans don't take to Elias is that he writes about European historical and cultural change and American sociologists don't feel comfortable with that sort of thing, except for [Jack] Goldstone and that small lot; and because he is theoretically very adventurous and synthetic, and they don't go for that; and because he trashed Parsons, who many of them liked back in the day; and because he could be mistaken for a closet Freudian, which they don't like; and because he brings up really obnoxious qualities of humankind, which they particularly don't like; and because he wrote a helluva lot of stuff, which takes a long time to read, they don't have time; and because 'figuration' is a word that has a distinctly effete connotations in this country, and sounds like art history . . .

Conclusion

Norbert Elias always declared that he did not want to found a 'school' of sociology. One good reason must have been that he sensed what Randall Collins (1998) was subsequently to demonstrate with massive evidence, that such schools typically last only a very few intellectual generations. In any case, he always saw his own work – even the central theory of civilizing processes – as only a beginning, something that would be revised, possibly even refuted, through future research. He did not command that 'Thou shalt have no other gods before me', even if figurational sociologists are sometimes accused of monotheism. He and Michel Foucault admired each other's work. The same was true, but more emphatically, with Elias and Pierre Bourdieu. This is shown in the use that figurational sociologists also make of those two authors. It may be argued that the sterile influence of structuralism lingered unhelpfully in both, but on the other hand Bourdieu's explicit anti-Kantianism very clearly puts him in the same camp as Elias in the struggle to emancipate the social sciences from the Western European philosophical mainstream.

What Elias wanted, rather, was for his *processual* way of thinking to become firmly entrenched, and for the central and vastly important questions with which he was preoccupied to return to their place among the central concerns of sociology. And not just sociology. Perhaps sociology is now too narrow a term to encompass what Elias was about; as it has become institutionalized in universities, many of us perceive that large tracts of it are now intellectually impoverished, characterized by an amnesia regarding its founding ambitions and by a damaging obsession with the pursuit of short-term 'impact' metrics and governmental approval (see Shilling and Mellor, 2001). If a new word, more encompassing than 'sociology', has to be invented to signify the theoretical–empirical study of the broadest questions of human co-existence, then so be it. We hope that, if only through the intellectual interconnections evident between the papers in this monograph, there may be apparent something of the scope of Elias's vision that so inspires some of us.

Notes

1 One Professor of Sociology, now deceased, described Elias to Stephen Mennell in the 1970s as 'an old bore'.

2 Quite understandably: after *Über den Prozess der Zivilization* in 1939, Elias published very little in either English or German until after his retirement from Leicester in 1962, and the flood of publications in English did not really get under way until the second half of the 1970s. For details of the very limited early reception of his work, see Goudsblom (1977a).

3 For a comparison of Parsons and Elias, see Mennell (1989).

4 This frequently occurring image in Elias's writings on knowledge and the sciences was derived from Plato, *Republic*, I, 328a, 'Passing the torch from hand to hand'. It refers to the custom at festivals in ancient Greece of runners handing lighted torches on to others in relays. Elias used the original quotation in 1921 in his first major published article, 'On seeing in nature' (Elias, 2006a [1921]: 21).

5 The name, 'Blue–White', was an allusion to the colours of a Jewish *Tallit* or prayer shawl, later represented in the flag of Israel. The organization was, to a certain extent, 'aping' (Elias's word) the *farbentragende Burschenschaften* – the 'colour wearing' student fraternities from which Jews were excluded.

6 The Frankfurt group were centred around Erich Fromm, Ernst Simon and Leo Löwenthal and were also associated with the 'circle around Rabbi Nobel': 'This man was a rabbi, originally from Hungary, who had also studied philosophy. He knew Hermann Cohen and represented a curious mixture of mystical religiosity, philosophical rigour, and quite likely also a more or less repressed homosexual love for young men. It really was a kind of "cult of community".' (Löwenthal, 1987: 21).

7 The Collected Works of Norbert Elias, containing many writings not hitherto available in English, are being published by University College Dublin Press, Dublin. Although some essays are included in other volumes, the bulk of them can be found in three volumes: Vol. 14, *Essays I: On the Sociology of Knowledge and the Sciences* (2009); Vol. 15, *Essays II: On Civilising Processes, State Formation and National Identity* (2008); Vol. 16, *Essays III: On Sociology and the Humanities* (2009). Specific essays to which we refer are listed in the references at the end of this introduction.

8 Some of those who worked with Elias have, however, joked among themselves that Elias often seemed very reluctant to let go of the torch.

9 This idea of the chain of generations being broken also occurs in *The Loneliness of the Dying*: 'When the chain of remembrance is broken, when the continuity of a particular society or of human society itself is ended, then the meaning of everything that its people have done throughout millennia, and of all that has ever seemed significant to them, is also extinguished' (Elias, 2010a [1985]: 28).

10 The questionnaires had been carefully preserved by Professor David Ashton; a partial report of the study appeared in Ashton and Field (1976).

19

11 See his interview with Elias conducted that year – Elias (1970).

12 Or maybe there had already been something about Dutch intellectual life that was receptive to Elias; Goudsblom (1977a) records that the original 1939 edition of *Über den Prozess der Zivilization* was favourably and prominently reviewed there immediately before the German invasion.

13 The Dutch title of Heilbron's thesis was *Het ontstaan van de sociologie* (Amsterdam: Prometheus, 1990) – 'the rise of *sociology*'. When it was translated into English, Polity Press exercised their contractual right to change the title to *The Rise of Social Theory*, which made total nonsense of Heilbron's study, which focused on the emancipation of *sociology* from philosophy in mid nineteenth-century France. See our remarks about the weasel-word term 'social theory' on p. 15. The moral of this story is that authors should always delete offensive clauses from publishers' contracts, and refuse to sign them unless the publisher agrees to that.

14 See Mennell's Note on the text, in Elias (2006c [1969]: xi–xv).

15 See Chartier's (2010) account of how a chance meeting with Elias at a conference at Wolfenbüttel led willy-nilly to him becoming possibly Elias's most consistent champion in France. Though an historian, Chartier – who was also close to Bourdieu – has written introductions to the French editions of even some of Elias's seemingly most purely sociological books.

16 See Goody (2006), and Liston and Mennell (2009).

17 Blok, however, later distanced himself from Elias's theories; see Mennell (1992: 89–90, 228–34).

18 Stephen Mennell, remarks in panel discussion chaired by Chris Rojek, at a conference on 'Elias in the Twenty-First Century', University of Leicester, 10–12 April 2006.

19 The boundary between the first and second generations can be a little blurred; for instance, in the partial list of Goudsblom's *promovendi* given above, all except Giselinde Kuipers also knew Elias personally – even though they perhaps (as Stephen Mennell [2006] admits) learned more about the significance of his ideas from Goudsblom than they did directly from Elias.

20 See http://www.norberteliasfoundation.nl/network/index.php.

21 In the 1980s, Norbert Elias came to prefer the term 'process-sociology' to 'figurational sociology', though his preference has not prevailed. It is not entirely clear whether 'figurational sociology' was first used by Elias's Dutch followers or by their Dutch opponents. What must be emphasized, though, is that 'figuration' is not a load-bearing structure in the Eliasian conceptual framework: it is not such a central concept as outside observers often assume.

References

Dates given in square brackets are those of first publication.

Ashton, David N. and David Field, (1976), *Young Workers*, London: Hutchinson.

van Benthem van den Bergh, Godfried, (1992), *The Nuclear Revolution and the End of the Cold War: Forced Restraint*, Basingstoke: Macmillan.

van Bottenburg, Maarten, (2001), *Global Games*, Champaign, IL: University of Illinois Press.

Brown, Richard, (1987), 'Norbert Elias in Leicester: some recollections', *Theory, Culture and Society*, 4 (2–3): 533–9.

Chartier, Roger, (2010), 'Pour un usage libre et respectueux de Norbert Elias', *Vingtième Siècle*, 106 (avril–juin): 37–52.

Chevalier, Sophie and Jean-Marie Privat, (eds), (2004), *Norbert Elias et l'anthropologie: 'Nous sommes tous si étranges . . .'*, Paris: CNRS Editions.

Collins, Randall, (1998), *The Sociology of Philosophies: A Global Theory of Intellectual Change*, Cambridge, MA: Harvard University Press.

Dalal, Farhad, (1998), *Taking the Group Seriously: Towards a Post-Foulkesian Group Analytic Theory*, London: Jessica Kingsley.

Elias, Norbert, (1970), 'Interview met Norbert Elias', *Sociologische Gids*, 17 (2): 133–40. [Reprinted as 'An Interview in Amsterdam', in Johan Goudsblom and Stephen Mennell, (eds), (1998), *The Norbert Elias Reader: A Biographical Selection*, Oxford: Blackwell: 141–51].

Elias, Norbert, (1978 [1970]), *What is Sociology?* London: Hutchinson [Collected Works, Vol. 5, forthcoming].

Elias, Norbert, (1991), *The Symbol Theory*, London: Sage [revised edn, Collected Works, Vol. 13, Dublin: UCD Press, 2011].

Elias, Norbert, (1994), *Reflections on a Life*, Cambridge: Polity [Collected Works, Vol. 17, Dublin: UCD Press, forthcoming].

Elias, Norbert, (1996 [1989]), *The Germans: Studies of Power Struggles and the Development of Habitus in the Nineteenth and Twentieth Centuries*, Cambridge: Polity Press [Collected Works, Vol. 11, *Studies of the Germans*, forthcoming].

Elias, Norbert, (2000 [1969]), 'Postscript (1968)', in *The Civilizing Process*, revised edn, Oxford: Blackwell: 449–83 [further rev. edn, *On the Process of Civilisation*, Collected Works, Vol. 3, forthcoming].

Elias, Norbert, (2006a [1921]), 'On Seeing in Nature', in *Early Writings*, Collected Works, Vol. 1, Dublin: UCD Press: 5–22.

Elias, Norbert, (2006b [1935]), 'The kitsch style and the age of kitsch', in *Early Writings*, Collected Works, Vol. 1, Dublin: UCD Press: 85–96.

Elias, Norbert, (2006c [1969]), *The Court Society*, Collected Works, Vol. 2, Dublin: UCD Press.

Elias, Norbert, (2007a [1987]), *Involvement and Detachment*, Collected Works, Vol. 8, Dublin: UCD Press.

Elias, Norbert, (2007b [1992]), *An Essay on Time*, Collected Works, Vol. 9, Dublin: UCD Press.

Elias, Norbert, (2008 [1990]), 'Fear of Death', in *Essays II: On Civilising Processes, State Formation and National Identity*, Collected Works, Vol. 15, Dublin: UCD Press: 256–66.

Elias, Norbert, (2009a [1985]), 'On the creed of a nominalist: observations on Popper's *The Logic of Scientific Discovery*', in *Essays I: On the Sociology of Knowledge and the Sciences*, Collected Works, Vol. 14, Dublin: UCD Press: 161–90.

Elias, Norbert, (2009b [1974]), 'Science or sciences? Contribution to a debate with reality-blind philosophers', in *Essays I: On the Sociology of Knowledge and the Sciences*, Collected Works, Vol. 14, Dublin: UCD Press: 191–211.

Elias, Norbert, (2009c [1977]), 'Address on Adorno: respect and critique', in *Essays III: On Sociology and the Humanities*, Collected Works, Vol. 16, Dublin: UCD Press: 82–92.

Elias, Norbert, (2009d [1972]), 'Theory of Science and History of Science: comments on a recent discussion', in *Essays I: On the Sociology of Knowledge and the Sciences*, Collected Works, Vol. 14, Dublin: UCD Press: 85–101.

Elias, Norbert, (2009e [1972]), 'Scientific Establishments', in *Essays I: On the Sociology of Knowledge and the Sciences* Collected Works, Vol. 14, Dublin: UCD Press: 107–160.

Elias, Norbert, (2010a [1985]), *The Loneliness of the Dying*, Collected Works, Vol. 6; volume also includes *Humana Conditio*, Dublin: UCD Press.

Elias, Norbert, (2010b), *Au delà de Freud*, Paris: La Découverte.

Elias, Norbert and Eric Dunning, (2008 [1986]), *Quest for Excitement: Sport and Leisure in the Civilising Process*, Collected Works, Vol. 7, Dublin: UCD Press.

Elias, Norbert and John L. Scotson, (2008 [1965]), *The Established and the Outsiders*, Collected Works, Vol. 4, Dublin: UCD Press.

Garland, David, (1990), *Punishment and Modern Society: A Study in Social Theory*, Oxford: Clarendon Press.

Garland, David, (2001), *The Culture of Control: Crime and Social Order in Contemporary Society*, Oxford: Oxford University Press.

Gerritsen, Jan-Willem, (2000), *The Control of Fuddle and Flash: A Sociological History of the Regulation of Alcohol and Opiates*, Leiden: Brill.

Gleichmann, Peter, Johan Goudsblom and Hermann Korte, (eds), (1977), *Human Figurations: Essays for/Aufsätze für Norbert Elias*, Amsterdam: Stichting Amsterdams Sociologisch Tijdschrift.

Glucksmann, Miriam, (1999), 'A Contingent Transmission of Sociology: Encounters with Norbert Elias', *Humanities Research*, 1, 1999: 55–61.

Goodwin, John and Henrietta O'Connor, (2006), 'Norbert Elias and the lost Young Worker project', *Journal of Youth Studies*, 9 (2): 159–73.

Goody, Jack, (2006), *The Theft of History*, Cambridge: Cambridge University Press.

Goudsblom, Johan, (1977a), 'Responses to Norbert Elias's work in England, Germany, The Netherlands and France', in Peter Gleichmann, Johan Goudsblom and Hermann Korte, (eds), (1977) *Human Figurations: Essays for/Aufsätze für Norbert Elias*, Amsterdam: Stichting Amsterdams Sociologisch Tijdschrift: 37–97.

Goudsblom, Johan, (1977b), *Sociology in the Balance*, Oxford: Basil Blackwell.

Goudsblom, Johan, (1992), *Fire and Civilization*, London: Allen Lane.

Hackeschmidt, J., (2004), 'The Torch Bearer: Norbert Elias as a Young Zionist' in *Leo Baeck Institute Yearbook*, 49(1): 59–74.

Heilbron, Johan, (1995), *The Rise of Social Theory*, Cambridge: Polity.

Hopkins, Keith, (1978), *Conquerors and Slaves*, Sociological studies in Roman history, Vol. 2, Cambridge: Cambridge University Press.

Hopkins, Keith, (1983), *Death and Renewal*, Sociological studies in Roman history, Vol. 2, Cambridge: Cambridge University Press.

Kapteyn, Paul, (1996), *The Stateless Market: The European Dilemma of Integration and Civilization*, London: Routledge.

Kempers, Bram, (1992), *Painting, Power, and Patronage: The Rise of the Professional Artist in Renaissance Italy*, London: Allen Lane.

Kilminster, Richard, (1998), *The Sociological Revolution: From the Enlightenment to the Global Age*, London: Routledge.

Kilminster, Richard, (2007), *Norbert Elias: Post-philosophical Sociology*, London: Routledge.

Korte, Hermann, (1994 [1974]), 'Norbert Elias and the theory of civilization', in Bernhard Schäfers, (ed.), *Sociology in Germany*. Opladen: Leske & Budrich.

van Krieken, Robert, (1998), *Norbert Elias*, London: Routledge.

Kuipers, Giselinde, (2006), *Good Humor, Bad Taste: A Sociology of the Joke*, Berlin: Mouton de Gruyter.

Lavie, Joshua, (2005), 'The lost roots of the theory of Group Analysis: "Taking interrelational individuals seriously!",' *Group Analysis*, 38 (4): 533–50.

Liston, Katie and Stephen Mennell, (2009), 'Ill Met in Ghana: Jack Goody and Norbert Elias on process and progress in Africa', *Theory, Culture and Society*, 26 (7–8): 52–70.

Löwenthal, Leo, (1987), *An Unmastered Past – The Autobiographical Reflections of Leo Löwenthal*, Berkeley, CA: University of California Press.

Mastenbroek, Willem F.G., (1999), 'Negotiation as emotion management', *Theory, Culture and Society*, 16 (4): 49–73.

Mennell, Stephen, (1989), 'Parsons et Elias', *Sociologie et société* 21 (1): 69–86. The original English text is available online at http://www.stephenmennell.eu/publications/journalArticles. php.

Mennell, Stephen, (1992), *Norbert Elias: An Introduction*, Oxford: Blackwell.

Mennell, Stephen, (2006), 'Elias and the Counter-ego', *History of the Human Sciences*, 19 (2): 73–91.

Mennell, Stephen, (2007), *The American Civilizing Process*, Cambridge: Polity.

Mouzelis, Nicos P., (1991), *Back to Sociological Theory*, Basingstoke: Macmillan.

Quilley, Stephen and Steven Loyal, (2005), 'Eliasian sociology as a "central theory" for the human sciences', *Current Sociology*, 53 (5): 807–28.

Shilling, Chris and Philip A. Mellor, (2001), *The Sociological Ambition*, London: Sage.

van Vree, Wilbert, (1999), *Meetings, Manners and Civilization: The Development of Modern Meeting Behaviour*, London: University of Leicester Press.

de Vries, Bert and Johan Goudsblom, (2002), *Mappae Mundi: Humans and their Habitats in Long-Term Ecological Perspective*, Amsterdam: Amsterdam University Press.

Waldhoff, Hans-Peter, (2007), 'Unthinking the Closed Personality: Norbert Elias, Group Analysis and Unconscious Processes in a Research Group: Parts I and II, *Group Analysis: the International Journal of Group-Analytic Psychotherapy*, 40, 3: 323–43 and 40, 4: 478–506.

Wilson, Bryan, (1982), *Religion in Sociological Perspective*, Oxford: Oxford University Press.

Wilterdink, Nico, (1990), *Where Nations Meet: National Identities in an International Organization*, Fiesole: European University Institute.

Wouters, Cas, (1976), 'Is het civilisatieproces van richting veranderd?', *Amsterdams Sociologisch Tijdschrift* 3, 3: 336–7.

Wouters, Cas, (2004), *Sex and Manners: Female Emancipation in the West 1890–2000*, London: Sage.

Wouters, Cas, (2007), *Informalization: Manners and Emotions since 1890*, London: Sage.

Three faces of civilization: 'In the beginning all the world was Ireland'

Robert van Krieken

Abstract: This paper outlines a refinement of the sociological usage of the concept 'civilization' by distinguishing between three different 'faces' of civilization – as the opposite of barbarism, as equivalent to culture, and in Elias's sense as capturing a particular trajectory of socio-historical development. I then illustrate how this distinction between three different faces of civilization can be deployed in relation to the history of the various attempts by the English to civilize the population of Ireland. Finally, I reflect on the centrality of the experience of the colonization of Ireland for the English conception of how 'barbarism' should be understood and opposed to 'civilization' (which was then later mobilized in the colonization of the New World), as well as on the ways in which the colonization of Ireland constituted a binding together of both civilizing and decivilizing processes.

Among social and political theorists and researchers, the concept of civilization leads a troubled existence, and this has always been one of the major concerns characterizing the reception of Elias's work and that of those who draw on his ideas. For example, in a recent review of Stephen Mennell's (2007) *The American Civilizing Process*, Randall Collins portrays Elias's conception of a process of civilization as a 'trend theory' heading for a 'dead end', claiming, despite all the evidence to the contrary, that 'The theory of the civilizing process, taken in the large, is an optimistic theory of social evolution along the lines of the Enlightenment liberals' (2009: 439). Of course, no self-respecting social scientist would want to be seen marching under that flag. The idea of 'the civilizing mission', as we all know very well, is firmly rooted in the history of colonization and imperialism, and it is precisely the normative dimensions of the concept of 'civilization' that has also driven social scientists to put it in quotation marks. The concept has always led an odd sort of double life in Western social and political thought, at one and the same time an organizing principle *and* an object of ongoing critique. As Jean Starobinski has said of the critique of civilization which immediately accompanied the word's original appearance in Mirabeau's writing, it 'took two forms: a critique *of* civilization and a critique formulated in the name of civilization' (1993: 8). Starobinski emphasizes how Mirabeau's usage suggested that 'instead of getting rid of the violence of "primitive" societies these civilizations perpetuate the brutality beneath deceptive exteriors. Instead of open barbarity, contemporary civilizations practice a dissimulated violence' (1993: 7). Alongside 'civilization' operating as a 'black box' concept that people use almost casually, relatively firm in the belief that it has a rock-solid, unambiguous meaning, it is also one of those essentially-contested concepts, like 'freedom' or 'progress', carrying many different meanings with sometimes entirely contradictory implications. Most people are much happier talking about liberalism, democracy, modernization, globalization, rationalization, post-modernization, or cosmopolitanism – even 'civility' is preferable to 'civilization'. This is why there is a widespread view in social and political theory that the concept is much better avoided (see for example Mazlish, 2004: 160–61; see also Goudsblom, 2006).

However, at the same time as there is little hesitation in mobilizing varying conceptions of 'barbarism' in reference to events, actions and forms of social organization we regard as immoral, unjust, cruel, inhumane or oppressive, the normative and rhetorical power of the opposition between barbarism and civilization remains enormous. Civilization continues to be an important conceptual and rhetorical reference point, the focus of whatever we understand by 'progress' or, if that word offends, the 'point' of any human action on the social and political world. Among social and political leaders and commentators, after 11 September 2001 there was a striking willingness to identify 'civilization' as being endangered by this particular terrorist act, in need of vigorous, armed defence, and the flag under which everyone is to rally, or risk being marked as a barbarian.

The promiscuous multiplicity of meanings and effects that the concept civilization can have is apparent in examples such as the discussion in Australia of the removal of Aboriginal children from their families throughout the twentieth century (van Krieken, 1999). *Both* the practice itself *and* the subsequent critique of that practice rely heavily on the concept of 'civilization' to legitimate themselves. Just as it was the duty of Europeans to cultivate the land to its maximum capacity, so too was it their duty to 'cultivate' and educate Aboriginal children to their 'maximum' capacity – that is, as assimilated and Europeanized. Civilized society is, in this usage, exactly what Aborigines are not part of, and it was this exclusion which supported the denial of their access to full citizenship until 1948. But the critique of Aboriginal child removal which has emerged over recent decades *also* presents itself as informed by an appropriate degree of civility, and the earlier administrators and officials as characterized by a barbarism which current generations should condemn as an example of cultural genocide.

Similarly on the other side of the world, in Ireland, in relation to the question of the treatment of children by those representing the Catholic Church, either in institutional care or in everyday pastoral life, what gives the issue a particularly sharp edge is the 'wolf in sheep's clothing' effect; the fact that it is precisely the institution which represented itself as the bearer of civilized morality which has appeared unable either to regulate the harms which its members have inflicted on the rising generation, or to recognize the role that its own processes and procedures have played in the infliction of those harms (Arnold, 2009; Raftery and O'Sullivan, 1999). In both cases, there is a need to understand the mentality of a civilizing mission which made it possible to inflict various sort of physical, emotional and psychological harms on people, especially children, and the criteria by which they are now understood as uncivilized, generating a profound sense of injustice about the adequacy of the institutional response to that experience.

In the past I have addressed this problem of 'promiscuous multiplicity' in the concept of civilization by drawing on Elias's much more elaborate theorization of how processes of civilization should be understood, how they should be linked to other processes such as urbanization, the development of capitalism, and state-formation more broadly (van Krieken, 1998). One would make a distinction between the common sense understanding of civilization, and Elias's theory of civilizing processes, and link Elias's approach to Max Weber's account of rationalization, or Foucault's portrayal of modern society as based on a particular kind of disciplining of the self (van Krieken, 1990; 2003). In this far less normative understanding of what civilization is, just as both Weberian and Foucauldian approaches could include a discussion of a 'dark side' so in relation to civilizing processes one could equally expand one's conceptualization to include discussion of processes of *de*civilization, the occasional and sometimes parallel breakdown of civility, the monopoly of violence, and social order (Mennell, 1990; Fletcher, 1995; Zwaan, 2003).

One of my own recent attempts to rework the way that the complexity of the relationship between civilization and decivilization can be grasped has been to distinguish between different senses of the word 'civilization', by attaching superscript numbers and speaking of civilization[1], civilization[2] and civilization[3], with the last being the understanding characterizing Elias's approach (van Krieken, 2002). However, this remains a relatively clumsy formulation and, in considering different ways of approaching the problem, I was reminded of the way that a similar question concerning the multiplicity of meanings of the concept 'power' has been addressed, beginning with Peter Bachrach and Morton Baratz's (1962) attempt to address the differing ways that political scientists and sociologists analysed power, by distinguishing between two 'faces' of power. A decade later Steven Lukes (2005) extended this account by formulating the idea of three 'faces' or dimensions of power (see also Abell, 1977; Boulding, 1989). Can we bring some useful order to the way we use the term civilization, then, as we have for the concept power, by thinking of it in terms of three 'faces', each of which captures a different aspect of what the idea of civilization can refer to?

First face of civilization – civilization vs. barbarism

One widespread sense of the concept of civilization revolves around a binary distinction between 'civilization' and 'barbarism', and concerns a particular way of organizing social and political life, the operation of power and the constitution of human subjectivity. In this sense, there is a linkage between civilization and what comes to be known as the 'rule of law', operating through the embedding of the exercise of power in impersonal rules and structures, rather than in the unregulated will of dominant individuals and groups, a 'government of laws, not of men'. The form taken by individual *subjectivity* plays a central role, and the mechanisms by which this is 'cultivated' are a core element of the ongoing production of governable citizens.

For David Hume, it was the application of human effort to practical, productive labour which would achieve this effect. 'Can we expect,' asked Hume, 'that a government will be well modelled by a people, who know not how to make a spinning wheel, or to employ a loom to advantage?' (Hume, 1987: 273). A central focus of Western political theory has been to argue that human beings are not born reasonable, and that some process of cultivation, refinement, education or formation of 'public reason' is a crucial dimension of a peaceful and productive civil society. Bauman argues that the *project* of civilization was centrally about the production of governable subjects (Bauman, 1987: 93).

By the end of the eighteenth century, it was this face of civilization which represented the form of human perfectibility to which European societies drove both their own populations and as much of the rest of the world as they could lay their hands on. As Elias wrote, civilization had come to be defined by Europeans 'simply as an expression of their own high gifts' (Elias, 2000 [1939]: 43). This first face of civilization had become a crucial part of Europeans' sense of superiority over all other peoples in the world: 'the consciousness of their own superiority, the consciousness of this 'civilization,' from now on serves at least those nations which have become colonial conquerors, and therefore a kind of upper class to large sections of the non-European world, as a justification of their rule' (see also Febvre, 1973 [1930]: 220).

In the subsequent twentieth and twenty-first centuries, American usage of 'civilization' in particular has come to encompass all and any types of 'progress', material and moral. In the US it came to mean not just mechanization and technology, free trade and welfare, but also individual liberty, democracy, and human rights, all of which were bound up with each other, in a universalistic conception that knew no cultural or national boundaries. As Charles and Mary Beard wrote in *The American Spirit*:

> This idea of civilization . . . embraces a conception of history as a struggle of human beings in the world for individual and social perfection – for the good, the true and the beautiful – against ignorance, disease, the harshness of physical nature, the forces of barbarism in individuals and in society. It assigns to history in the United States, so conceived, unique features in origins, substance and development. (1942: 580–81)

This understanding of civilization has, since the Tiananmen Square massacre of 1989 and the attacks on New York and Washington in 2001, come to function as 'an overarching indication of the inviolable basic rights of every individual regardless of sex, skin colour or religion, for a democratic political structure and for an independent legal system' (den Boer, 2001: 78).

Second face of civilization – civilization = culture

This first hierarchical approach to civilization as progress and colonialism is often seen as primarily ideological (for example, McVeigh and Rolston, 2009), however, and there has been a consistent concern in social science to develop a less value-laden construction of it. In order to achieve this, as Lucien Febvre observed, it came also to have an 'ethnographic' meaning, referring simply to a way of life, a particular assembly of cultural, moral, political and economic forms. The second face of civilization came to be interchangeable with 'culture' or 'society', and it allows for multiple 'civilizations'. In this sense it is pretty well interchangeable with 'culture' or 'society', and this is how it is being used when people talk about a 'clash of civilizations', or 'civilizational analysis'. Huntington makes it clear that he sees no need to distinguish between civilization and culture: 'A civilization is . . . defined both by common objective elements, such as language, history, religion, customs, institutions, and by the subjective self-identification of people' (1993: 24). As Goudsblom (2006) notes, the conflation of civilization and culture had become characteristic of the attempts to develop a scientific understanding of human society in history, ethnology and anthropology from the late nineteenth century onwards. Many twentieth-century anthropologists, such as Ruth Benedict in *Patterns of Culture* (1934), were quite unconcerned about any distinction, treating the two words as interchangeable 'standard tools of their trade' (Goudsblom, 2006: 292).

The problem with the second face is precisely this conflation of civilization and culture, which for certain purposes need to be kept distinct. Roland Robertson, for example, speaks of the need to 'distinguish between civilization as a socio-cultural complex – more loosely, a bounded way of life – on the one hand, and civilization as a process, on the other' (2006: 421). The opposition between *Kultur* and *Zivilisation* is more than just a relic of nineteenth-century nationalism, a German reaction to Napoleonic imperialism: it does capture an important distinction of continuing salience. There are different things to talk about, and if 'civilization' is used in a way that equates it with culture, we lose the ability to distinguish between different dimensions of particular political developments, movements, and forms of thought. As Reinhold Niebuhr (1952) suggested, the opposition basically overlaps with that between Ancient Greece (culture) and the Roman Empire (civilization). Or as Brett Bowden puts it (2004: 38), it parallels the distinction between the social and political thought of the Enlightenment (civilization) and that of the Counter-Enlightenment (culture).

For example, Ian Buruma (2004) has argued, in his critique of how writers like Bernard Lewis (1956) understand social and political thought in the Muslim world, it is a mistake to see things entirely in terms of 'culture' or ideology, and to lose sight of the underlying issues related to political, military and economic institutions. Rather than being determined by cultural concerns such as the relationship between Islam and the modern world, it is more likely that Pakistan can be most effectively understood in terms of 'a history of authoritarian rule by a small landowning class and military juntas than with any "millennial" rivalry between two world religions'. The two concepts of culture and civilization simply 'work' differently in political discourse, and this relates to the continued salience of the first face of civilization, as the opposite of barbarism. One can conceivably describe the attack on the Twin Towers on 11 September 2001 as an attack on 'civilization itself', but not as an attack on 'culture itself'.

Third face of civilization – processes of civilization and decivilization

It is Elias's approach to civilization which identifies its third face, namely its character as a process – as civil-*ization*. For Elias the process of civilization in the history of Western European state-formation was not simply about a progressive movement from barbarism to civility, but about a number of much more specific lines of social, political and economic transformation. The third face of civilization thus concerns those social and political conditions, practices, strategies and figurations which *produce* whatever ends up being called civilization, and its utilization depends on a reflexively critical awareness of the way in which particular conceptions and experiences of 'being civil' get constructed and produced in one way or another.

The aspects of Elias's conception of civilization that I would like to concentrate on here are, first, his emphasis on long-term historical trends towards the concentration and monopolization of the means of violence, and, second, the gradual assimilation of a larger number of relatively small political and military units into a decreasing number of large ones. Town, communities, lordships and fiefdoms have over time been caught up in a powerful 'logic'[1] pushing towards an increasing monopolization of power and, correspondingly, of the means of violence by increasingly centralized political authorities, eventually in the form of the sovereign nation-state with its army, police and legal apparatus. This centralization process is in turn driven by two historical mechanisms. The 'monopoly mechanism', in which competitive dynamics will tend towards the elimination of weaker competitors and the consolidation of 'players' into a smaller number of larger units, and the associated 'royal' mechanism, in which power tends to concentrate in a single actor because of the systemic salience of any *nodal point* for the conflicts between the other groups in society. Such 'strong actors' can neither individually overcome any of the others, nor stop competing to the degree required to form an effective alliance with each other.

Second, he focused on the effects of what he called lengthening chains of social interdependence, which can also be understood as a steady increase in social differentiation and social density. Elias noted that one could observe, as a constituent aspect of the process of civilization, ever-expanding networks of interdependence and mutual influence in Western European society. This in turn lengthened the social 'conveyor belts' running through individuals' lives and made them more complex, which generates increasing demands on individual subjectivity and social pressures towards a particular kind of psychological disposition or *habitus* – a disposition that Weber and Foucault would refer to as 'discipline' (van Krieken, 1990, 2003). What we experience as 'civilization' is thus founded on a particular *habitus* which is linked to the forms taken by broader social and political relationships and institutions.

Over the longer term these processes tended, Elias argued, to produce 'a transformation of the whole drive and affect economy in the direction of a more continuous, stable and even regulation of impulses and emotions in all areas of conduct, in all sectors of his life' (Elias, 2000 [1939]: 374). Central to this face of civilization is the question of the extent to which social structures do indeed generate a stable and even regulation of emotions and impulses,[2] not simply whether there is a dominant self-perception of oneself as civilized. Later, however, he would also draw attention to the ways in which shifts in social structure can also generate a *destabilization* of the regulation of impulses and affects which could be understood as constituting processes of *decivilization* (Elias, 1996 [1989]). He raised the possibility that civilization and decivilization can occur simultaneously, with monopolies of force being capable of violence as extreme as situations where the 'means of violence' are more diffusely controlled (Mennell, 1990; Fletcher, 1995; 1997; Zwaan, 2003).

Elias's linkage of the historical formation of subjectivity with state formation, as well as with more general processes of social development, constitutes a conceptual basis for analysing the civilizing mission itself, using a conceptualization of a third face of civilization to analyse what was understood as its first two faces. The normative assessment of peoples constructed as uncivilized barbarians can then be seen to be rooted in the psychic, social and political dynamics of civilizing processes themselves, the negative image of the 'savage' being a projection of the civilized person's own feared internal barbarism, at either the individual or collective level.

Irish state formation and processes of civilization and decivilization

In illustrating how the concept of the three faces of civilization can be mobilized in historical sociological research, one could begin with the comparison that I used to open the paper, between the Australian and Irish experiences of the abuse of children in institutional care throughout the twentieth century. In the Australian setting, an important element of the policies underpinning the removal of Aboriginal children from their families was what you could call a 'colonial imagination', a sense of a need to transform the children of Aboriginal parentage so as to civilize them, to bring them to a European way of life, a

European *habitus*. There is scope, then, to examine the parallels in that arena, to what there might be about the Irish experience that could be addressed in terms of the relation between colonizer and colonized. But as soon as one begins this analysis, it becomes clear that there are aspects of Irish history that make it necessary to re-think how we have generally thought about the psychology of colonization.

There is a tendency to frame colonialism in terms of a relationship between Europeans and 'the rest', beginning with the inhabitants of South and North America. So Anthony Pagden (1982) may acknowledge the roots of the opposition between civility and barbarism in Ancient Greece and Rome, but he quickly jumps to the Spanish *conquistadores*, de las Casas and de Vitoria, and the story unfolds from that point onwards. To the extent that Irish historians make the connection between the Irish experiences and the colonization of the New World, it is often seen as the latter influencing the former (Canny, 1973, although a little later Canny reverses the relationship: 1976: 160).

However, it is important to get the timing right, and to see that the experience of the English in Ireland *preceded* their ventures into the New World, and provided both the conceptual, psychological and practical foundations for their relationships with non-Europeans. So what it means to be 'non-European' was first constructed *within* Europe – albeit, in the Irish (and Welsh and Scottish) case, on Europe's outer frontiers – not *between* Europeans and those living beyond Europe. The question of 'race' was in the first place not about skin colour, but about other sorts of divisions between human beings and their differently structured psychologies according to other sorts of criteria.

Any cursory look at Irish history makes it clear that it is closely bound up with English state and cultural formation, and that a central element of the English perception of Ireland was a persistent distinction between civility/ civilization and barbarism being equivalent to the distinction between the English and the Irish. Indeed English civility was in many respects defined precisely in opposition to Irishness – it was everything that the Irish were not. And the Irish later returned the favour, seeing themselves from around the eighteenth century onwards likewise as the morally superior representatives of an ancient Celtic/Catholic civilization that had resisted the temptations of modernization and their associated descent into moral turpitude, decadence and degradation (Augusteijn, 2006: 274–77).

There is a tendency to construct the social history of Ireland and England in national terms as distinct histories, and in terms of the first two faces of civilization, as being either about disputed conceptions of 'progress' or about cultural difference. Irishness was defined in the eighteenth/nineteenth century in opposition to the English, and indeed framed as a 'clash of civilizations', drawing on both the first and second faces of the concept of civilization, with Irish identity rooted in a conception of an ancient Irish culture, way of life and, of course, language. To the extent that the concept of 'civilization' is used at all, it is used in terms of its first two 'faces', especially the first, so producing a critique of the hypocrisy and internal contradictions of a conception of civilization that rests on such clearly barbaric practices. Frequently it was framed in terms of an idealized rural way of life in opposition to the decadent, immoral lifestyle of England and Europe – in many respects, 'culture' versus 'civilization'. 'This was a spiritual, morally superior nation that had developed and maintained itself in a Europe that increasingly succumbed to barbarism' (Augusteijn, 2006: 281).

But it is worth going beyond thinking in horizontal terms of Ireland and England, to see things in vertical terms that cut across the national differences and help us to see the development of social and political life in Ireland as part and parcel of a set of transnational processes, especially those of monopolization of the means of violence (and law and administration), and increasing orientation towards central sets of norms and values (today, human rights). This is what a utilization of the third face of civilization makes possible, because it is not wedded to the concept of 'progress' and 'improvement'.

The arguments often ran as much *within* a particular country as *between* countries. The question of the English attempts to pacify and civilize the Irish was as much a concern *within* England (see also Eugen Weber, 1979, on France). For example, in England there were also those who yearned for a glorious pre-Norman conquest past, which they felt had been ruined and debased by invaders too brutish and insensitive to understand the true value of authentic English, Saxon culture.[3] Rather than seeing the course of Irish history as revolving around the conquest and domination of Ireland by a foreign power, in terms of 'the English' and 'the Irish', it may be more useful to think in terms of clashes between differing ways of doing things – governing a population, constructing one's identity, managing commercial and political activity, managing family life, maintaining social order and integration, structuring political and administrative institutions, and so on – clashes which took place as much within England as between England and the peoples of its 'Celtic fringe'.

The history of Ireland and its role within English state-formation also casts a particular kind of light on how we understand the state's monopolization of violence and the nature of court society. Elias's original formulation in *The Civilizing Process* emphasized the more general long-term trend towards the centralization of military and political power. He wrote, for example, of 'a quite simple social mechanism which, once set in motion, proceeds like clockwork', in which the dynamics and logic of competition will push any large number of social and political units towards a centralization of power and authority into an ever-decreasing number of units (2000 [1939]: 264).

However, as Rees Davies has suggested, 'issues raised by the precociousness of the early English state might well be brought into sharper focus by considering the contrasting experiences of the societies and polities which bordered on it' (1993: 3). It is important to include the relationship between England and Ireland in one's understanding of such processes, because it highlights how rough, uneven, and often very tenuous and tortured the process of the monopolization of violence was, how the relationship between the centre and the periphery was fought out on a regular basis along shifting frontiers (Ellis, 1995; 1999; Lydon, 2008; Muldoon,

2003; 2009), and how this generated a particular configuration of the relationship between civilization and decivilization.

Looking at Irish history from this perspective makes it possible to see the extent to which the English conception of 'the savage' and indeed of the whole colonial project, was anchored in the perception of the Irish and 'Irishness' dated back to the twelfth century, as well as the experiments in colonial settlement attempted in Ireland in the fifteenth and sixteenth centuries. The concept of the opposition between barbarism and civilization does have its roots in the Ancient World, but in the process of those concepts being rediscovered in the Renaissance of the twelfth century, they were fleshed out and given particular form in the attempts of the English state to incorporate its Celtic fringe into a centralized polity and society with a relatively homogenous type of 'English self'.

The English encounter with the people of Ireland, Wales and Scotland constituted an important watershed in the development of what both civilization and barbarism were, the former defined in relation to the latter, and formed the basis for their subsequent encounters with the Indigenous population of North America. The relationship of the English to their Celtic fringe was also in turn an aspect of the larger expansion of Latin Christendom from the eleventh century onwards to England itself and then on to Wales, Scotland and Ireland, to the Baltic region, the Balkans, southern Italy and Sicily, Spain and Portugal, Poland and Hungary – what Robert Bartlett (1993: 269–91) calls the 'Europeanization of Europe'.

To get a feel for the thinking behind the perception of the Irish as 'wild' and 'savage', there are a number of writers one can turn to. One can begin with the Greeks and the Romans, who saw all the regions furthest from themselves, such as Ireland, Scotland, and Norway, as barbarous. The Greek geographer Strabo said Irish men were cannibals, eating their fathers when they die and then holding an orgy with numerous women including their mothers and sisters. Solinus (300 AD), the Latin grammarian, said Ireland was

> an inhuman place due to the ferocious behaviour of its inhabitants . . . the people are inhospitable and warlike. Victors in battle, having first drunk of the blood of those they kill, then paint their faces with it. Right and wrong is all one to them. There are no bees . . .' (cited in Haywood, 1996: 470)

However, the Roman perception of Ireland arose more from a geographic bias in that the further any people lived away from Rome, the less virtuous and more barbaric they must be. The accounts based on actual observation and real experience came later.

Much of the discussion begins in the sixteenth century with Edmund Spenser (1552–99), especially his *View of the Present State of Ireland* (1934 [1596]) which complains about Irish hairstyles and mantles, which he seemed to regard as making the Irish the original hoodies, functioning to disguise their 'thevishe Countenaunce' (p. 70). Spenser's portrayal of Ireland is characterized by a combination of looseness and wildness on the one hand, and excessive control and repression on the other. In Spenser, as Patricia Coughlan observes, the

Irish, 'swerve', 'straggle', 'miche in corners', 'break forth', 'walk disorderly', are 'loose', 'wandering', 'idly roguing', 'loitering', they are a 'rebellious rout of loose people . . . infesting the woods and spoiling the good subject' (Coughlan, 1989: 53)

But Spenser was largely extending the account of a twelfth-century English monk, Gerald de Barri (Giraldus Cambrensis – Gerald of Wales) (1146–1223), whose *Topographica Hibernica* (1185) became the foundation of all the later accounts, which would only deviate slightly from his representations. He drew a picture of a people who regularly had sex with animals, were constantly killing, maiming and torturing each other, knew no taboo on incest, had no respect for marriage and family life, and were dishonest and untrustworthy. Gerald formulated a theory of human development and progress, from the woods to the fields, to settlements and communities organized around disciplined forms of work and 'the money-making of towns' composed of citizens with both rights and privileges, and obligations to their civic community. The Irish people, thought Gerald, appeared to be resolutely wedded to 'the life which it has been accustomed to lead in the woods and countryside', and this was a problem that needed to be dealt with.

Robert Bartlett observes that Gerald wasn't especially unique, that his accounts of the Irish and Welsh are largely consistent with the observations made from within Latin Christendom about other peoples on its margins and frontiers – Adam of Bremen on the Baltic Scandinavian peoples, Helmold of Bosau on the Slavs, Otto of Freising on the Bohemians and Magyars, Gunther of Paris on the Poles. On the whole, scholars in Anglo-Norman and German society tended to see the world beyond their borders as:

> economically backward, dominated by a rough, pastoral way of life; politically fragmented, mauled by civil wars and bloody tyrants; inhabited by fierce, lawless raiders, who could not be trusted; given over to superstition and black magic; pagan or semi-pagan; indulging in human sacrifice and sexual excess. (2006 [1982]: 141)

Nor was Gerald especially original. A generation before, the English historian William of Malmesbury (1080/95–1143) had been very active in reviving the classical distinction between civilization and barbarism. He gave it new life by taking the definition of barbarism beyond that of equating it with paganism, and identifying the ways in which nominally Christian populations could still be uncivilized, focusing on the degree of urbanization and commercialization as indices of civilization (Gillingham, 1992, 2001, 1995: 60).

If we consider the conceptualization of writers like William of Malmesbury, Gerald de Barri and Edmund Spenser as windows on to the thinking of administrators and rulers, it is clear that it was very firmly organized in terms of the first face of civilization, on civilization as barbarism's opposite, to be imposed as effectively as possible, no matter how much violence might be needed. If you think of your omelette in a particular kind of way, then you don't worry too much about the eggs being broken. But if we think in terms of the third face of civilization, there was clearly a range of long-term processes in motion, regardless of what particular kings, lords or adventurers might be thinking and doing as actors within those processes.

For example, a number of political, economic and social developments, which were essentially European processes of social change originating in Paris and Rome, were in train in lowland England that were yet to have real effect in Ireland:

- Religious – changes in Church doctrine and practice, including family life and Church organization.
- The shift from pastoralism to agriculture
- Urbanization
- Commercialization
- Advances in military technology
- Centralization of state administration and political power
- Pacification of the aristocracy – 'courtization of warriors'
- Pacification of inheritance and succession

The Anglo-Normans in many respects 'represented the triumph of a vibrant, confident, aggressive economic mentality which had come to dominate north-western Europe from the second half of the eleventh century' (Davies, 1990: 10). As Davies observes:

> the world would never be the same again. A confident, expansive, exciting and rich international culture had come to occupy centre stage in northern Europe; its drawing power and its enticing supremacy were irresistible. Indeed those who dared to withstand its charms could be dismissed as barbarians: when Stephen of Lexington, dispatched to investigate Cistercian observance in Ireland, decreed that knowledge of French or Latin was a prerequisite for a monk and added, crushingly, that 'no man can love the cloister and learning if he knows only Irish', he was proclaiming the values of a European cultural and religious world into which the 'Celtic' countries were being dragged willy-nilly. (1990: 19)

Even without the colonization efforts of the Anglo-Normans and the English, suggests Davies, it is highly likely that regions such as Ireland would have eventually found themselves drawn to the shifts in cultural, political, administrative and social practices throughout Europe (1990: 15–16).

I will focus here on just two aspects of those broader processes of social change – (1) the transformations of marriage and family life; (2) the monopolization of violence and centralisation of political power, and formation of court society.

1 Marriage practices

One of the sorest points in the relationship between the Gaelic Irish and the Roman Catholic church was the realm of marriage and sex (Bartlett, 2006 [1982]: 42; Byrne, 1993: 41). Archbishop Lanfranc of Canterbury (1070–89) complained in 1074 that the Irish law of marriage was 'rather a law of fornication': an Irish man would abandon his wife apparently at will and proceed to 'form a criminal alliance . . . with any other woman he pleases, either a relative of his own or of his deserted wife or a woman whom somebody else has abandoned in an equally disgraceful way' (cited in Duffy, 1997: 25). His successor, Archbishop Anselm (1093–1109) wrote that 'men exchange their wives as freely and publicly as a man might exchange his horse' (cited in Duffy, 1997: 25). When Pope Alexander III wrote to Henry II after his assumption of control over the Anglo-Norman invasion of Ireland, he emphasized how necessary the intervention was because he had heard that Irish men 'openly cohabit with their stepmothers and do not blush to bear children by them', Irish men had sex with their brother's wife and lived with two sisters, and 'many have intercourse with daughters of mothers they have deserted' (cited in Duffy, 1997: 25). For the Church, Ireland was the Jerry Springer Show writ large.

What all this was about was primarily the same issue that led to Henry VIII breaking with Rome, namely the aristocratic concern with political alliance and control over inheritance. The Church's restrictions of those permitted to marry undermined the role of marriage in the formation of aristocratic political allegiances, and the ban on divorce stood in the way of the maintenance of family lineages. Also at issue was property and the accumulation of wealth. In what John Goldthorpe (1987) termed the 'Christian revolution' in family life, the Church had set about changing a number of common practices in European family life – marriage between close kin, remarriage with affinal kin (those of their former spouse), remarriage after divorce, concubinage (the practice of men taking a 'childbearing wife', often in addition to a childless first wife), adoption and fostering.

The significance of all these changes, argues Jack Goody (1983), was that they all weakened kinship ties beyond the immediate nuclear family and had the effect of vastly increasing the property that came into the Church's hands. All the practices it prohibited were what Goody called 'strategies of heirship', ways of ensuring that accumulated property and wealth stayed within the kinship network in the face of the usual barriers to the transmittal of inheritance from one generation to the next – childlessness, absence of male heirs, death of one parent, separation of parents. If one prohibits the usual ways of providing 'fictional' heirs – children from a new marriage, a marriage to a widow's brother-in-law or a concubine, a fostered or adopted child – then roughly 40 per cent of the population would be left with no male heirs.

Add a Church ideological strategy of promoting the provision of bequests to the Church as a means of saving one's soul, and one saw a massive increase in property being inherited by the Church. Whether or not this was the intention motivating the Church's policies on marriage and the family, certainly, wrote Goody, 'one of the most profound changes that accompanied the introduction of Christianity was the enormous shift of property from private ownership to the hands of the Church, which rapidly became the largest landowner in England (as in most other European countries) a position it has retained to this day' (1983: 45–6). Unlike England and the Continent, however, at that time the Church did not have enough of an institutional presence in Ireland to be able to provide forms of compensation for what the Gaelic aristocracy would lose by conforming to such rules.

2 *Monopolization of violence and centralization of administration, power, authority, law (conflict management)*

A difficulty with much theorization of the development of the modern state is the assumption that the state's boundaries are clearly fixed and that problems of pacification and centralization take place inside those boundaries. However, in reality English state formation was distinctive in being characterized by a persistent instability at its borders with the Celtic world. The Irish experience raises the whole problem of the *frontier* in state formation,[4] and the difficulties it placed in the path of the monopolization of violence and the centralization of authority, politics, law and sovereignty.

Gaelic Ireland was essentially an aristocratic warrior society, with its politics and society organized around military competition among an ever-shifting array of chiefs and kings. It was a fragmented, decentred polity characterized by marriage and inheritance practices that encouraged constant competition between warring clans composed primarily of pastoralists. Nicholas Canny speaks of the 'balkanized' nature of Gaelic political life (1989: 107). William of Newburgh (1136–1201), compared the political condition of Ireland to that of England before the coming of the Normans. He wrote that 'Ireland was divided into a number of kingdoms and had many kings like the ancient practice in England and is commonly torn apart by these divisions' (cited in Muldoon, 2003: 78). The Anglo-Normans saw a lot more potential in a settled political order based on agriculture and urban life, so they set about displacing the indigenous population into the woods and bogs and replacing them with settlers who would farm the land properly. But the displacement was always partial, forcing ongoing strategies of accommodation and compromise, and a mixing of cultures and ways of life, which came to be understood by the English as the 'problem of degeneracy'.

The model for court society that underpinned the formation of centralized European states depended on the ongoing transformation of warrior-knights into courtier-knights.[5] Corrigan and Sayer speak in relation to England of the 'demilitarization of the nobility', observing that 'by 1576 only a quarter of the peerage had seen active service' (1985: 63). There was a shift away from the 'warrior' paradigms of aristocracy to politics and law; in the first year of Elizabeth's reign, Star Chamber heard 67 cases; in the last, 732 (p. 63). The control over armed force increasingly came to be monopolized by the Crown, and Corrigan and Sayer refer to this as 'a civilizing process of considerable importance' (p.63). The control that the English state tried to exercise over its Celtic neighbours was in many respects an attempted extension of its growing control internally of its own population (Davies, 1993: 7).

However, Ireland and the Celtic fringe posed a particular problem for English state formation, in that the English crown was faced with a dual task – how to pacify not only the Gaelic lords, but also the English lords they needed to use for that purpose. The English Crown was faced with what Machiavelli called the problem of governing a mixed principality, particularly that 'even if one has a very strong army, [a new ruler] will always need the good will of the inhabitants' (Machiavelli, 1961 [c. 1514]: 18). The mechanisms and processes by which court society was formed and developed in lowland England worked much less effectively at a greater distance from Westminster, along rather long borders in terrain (highlands, woods, bogs) that was difficult – i.e., more expensive – to pacify. The shift in the nature of aristocratic conduct depended on their incorporation into court society, and this required their physical presence, something harder to achieve the further away from court one was located (Canny, 1976: 28). The successful pacification of the borderlands depended precisely on local rulers who were both militarily strong in their own right, and possessed of the capacity to forge local allegiances and compromises with the native population to secure their cooperation (Cosgrove, 2001: 132). Both of these constituted centrifugal forces that contradicted the centripetal requirements of the formation of court society. As Machiavelli (1961 [c. 1514]) observed, a Prince governing a 'country differing in language, customs, or laws', if he does not reside there himself, has to rely on local allies, but in so doing,

> He has to see to it that they do not gain too much strength and authority. With his own forces and their support, he can very early reduce the stronger powers and then become arbiter of the entire province. Any ruler who does not succeed in doing this will soon lose what he has won, or so long as he does manage to hold it, will have a host of difficulties and annoyances. (p. 21)

Throughout the history of Ireland's relationship with the English crown, one sees a constant to-ing and fro-ing between these two forces – investment in improved military defence of the border administered by able lords, producing increased threats to the crown in the form of 'overmighty subjects' (Ellis, 1999: 168), alternating with constraints placed on the status and power of the local lords, reducing their effectiveness or encouraging them to rely on brute force, in turn increasing the threats to the English crown's economic and security interests. Walter Raleigh, for example, could only remain a good courtier by restricting his involvement to the occasional military campaign and slaughter of captured combatants, and moving quickly on to the New World.

Law was a crucial aspect of this confrontation between the two different ways of structuring social, political and economic life, and from the thirteenth century onwards, the extension of the common law to the Irish had been seen as an important aspect of pacifying and civilizing Ireland (Otway-Ruthven, 1950; Pawlisch, 1985: Muldoon, 2003: 81–91). The Irish who lived among the English or who wished to become assimilated employed the common law. The Brehon law maintained and supported the tribal way of life that the English wanted to displace (Pawlisch, 1985; Patterson, 1991). One of the more important legal concerns was ownership and inheritance of land – the Gaelic system of partible inheritance and communal ownership was in sharp conflict with English conceptions of private property and all that that meant for their capacity to engage in stable and productive economic activity. They also saw the Gaelic practices of landholding as undermining the development of stable and productive economic activity, the formation of towns based on expanding commercial incorporation in broader markets, and so on.

The Gaelic legal system was inherently resistant to a Hobbesian centralization of sovereignty – Brehons were more akin to what we would today call arbitrators as opposed to magistrates or judges, and practices and principles would often vary significantly from one region to another. Where there were consistent practices, the English also found them ill-suited to what they regarded as good order and civility – a system of fines for capital crimes they found an inadequate deterrent, and the ease of marriage and divorce a recipe for ongoing feuding over inheritance and political control (Gillingham, 1992: 404). These and other features of the lack of fit between English and Gaelic ways of life seriously undermined the English state's capacity to ally itself with the indigenous society and culture, a central element of its own development and expansion (Davies, 1993: 12).

In principle demilitarization involved both the exercise of violence and attempts to transform the psychology of the Irish population, an important part of which was the placement of all conflict within the framework of English law. The disciplining and pacification of a population generally drew on two different strategies – the word and the sword, persuasion and coercion (Bradshaw, 1978). In England a particular combination of the two worked more or less successfully, but in Ireland the sword became the English strategy of choice. Gerald's recommendation in 1189 was 'First tame them, then govern them'; the Irish were to be 'either disabled or destroyed' (cited in Gillingham, 1993: 27). Despite having some reservations about the brutality of the Anglo-Normans, he ends up agreeing that Irish rebels 'should be killed in order to inspire fear, so that as a result of the example we make of them this lawless and rebellious people may shrink from engaging our forces in future' (in Gillingham, 1993: 27). Perhaps Gerald and the English governors were persuaded of Machiavelli's observation 'that men must be either pampered or annihilated. They avenge light offences; they cannot avenge severe ones; hence, the harm one does to a man ought to be such as to obviate any fear of revenge' (Machiavelli, 1961 [c. 1514]: 20). The second option certainly became the dominant logic of the English forces occupying Ireland up to the end of the seventeenth century.

The pacification of the Irish aristocracy was pursued in a highly militarised and exceptionally violent way, reaching new depths from the assertion of Henry VIII's kingship of Ireland in 1534. English Lords Deputy made liberal usage of massacres, treachery and atrocities to subdue the native population, turning the whole English civilizing mission into exactly the sort of enterprise that suggests the need to put the word 'civilization' in inverted commas (Carey, 1999; Edwards, 2007). Rather than capturing prisoners to claim a ransom, the English, beginning with Sir William Skeffington (1465–1535), Lord Deputy (1534–5), started putting them all to death, even long after hostilities had ceased, not just in the heat of battle. The phrases 'the pardon of Maynooth' and 'Grey's pardon' came to represent treachery, the slaughter or execution of prisoners who had given themselves up in exchange for the promise of pardon. This is particularly striking because the overall historical trend in the conduct of warfare in Europe had been in the opposite direction, toward chivalry in the treatment of prisoners (Gillingham, 1993; 1999), and Gerald's complaint in the late twelfth century about the Irish and the Welsh was precisely that they, in contrast to the French habit of capturing and ransoming soldiers, 'butcher and decapitate them' (Gerald of Wales, 1978: 269).

One of the widely cited examples of the violence of English state terrorism is Thomas Churchyard's account of the habit of Sir Humphrey Gilbert (1537–83) to line the approach to his tent with the heads of recently killed Irish rebels:

> So that none could come into his tent for any cause but commonly he must pass through a lane of heads which he used *ad terrorem*, the dead feeling nothing the more pains thereby: and yet it did bring great terror to the people when they saw the heads of their dead fathers, brothers, children, kinsfolk and friends, lie on the ground before their faces, as they came to speak with the said colonel. (cited in Canny, 1973: 582)

Robert Williams suggests that one way to capture Gilbert's style is to 'imagine Genghis Khan supplemented by the lessons of Machiavelli's Prince' (1990: 152).

Sir Henry Sidney (1529–86) was the first to attempt a systematic re-structuring of political power in Ireland (1565–71, 1575–8), identifying the nobility and their dynasties as the principal source of political instability, and set about disarming them and re-shaping Irish political structures. The Irish aristocracy split, some (such as Lord Ormond) compromised and became good, pacified courtiers. Others maintained their warrior resistance, partly because the savagery with which English soldier-settlers pursued their dispossession of the native Irish, a savagery that was to a large extent a result of the deeply-rooted construction of the Irish as barbaric, sub-human, and in need of 'breaking', which appeared to legitimize in the English colonists' minds their extreme violence. It appears that the 'courtisation of warriors' (Elias, 2000 [1969]: 465–75), the restraint of violence in relation to the English monarch (with greater or lesser degrees of success) or the 'demilitarization of the nobility' to which Corrigan and Sayer (1985) refer, *within* English society was accompanied, perhaps even enabled, by the existence of Ireland as a field for the projection of that onto a recalcitrant Irish colonial population. English pacification and civility were to a large extent interdependent with the continuation of warrior violence, atrocities and massacres until at least the end of the seventeenth century, alongside the ruthless economic exploitation which was to continue to the end of the nineteenth century.

Conclusion – Ireland as 'laboratory of Empire'

I shall conclude by returning to my sub-title, 'In the beginning all the world was Ireland'. As you will know, this is a reference to John Locke's observation on the absence of money in the New World (1960 [1690]: 319), and is an attempt to convey a sense of the nature of the primal social order from which all civilized society had advanced, and which all societies share, no matter what their sub-sequent historical trajectory. America is how we all once were. Just as Europeans advanced beyond that barbaric condition to their current civilized state, it is clear that the New World must undergo the same transformation – this is often seen as lying at the heart of the colonial imagination.

However, Ireland's experiences in the context of English state formation show that the history of the colonial imagination does not begin in 1492 with Columbus's arrival in America. The modes of thinking about civilization and barbarism that underpinned the colonization of the world beyond Western Europe did not commence with the contact with the Amerindians in the New World, but with the initial period of self-confident expansion of European societies into their frontier regions during the twelfth-century renaissance (Quinn, 1947). The concepts used to legitimize the colonial enterprise in royal charters to colonizers first took shape in the papal bull encouraging Henry II to take possession of Ireland. Before 1641, observes Jane Ohlmeyer, 100,000 people had migrated to Ireland from Britain (30,000 Scots, the rest Welsh or English); the corresponding numbers of migrants crossing the Atlantic were: c.6,000 settlers in Massachusetts by 1636 and c.8,000 in Virginia by 1640 (Ohlmeyer, 1998: 139). Colonial adventurers like Walter Raleigh (1554–1618) and Humphrey Gilbert (c.1539–83) cut their teeth in Ireland, experimenting there with subduing an indigenous population with an alien culture and the mechanics of displacing the natives by establishing plantations of imported, already civilized and disciplined, settlers before they set sail for the more lucrative New World (Muldoon, 2003: 91–2).

The psychology and practicalities of colonization and the resort to violence as the mechanism by which civilization, in its first face, is to be achieved were a lesson that English administrators thought they had learned in Ireland (and Wales and Scotland) from 1169 onwards, and which they then applied in the New World in the sixteenth century (Gillingham, 1992; Muldoon, 2003: 152; Harding, 2005). As Michael Hechter observed, 'The case of Ireland is an almost ideal-typical example of a colonial situation, and it provided England with practical experience by which to evaluate later colonial policies' (1975: 73).

In the end, though, the overt attempts at civilizing offensives on England's frontiers proved only partially effective in bringing about the kinds of transformations that were already in motion, and to the extent that they drew on decivilizing techniques of escalating rather than reducing violence, they actually slowed those changes down (see, for example, Tait, Edwards and Lenihan, 2007). In fact, the local aristocracy was relatively quick to adapt to the third face of civilization, such as the requirements of urban, commercial,

Europeanized society, and did not in principle have very many objections to becoming subjects of the English crown. What they objected to was the wholesale expropriation of their lands (Davies, 1990: 60), driven on the English side both by sheer greed and a sense that the Gaelic Irish failed to extract nearly enough value from their landholdings – the two concerns that would also later drive the colonization of the New World and Australasia.

When one examines the three major elements of what Elias understood as the civilizing process – (1) a shift in the balance between external and internal constraint towards the latter, (2) a tendency towards a more stable and differentiated pattern of self-restraint, and (3) increasing mutual identification across group boundaries – it is clear that the peculiarities of the English state's Celtic frontier produced a much more complex, in many respects perverse, unfolding of all three tendencies than we are used to considering when we look at English state formation in isolation. To the extent that mutual identification across racial or ethnic boundaries, or between settler-colonists and indigenous populations, is either absent or weak, the Irish experience is a complex example of what Abram de Swaan (2001) calls 'dyscivilization' – a partial unfolding of some but not all possible aspects of processes of the third face of civilization, with the Irish people having been subjected to a process of psychological and cultural 'compartmentalization' precisely within the process of forcing their political integration with England and Europe.

An understanding of the third face of civilization makes it possible to see 'the civilizing mission' as *itself* subject to processes of civilization, in the sense of its third face. 'The way we civilize' can be seen as more or less organized around the restraint of emotion and visceral responses, and a greater or lesser responsiveness to lengthening chains of social interdependency, to the long-term implications of individual actions and organized interventions, and to what I have here framed as the third face of civilization.

Notes

1 Although, it should be noted that Elias himself would have disputed the use of the word 'logic' in this context; see Elias (2009a [1985]) and Elias (2009b [1985]).
2 For an argument against any significant linkage between particular forms of society and distinctive personality types, see Bendix (1952).
3 See, for example, Chibnall's (1999) discussion of the notion of the 'Norman yoke'.
4 See also Mennell's (2007: 193–209) discussion of the frontier in American state formation.
5 Elias refers to this process as 'the taming of warriors' (Elias, 2006 [1969]: 160–1, 230–2) and as 'the courtisation of warriors' (2000 [1939]: 387–97).

References

Dates given in square brackets are those of first publication.

Abell, Peter, (1977), 'The many faces of power and liberty: revealed preferences, autonomy and teleological explanation', *Sociology*, 11: 3–24.

Arnold, Bruce, (2009), *The Irish Gulag*, Dublin: Gill & Macmillan.

Augusteijn, Joost, (2006), 'Ireland and Europe: A Dutch perspective', *Radharc: A Journal of Irish and Irish-American Studies*, 5/7: 265–86.

Bachrach, Peter and Morton S. Baratz, (1962), 'Two Faces of Power', *American Political Science Review*, 56, 4: 947–52.

Bartlett, Robert, (1993), *The Making of Europe: Conquest, Colonization and Cultural Change 950–1350*, London: BCA.

Bartlett, Robert, (2006 [1982]), *Gerald of Wales: A Voice of the Middle Ages*, Stroud: Tempus.

Bauman, Zygmunt, (1987), *Legislators and Interpreters*, Cambridge: Polity.

Beard, Charles A. and Mary R. Beard, (1942), *The American Spirit: a study of the idea of civilization in the United States*, New York: Collier Books.

Bendix, Richard, (1952), 'Compliant behaviour and individual personality', *American Journal of Sociology*, 58, 2: 292–303.

Benedict, Ruth, (1934), *Patterns of Culture*, London: Routledge & Kegan Paul.

Boulding, Kenneth E., (1989), *Three Faces of Power*, Newbury Park: Sage.

Bowden, Brett, (2004), 'The Ideal of Civilisation: its Origins and Socio-Political Character', *Critical Review of International Social & Political Philosophy*, 7, 1: 25–50.

Bradshaw, Brendan, (1978), 'Sword, word and strategy in the Reformation in Ireland', *The Historical Journal*, 21, 3: 475–502.

Brannigan, John, (1998), 'A particular vice of that people: Giraldus Cambrensis and the discourse of English colonialism', *Irish Studies Review*, 6, 2: 121–30.

Buruma, Ian, (2004), 'Lost in translation: the two minds of Bernard Lewis', *The New Yorker*, 14 June.

Byrne, John F., (1993), 'The trembling sod: Ireland in 1169', in Art Cosgrove, (ed.), *A New History of Ireland, Vol. II: Medieval Ireland 1169–1534*, Oxford: Clarendon Press: 3–42.

Cambrensis, Giraldus, (1982), *The History and Topography of Ireland*, Mountrath: Dolmen Press.

Canny, Nicholas P., (1973), 'The ideology of English colonization: From Ireland to America', *The William & Mary Quarterly*, 30, 4: 575–98.

Canny, Nicholas P., (1976), *The Elizabethan Conquest of Ireland: A Pattern Established 1565–76*, Hassocks: Harvester Press.

Canny, Nicholas P., (1989), 'Early modern Ireland c.1500–1700', in Robert F. Foster, (ed.), *The Oxford Illustrated History of Ireland*, Oxford: Oxford University Press: 104–60.

Carey, Vincent P., (1999), 'John Derricke's 'Image of Irelande', Sir Henry Sidney, and the massacre at Mullaghmast, 1578', *Irish Historical Studies*, 31, 123: 305–27.

Cavanagh, Sheila T., (1993), 'The fatal destiny of that land: Elizabethan views of Ireland', in Brendan Bradshaw, Andrew Maley and Willy Maley, (eds), *Representing Ireland: Literature and the Origins of Conflict, 1534–1660*: 116–31, Cambridge: Cambridge University Press.

Chibnall, Marjorie, (1999), *The Debate on the Norman Conquest*, Manchester: Manchester University Press.

Collins, Randall, (2009), 'A dead end for a trend theory', *Archives Européennes de Sociologie*, 50, 3: 431–41.

Corrigan, Philip and Derek Sayer, (1985), *The Great Arch: English State Formation as Cultural Revolution*, Oxford: Basil Blackwell.

Cosgrove, Art, (2001), 'The Gaelic resurgence and the Geraldine supremacy c. 1400–1534', in Theodore W. Moody and Francis X. Martin, (eds), *The Course of Irish History*, (revised edn.), Dublin: Mercier Press/RTÉ: 125–38.

Coughlan, Patricia, (1989), 'Some secret scourge which shall by her come unto England': Ireland and incivility in Spenser', in Patricia Coughlan, (ed.), *Spenser and Ireland: an interdisciplinary perspective*, Cork: Cork University Press: 46–74.

Davies, Robert R., (1990), *Domination and Conquest: the Experience of Ireland, Scotland and Wales 1100–1300*, Cambridge: Cambridge University Press.

Davies, Robert R., (1993), 'The English state and the 'Celtic' Peoples 1100–1400', *Journal of Historical Sociology*, 6 (1): 1–14.

Davies, Robert R., (1994), 'The Peoples of Britain and Ireland 1100–1400. I. Identities', *Transactions of the Royal Historical Society, Sixth Series*, 4: 1–20.

Den Boer, Pim, (2001), 'Vergelijkende begripsgeschiedenis', in Pim Den Boer, (ed.), *Beschaving: Een geschiedenis van de begrippen hoofsheid, heusheid, bechaving en cultuur*, Amsterdam: Amsterdam University Press: 15–78.

Duffy, Seán, (1997), *Ireland in the Middle Ages*, Houndmills: Macmillan.

Edwards, David, (2007), 'The escalation of violence in sixteenth-century Ireland', in David Edwards, Padraig Lenihan and Clodagh Tait, (eds), *Age of Atrocity: Violence and Political Conflict in Early Modern Ireland*, Dublin: Four Courts Press: 34–78.

Elias, Norbert, (1996 [1989]), *The Germans: Studies of Power Struggles and the Development of Habitus in the Nineteenth and Twentieth centuries*, Cambridge: Polity Press.

Elias, Norbert, (2000 [1939]), *The Civilizing Process: Sociogenetic and Psychogenetic Investigations*, Oxford: Blackwell.

Elias, Norbert, (2000 [1969]), 'Postscript (1968)', in The Civilizing Process, rev. edn, Oxford: Blackwell: 449–83 [further rev. edn On the Process of Civilisation, Collected Works, Vol. 3, forthcoming].

Elias, Norbert, (2006 [1969]), *The Court Society*. Collected Works, Vol. 2, Dublin: UCD Press.

Elias, Norbert, (2009a [1985]), 'On the creed of a nominalist: observations on Popper's *The Logic of Scientific Discovery*', in *Essays I: On the Sociology of Knowledge and the Sciences*, Collected Works, Vol. 14, Dublin: UCD: 161–90.

Elias, Norbert, (2009b [1985]), 'Science or sciences: contribution to a debate with reality-blind philosophers', in *Essays I: On the Sociology of Knowledge and the Sciences*, Collected Works, Vol. 14, Dublin: UCD Press: 191–211.

Ellis, Steven G., (1995), *Tudor Frontiers and Noble Power: the Making of the British State*, Oxford: Clarendon Press.

Ellis, Steven G., (1998), *Ireland in the Age of the Tudors 1447–1603: English Expansion and the End of Gaelic Rule*, London: Longman.

Ellis, Steven G., (1999), 'The English state and its frontiers in the British Isles, 1300–1600', in Daniel Power and Naomi Standen, (eds), *Frontiers in Question: Eurasian Borderlands 700–1700*: Houndmills: Macmillan: 153–81.

Ellis, Steven G., (2003), 'Racial discrimination in late medieval Ireland', in Gudmundur Hálfdanarson, (ed.), *Racial Discrimination and Ethnicity in European History*, Pisa: Università di Pisa: 21–32.

Febvre, Lucier, (1973 [1930]), 'Civilisation: Evolution of a word and a group of ideas', in Peter Burke, (ed.), *A New Kind of History: From the Writings of Lucien Febvre*. London: Routledge & Kegan Paul: 219–57.

Fletcher, Jonathan, (1995), 'Towards a theory of decivilizing processes', *Amsterdams Sociologisch Tijdschrift*, 22, 2: 283–96.

Fletcher, Jonathan, (1997), *Violence and Civilization*, Cambridge: Polity.

Frame, Robin, (1981), *Colonial Ireland, 1169–1369*, Dublin: Helicon.

Frame, Robin, (1995), 'Overlordship and reaction, c.1200–c.1450', in Alexander Grant and Keith J. Stringer, (eds), *Uniting the Kingdom? The Making of British History*, London: Routledge: 65–84.

Gerald of Wales, (1978), *The Journey through Wales and the Description of Wales*, Harmondsworth: Penguin Classics.

Gillingham, John, (1987), 'Images of Ireland, 1170–1600: the origins of English imperialism', *History Today*, 37, 2: 16–22.

Gillingham, John, (1992), 'The beginnings of English imperialism', *Journal of Historical Sociology*, 5, 4: 393–409.

Gillingham, John, (1993), 'The English invasion of Ireland', in Brendan Bradshaw, Andrew Hudfield and Willy Maley, (eds), *Representing Ireland: Literature and the Origins of Conflict 1534–1660*. Cambridge: Cambridge University Press: 24–42.

Gillingham, John, (1994), '1066 and the introduction of chivalry into England', in Garnett, George and John Hudson, (eds), *Law and government in medieval England and Normandy: essays in honour of Sir James Holt*, Cambridge: Cambridge University Press: 31–55.

Gillingham, John, (1995), 'Foundations of a disunited kingdom', in Alexander Grant and Keith J. Stringer, (eds), *Uniting the Kingdom? The Making of British History*, London: Routledge: 48–64.

Gillingham, John, (1999), 'Killing and mutilating political enemies in the British Isles from the late twelfth to the early fourteenth century: a comparative study', in Brendan Smith, (ed.), *Britain and Ireland 900–1300: insular responses to medieval European change*, Cambridge: Cambridge University Press: 114–34.

Gillingham, John, (2001), 'Civilizing the English? The English histories of William of Malmesbury and David Hume', *Historical Research*, 74: 17–43.

Gillingham, John, (2002), 'From Civilitas to Civility: codes of manners in medieval and early modern England', *Transactions of the Royal Historical Society, Sixth Series*, 12: 267–89.

Goldthorpe, John H., (1987), *Family Life in Western Societies: A Historical Sociology of Family Relationships in Britain and North America*, Cambridge: Cambridge University Press.

Goody, Jack, (1983), *The Development of Family and Marriage in Europe*, Cambridge: Cambridge University Press.

Goudsblom, Johan, (2006), 'Civilization: the career of a controversial concept', *History & Theory*, 45: 288–97.

Hadfield, Andrew, (1993), 'Briton and Scythian: Tudor representations of Irish origins', *Irish Historical Studies*, 28, 112: 390–408.

Hadfield, Ardrew, (1999), 'Rethinking early-modern colonialism: the anomalous state of Ireland', *Irish Studies Review*, 7, 1: 13–27.

Harding, David, (2005), 'Objects of English colonial discourse: The Irish and Native Americans', *Nordic Irish Studies*, 4: 37–60.

Haywood, Eric G., (1996), 'Is Ireland worth bothering about? Classical perceptions of Ireland revisited in Renaissance Italy', *International Journal of the Classical Tradition*, 2, 4: 467–86.

Hechter, Michael, (1975), *Internal Colonialism: The Celtic Fringe in British National Development, 1537–1966*, London: Routledge & Kegan Paul.

Hume, David, (1987), 'Of refinement in the arts', in *Essays Moral, Political and Literary*, Indianapolis: Liberty Classics.

Huntington, Samuel P., (1993), 'The clash of civilizations?', *Foreign Affairs*, 72, 3: 22–49.

Johnston, Dorothy, (1980), 'Richard II and the Submissions of Gaelic Ireland', *Irish Historical Studies*, 22, 85: 1–20.

Jones, William R., (1971), 'The image of the barbarian in medieval Europe', *Comparative Studies in Society & History*, 13, 3: 376–407.

Kenny, Gillian, (2006), 'Anglo-Irish and Gaelic marriage laws and traditions in late medieval Ireland', *Journal of Medieval History*, 32: 27–42.

van Krieken, Robert, (1990), 'Social Discipline and State Formation: Weber and Oestreich on the Historical Sociology of Subjectivity', *Amsterdams Sociologisch Tijdschrift*, 17, 1: 3–28.

van Krieken, Robert, (1998), *Norbert Elias*, London: Routledge.

van Krieken, Robert, (1999), 'The barbarism of civilization: cultural genocide and the "stolen generations",' *British Journal of Sociology*, 50, 2: 297–315.

van Krieken, Robert, (2002), 'Reshaping civilization: liberalism between assimilation and cultural genocide', *Amsterdams Sociologisch Tijdschrift*, 29, 2: 1–38.

van Krieken, Robert, (2003), 'The organization of the soul: Elias and Foucault on discipline and the self', in Eric Dunning and Stephen Mennell, (eds), *Norbert Elias, Vol. 1 (Sage Masters of Modern Social Thought)*, London: Sage: 135–53.

Leerssen, Joep, (1995), 'Wildness, wilderness, and Ireland: medieval and early-modern patterns in the demarcation of civility', *Journal of the History of Ideas*, 56, 1: 25–39.

Lennon, Colm, (2005), *Sixteenth-Century Ireland: The Incomplete Conquest*, Dublin: Gill & Macmillan.

Lewis, Bernard, (1956), 'The Middle East reaction to Soviet pressures', *The Middle East Journal*, 10, 2: 125–37.

Lewis, Bernard, (2001), 'The revolt of Islam', *The New Yorker*, 19 November 2001.

Locke, John, (1960 [1690]), *Two Treatises on Government*, Cambridge: Cambridge University Press.

Lukes, Steven, (2005), *Power: a Radical View*, Houndmills: Palgrave Macmillan.

Lydon, James, (1993), 'A land of war', in Art Cosgrove, (ed.), *A New History of Ireland, Vol. II: Medieval Ireland 1169–1534*, Oxford: Clarendon Press: 240–74.

Lydon, James, (1995), 'Ireland and the English Crown, 1171–1541', *Irish Historical Studies*, 29, 115: 281–94.

Lydon, James, (1997), 'Ireland in 1297: "At peace after its manner" ', in James Lydon, (ed.), *Law and Disorder in Thirteenth-Century Ireland: The Dublin Parliament of 1297*, Dublin: Four Courts Press: 11–24.

Lydon, James, (2001), 'The medieval English colony (1300–c. 1400)', in Theodore W. Moody and Francis X. Martin, (eds), *The Course of Irish History*, rev. edn., Dublin: Mercier Press/RTÉ: 113–24.

Lydon, James, (2008), 'The problem of the frontier in medieval Ireland', in Edmund Curtis, Annette J. Otway-Ruthven and James Lydon, (eds), *Government, War and Society in Medieval Ireland*, Dublin: Four Courts Press: 317–31.

Machiavelli, Nicolò, (1961 [c.1514]), *The Prince*. Harmondsworth: Penguin.

Mazlish, Bruce, (2004), *Civilization and its Contents*, Stanford: Stanford University Press.

McVeigh, Robbie and Bill Rolston, (2009), 'Civilising the Irish', *Race & Class*, 51, 1: 2–28.

Mennell, Stephen, (1990), 'Decivilizing processes: theoretical significance and some lines of research', *International Sociology*, 5, 2: 205–23.

Mennell, Stephen, (2007), *The American Civilizing Process*, Cambridge: Polity.

Morrill, John, (1995), 'Three kingdoms and one commonwealth? The enigma of mid-seventeenth-century Britain and Ireland', in Alexander Grant and Keith J. Stringer, (eds), *Uniting the Kingdom? The Making of British History*, London: Routledge: 170–90.

Muldoon, James, (2003), *Identity on the Medieval Irish Frontier: Degenerate Englishmen, Wild Irishmen, Middle Nations*, Gainesville, FL: University Press of Florida.

Muldoon, James, (2009), *The North Atlantic Frontier of Medieval Europe*, Aldershot: Ashgate.

Murphy, Andrew, (1999), *But the Irish Sea Betwixt Us: Ireland, Colonialism, and Renaissance Literature*, Lexington, KY: University Press of Kentucky.

Murphy, Andrew, (1999), 'Ireland and ante/anti-colonial theory', *Irish Studies Review*, 7, 2: 153–61.

Niebuhr, Reinhold, (1952), 'Culture and civilization (a summary)', *Confluence*, 1, 1: 66–76.

Ohlmeyer, Jane H., (1998), 'Civilizinge of those Rude Partes': Colonization within Britain and Ireland, 1580s–1640s', in Nicholas Canny, (ed.), *The Origins of Empire; British Overseas Enterprise to the Close of the Seventeenth Century, Oxford History of the British Empire*, Oxford: Oxford University Press: 125–147.

Otway-Ruthven, Annette J., (1950), 'The native Irish and English law in medieval Ireland', *Irish Historical Studies*, 7, 25: 1–16.

Pagden, Anthony, (1982), *The Fall of Natural Man: The American Indian and the Origins of Comparative Ethnology*, Cambridge: Cambridge University Press.

Patterson, Nerys, (1991), 'Gaelic Law and the Tudor Conquest of Ireland: The Social Background of the Sixteenth-Century Recensions of the Pseudo-Historical Prologue to the Senchas Már', *Irish Historical Studies*, 27, 107: 193–215.

Pawlisch, Hans S., (1985), *Sir John Davies and the conquest of Ireland: A Study in Legal Imperialism*, Cambridge: Cambridge University Press.

Quinn, David B., (1947), *Raleigh and the British Empire*, London: Hodder & Stoughton.

Quinn, David B., (1958), 'Ireland and sixteenth-century European expansion', *Historical Studies*, 1.

Raftery, Mary and Eoin O'Sullivan, (1999), *Suffer the little children: the inside story of Ireland's industrial schools*, Dublin: New Island.

Robertson, Roland, (2006), 'Civilization', *Theory, Culture & Society* 23, 2–3: 421–7.

Spenser, Edmund, (1934 [1596]), *A View of the Present State of Ireland*, London: Eric Partridge.

Starobinski, Jean, (1993), 'The word *civilization*', in *Blessings in Disguise; or, The Morality of Evil*, Cambridge, MA: Harvard University Press: 1–35.

de Swaan, Abram, (2001), 'Dyscivilization, Mass Extermination and the State', *Theory, Culture & Society*, 18, 2–3: 265–76.

Taatgen, Hendrik A., (1992), 'The Boycott in the Irish Civilizing Process', *Anthropological Quarterly*, 65, 4: 163–76.

Tait, Clodagh, David Edwards and Padraig Lenihan, (2007), 'Early modern Ireland: a history of violence', in David Edwards, Padraig Lenihan and Clodagh Tait, (eds), *Age of Atrocity: Violence and Political Conflict in Early Modern Ireland*, Dublin: Four Courts Press: 9–33.

Weber, Eugen, (1979), *Peasants into Frenchmen: The Modernization of Rural France, 1870–1914*. London: Chatto & Windus.

Williams, Robert A., Jnr, (1990), *The American Indian in Western Legal Thought: The Discourses of Conquest*, New York: Oxford University Press.

Zwaan, Ton, (2003), 'On Civilizing and Decivilizing Processes: A Theoretical Discussion', in Eric Dunning, and Stephen Mennell, (eds), *Norbert Elias – Vol. 4 (Sage Masters of Modern Social Thought)*, London: Sage: 167–75.

Process sociology and international relations

Andrew Linklater

Abstract: Norbert Elias was unusual amongst sociologists of his generation in placing international relations at the centre of sociological analysis – and he was ahead of various theorists of the state who argued in the 1970s and 1980s for enlarging the boundaries of sociology to include relations between states. In Elias's process sociology, international competition for power and security, and 'elimination struggles', have led to larger territorial monopolies of power. In the case of 'civilized' societies, inner pacification has developed alongside preparation for, and repeated involvement in, interstate war. Elias argued that there is no parallel to the 'civilizing process' in international relations, but he observed that higher levels of human interconnectedness have created pressures on people to become better attuned to each other's interests over greater distances. However, many groups react against perceived threats to power, autonomy and prestige and, in general, everyday orientations have lagged behind advances in international interdependence. For Elias, the sociological challenge was to understand how the species can acquire greater control over the processes of global integration. This paper discusses the place of international relations in Elias's account of the civilizing process; it maintains that the approach should be linked more closely with the 'English School of international relations' and its analysis of 'civility' and 'standards of civilization' in world affairs.

Introduction

Over roughly the last two decades, theorists of international relations have drawn extensively on sociology and social theory in an attempt to bring greater sophistication to the field. Elias's writings have not gone unnoticed in that development, but they have had little influence on central theoretical directions.[1] Few have recognized that the analysis of international relations was central to Elias's study of the civilizing process – or that his writings devoted more attention to relations between societies than did many prominent works in social theory and sociology that have influenced International Relations.[2] An assessment of the value of Elias's writings for that field of inquiry is overdue, particularly because his analysis of the civilizing process contains many insights into how international relations over the last few centuries have influenced, and been influenced by, the larger, ongoing transformation of human society. Also overdue is the discussion of how process sociology can profit from engaging with leading approaches in International Relations – particularly 'English School' reflections on 'international society'.[3] Of special relevance is the latter's analysis of the nineteenth century 'standard of civilization'. European states employed that principle to defend their domination of non-European societies, to stand in judgment of their social practices, and to justify controlling their future paths of development.[4] Elias alluded to such developments when he noted in the 1930s that 'the latest phase of the continuing civilizing movement that we are able to observe' is evident in efforts by many non-European elites to emulate the European establishment (Elias, 2000 [1939]: 386, 431–2). He added that the British Empire might succumb to the forces of disintegration but, in his later writings, he did not consider the implications of the anti-colonial revolution for international relations (see below p. 58). By contrast, the English School approach to world politics has analysed the impact of the collapse of the overseas empires on international society, and it has concentrated on 'Third World' struggles to replace 'the standard of civilization' with the idea of a plurality of civilizations that face one another as equals. Leading English School theorists have pointed to success in creating a level of 'civility' that spans the differences between the former colonial powers and the colonised peoples (Jackson, 2000). Their analysis invites the observation that the most recent phase of civilization is evident in the reality that most non-European peoples have accepted Western principles of international relations that are predicated on the idea of the sovereign state, on the duty of non-intervention, and on the practices of diplomacy and international law that denote the existence of an international society of states (Bull and Watson, 1984).

Those introductory comments raise large questions about the relationship between the civilizing process, the European society of states and its global expansion. To explore these matters in more detail, this article focuses on those sections of Elias's writings that deal explicitly with international relations. It is important to add that the relevant passages are not appendices to his account of the civilizing process but are central to the entire analysis. Elias's explanation of that process considered the rise of the modern state *and* the simultaneous division of Europe into sovereign units that had only limited commitments to restraining the use of force in their external relations. State formation and the development of an international political system were two sides of the same coin – although governed by very different principles. There is a parallel with classical realist thought in International Relations which argues that there is a fundamental difference between hierarchical political orders where security is provided by the state, and the anarchic condition in which states must provide for their own security and survival, and where they often find themselves trapped in spiralling geopolitical competition and engulfed in major war as a result. There is also a parallel between the idea of the 'security dilemma' which has been central to realist explanations of tensions between states (see Booth and Wheeler, 2008) and the idea of the 'double-bind process' which Elias employed to explain geopolitical competition (as well as human responses to natural forces). Elias's realism is exemplified by the claim that the 'elimination contests' which states have been involved in for millennia may only end when the species comes under the dominion of a world state (Elias, 2000 [1939]: 445–6; see Elias, 2010b [1987]: 202ff. and Elias, 2010a: 134–5 for a different view. For parallel themes in International Relations, see Wendt, 2003).

Stressing similarities between Elias's writings and approaches to world politics invites the question of whether his reflections contribute anything new to understanding international relations (the question also arises because there is little evidence that he was familiar with leading writings in the field). A different conclusion is suggested by Elias's observations about how the civilizing process grew out of the 'preceding social phase', how it bound people together in new ways, and how the internal pacification of societies led to a new round of elimination struggles and unprecedented levels of interconnectedness that have resulted in tensions between national ways of life and the need for 'global steering mechanisms' that can increase the level of control over largely unregulated processes. Elias's analysis of those tensions brings fresh insight to the study of relations between modern societies by showing that they are part of longer-term patterns of development that include the rise of larger territorial monopolies of power, lengthening webs of interconnectedness, and the pressures to learn how to become better attuned to the needs and interests of people over greater distances that exist alongside familiar struggles for power, autonomy and prestige.

Limits of civility

There is no need to summarize the argument of *The Civilizing Process* here, but it is necessary to identify those features of the investigation that are most significant for Elias's reflections on international politics. In that work, Elias (2000 [1939]: 87ff.) showed how the idea of *courtoisie* was replaced by the idea of civility which was then superseded by the idea of civilization. In examining the second transition, Elias stressed the standard-setting role of the eighteenth century French absolutist court. Earlier medieval courts were described as the first 'societies' in which warriors were slowly turned into courtiers with responsibility for the tasks associated with the increasing administrative burden of emerging states. Members of court society found that their struggles for power and prestige became woven together in ways that required closer self-monitoring and the detailed scrutiny of others' actions, the careful observation of the rules of etiquette under the watchful eye of the king, and the more general control of impulses that enabled members of the court to co-exist without the levels of force that had earlier characterized the lives of warriors. The court of Louis XIV was exemplary because it was the model that adjacent societies sought to emulate (see Elias, 2006 [1969]).

Court societies in Western Europe were bound together by familial ties that were reinforced by elite intermarriage, and the interweaving of courts influenced the ways in which societies behaved towards each other. An aristocratic code underpinned the belief that warfare should resemble the duel, and that force should comply with honourable or chivalrous ideals. Ruling groups identified more closely with each other than with the lower strata in their societies. It is worth noting some parallels with International Relations scholarship. Writing in the 1940s, Carr (1945) and Morgenthau (1973) commented on the 'aristocratic internationalism' of an earlier era, and described how the recent fusion of state and nation eroded the old aristocratic restraints on inter-state violence. Elias referred to a similar process in which bourgeois efforts in the nineteenth century to rally popular support for the nation weakened transnational ties. Bourgeois universalistic and egalitarian ideas sharpened the tension between higher moral principles and the conduct of foreign affairs (Elias, 1996 [1989]: 161). Rising middle-class groups used the new egalitarian ethic to challenge the power of the nobility, but most fell back into the standard ways of conducting international relations.

Parallels to the realist view that little of substance changes in international politics abound in Elias's writings. Two examples are the comment that all that has changed over the millennia are the methods of killing and the number of people involved, and the remark that, in many respects, modern states behave in much the same way as their ancestors did in the so-called age of 'barbarism' (Elias, 1996 [1989]: 176). Elias added that because of the civilizing process, pleasure in killing has declined. Reflecting general trends in impersonal, bureaucratic systems, aggressive impulses have been suppressed in the shift towards the disciplined performance of specialist tasks that require highly-technical training in the art of warfare. But the dangers of war had not declined significantly. A central theme in Elias's writings is that geopolitical conflicts are highly probable, but not inevitable, when states are forced to compete for power and security – that is, when no higher monopoly of power can provide for their security (Elias, 2000 [1939]: 264, 312). There are clear parallels between Elias's emphasis on the recurrence of conflict as societies struggle for security, and realist or neo-realist approaches to world politics that maintain that war and geopolitical rivalries have dominated relations between states for millennia.[5]

As noted earlier, the reasons that Elias gave for that immanent tendency bring to mind realist notions of the security dilemma. First coined by John Herz in the 1950s, that concept refers to the bind in which states often find themselves. Responsible for their security, they must accumulate sufficient military power to withstand immediate threats and prepare for likely challenges. Intentions may be defensive, but other societies cannot assume that the instruments of violence will never be turned against them. The rational calculation of interests dictates that they take similar measures, also for defensive reasons, although others can no more assume that the ability to inflict violent harm will stay in reserve and be used only to resist aggression. Without any actor intending to bring such circumstances about, states (and particularly the great powers) find themselves entangled in geopolitical struggles that generate fear and mutual suspicion, and increase the danger of war.

Elias used the notion of the 'double-bind process' to describe such tensions that arise in international affairs and in human relations with the natural world. As part of a larger study of the role of the emotions in social life, the concept was used to highlight the influence of collective fantasies on relations between societies. States that are caught up in double-bind processes often exaggerate threats. Exposed to danger, they act on highly-emotive images of reality, and reinforce feelings of distrust and fear in others that can trap them all in cycles that are hard to disrupt (Elias, 2007a [1987]: ch. 3). Elias argued that the high fantasy-content of national images can block the 'realistic assessment' of critical forces and 'realistic practice'. Similar responses are promoted in others with the result that, collectively, they fail to make progress in understanding how key dynamics might be brought under control. The resulting circularity invariably binds people more intensely to their 'survival units' and locks them into insider– outsider dualisms that make it harder to attain 'reality-congruent' knowledge of international processes (see Kaspersen and Gabriel, 2008). Those problems are magnified by forms of 'group love' that celebrate using force against others and towering over them. Such attachments are intensified when societies believe that they have been denied the respect and the standing that is their right – as in the case of post-First World War Germany where the idea of the 'stab in the back' was linked with 'idealized' self-images and distorted views of competitors that revealed how societies can succumb to a collective illness that leads to their downfall and to the devastation of other peoples (Elias, 2010a: 95, 101; Elias, 2008 [1976]: 28–9).

Elias's ingenious commentary on the problem of involvement and detachment in relations between peoples informed the discussion of how advances in 'reality-congruent' knowledge can increase the potential for mastering processes that seem beyond control. Societies caught up in double-bind processes may be so emotionally involved in the moment that the detached analysis of the pressures they face escapes them.[6] Each can be so caught up in asking what specific events mean for its own interests that none can acquire the distance required to comprehend the intrinsic nature of these events and their meaning for all the societies involved (Kilminster, 2007: 118). Elias believed that social science has a unique role to play in promoting the requisite detachment from short-term horizons that is essential for understanding general social processes and for learning how to gain control over them. Firmly committed to non-partisan sociological inquiry that checks tendencies to place prognosis ahead of diagnosis, he believed that the 'detour of detachment' could provide societies with a fund of reality-congruent knowledge that could be used to regulate unmastered processes.

Elias (2000 [1939]: 35ff.) observed that the late eighteenth-century physiocrats instigated one of the great breakthroughs in the social sciences by portraying the economy as a system of laws that societies could to some degree manipulate to their common advantage. He referred to perspectives on the natural world that acquired levels of detachment superior to the more involved standpoints that prevail in social inquiry, blocking similar accomplishments. The point can be applied to the study of international relations by noting that thinkers of the Italian Renaissance constructed the idea of an interdependent states-system with laws or tendencies that could be regulated to some degree if the great powers refrained from seizing every opportunity to gain short-term advantage and cooperated to maintain the balance of power. The emergence of the new diplomatic system which revolved around resident ambassadors with agreed immunities was linked to an appreciation of the need for restraint and foresight in foreign policy, and with an understanding of the politics of *raison de système* (the politics of curbing national ambitions that threatened the survival of the balance of power). In the seventeenth century, accounts of the laws that governed the universe may have been influential in the quest for a more detached understanding of the systemic forces that dominate international politics and in the search for consistency between foreign policy practice and 'reality-congruent' knowledge (Butterfield, 1966).

Elias described international relations as the realm in which the fear of the possible consequences of failing to outmanoeuvre or defeat specific adversaries has often barred the way to even the imperfect levels of detachment that have appeared in some other spheres of social interaction. As noted earlier, the approach has much in common with realist and neo-realist perspectives that highlight the differences between domestic and international politics, and specifically the dangers and constraints that exist when political actors must compete for security. It is important to add that Elias did not share the classical realist belief that struggles for power are inherent in human nature (Mennell, 2010). Nor was he sympathetic to the mode of reasoning, evident in the neo-realist explanation of geopolitical rivalries, that focuses on the constraining role of the international system. Elias argued that analyses that emphasize unchanging systemic forces correctly point to structural features of the social world, but they are guilty of a 'process reducing' orientation that is avoided in advanced social inquiry (Elias, 2000 [1969]: postscript; see Waltz, 1979, for an example of process-reduction in neo-realism). Elias's perspective strongly advises against assuming that states are part of an international system that forces them, as if from outside, to compete for power and security; in the end, structural restraints are no more than the pressures that people impose on each other. An alternative starting-point begins with the question of how societies with diverse civilizing processes and different assumptions about the levels of self-restraint that are appropriate in the foreign policy realm are drawn into webs of mutual dependence that none control (Elias, 2000 [1939]: 410). Such entanglements create pressures to become more responsive to the interests of other peoples, but advances rarely take place where competition for power and prestige leads to national images with a high 'fantasy content'. Such struggles cannot be understood without analysing the history of the relations between the societies involved, the rivalries over what they regard as their due respect and recognition, and their conceptions of superiority over, or inferiority to, others. They cannot be explained without understanding different civilizing processes that reflect the influence of 'domestic' and 'international' forces – processes that systems-theorizing ignores. A central theme in Elias's writings was that those forces are inseparable, although the social sciences had yet to develop an adequate vocabulary for explaining their interpenetration.

The dualism of nation states' normative codes

A central question is whether Elias believed that core elements of the civilizing process have left a lasting impression on world politics – or whether it is at all meaningful to refer to a *global* civilizing process. His more pessimistic comments about international relations stem from the claim that the European civilizing process was linked with the rise of territorial concentrations of power that imposed external constraints, which slowly turned into internal restraints as more and more people became tied together in longer webs of interconnectedness and subject to closer self-monitoring. State monopolies of power suspended earlier elimination contests between nobles and set in motion long-term patterns of change that tamed the warriors. However, states entered into new struggles for power, and new 'elimination contests', now fought out at the international level (see the discussion of the 'monopoly mechanism', in Elias (2000 [1939]: 268ff.). The upshot was the 'Janus-faced' condition in which states are inwardly pacified but prepared for war (Elias, 1996 [1989]: 175). As with warring lords, states rarely tried to extend their power as far as they could. Motivation was usually defensive, the aim being to deny strategically significant territory to adversaries.[7] States were prepared however to inflict levels of harm on enemies that were largely outlawed in relations between citizens. They operated with a double standard of morality, not only tolerating but at times celebrating acts of violence that were prohibited within state boundaries. For that reason, Elias (1996 [1989]: 177) maintained that there was a 'split' at the heart of the civilizing process. In the final pages of *The Civilizing Process* he cited with apparent approval Holbach's comment that humans will only earn the right to call themselves civilized when they succeed in eradicating warfare (Elias, 2000 [1939]: 446–7).

It would be peculiar if the changing sensibilities to violence which emerged with the civilizing process have not influenced foreign policy behaviour to some extent. Elias (1996 [1989]: 405) observed that information about the atrocities that were committed in the Nazi death camps produced shock and repugnance, and he pointed to a contrast with classical antiquity where what is now called genocide was commonplace and rarely attracted condemnation. Modern attitudes to war reflected broader patterns of change that led the slaughter of animals to be hidden 'behind the scenes', that involved the abolition of judicial torture and capital punishment, that produced new sensibilities regarding violence to women and children or cruelty to animals, and which relocated force to the barracks where it was 'stored' for use in emergencies. The point was that modern peoples are accustomed to living in pacified societies. Unlike the members of warrior societies who carry weapons and use them in everyday life, and who are trained from infancy to take part in war, the citizens of modern states need special training to prepare them for the demanding transition from peace to war. They are less attuned to violence from an early age, and less likely to encounter death and the dying in everyday life (Elias, 2010a). Killing and wounding, or witnessing the horrors of war, can lead to psychological disorders on returning to 'normal' society, as encapsulated by the idea of post-conflict traumatic syndrome. Because of the civilizing process, the earlier qualities of the warrior that included the zest for battle and the joy in killing are less central to modern organized warfare. The warrior in civilized society is required to demonstrate something of the same levels of emotion control and restraint that modern bureaucratic structures impose on officials. The essential claim is captured by the observation that Holocaust deniers miss the central point when they argue that the killing of Jews occurred because of sporadic outbursts of hatred and violence by sections of the military. Fewer Jews would have been killed had the Nazi regime not been able to harness bureaucratic power to murder millions of people (Mennell, 1998: 249).

Civilizing processes and international society

One of the paradoxes of the bipolar era, Elias (2007b [1992]: 129) observed, was that millions of people co-existed amicably in their society, but lived with the possibility of large scale slaughter as a result of nuclear war. From one critical standpoint, that observation failed to recognize the extent to which the nuclear revolution had introduced the 'functional equivalent' of a monopoly of power that compelled the great powers to show greater foresight and to display higher levels of self-restraint lest they were drawn into a nuclear conflict (van Benthem van den Bergh, 1992). On that argument, nuclear weapons have had a 'civilizing' role in world politics since they have created pressures to tame violence, to acquire more realistic understandings of adversaries, and to treat them with respect (for a more pessimistic view, see Elias, 2010a: 119).

Students of international relations can develop that critique of Elias's position by pointing to the high level of order that exists in international politics even in the condition of anarchy, understood as the absence of a higher power monopoly rather than as chaos and conflict (Bull, 1977). The 'English School of International Relations' or 'international society perspective' has been centrally involved in understanding the foundations of international order. Indeed, some of its exponents have referred to 'civility' and to 'civilizing processes' in world politics, although there is no evidence that their choice of terms was influenced by reading Elias (see Linklater, 2004; also Linklater and Suganami, 2006). Their explanation of global civility stressed that most states have an interest in preserving the larger order on which their security depends. There is a parallel with the notion of the 'ambivalence of interests' that Elias (2000 [1939]: 312ff) used to explain the survival of stable monopolies of power in modern Europe. Necessity, his argument was, created incentives to moderate self-interest; the fear was that the lack of restraint would provoke others into aggressive responses that would endanger the political order that different groups had an interest in preserving. Initially, compromises were grudging, but the fact that they were made at all revealed how people can develop more realistic understandings of each other along with new patterns of foresight and self-restraint. Similar reasoning underpins the study of international society. Process sociology and the English School are similar in stressing that advances in civility largely occur between states that can respond to threats by imposing an equivalent cost on those that have harmed or can harm them (see the discussion of functional democratization in Elias 2000 [1939], and the analysis of the importance of the balance of power for international society in (Bull, 1977: ch. 5).

Leading members of the English School have argued that the sense of belonging to a civilization that is sharply differentiated from the 'barbarian' world has often made it easier for states to rely on diplomacy to establish basic principles of global co-existence (Wight, 1977). Order between the European powers in the nineteenth century was strengthened by the 'standard of civilization' that maintained that only European powers had the right to belong to an international society of sovereign states. According to that idea, 'backward' non-European societies were appropriately colonies, or in some other way subject to the imperial powers that claimed the right to set the conditions that they would have to satisfy before they could be considered for admission to the society of states. The 'standard of civilization' invites the question of whether European ideas about civility and civilization influenced the modern states-system in other ways. Its impact on European attitudes towards the non-European world is evidence of how the civilizing process has influenced international relations. But to what extent did ideas about civility and civilization shape relations between the European powers themselves, and the long-term development of international society?

A window onto the link between the civilizing process and the idea of international society is provided by the writings of Francois de Callières (1983 [1716]), which demonstrated that the French absolutist court was standard-setting in the diplomatic realm as in other spheres.[8] No higher authority, he argued, could restrain sovereigns in the world that had replaced the *respublica Christiana*, but states were nevertheless 'parts of a civilization' that were able to promote 'order and adjustment by civilized means' (Keens-Soper and Schweizer, 1983: 35). As custodians of 'civilized' statecraft, ambassadors had special responsibilities for displaying self-restraint and foresight. It was incumbent on them to avoid 'a severe rugged manner' that 'commonly disgusts and causes aversion'; it was crucial that they were recruited not from the 'naturally violent and passionate' whose sensibilities had been coarsened by war, but from the 'civilized' ranks of the lower nobility who could understand other courts in their own terms, setting aside any personal hostilities to alien customs (Callières, 1983 [1716]: 75, 86, 150, 166ff.). Highly attuned to court rationality, the skilled ambassador could think from the standpoint of others and recognize the value of a reputation for honesty (Callières, 1983 [1716]: 83,

139). Securing 'mutual advantages' required self-restraint; the disputatious amplification of differences, and any temptation to highlight others' weaknesses, had to be resisted (Callières, 1983 [1716]: 110). The underlying reason for civility was that states had become so intertwined in 'one and the same Commonwealth' that change in one place was 'capable of disturbing the quiet of all the others' (Callières, 1983 [1716]: 68, 70). The compulsions of interdependence therefore created incentives to replace impulsive conduct with a dispassionate calculation of common interests (Callières, 1983 [1716]: 97, 138). With heightened interconnectedness, the old adage of the prince, *sic volo, sic jubeo, stat pro ratione voluntas*, ('let the fact that I wish this, be sufficient reason') could no longer suffice as the first principle of statecraft (Callières, 1983 [1716]: 62).

De Callières did not live in an era that was greatly troubled by tensions between statecraft and universal principle, or that was anxious about removing the imperfections of international society by advancing towards perpetual peace (Keens-Soper and Schweizer, 1983: 39). It was thought that a balance had to be struck between the quest for 'mutual advantages' and the ambassadorial duty to serve the 'honour and interest of his Prince' (Callières, 1983 [1716]: 111). But what is striking is the vision of bringing an element of restraint to world politics that drew on many of the qualities that Elias regarded as emblematic of court society and which, as already noted, underlined the exemplary, standard-setting, role of the French court (Elias, 2006 [1969]; Keens-Soper and Schweitzer, 1983: 23).

Those observations bring to mind Elias's comments about the link between court society and European standards of self-regulation that were evident in the idea that warfare should have the hallmarks of the aristocratic duel. Crucially, however, Elias believed that such restraints are brittle when societies fear for their survival or security. The same conviction runs through English School writings, and is evident in the statement that international order may ultimately depend on the balance of power, and is threatened by the rise of a hegemon (see Dunne, 2003; also Elias, 2010a: 101 on 'hegemonic intoxication'). The assumption is that what there is in the way of a global civilizing process depends largely on the restraints that states impose on each other, cognisant of the dangers of behaving otherwise. That is not to suggest that internal restraints are wholly lacking – only that for the English School they may prove to be insufficiently strong to curb the ambitions of the great powers and to constrain hegemonic aspirations (Clark, 2009; Elias, 2010a). There are unmistakable parallels with Elias's claim that civilizing processes are brittle, unevenly developed and susceptible to sudden reversal under conditions of threat and instability.

Integration and disintegration in the current phase of globalization

Elias (2000 [1939]: 386) described the most recent phase of the civilizing process as one in which the outlook of a global establishment – the Western colonial powers – had won acceptance amongst many colonized elites. Earlier patterns in relations between 'the established and the outsiders', in which the former encouraged the latter to internalise feelings of inferiority, and the latter sought to emulate the former's 'civilized' practices, had fuelled those changes. The spread of 'civilized' norms was evidence of the globalization of social relations, although Elias (2000 [1939]: 266–7) was quick to add in the 1930s that the British Empire seemed to be nearing the end of the road, just as earlier empires had succumbed to the disintegrative tendencies that appear whenever diverse peoples are forced together against their will (also Elias, 2010a: 134–5).

Those comments about the recent phase of globalization require discussion of a central theme in Elias's later writings, which is the overall trend over thousands of years of human history towards the establishment of ever-larger territorial concentrations of power along with associated pressures on the people who have been drawn together to become better attuned to each other's interests and to widen 'the scope of emotional identification' to others within the new 'survival unit' (see de Swaan, 1995; Mennell, 1990; 1994). The analysis of the civilizing process explained how changing conceptions of civilized conduct – and specifically shared understandings about the sources of shame and embarrassment – had helped bind people together in modern political communities. With the rise of the idea of the nation, members of the same state began to identify with each other to a greater extent than before, irrespective of social origin. Elites that had self-consciously distanced themselves from the lower strata began to claim to represent the entire nation. The civilizing process took different forms in societies such as France and Germany where particular national histories and collective identities found expression in specific internal tensions and distinctive orientations towards the wider world (Elias, 1996 [1989]: 160ff.). But in general, closer emotional identification between the members of particular societies developed in tandem with sharp contrasts between European peoples, and also with perceptions of major differences between the European and non-European worlds. As noted earlier, the most recent phase of the civilizing process is inextricably linked with the fact that more and more people across the world have been drawn together. Incentives to moderate ambitions have increased as a result – in a parallel to the forms of responsiveness between people who were earlier forced to live together within the same nation-state. However, longer webs of social and economic interconnectedness often provoke hostile reactions as groups respond to threats to their power and status – and rivalries between states certainly do not end with increasing interdependence. There was no guarantee, Elias argued, that a global civilizing process marked by increasing pacification and higher levels of emotional identification between peoples will define the future course of events.

The reality that 'integration–disintegration' tensions are now worked out at the level of humanity required the supersession of conventional sociological analysis. Sociologists, Elias (2010b [1987]: 147) argued, can no longer close their 'eyes to the fact that in our time, in place of the individual states, humanity split up into states is increasingly . . . the framework of reference, as a social unit, of many developmental processes and structural changes'. It had become essential to analyse long-term social processes that profoundly influence the lives of human beings in their different societies. Such re-orientations did not just involve an inquiry into the forces that, in the last few centuries, and especially since the industrial era, have drawn people more closely together. It was important to adopt a world-historical perspective on global civilizing processes such as the emergence of the linguistic or symbolic powers that made the following phenomena possible: the replacement of biological with cultural evolution as the main influence on human development; the elimination of rival species and the large-scale pacification of nature; the evolution of longer social and political webs so that now virtually the whole of humanity is tied by 'its hand and feet' in relations that none control; the remarkable levels of pacification that exist in stable societies; and the dangers that people now confront as a result of successive revolutions in the capacity to cause harm over greater distances. The latter may have brought humanity closer to the 'end of the road' and to the point where, without a new civilizing process, there is a very real possibility of a return to the cave (Elias, 2010a: 78, 128). Against this background, Elias (2010a: 144ff.) maintained that human beings now face an entirely new problem, which is how to pacify humanity as a whole and how to end 'hegemonic wars'.

A recurrent theme in Elias's examination of very long-term processes of change is the co-existence of greater collective power over nature and an increase in the threats that people pose to one another by belonging to different 'survival units'. Time and again, societies have been faced with the question of whether their modes of orientation can keep pace with the demands of increased interconnectedness. Often, the *habitus* has had a 'drag effect' on the emergence of multiple loyalties in more inclusive associations that exercise greater power over the forces that chain people together. In modern states, centralized institutions have often been created to deal with the problems that stem from higher levels of interconnectedness. With respect to the modern international system, Elias (2010b [1987]: 147, 181, 195–7) argued that the rise of 'unions of states' may eventually replace 'individual states' as 'the dominant social unit'. But movement in that direction is not straightforward. As a result of the parochial attachments encouraged by 'natio-centric socialization', many people are hostile to higher political arrangements that challenge 'traditional national self-images'; they may recognize the utility of such unions while admitting that they do not derive much 'emotional warmth' from them (Elias, 2000 [1939]: 551).

Elias (2010b [1987]: 222) argued that the transition to post-national communities may be more difficult than the transition from tribe to state was. No explanation is offered, but perhaps the interplay between 'natio-centric socialization', the part that double-bind processes play in perpetuating insider–outsider dualisms, and anxieties about losing power and autonomy to higher political authorities provides the answer. In combination, those forces prevent levels of detachment from the problems of the hour that can enable societies to establish 'global steering mechanisms' that allow them to plan their lives together more successfully. The reality is that the idea of humanity is a 'blank' space on the 'emotional map' of most people (Elias, 2010b [1987]: 181, 198–9). More are aware of the misery of the world's vulnerable communities, and many believe that something should be done about it, but there is little effective action (Elias, 1996 [1989]: 26). Looking back on modern times, future generations may conclude that the affluent in contemporary societies were amongst the 'late barbarians' (Elias, 2010b [1987]: 146–7). Wrapped up in the observation is the hope that people will find ways of organizing their existence so that all can live without the burden of relievable suffering and unnecessary harm. But there is no guarantee of progress. The 'immense process of integration' which the species is undergoing may give way to a 'dominant disintegration process' (Elias, 2010b [1987]: 148). Forward movement would be easier if people could shed feelings of cultural superiority and acquire more realistic understandings of other groups. An appreciation of the 'senselessness of wars', and the urgency of combining old loyalties to nation-states with new attachments to post-national associations, might develop if people held before them an 'image of humanity' clinging to life 'on the small solar planet Earth' in a universe that is indifferent to their fate (Elias, 2010a: 82).

The importance of Elias for international relations theory today

It is important to conclude with some observations about the relationship between Elias's discussion of elimination contests, double-bind processes, integration–disintegration tensions and so forth, and some leading theories of international relations. What, in short, does process sociology contribute to those theories? What might it learn from them?

The focus on long-term perspective is one of the great strengths of Elias's processual approach. There is a parallel with Elias's lament about the 'retreat into the present' (which is evident in much social and political analysis) and the critique of 'presentism' in international relations theory (Buzan and Little, 2000; Elias, 2009 [1987]). Support for long-term perspectives in the study of world politics has emerged as part of a critique of neo-realism – specifically its failure to explain changes in the principal forms of political unit as well as different levels of interconnectedness in international history and recent shifts in the importance of economic as opposed to geopolitical interaction (Buzan and Little, 2000). What Elias's writings contribute to that discussion is a sophisticated explanation of long-term patterns of development over centuries and millennia that revolves around the comparative analysis of civilizing processes. It is important to add that very little work in International Relations views long-term trends in relations between states in conjunction with the long-term transformation of human society. There is a tendency, which is most evident in neo-realism, to regard the international system as a domain existing apart from other spheres of social and political existence, and to ignore crucial questions about how domestic and international processes are closely interwoven and evolve over time (Waltz, 1979).[9]

It is essential to stress that the realist tradition has long dealt with the themes that lie at the heart of Elias's approach to international relations: with elimination contests, double-bind processes, monopolistic tendencies and so on. Undoubtedly, process sociologists can profit from engaging with the realist literature. However, students of international relations could also usefully engage with Elias's critique of systems theorizing and indeed with all 'process-reducing' orientations to society and politics. It is important to note that *The Civilizing Process* explicitly discussed many issues that have been central to innovative scholarship in International Relations in the recent period, including the reasons for the emergence of states (the *sine qua non* of international politics), for the divisions between domestic and international relations, and for the separation between 'economics' and 'politics'. Shared ground is the belief that systems approaches cannot explain such long-term patterns of development (Rosenberg, 1994; Ruggie, 1983).

Elias organized his account of those phenomena around the study of the civilizing process – that is, around the analysis of changing attitudes to violence in relations within, if not in relations between, states. English School approaches to the society of states contribute to understanding civilizing and decivilizing processes in international relations. Closer ties between process sociology and the study of international society can shed new light on how the rise and evolution of the modern society of states has been part of a larger transformation of human existence – more specifically, how it has been influenced by, and has influenced, the European civilizing process.

There is no space to consider a raft of perspectives including studies of the 'liberal peace' and 'security communities' such as the European Union, as well as investigations of the rise of the universal human rights culture and innovations in international criminal law, that are pertinent to taking that investigation further. Nor is there an opportunity to consider possible future linkages between process sociology and the critical or normative approaches to international relations that have developed over the last three decades. Elias was opposed to partisan sociology. But unambiguously normative – and indeed internationalist – convictions are evident in his claim that there may come a time when those who commit atrocities against others are judged to be either 'criminal or insane' (Elias, 2007a [1987]: 13). Efforts to build connections between process sociology, critical-theoretical standpoints and the English School approach to international relations are currently under way (Linklater, 2010; 2011). Whether that development is wholly consistent with Elias's overall approach is another matter (see Kilminster, 2007: ch. 5). It is mentioned as evidence of Elias's importance for the study of international relations, and of his belated, but inevitable, rise to prominence in the field.

Acknowledgements

I wish to thank Godfried van Benthem van den Bergh, Florence Delmotte, Stephen Mennell, Norman Gabriel and Chris Shilling for their comments on an earlier draft of this paper.

Notes

1 Van Benthem van den Bergh (1992) was the first major work published in English to use Elias's writings in the study of international relations, though he had made the connection in essays written in Dutch in the 1970s – see his book *De staat van geweld en andere essays* (1980). See also Linklater (2004, 2007, 2010) on the relevance of Elias's work for analysing the problem of harm in world politics.
2 The custom is followed here of distinguishing between International Relations (with capital letters) as a field of inquiry and international relations (lower case) as the sphere of strategic, diplomatic and economic relations between states.
3 Elias (2010a: 130) refers to 'solidarity' between states based on respect for sovereignty, but this is a very occasional reference to the existence of an international society.
4 See Elias (2000 [1939]: 43) for a discussion of Napoleon's attitude towards the conquest of Egypt and the idea of the civilizing mission.
5 Donnelly (2000, 2009) explains the differences between realist and neo-realist approaches.
6 The context is such cognitive advances in the natural sciences as the rise of the heliocentric universe and the Darwinian dethroning of the species that displayed the remarkable advances in 'self-distancing' that have given human societies unrivalled mastery of the physical world (Elias, 2007a [1987]: Section VII).
7 In the language of international relations theory, Elias was a 'defensive realist' who focused on strategies of denying others control over vital strategic areas. 'Offensive realism' maintains that expansionist ambitions shape the behaviour of the great powers (Donnelly, 2009). The latter theme was central to the discussion of 'hegemonic fever' and 'hegemonic intoxication' in Elias (2010a: 91–2, 101).
8 De Callières was a member of Louis XIV's court who served as French ambassador to Spain.
9 Elias did not discuss ways in which diplomacy, the managed balance of power and other institutions of international society made it possible for states to escape double-bind processes or to mitigate their effects. See however the discussion of the relationship between civilization and diplomacy in Elias (1996 [1989]: 139ff.).

References

Dates given in square brackets are those of first publication.

van Benthem van den Bergh, Godfried, (1980), *De staat van geweld en andere essays*, Amsterdam: Meulenhoff.
van Benthem van den Bergh, Godfried, (1992), *The Nuclear Revolution and the End of the Cold War: Forced Restraint*, Basingstoke: Macmillan.
Booth, Ken and Nicholas J. Wheeler, (2008), *The Security Dilemma: Fear, Cooperation and Trust*, Basingstoke: Palgrave Macmillan.
Bull, Hedley, (1977), *The Anarchical Society: A Study of Order in World Politics*, Basingstoke: Macmillan.
Bull, Hedley and Adam Watson, (eds), (1984), *The Expansion of International Society*, Oxford: Clarendon Press.
Butterfield, Herbert, (1966), 'The Balance of Power', in Herbert Butterfield and Martin Wight, (eds), *Diplomatic Investigations: Essays in the Theory of International Relations*, London: Allen & Unwin.
Buzan, Barry and Richard Little, (2000), *International Systems in World History: Remaking the Study of International Relations*, Oxford: Oxford University Press.
Callières, Francois de, (1983 [1716]), *The Art of Diplomacy*, Leicester: University of Leicester Press.
Carr, Edward Hallett, (1945), *Nationalism and After*, London: Macmillan.

Clark, Ian, (2009), 'Towards an English School theory of hegemony', *European Journal of International Relations*, 15, 2: 203–28.

Donnelly, Jack, (2000), *Realism and International Relations*, Cambridge: Cambridge University Press.

Donnelly, Jack, (2009), 'Realism', in Scott Burchill and Andrew Linklater, (eds), *Theories of International Relations*, Basingstoke: Palgrave.

Dunne, Tim, (2003), 'Society and hierarchy in international society', *International Relations*, 17: 303–20.

Elias, Norbert, (1996 [1989]), *The Germans: Power Struggles and the Development of Habitus in the Nineteenth and Twentieth Centuries*, Cambridge: Polity Press. [Collected Works, Vol. 11, forthcoming].

Elias, Norbert, (2000 [1939]), *The Civilizing Process: Sociogenetic and Psychogenetic Investigations*, Oxford: Basil Blackwell. [*On the Process of Civilisation*, Collected Works, Vol. 3, forthcoming].

Elias, Norbert, (2000 [1969], 'Postscript (1968)', in The Civilizing Process, revised edn, Oxford: Blackwell: 449–83.

Elias, Norbert, (2006 [1969]), *The Court Society*, Collected Works, Vol. 2, Dublin: University College Dublin Press.

Elias, Norbert, (2007a [1987]), *Involvement and Detachment*. Collected Works, Vol. 8, Dublin: University College Dublin Press.

Elias, Norbert, (2007b [1992]), *An Essay on Time*, Collected Works, Vol. 9, Dublin: University College Dublin Press.

Elias, Norbert, (2008 [1976]), 'Towards a theory of established–outsider relations', in Norbert Elias and John L. Scotson, (2008 [1965]), *The Established and the Outsiders*, Collected Works, Vol. 4, Dublin: University College Dublin Press.

Elias, Norbert, (2009 [1987]), 'The retreat of sociologists into the present', in Norbert Elias, *Essays III: On Sociology and the Humanities*, Collected Works, Vol. 16, Dublin: University College Dublin Press.

Elias, Norbert, (2010a), *The Loneliness of the Dying* and *Humana Conditio*, Collected Works, Vol. 6, Dublin: University College Dublin Press.

Elias, Norbert, (2010b [1987]), *The Society of Individuals*, Collected Works, Vol. 10, Dublin: University College Dublin Press.

Gong, Gerrit, (1984), *The Standard of 'Civilization' in International Society*, Oxford: Clarendon Press.

Jackson, Robert, (2000), *The Global Covenant: Human Conduct in a World of States*, Oxford: Oxford University Press.

Kaspersen, Lars B. and Norman Gabriel, (2008), 'The importance of survival units for Norbert Elias's figurational perspective', *Sociological Review*, 56, 3: 370–87.

Keens-Soper, H.M.A. and Karl W. Schweizer, (1983), 'The Life and Work of Francois de Callieres', in Francois de Callières, *The Art of Diplomacy*, New York: Holmes & Meier Publishers.

Kilminster, Richard, (2007), *Norbert Elias: Post-Philosophical Sociology*, Abingdon: Routledge.

Linklater, Andrew, (2004), 'Norbert Elias, the civilizing process and International Relations', *International Politics*, 41, 1: 3–35.

Linklater, Andrew, (2007), Torture and civilization', *International Relations*, 23, 1: 119–30.

Linklater, Andrew, (2010), Global civilizing process and the ambiguities of human inter-connectedness', *European Journal of International Relations*, 16, 2: 155–78.

Linklater, Andrew, (2011), *The Problem of Harm in World Politics: Theoretical Investigations*, Cambridge: Cambridge University Press.

Linklater, Andrew and Suganami Hidemi, (2006), *The English School of International Relations: A Contemporary Assessment*, Cambridge: Cambridge University Press.

Mennell, Stephen, (1990), 'The globalization of human society as a very long-term social process: Elias's theory', *Theory, Culture and Society*, 7, 2: 359–71.

Mennell, Stephen, (1994), 'The formation of we-images: a process theory', in Craig Calhoun, (ed.), *Social Theory and the Politics of Identity*, Oxford: Blackwell: 175–97.

Mennell, Stephen, (1998), *Norbert Elias: An Introduction*. Dublin: University College Dublin Press.

Mennell, Stephen, (2010), 'Abschiedsvorlesung: Realism and reality congruence – International Relations and Sociology'. Paper delivered at the Conference on *Globalization and Civilization in International Relations: Towards New Models of Human Interdependence*, University College Dublin.

Morgenthau, Hans, (1973), *Politics Among Nations: The Struggle for Power and Peace*. New York: Alfred Knopf.

Rosenberg, Justin, (1994), *Empire of Civil Society: A Critique of the Realist Theory of International Relations*, London: Verso.

Ruggie, John, (1983), 'Continuity and transformation in the world polity: toward a neo-realist synthesis', *World Politics*, 35, 2: 261–85.

de Swaan, Abram, (1995), 'Widening circles of identification: emotional concerns in sociogenetic perspective', *Theory, Culture and Society*, 12, 2: 25–39.

Waltz, Kenneth, (1979), *Theory of International Politics*, New York: Addison-Wesley.

Wendt, Alexander, (2003), 'Why a world state is inevitable', *European Journal of International Relations*, 9, 4: 491–542.

Wight, Martin, (1977), *Systems of States*, Leicester: University of Leicester Press.

Entropy, the anthroposphere and the ecology of civilization: An essay on the problem of 'liberalism in one village' in the long view

Stephen Quilley

Abstract: In his theory of civilizing processes Elias drew attention, albeit obliquely, to the interweaving connections between ecological, biological, social and psychological processes operating at a variety of nested temporal scales. Elucidating a series of fundamental propositions, this paper is an attempt firstly to explicate the parameters of the general theory of humanity that is implicit in his concrete historical studies, and secondly to apply this theory to linked problems of global sustainability and cosmopolitan democracy. Building on Goudsblom's concept of the 'anthroposphere', I argue that long-term processes of social development have always been synonymous with a specific process of ecological transformation defined by 'trophic expansion'. This Eliasian approach to human ecology is then used to explore the global environmental ecological crisis through the lens of the *longue durée*. From this perspective, I question liberal assumptions about the natural affinity between democracy and ecological sustainability and, more specifically, the possibility of 'low energy cosmopolitanism'. Developing ideas hinted at by C. H. Waddington in the 1960s and more recently by James Lovelock, I argue that any long-term future for complex, cosmopolitan societies and a sustainable rapprochement between the biosphere and the anthroposphere, will depend on the emergence of technologies of 'trophic detachment'.

Introduction

This essay is an attempt to explicate the general theory of human development that is implicit in Elias's theory of civilizing processes. The immediate purpose is to explore the connected problems of sustainability on the one hand and democratic pluralism and social liberalism on the other, through the lens of very long-term processes of social-ecological development. It is useful to start with two definitions.

The Anthroposphere 'is that part of the biosphere which is inhabited and influenced by humans. The most fundamental trend in human history has been the expansion of the anthroposphere within the biosphere – at first slow and almost imperceptible, later at an increasingly more rapid pace'. (Goudsblom, 2003b: 3–4)

Trophic expansion is the process through which a steadily increasing proportion of the annual productivity of the biosphere is diverted to fund long-term processes of human social development. It is a measure of the relative encroachment of the anthroposphere on the biosphere. (Quilley, 2004b)

Cosmogenesis and Elias's theory of knowledge

In *Involvement and Detachment* (2007 [1987]: 179–233) Elias used the term 'the great evolution' to refer to an overarching process of cosmogenesis. In his 'comprehensive process model' (see Quilley, 2004a), a Comtean *hierarchy of scientific disciplines* corresponds to a *spectrum of fields of investigation* arranged according to their degrees of complexity and 'levels of integration'. But these fields also form a *temporal sequence* in an overarching evolutionary process: the Big Bang being followed by the formation of stars and planets, the evolution of life and, at least on our planet some 40–100 thousand years ago, the emergence of a culture-bearing species capable of manipulating symbols and developing a social stock of knowledge (Elias, 2011 [1991]).

In this sense, the science of sociology and its subject matter have a broader place and significance in an overarching process of cosmogenesis. Anticipating the current biological thinking in relation to complexity theory (Kaufman, 2000), Elias argues that, in the 'great evolution' there is an unambiguous direction towards increasing complexity. By creating matter, 'the Big Bang' set in train the physical processes that constitute the first dimension in the ongoing transformation and evolution of the universe. This process of physical expansion provides the field of investigation for cosmology. Successive dimensions form a temporal sequence, with evolutionary-biological processes, and the plane of integration that we call 'life', emerging (on our planet) only 3.5 billion years ago. With human symbol emancipation, biological evolution eventually engenders the plane of integration we understand as culture: the '*anthroposphere* within the biosphere' (Goudsblom, 2002).

> *Proposition 1: For Elias civilization is an aspect of an overarching process of cosmogenesis. Such continuity is the point of what David Christian (2005) calls 'big history'.*

Interweaving processes operating at variable scales and in relation to different units of analysis (person, organism, social group, species, ecological community, biosphere)

Elias was famously concerned with very long-term processes of social development. The theory of civilizing processes was advanced in relation to changes in state formation (*sociogenesis*) and personality structure (*psychogenesis*) in Western Europe taking place over a thousand years. But at the same time he recognized that to account fully for the dynamics of human development both in terms of the growth and development of (biological, psychological, social) individuals and also societies, even this extended timeframe is not fully adequate. *Social individuals* are moulded by their immersion in symbols and the intergenerational transmission of a social stock of knowledge. As *organisms*, individuals are also moulded by genetic inheritance and (ongoing) processes of Darwinian evolution unfolding over millions of years. Social development at the level of *communities* is necessarily tied to systematic ecological transformations in the relationship with and between other species.

On this basis, taking the widest possible view of human development, we might extend Elias's conceptual couplet and refer to a family of processes involving different temporal scales and units of analysis.

- *Psychogenesis* – the moulding of the psyche and the formation of the average personality structure
- *Sociogenesis* – the formation of states, markets and other societal institutions, over centuries.
- *Phylogenesis* – the evolution of species ('human nature') [ongoing – see Wills, 1998]
- *Biogenesis* – the somatic development of individual human organisms in relation to particular social-ecological regimes. Examples might include the putative intergenerational changes in IQ, posture, or diseases of affluence such as obesity and cancer.
- *Ecogenesis* – the anthropogenic evolutionary/ecological transformation of regional and later global ecosystems

> Proposition 2: *Just as it involves the ongoing formation of both psychological habitus, state and society, civilization necessarily involves the formation of species – both our own and those in the wider ecological community (Coppinger and Smith, 1983) – and the transformation of ecological communities and ecosystems.*

The 'anthroposphere' and 'levels of integration'

Elsewhere (Quilley, 2010) I have argued that Elias absorbed the 'levels of integration' framework from the organicist tradition in biology, and probably directly from the work of Joseph Needham (1937). At various times during the twentieth century, otherwise respectable biologists have speculated that the earth was entering a new phase of evolution led by humanity. Julian Huxley, Vladimir Vernadsky and Édouard Le Roy all saw the humanization of the biosphere as a new 'psycho-social' phase of a broader evolutionary process. The underlying conception of biological life and human culture as phases in an encompassing process of cosmic evolution was rooted in an organicist philosophy of biology which, at the time, constituted the background orthodoxy for the life sciences (Quilley, 2010). The defining feature of organicism was the recognition of processes working at different 'levels of integration' (Needham, 1937). In complex biological and social systems, the pattern organization could engender emergent dynamics that had an autonomous structure irreducible to processes at lower levels. The functioning of a complex biological structure such as a fly could not be deduced simply by aggregating the functional properties of its constituent cells. The organization and pattern of interdependence between those cells is decisive. Likewise, the characteristics of a human social group cannot be derived by simply aggregating those of its individual members. Rather 'personality' and behaviour of the group is an emergent and variable quality engendered by the pattern of organization and dynamic interdependence between such individuals. A second postulate of organicist biology is that higher-level processes frequently transform those at lower levels. For instance, just as the emergence of biological life had transformed the chemistry and geology of the planet, so the emergence of social processes would transform biological processes at lower 'levels of integration'.

The notion of the evolution of humanity as an aspect of a broader process of cosmic evolution and the latest stage in the evolution of the Earth was widely held by evolutionary humanists of the early to mid twentieth century, notably Julian Huxley ('the era of psycho-social evolution'), Vernadsky (the 'psychozoic era'), Le Roy (the era of 'hominisation'), Teilhard de Chardin (the 'vitalization of matter' and the 'hominization of life'), and more recently the theologian Thomas Berry who refers to an emerging 'ecozoic era' in which biological life becomes self-aware (Berry, 2005; Sampson and Pitt, 1999). The idea is also highly resonant with contemporary developments in complexity theory and particularly Stuart Kaufman's (1995; 2000) notion of a 'general biology' that starts from the premise of an immanent, cosmic process of complexification.

> *Proposition 3: From the organicist perspective the process of civilization is a natural dimension of an immanent cosmic potential for (and possibly a tendency towards) complexity. But, as Elias stresses in relation to social complexity, such a trajectory is neither automatic nor irreversible. 'Decivilization' or an overall reduction in complexity is always a possibility, certainly in any particular locus (see Mennell, 1990).*

Civilization and the deep continuity of our environmental problems

It goes without saying that civilization is understood as a process and not a state. More subtly, in the technical Eliasian sense, civilization does not equate with the complex, static, urban societies that emerged on the back of agriculture.[1] As Goudsblom (1992) showed in relation to fire culture among our hominid forbears, civilization is a concomitant of human social life and the capacity, through the use of symbols (Elias, 2011 [1991]) to generate an inter-generational, social stock of knowledge which, in a very real sense, forms the psychic habitus and personality structure of individual people. In this sense the process of civilization is a necessary correlate of the 'expanding anthroposphere' (Goudsblom, 2002).

One implication of this conception concerns the ecology of civilization. Green-anarchistic and primitivist critiques of civilization (Bookchin, 1982; Zerzan, 2005; Heinberg, 1995; Quinn, 1995) habitually equate civilization with agriculture and imply a deep discontinuity in human development. From this perspective, our present global ecological problems derive ultimately from agrarianization, construed as a bad, and possibly even reversible, *choice*. This position is rhetorically satisfying and emotionally compelling. It also expresses cogently an immanent truth that complex, technological societies may prove, in the end, to be an unsustainable cosmic blip. But the implication of a fork in the road, implying some back-pedalling path to ecological redemption, is itself completely wrong.

Anthropology and evolutionary biology increasingly point to the deep continuity in human engagements with non-human nature. Agriculture and domestication evolved quite naturally and independently of any human intentions or choices (Tudge, 1998; Budiansky, 1998; Coppinger and Smith, 1983). This perspective is less than comforting. It provides no easy target for environmentalist rage.

Proposition 4: The problem of global ecology is, in a very real sense, a problem of human nature. Trophic expansion is a function of language and the human capacity for culture. Inter-generational transmission of a social stock of knowledge allows humanity continually to improve its cognitive mapping and understanding of non-human nature. In ecological terms this is extremely disruptive, allowing our species to move into new niches, continually extracting more energy from more nodes in ever more diverse ecosystems. Trophic expansion is what we do and have always done as a species. Without losing our evolved capacity for language, there is no easy way back into the Garden of Eden. Humanity cannot become once again, just another 'self-effacing ape' (Eisenberg, 2000).

Entropy and Complexification

'Energy flow takes the sting out of time . . . taming its degrading influence' (Chaisson, 2001: 214)

Governed by the first and second laws of thermodynamics, the universe is winding down. The temperature and pressure differentials that are a prerequisite for the formation of 'free energy' are slowly, but inexorably equalizing. The entropy of the universe as a whole is increasing. 'In the long run, we are all dead': Keynes could as well have been writing about cosmology as economics. But even as this decaying universe winds down, order abounds. The very expansion of the universe seems also to ensure the existence of pockets of entropy-defying order, complex systems able to export negative entropy and exist in dynamic but stable 'far from equilibrium' states. Here, evolutionary dynamics seem to foster a secular trend towards complexity and away from equilibrium. Human beings, human culture and the ecological crisis resulting from anthropogenic changes to the biosphere are all part of this countervailing trend.

Harmony and balance are very much in the time-horizons of the beholder. In a thermodynamic sense the persistence of any kind of order or structure at a particular spatial/temporal locus must be associated with a corresponding increase in external disorder (that is, in the wider system). From a cosmic timescale any ordered state of complexity persisting and reproducing itself far from thermodynamic equilibrium, is necessarily fragile and ultimately unsustainable. Low entropy harmony is a figment of a very ephemeral imagination. A species that measured longevity in eons would in all likelihood think about sustainability in very different ways.

Nevertheless, from a human perspective differences measured in centuries and millennia are likely to prove to be profoundly important, perhaps even determining whether or not our species has any kind of future at all. The important question is not whether this or that form of economy and society is sustainable in any absolute sense, but how long a particular configuration can persist and how abrupt or drawn out any changes are likely to be. For humanity, the critical factor will be whether the duration and speed of ecological transformations outstrips our social capacity to understand and adapt.

A pioneering advocate of 'big history', David Christian, argues that the significance of human-scale events and problems can only be grasped in relation to an over-arching cosmic evolutionary process that started with the big bang and encompasses unfolding natural and historical developments at all spatial and temporal scales.[2] The Odyssey of human development is likened to one tiny segment of a 'desert caravan', spiralling back 13 billion years into the past and reaching forward into an unknowable future.

> Modern science tells us that the caravan is vast and varied and our fellow travellers include numerous exotic creatures from quarks to galaxies. (Christian, 2005: 1)

Popular understanding of Darwin's theory of evolution is probably sufficient that the idea of a chimpanzee and even an oak tree, an *E. coli* bacterium or an HN51 virus, as 'fellow travellers' may not seem outlandish or offensive. Most people are familiar with the idea that we share genes with other species and are by definition, albeit very far removed, kith and kin. But what does it mean to say that we are fellow travellers with 'quarks' or 'galaxies'? It means a great deal, as it turns out, and has enormous significance for our view of ourselves as well as the meaning of common place terms such as 'sustainability'.

In his evocation of a scientific origin myth, Christian identifies the endless 'waltz of chaos and complexity' as the central drama in the evolution of the universe, of life and of people. In identifying orderliness as the central plotline, he intimates what many natural scientists and anthropologists have elaborated at great length (for example White, 1943; Smil, 2008) – that is, that the dissipation and accumulation of free energy drives historical dynamics at all levels, from the creation of stars, to the drama of biological evolution and even processes of civilization and state formation. As Christian points out in his own summary, 'creating and maintaining patterns requires work' (2005: 506). Any complex system, such as a pack of cards, has more disordered than ordered states. Understanding how any kind of patterning or ordering process works involves understanding the dynamics of energy.

Whilst the first law of thermodynamics dictates that energy can never be lost, the second law says that in a closed system, the amount of energy available to do work (that is, available to create order and complexity) will decline over time. 'Free energy' is a measure of the energy available to do patterning or ordering work. Such usable energy requires some form of difference in potential. This could be literally a gradient, as in the case of water stored uphill, behind a dam. The potential energy of the damned water represents high-grade solar energy that has been absorbed from the sun during the process of evaporation. The process of cloud formation and raining effectively lifts the water onto the hills, locking up a proportion of the solar energy in the form of potential kinetic energy. This energy can be used to drive turbines and produce electrical energy.

According to the second law, an inexorable process of 'entropic decay' means that in the universe as a whole (a closed system which no energy leaves or enters), over a staggeringly long period of time, all such differentials and gradients will diminish, eventually to zero. This tendency towards thermodynamic equilibrium means that over time entropy must increase and complexity must everywhere decrease, theoretically to a point of chaos defined by an absolute absence of order or patterning of any kind. This is what Christian pithily refers to as the 'down-escalator of entropy'.

The second law is fundamental to modern physics. But it raises two pretty fundamental problems. The first is how order is possible at all. What was the original source of all the free energy that has driven the formation of galaxies, stars, planets and, on Earth, the evolution of life? One possible explanation is that it was the expansion of the universe that engendered the temperature and pressure differentials that in turn define free energy and make it available for ordering and patterning processes (see Christian, 2005: 508).

The second problem has greater immediate relevance to the problem of sustainability and the wider cosmological significance of humanity. If there is a universal tendency towards disorder and increasing entropy, why does it appear that complexity and order has actually increased – albeit in very localized arenas? Compared with the infinitely larger backdrop of expanding space, the formation of stars and galaxies is clear evidence of increased order and patterning. Likewise, in at least one small place in the universe, we know that geochemical order has engendered life and processes of *biological* evolution involving a quantum leap in the levels of complexity. And finally life itself has given rise to a species capable of manipulating symbols and generating an inter-generational, social stock of knowledge which provides the basis for a new, emergent form of complexity, plumbing the depths of entropy yet further. Although the Second Law of thermodynamics dictates an inexorable trajectory of entropic decay and disorder – a 'cooling down' of the universe that will end in 'heat death' – entities as different as stars, crystals, living organisms and human culture all exhibit a capacity to 'climb the down escalator of entropy'. How are these local, pinprick explosions of order and complexity possible? Where does the free energy come from? How is it concentrated?

The answer is elegant and even simple and relates to the relationship between open and closed systems (Christian, 2005: 509–11; Daly and Farley, 2004). The second law of thermodynamics relates to closed systems such as the universe. Entities such as stars, crystals, biospheres or organisms are open systems. Order within an open system such as a biosphere is achieved at the expense of increased disorder – increased entropy – in the wider system. In his groundbreaking thermodynamic definition of living systems, Schrödinger (1944) argued that organisms effectively export negative entropy (or 'negentropy').[3] In this way, by accelerating the transformation of free energy in the form of solar flux into ambient, low-grade and unusable heat energy the evolution of complexity actually speeds up the entropic decay of the wider system. To extend Christian's metaphor, it is as if by climbing up the 'down escalator' of entropy, complex entities actually speed up its rate of descent.

This emphasis on the nesting of open and closed systems and flows of energy and matter has become an organizing insight in the discipline of ecology and cognate 'trans-disciplines' such as ecological economics (Daly and Farley, 2004). It allows us to focus very clearly on the relationship between order and the dynamic stability of nested systems and subsystems at different spatial and temporal scales. Most critically, in relation to the problem of the sustainability of human activities, it allows us to identify the nature of the relationship between the biosphere and the expanding domain of human activities or the 'anthroposphere' over time (Goudsblom, 2002). Prigogine (Prigogine and Nicolis, 1977; Prigogine and Stengers, 1984) famously identified complex systems as 'dissipative structures' defined by large energy which allow them to persist in stable states 'far from equilibrium'. This definition helped to launch interdisciplinary studies of complexity and self-organizing systems (Kaufman, 1995, 2000). There are many examples of non-living, inorganic complex systems that can be characterized as dissipative structures in this sense – for example, the vortex formed by water in the plug hole of an emptying bath. However, it is living systems and organisms that provide the examples most complex, fragile and furthest from thermodynamic equilibrium. The glorious, kaleidoscopic, creative and destructive complexity of human culture may turn out to be the most fleeting and fragile of them all, burning itself out in a cosmic millisecond.

Proposition 5: It is a feature of all complex living systems (organisms, ecosystems, cities, biospheres) that they persist in a state of low entropy, far from equilibrium – i.e., they become more internally ordered and complex – to the extent that they export disorder elsewhere. The expanding anthroposphere is no different from the biosphere upon which it depends – except that the entropic disorder engendered by processes of social development and economic growth must be absorbed by the biosphere without undermining its integrity. And so far, human systems have not been able to sustain their far from equilibrium state without the biosphere. These are the twin problems of 'trophic expansion' and 'trophic dependence'. This is the thermodynamic truth underlying the 'limits to growth'.

Biosphere–anthroposphere dynamics: the process of civilization and sustainability

One of the major advantages of the levels of integration perspective is that it draws attention to the interweaving of processes operating at sometimes wildly different spatial and temporal scales. Human organisms are subject to the constraints of the physical universe: gravity requires that we do not grow too large. Human nature evolved by processes of Darwinian evolution: we bear characteristic traits of quadrupeds, mammals, primates and hominids, through all of which we express even the most modern and technologically sophisticated behaviours, such as driving a car. Human ecology is defined, as for any species, by social interactions with other humans as well as interdependence with a wider community of species. An individual's personality is informed simultaneously by genetics, by social interaction, by history and – as we shall see – by ecology.

Consider for example current dilemmas in relation to global warming through an Eliasian frame. In *The Civilizing Process* (2000 [1939]), the analysis centres on the relationship between the *psychogenesis* of the average personality structure and the *sociogenesis* of the market economy and state. But we can expand on this. In *What is Sociology?*, Elias referred to the 'triad of basic controls' – social controls operating between people, psychological controls regulating individual behaviour and ecological controls operating between groups of people and non-human nature.[4] Specifically, Elias shows that the stage of development of a society can be determined:

(1) by the extent of its control-chances over extra-human nexuses of events, that is, over what we sometimes refer to rather loosely as 'natural events';
(2) by the extent of its control-chances over inter-human connections, that is, over what we usually refer to as 'social nexuses';
(3) by the extent to which each of its individual members has learned, from childhood onwards, to exercise self-control.

Scientific and technological developments correspond to the first of these basic controls; the development of social organization to the second; and the personality structure to the third. According to Elias, the three are interdependent both in their development and in their functioning at any given stage. However, he warns against 'the mechanistic idea that the interdependence of the three types of control is to be understood in terms of the parallel increases in all three' (1978 [1970]: 157). More particularly, the development of the three types does not occur at the same rate, and the development of one type can contradict, impede or threaten developments regarding the others. For example, it is highly characteristic of modern societies that the extent of their control-chances over extra-human natural nexuses is greater and grows more quickly than that over inter-human social nexuses (1978 [1970]: 156). This is evident in the fact that the developments in the 'natural' sciences have proceeded more quickly than development in the 'social' sciences, with the result that our ability to predict, intervene and control the natural/physical world is greater at present than our ability to control social processes. A corollary of this is the fact that the less amenable a sphere of events is to human control, the more emotional and fantasy-laden people's thinking about it tends to be. For Elias, such emotional and fantasy-laden thinking about the social world represents a significant obstacle to the development of a more reality-congruent stock of social scientific knowledge.

As Goudsblom (1992, 2003a) shows in relation to early hominid fire culture, at all stages of human development the development of complexity in social relations is intimately tied to energy. Like all life forms, this relates firstly to chemical energy acquired through individual and collective food provisioning strategies and regimes. With fire, humanity acquired the capacity to utilise the exo-somatic energy locked up in wood and later, cow-dung, peat, oil and coal. In short, advances in the division of labour (what Elias referred to as the 'social division of functions') progress in tandem with trophic and energy regimes. Thus, during the (European) early modern period the processes of sociogenesis and psychogenesis described in *The Civilizing Process* were intimately tied up with transforming socio-ecological and energy regimes (Fischer-Kowalski and Haberl, 2007). Shortages of firewood in England leading to the systematic exploitation of coal were connected with the development of steam engines, pump priming the early process of industrialization. Energy flows per capita, which had been rising steadily throughout human history, began to rise more rapidly. Over the last three hundred years this energy throughput has made possible an almost exponential increase in the circulation of goods, people and information. To a large extent this is what economic growth is: the escalating flows of things and signs (Lash and Urry, 1993).

In short, the *sociogenesis* and *psychogenesis* of our highly individuated personality structure, upon which liberal societies are constructed,[5] has also involved a wide-ranging process of *ecogenesis*. Near-exponential demographic growth, rapid urbanization, accelerating loss of habitat, deforestation, escalating pressure on aquifers, crashing biodiversity – are all symptoms of the process of ecogenesis associated with this new phase in the expansion of the anthroposphere in which the zero-sum limits come into play. But most of all, capitalist modernization has an intrinsic dependence on the burning of fossil fuels. So here in *The Civilizing Process*, processes of individual psychological development, unfolding over decades, are linked to a process of societal formation unfolding over centuries, which is linked to changes in the carbon cycle, atmospheric chemistry and climate regulation playing out over millions of years. This is the truth underlying Vernadsky's notion of humanity inaugurating a new geological (psychozoic) epoch (Vernadsky, 1998 [1926]).

Proposition 6: The process of civilization involves the elaboration of social, psychological and ecological controls, the extent of which provides a broad measure of the stage or level of complexity. Long-term processes of social development are characterized by a steady acceleration in the circulation of goods, people and information – a circulation that corresponds to the overall energy and material throughput. Given that the anthroposphere is dependent on and expands within a finite and limited biosphere, the relationship between the process of civilization and the biosphere must be defined, ultimately, by a zero sum game. The psychogenesis of the modern, individuated personality structure and the sociogenesis of the modern state depend on a process of ecogenesis that is, in the long run, untenable.

Low energy cosmopolitanism: on the tensions between ecology, democracy and civilization

Now here we have an interesting vantage point from which to view the ecological problems of twenty-first century global society. Sociologists have always been preoccupied with modernity – the idea of a break with traditional society. Tönnies's (2002 [1887]) distinction between *Gemeinschaft* and *Gesellschaft* set the tone for sociological commentary on the process of modernization for the next hundred years. But for most of this time critics of capitalist modernization ignored the underlying social-ecological regime and the energetic basis of petro-capitalism. In *The Communist Manifesto* Marx and Engels (1998 [1848]) were more honest than most. They celebrated the power of the new bourgeois order precisely because of its capacity to demolish the traditional order (the 'idiocy' of peasant society) and sweep away the binding ties of feudalism. Capitalist modernization was clearing the way for socialism and the emergence of a new socialist man. And in his more whimsical moments, a younger Marx imagined this new denizen of the socialist order to be thoroughly individuated and even bourgeois in his desire to express a variety of creative potentials at various times through the working day and week. Since then critics, and especially green critics, have been less honest than Marx. Left, green and liberal utopian thinking has often taken for granted the social and functional complexity of modern societies, without recognizing just how much this owes to capitalist industrialization. Elias has been one of the few to have fully appreciated the extent to which the highly individuated and constrained personality structure that underpins modern consumer societies is relatively new, and historically contingent. Liberal-democratic polities, consumer economies, contemporary aesthetics, high and low forms of artistic endeavour, tolerant and expressive sexual politics, egalitarian gender relations – all assume a degree of psycho-social individuation that was and is literally unthinkable in more traditional societies.[6]

But of course capitalism has always been fossil-fuelled. A non-capitalist form of cosmopolitanism is thinkable, if not very plausible. But whereas a socialist, social democratic or anarchistic form of *Gesellschaft* must be at least considered a possibility, an ecological *Gesellschaft* seems, at first sight, almost oxymoronic.

Why? Because the circulation of goods, people and information is just as intrinsic to capitalist modernization as the wage relation (after Marx), the institution of markets (after Polanyi) or the modern state (after Weber). Economic growth is indivisible from this circulation. The process of individuation and associated relative freedoms of movement and expression that defined Tönnies's *Gesellschaft* are inconceivable without this continuing and growing throughput of energy.

Historically there never has been a 'low-energy cosmopolitanism' (see Hayes and Dobson, 2008). Just about all of those aspects of modern societies that we most cherish – individualism, social liberalism, tolerance, cosmopolitanism, democracy, complexity – emerged in the wake of capitalism and depend absolutely on the circulation of goods, people and information, and so on energy throughput.

So what happens if the energy is not available? Climate change scenarios suggest that if we burn remaining stocks of fossil fuel, disastrous climate change may be sufficient to destroy global civilization, and even the human species (Lynas, 2007). Peak oil pundits suggest that we are likely to experience an imminent, chronic energy shortfall with the peaking of global oil production (Kunstler, 2005; Heinberg, 2005). Neither scenario provides much ground for optimism. For instance in his 'Olduvai theory', Richard C. Duncan (2007) argues that the absolute dependence of capitalist modernity on a one-off, non-renewable bounty of oil makes collapse a certainty. For Duncan, our global civilization based on petro-capitalism can only last just over a century. In his magisterial study, Smil (2008) is more circumspect but still acknowledges the absolutely limited duration of a fossil-fuelled global society.

I don't want here to debate whether or not either scenario is possible or even likely, but merely to note that for much of the environmental movement, over the last decade both catastrophic climate change and peak oil have become routine expectations. Just how routine these expectations are is made clear by the viral growth of the 'Transition Town' movement (Hopkins, 2008). Inspired by Rob Hopkins's experiment in community resilience in Totnes, Devon, hundreds of Transition Initiatives are now springing up across the UK, Europe, Australia, New Zealand, Canada and the United States. The Transition strategy is absolutely premised on both peak oil and catastrophic climate change, and Richard Heinberg, a guru of the American peak oil movement, has now become one of its leading figures. Transition politics is not anti-capitalist nor anti-globalization precisely because the expectation is that an energy shortfall will lead to a rapid relocalization and simplification of economic life within a few decades. Transition speaks the language of localism and sufficiency, and taps a deep frustration with consumer society. The expectation is that in the post-carbon, post-capitalist order, citizens will live more familial, authentic and creative 'hand made' lives, recovering a range of artisanal 'Transition skills' (Quilley, 2009a) and more rewarding *gemeinschaftlich* forms of community (see Barry and Quilley, 2008).

Besides the rapidity of its emergence as perhaps the dominant environmental movement in the West, what is striking about this movement is its hybrid Anglo-

American origin. In the UK there is no 'survivalist movement' pretty much because there are no hills to run to. Transition is very much a social, collective response geared towards communities and working alongside, but not under, local authorities. In many ways it fills the political gap left by the seeming failure of Agenda 21 engagement with climate change mitigation after the Kyoto summit. Communities recognize an imperative to face up to disruptive and possibly catastrophic climate change that is now perceived as unavoidable. But at the same time, the movement is informed by the concept of peak oil. Now, despite the fact that some of the most significant contributions to the technical debate have come from the UK and Europe (not least the role of Colin Campbell and Kjell Aleklett in the *Association for the Study of Peak Oil and Gas* [ASPO] see http://www.peakoil.net/), the politics of peak oil have very much been coloured by a strain of American survivalism. Since the height of the cold war many thousands of Americans have been expecting 'the system' to collapse and there is a whole infrastructure of militaristic training, homesteading and community networking geared to this eventuality – informed variously by fundamentalist Christianity, primitivist anarchism and other strains of environmentalism. Peak oil has now taken over from nuclear war as the primary scenario of collapse (for a taste, see James Wesley Rawls, 2009a & b). But what is significant about the last decade has been the proliferation of a more respectable popular and academic literature advancing fundamentally similar scenarios (Tainter, 1990; Heinberg, 2005; Diamond, 2006; Kunstler, 2005; Rees, 2004; Homer-Dixon, 2006; Hansen, 2007; Lynas, 2007; Lovelock, 2007; 2009; Martin, 2007). Many of these contributions are by heavyweight scientists – such as James Hansen of NASA or the UK's Astronomer Royal Martin Rees – from the heart of the scientific establishment. Reinforced by a raft of environmental science fiction (most recently the film of Cormac McCarthy's *The Road*) the prospect of collapse has emerged to become a routine part of the psycho-political landscape (for recent novels see Theroux, 2009; Wilson, 2009; Scarrow, 2007).

Despite its roots in the peak oil movement, and although premised fairly overtly on the implosion of the global economy and the failure of nation-state institutions, the Transition Network remains obdurately disinclined to focus on the problem of violence. This is surprising. The re-emergence of famine in Western countries combined with a failure of state institutions would certainly result in appalling violence between individuals and communities. This problem would be especially acute in a densely populated country like the UK, which is so dependent on imported food. In any collapse scenario, it is difficult to see how the denizens of Totnes might protect their newly planted nut trees. But at the same time it is impossible to imagine that resource shortages on the scale anticipated by the peak oil and Transition movements would not result in geo-political violence and regional and even global wars.

Since none of this is very pleasant to contemplate, a Polyannaish avoidance of the issue is perhaps unsurprising. But in the medium and longer term the prospect of collapse and relocalization also raises the question of what kind of society will emerge in place of the global, connected, hyper-mobile society of flows that we created on the back of cheap oil (Lash and Urry, 1993). What seems certain is that the spirit of cosmopolitanism is likely to give way to more communitarian forms of political life. What is more, the open and mobile *gesellschaftlich* forms of social life which we take so much for granted, societal forms underpinned ultimately by relatively disembedded markets, are likely to give way as traditional, socially embedded, highly conventional *gemeinschaftlich* social forms re-emerge. For those modern refuseniks disenchanted with the shallow, unsustainable idiocy of consumer society, there may well be cause to celebrate, with the resurrection of family and community as the primary vehicles of social support and solidarity. Those who survive the putative 'long emergency' might well be healthier, enjoy better and more authentic food and perhaps even benefit from more rounded social relationships and a less strained relationship between domestic life and work. Under these circumstances, many would indeed find fulfilment in the re-invented artisanal roles and functions that once again service a relocalized and more self-sufficient division of labour. But there can be no doubt that, with regard to the long march of political and social enfranchisement, such a neo-traditionalism would be politically and socially regressive. Traditional agrarian society, with more and possibly most people working on the land, implies a world of landowners and serfs, ascriptive social identities and lives determined by the circumstances of one's birth – class, gender, religion, ethnicity and caste. In this brave new world there would be plenty of work (although no jobs) for sociologists. In his novel *A World Made by Hand*, one of the most well known and vocal peak oil pundits, James Howard Kunstler (2008), is surprisingly honest. He doesn't shy away from what the politics of such a newly agrarian society might look like. Without energy slaves in the form of internal combustion engines, most of the population become peasants and old social hierarchies, including gender inequalities, reassert themselves.

> All the trustees [of the reformed town council] were men, no women and no plain laborers. As the world changed, we reverted to social divisions that we'd thought were obsolete. The egalitarian pretences of the high-octane decades had dissolved and nobody even debated it any more, including the women of our town. A plain majority of the town's people were labourers now, whatever in life they had been before. Nobody called them peasants, but in effect that's what they had become. That's just the way things were. (2008: 101)

But most anti-capitalist, anti-globalization and environmentalist prognoses of relocalization flatly refuse to engage with the implications of this neo-traditionalist, post-liberal society. Politics and social life will be pretty much like it is now, just more local.

Proposition 7: The failure of the revolution in Germany presented Lenin's regime with the impossible choices summed up by the phrase 'socialism in one country'. Anticipating ecological collapse, environmentalists are now faced with a similar dilemma in relation to 'liberalism in one village'. If the process of civilization cannot bypass bio-physical limits to growth – if the biosphere cannot sustain current forms of social complexity – a process of de-civilization will throw into reverse those patterns of socio-psycho-genesis described in Elias's The Civilizing Process. *With declining flows of people, goods and information, pronounced relocalization would engender a less individuated personality structure, bound by looser psychic constraints but subject to more intrusive forms of social control. High energy cosmopolitanism would give way to low energy communitarianism. In such a scenario, gender equality, class egalitarianism and sexual permissiveness and other paraphernalia of* gesellschaftlich *societies would not endure. Youth culture would not exist.*

Lovelock's lifeboats: trophic detachment and the future of civilization

So here is the prospect for humanity and for civilization at the start of the twenty-first century. Language and social processes evolved out of the biosphere as a new level of integration, expressing an immanent cosmic tendency towards complexity. Like other complex systems that persist in states 'far from thermodynamic equilibrium' and which habitually climb the 'down escalator of entropy', the anthroposphere is a 'dissipative structure'. Its internal order depends on a continuing throughput of energy and is achieved at the cost of disorder in the wider system. In the case of the anthroposphere, 'the wider system' is (currently) the biosphere. The biosphere, however, can only absorb a certain amount of entropic disorder. This places an absolute limit on the expansion of the anthroposphere – at least in so far as the latter is parasitic on the life support systems of the Earth. The propensity for trophic expansion makes human social development intrinsically unstable – a dynamism that is the motive force for history. Civilization always entails simultaneous processes of eco-genesis. Unfortunately, for our children, after thousands of generations, humanity is now reaching the biophysical limits to growth. The expansion of the anthroposphere is increasingly in a zero-sum relation to the biosphere as a whole: deforestation in the Amazon, a brutal and poignant swathe of extinctions, the destruction of coral reefs . . . these are only the most visible examples of a global ecosystem in distress.

Unfortunately or fortunately, depending on your point of view, the global economy will implode before any terminal collapse of the planet's life support systems. It seems likely that the combination of peak oil and climate change will, at some point over the next half-century, seriously curtail the expanding circulation of goods, people and information. This circulation has characterized the expanding anthroposphere for tens of thousands of years. Any hiatus would be epochal in its significance. As well as the economy, it would also have an immediate impact on all areas of political and cultural life and even the average personality structure. No area of human experience would remain unchanged. The implosion of globalism would signal a dead end for cosmopolitan, *gesellschaftlich* societies characterized by expanding, disembedded markets. Instead we would see a resurgence of defensive, inward looking, place-bound *gemeinschaftlich* communities. The new age will not be liberal.

This seems to be a fairly catastrophic prognosis. Liberal society, based on a respect for the individual, on human rights, on social tolerance, seems to have a fatal umbilical connection to petro-capitalism and economic growth. Is there any alternative?

Logically the problem seems to be the relationship between the anthroposphere and the biosphere. On the one hand, the expanding anthroposphere seems to represent a new level of integration and the latest phase in an unfolding process of cosmogenesis. On the other hand, there is nothing guaranteed about the trajectory of complexification. In the history of the cosmos, each successive level of complexity seems to be less assured and more vulnerable to collapse and reorganization around lower levels. The dependence of the anthroposphere upon a vibrant, integral biosphere which it, in turn, systematically undermines, is a good example. Possibly, the long-term solution suggests detachment: anthroposphere without biosphere, or rather sustained by an artificial biosphere. But the only attempt to create an artificial anthropic life support system, the Biosphere II experiment, failed almost immediately (Allen, 1997; see http://www.biospherics.org/).

In his recent books James Lovelock paints a picture of cataclysmic global warming destroying the capacity of most human societies to feed themselves (2007, 2009). By the end of the present century a residual civilization will be gravitating towards new lifeboat cities around the poles. Island societies such as Britain and New Zealand, and those with extensive circumpolar polar territory will fare the best (although 'best' is an extremely relative term). Although his gloomy scenario assumes a brutal cull of the human population, he is in little doubt that humanity will survive as a species. However, for Lovelock, the real question is whether *civilization* can survive beyond the present century.[7]

In Lovelock's view, the evolution of a symbolizing species with a capacity for culture, amounted to an 'infection' for the Earth – an affliction he dubs 'polyanthroponemia.' But referring implicitly to the symbiogenesis theory of cellular evolution, pioneered by his close collaborator Lynn Margulis, he argues that a relationship of virulent parasitism could develop into a more stable, and mutually beneficial, symbiosis.[8] If humanity can learn to live with Gaia, we can develop as the mind and regulatory guidance mechanism for a self-aware and sentient planetary organism. This vista is, however, only possible on the basis of civilization. Humanity cannot revert and become, once again, 'just another self-effacing ape' in the forest (the phrase is Eisenberg's, 2000) A flexible 'prosthetic ecology' based on technology is an integral dimension of our 'eco-morph' – the fit between our evolved nature and the environment. For Lovelock, the danger of 'deep green' fantasies of simplicity are that they cannot preclude, indefinitely, a resumption of social development, trophic expansion and the demographic ratchet, and 'if anytime in the new world we recommence carbon fuel gathering we would be in danger of destroying ourselves and most of non-microbial life' (2009: 160). In the long term, our future and that of the planet will depend on our ability to use technology selectively and reflexively, in such a way as to leave Gaian regulatory mechanisms undisturbed.

We humans are vitally important as a part of Gaia, not through what we are now but through our potential as a species to be the progenitors of a much better animal. Like it or not we are now its heart and mind, but to continue to improve in this role we have to ensure our survival as a civilized species and not revert into a cluster of warring tribes that was a stage in our evolutionary history. . . . [We might become] a species closer to Gaia . . . [serving within her] as our brains do in each of us. We would be an important part of what had become in effect an intelligent planet better able to sustain habitability. (2009: 21, 161)

Lovelock's scenario is immediately suggestive of one way out of partially resolving the tension between the anthroposphere and the biosphere. The evolution of language and culture has made ecological disturbance an innate characteristic of human ecology. Only a further development of civilization, enhanced technological capabilities and greater scientific understanding of Gaian physiology and humanity's place within it, would make it possible to curb and channel this propensity for ecological disruption.

This may seem an oddly teleological and metaphysical idea to come from one of the world's most eminent natural scientists. But it is entirely concordant with the process of cosmogenesis implied by organicist biology. It is also resonant with an ongoing paradigm shift in biology as well as developments in complexity theory (Kaufman, 2000; Jablonka, Lamb and Zeligowski, 2005).

So how does Lovelock reconcile the expanding anthroposphere with the fragile Gaian physiology of the Earth? Essentially, he envisages a 'high-tech, compact civilization' emerging from the collapse of twenty-first century global society and organized on the basis of a kind of trophic detachment. He says:

My dream is that we will discover how to synthesize all the food we need from carbon dioxide, nitrogen and water and a few minerals . . . Perhaps a biopsy sample of the leg muscle of a single Aberdeen Angus bull would in this way provide steaks for a multitude. . . . Then the footprint of food production would shrink until whole swathes of land could return to Gaia. Maybe we could redeem technology and return this way to the natural world that was there before we began to use fire. Massive crop failure in future adverse climates would give food synthesis an immediately vital role. But like other technological dreams we do not have the time to do it now. (2009: 87)

And later,

Food synthesis would lessen its impact on the planet and the widespread desert of this calorific planet would be an ample provider of solar electricity. Such a civilization gives us a chance to cease being a burden on Gaian regulation and time to learn how to complement it. A high standard of living with women empowered and well educated would perhaps provide an automatic curb on population growth. If this were global in extent disruption by war might be less likely. (2009: 91)

In fact Lovelock is by no means the first to suggest such a scenario. For instance as far back as 1967 Nicholas Calder, who was one of the first to use the image of the earth as a space-ship, presented a bold and science-fiction-like scenario in which agricultural production was replaced with closed system food production based on the breakthroughs in genetic science which were in the 1960s beginning to transform the technological imagination. Calder recognized that ultimately the problem of food production was about carbon fixation and the utilization of solar energy. Drawing on the ideas of eminent biologist Conrad Waddington (1957), Calder argued for in-vitro photosynthesis, using 'artificial leaves' to deliver an industrial scale of synthetic carbon fixation and phosphorylation (1967: 152–7). This would provide the substrate for in-vitro synthesis of complex food tissues using the new science and technologies of molecular genetics. On this basis it would be possible, he enthused, to 'grow a beef-steak without a cow' (1967: 157). But the greatest advantage of the envisaged paradigm shift was that it would allow for the liberation of huge areas of the Earth's surface from the long-tightening grip of agriculture. Calder's vision was certainly eccentric but even in his most science-fictional moments, there is an appreciation of the fundamental tension between the Promethean logic of social development that is hardwired into the inventive, discursive and collective human mind, and the ecological systems through which we evolved.

Here then is one radical and disturbing vision of 'resilience'. It is green. It is holistic. But it challenges not just the displacement of natural ecosystems by intensive, prosthetic, agro-ecological systems, but also the more gentle organic/ permaculture vision of food production systems in symbiotic harmony with natural ecosystems. For Lovelock the resilience of both human food and energy systems and the Gaian physiology upon which we all depend will, in the long term, require their radical separation. In essence he envisages a technologically-mediated process of *trophic detachment* (see Quilley, 2004b).

Fifty years after Calder and Waddington's speculations, technologies for possible trophic detachment are now coming into view. '*Vertical farming*' (Despommier, 2008; Grover, 2009)[9] would involve stacking farming and horticultural operations into a closed loop, artificial eco-system, generating little or no waste and producing vast quantities of basic foods in highly concentrated and localized urban locations. *Artificial photosynthesis* (Smith, Friedman and Venter, 2003) would make possible the synthetic production of both energy and basic food substrates using only water, atmospheric CO_2 and light energy. The ongoing revolution in *molecular engineering* promises to make possible the in vitro synthesis of complex food proteins from basic organic substrates ('meat in a test-tube'). Advances in *horticultural and ecological engineering* are generating sophisticated technologies and systems for the creation and management of closed, artificial eco-systems. In the future such systems may provide the basis for *autotrophic urban systems* based on the integration of architecture, food production and ecological management.

This emerging cluster of technologies and the associated urban-architectural and social regimes that they imply, may prove decisive in both *mitigating climate change as well as adapting food provisioning systems to adverse future growing conditions*. If Lovelock is right, global civilization is about to see a profound collapse and retrenchment. Trophic detachment may allow residual 'lifeboat' cities in the polar regions of a much hotter and less climatically stable world to renew the relationship between civilization and the biosphere on a truly sustainable basis. Such technologies have the potential to transform the relationship between humanity and the biosphere as fundamentally as did fire culture and agrarianization. For a million years, the grip of humanity on the biosphere has been tightening. For the first time in the history of our species, this grip might be relaxed. Industrial scale, urban food synthesis, at least in the long term, might allow large areas of agricultural land to revert back to non-human nature, enhancing and restoring the resilience of the planetary life support systems (Waddington, 1957; Calder, 1967; Soleri, 1969). Inspired by Soleri's vision of 'arcology', the prospect of turning every architectural surface into a metabolic processing site now also animates the work of Richard Register and the Eco-Cities movement (2006; see Downton, 2009). For James Lovelock only such an approach to urban food systems will be able to provide the basis for a Gaian civilization, symbiotic with the biosphere and capable of enduring into the far future (2009).

Taking their cue from climatologists, natural scientists are beginning to concede the scale of humanity's terraforming activities. In 'geo-speak' the Holocene has given way to the 'Anthropocene', an evolutionary–geological era defined by one species. There is an enormous irony in this transition. Just as scientists have achieved the technological capacity to view the earth and humanity as a whole, and just as global connectivity of the internet makes such images universally available, the images themselves reveal the fragile beauty of the biosphere desecrated and global ecosystem services on the point of implosion due to a distinctive human ecology of Malthusian overshoot. Just as, for the first time, our species becomes aware of itself as a whole ('humanity', 'human rights', and so on), a combination of ecological and economic meltdown threaten the end of civilization, and with it not just the glimmering natural scientific understanding of the biosphere in all its complexity, but the even more fragmentary sociological insight that comes with the recognition of 'humanity' as a frame of reference or a survival unit. Whether or not Lovelock turns out to be right in thinking that Gaia might 'take revenge' (figuratively speaking) and shrug off civilization, between them the concept of the 'Anthropocene', the science of climate change, the emerging paradigm of ecological economics and the recognition of the significance of entropy in the disciplines of history and sociology, all contribute to a 'double-bind' in humanity's self-understanding. As a species with an evolved propensity for language and culture, it seems that long-term processes of social development and the concomitant process of trophic expansion and ecological domination are an inevitable consequence of 'human nature'. If sustainability requires humans to become a self-effacing ape, just one among many species, then it becomes an ever-receding utopia. In the trajectory of humanity as a whole, myriads of smaller-scale, more sustainable, less intensive societies have consistently given rise (one way or another) to larger scale, more expansive, more intensive and more energetic societies. Trophic detachment may be the only way to achieve a stable relationship with our Earth.

Proposition 8: Thinking productively about the problem of sustainability requires us to extend our habitual time horizons, but also to question the relevant units of analysis. In the short run, it seems likely that civilization[10] is heading for a period of contraction if not collapse. But if humanity does manage to come through the present century with a complex, science-based civilization intact, the future may open up a new symbiotic relationship between humanity and the biosphere. In the long view, developing technologies of trophic detachment may allow the expansion of the anthroposphere to continue with a more muted and manageable impact on the fragile ecosystems of the earth. Autotrophic, self-provisioning eco-cities would release large areas of the Earth's surface from the ecological tyranny of agriculture, re-invigorating the self-regulatory Gaian physiology of the Earth. In such a scenario humanity would become a part of a new sentient, self-aware, reflexive organ regulating the biosphere. In short, one future and possibly the only future for civilization is to function as the mind for a planetary-wide super-organism called the Earth.

Conclusion

In attempting, very much in the spirit of Auguste Comte, to develop a general science of humanity, Elias anticipated more recent work in the area of complexity theory (Kaufman, 1995, 2000). Both Elias and Kaufman have dared to suggest that there is pattern in the 'great evolution' – an order amenable to scientific investigation. In identifying systemic, recurring relationships between processes operating at wildly varying temporal scales (each with their own academic disciplines – evolutionary biology, archaeology, history, sociology), Elias also opened the way to a very different understanding of the global ecological crisis: the problem of environmental sustainability as it might be viewed retrospectively one day (we hope), by our descendents in the deep future; or perhaps comparatively with much greater detachment than could ever be easy for an Earthling (of any geological period or species) by an alien ecologist of civilizations.

As Lovelock seems to grasp intuitively, sustainability in the *longue durée* implies an entirely new geological epoch, defined by a new level of integration and an evolutionary transformation as fundamental as the evolution of life (the biosphere), some 3.5 billion years ago, or the evolution of language (and with it the anthroposphere), one hundred millennia before the present. The emergence of an 'anthro-ecosphere' and a Gaian civilization playing a full and integral role in the evolution and biodiversity of the planet is hypothesized in Figure 1.[11]

If our species fails to make such a transition it is difficult to see how cosmopolitan liberal societies, which are premised on the ever-faster circulation of goods, people and information, can ever be sustainable and provide a long-term framework for the organization of societies and social life. This is the problem of 'liberalism in one village'.

On the other hand, as Lovelock seems to intuit, the emergence of the Level 9 anthro-ecosphere as a higher level of integration is likely to involve a radical reconfiguration of the relationship between the whole and the parts. In the very

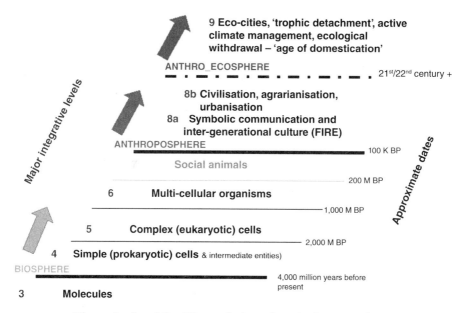

Figure 1: *Level 9 – The evolution of an Anthro-ecosphere.*

long term the biological co-evolution of our species and the planet suggests, at the very least, a more restrained, ecological and collectivist personality structure emerging on the back of an 'ecological civilizing process' (Quilley, 2009b).

In this scenario the individuated personality structure which animates so much of our politics and culture will succumb to a further internalization of restraints resulting in something which looks much more like a 'collective conscience'. In such circumstances it might be that terms like 'social liberalism' and 'cosmopolitanism' would feel like anachronisms relevant to a 'primitive mentality', as future humans play Dr Spock to our present day, partly-civilized but emotional, Captain Kirk. Lovelock speculates as much:

> Social insects such as bees, hornets, ants and termites evolved to form nests – communities far stronger than crowds of individuals – but in doing so they lost personal freedom and became subjects of their queens. Perhaps in a similar way we would lose freedom at the same time that Gaia gained strength . . . We cannot now know the chances of this happening, how long it will take or what it will be like to be a Gaian subject. The only near certainty is that we will never evolve this way if we allow ourselves, through inaction or improper response, to be made extinct by global heating . . . Let us look ahead to the time when Gaia is a truly sentient planet through the merging with her of our descendents. (Lovelock, 2009: 161–2)

Unfortunately an ecological civilizing process, and the inculcation of much more demanding standards of habitual self-restraint, though possible, seems unlikely.

Notes

1 In common parlance 'civilization' is a static concept that refers to a certain type of complex society characterised by a defined agrarian, territorial base, relatively high technology, an advanced social and technical division of labour, extensive forms of social stratification and corresponding military, religious and state apparatuses. Elias's technical concept of civilization is processual, relative (that is, marked by degrees – more or less) and characteristic of all human societies (see Goudsblom, 1992). It is defined by the interweaving of three sets of controls – social controls between people, ecological controls in relation to non-human nature, and psychological controls internalized by individuals during the course of childhood socialisation. In this article I use the term in both senses depending upon, and made clear by, the context.

2 Here I rely on David Christian's *Maps of Time* (2005: Appendix 2, pp. 505–11), and more detailed accounts provided by Eric Chaisson (2001) and Prigogine and Stengers (1984) on the cosmological and evolutionary significance of complexification; the work of Stuart Kaufman (1995, 2000) on more recent developments in complexity theory and self-organizing systems; and on Daly and Farley (2004) on the relationship between thermodynamics and economics.

3 The contraction of the word is attributed to Leon Brillouin (1953).

4 See Elias, 1978 [1970]: 156–7 for a discussion of this concept. Also see Mennell, 1998: 169–72, 236.

5 Since World War II, attempts to build liberal polities in societies that have not developed such an individuated personality structure have usually failed, often with grim results. Afghanistan is a case in point. Africa provides many examples. China and Iran are instances of modern societies where individuation through economic growth has engendered movements for democracy and a liberal sensibility among the urban middle classes but not, thus far, a stable liberal polity.

6 Consider, for example, the simple act of naming a child. Three hundred years ago sons were often named purely as a function of a social locus defined by their father (for example Stevenson, Johannson – literally Steven's son, Johan's son). By the early twentieth century parents chose from a wide but nevertheless limited set of conventional (often 'national') names – expressing the considerable but limited extent of individuation. The involvement of the state in setting such limits continued in France until well into the twentieth century. But in twenty-first century Britain, the art of naming has become a national obsession, with an overt emphasis on individual expression. It has even been suggested that the name functions as a 'brand' and might be instrumental in individual social advancement (Marsh, 2007: 'The names that will get your baby into Oxbridge'). My own children are perhaps a case in point: Tuuli (Finnish, meaning 'wind'), Jem (American, from *To Kill a Mockingbird*), Arlo (after American folk singer Arlo Guthrie) and Romy (tragic film heroine Romy Schneider).

7 By 'civilization' he means a complex society with an extended division of labour and highly developed scientific and technological capabilities.

8 Margulis confirmed that complex, eukaryotic cells are the result of an original process of symbiogenesis, whereby free-living bacteria became incorporated into host cells (on the back of either predatory ingestion or parasitic invasion) as functional organelles such as mitochondria or chloroplasts. Formerly independent bacteria retained their own DNA but became specialized cellular organs, increasing the complexity and evolutionary potential of the new, symbiotic complex (1992). See *The Symbiotic Planet* (1998) for her understanding of the relevance of symbiogenesis to the evolution of the biosphere and Lovelock's Gaia hypothesis.

9 The Paignton Zoo vertical farm is being developed by Valcent Verticrop High Density Growth Systems http://www.valcent.net/s/HDVGS.asp?ReportID=264273 – accessed 20 January 2010.

10 Here I use the term as a noun – that is, in the vernacular sense of a complex, technological society with an advanced division of labour.

11 Figure 1 is a modification of a schema advanced by Max Pettersson (1996), who in turn modified Joseph Needham's theory of integrative levels (1937) which was familiar to Elias.

References

Dates given in square brackets are those of first publication.

Allen, John, (1997), 'Biospheric theory and report on overall biosphere 2: design and performance during Mission One (1991–1993)', *Journal of Life Support and Biosphere Science*, 4: 3–4.

Barry, John and Stephen Quilley, (2008), 'Transition Towns: "survival", "resilience" and the elusive paradigm shift in sustainable living', *Eco-Politics Online*, 1, 2: 12–31.

Berry, Thomas, (2005), 'The EcoZoic Era', Lecture delivered to the E. F. Schumacher Society, available online at www.schumachersociety.org/publications/berry_91.html. Accessed 12 September 2007.

von Bertalanffy, Ludwig, (1952), *Problems of Life: An Evaluation of Modern Biological Thought*, London: Watts.

von Bertalanffy, Ludwig, (1956), 'A biologist looks at human nature', *Scientific Monthly*, 82: 33–41.

von Bertalanffy, Ludwig, (1965), 'On the Definition of the Symbol', in Joseph R. Royce, (ed.), *Psychology and the Symbol: An Interdisciplinary Symposium*, New York: Random House: 28–71.

von Bertalanffy, Ludwig, (1969), *General System Theory: Foundations, Development, Applications*, New York: George Braziller.

Bookchin, Murray, (1982), *The Ecology of Freedom. The Emergence and Dissolution of Hierarchy*, Palo Alto, CA: Cheshire Books.

Brillouin, Leon, (1953), 'Negentropy principle of information', *Journal of Applied Physics*, 24, 9: 1152–63.

Budiansky, Stephen, (1998), *The Covenant of the Wild*, London: Phoenix.

Calder, Nigel, (1967), *The Environment Game*, London: Secker & Warburg.

Chaisson, Eric J., (2001), *Cosmic Evolution: The Rise of Complexity in Nature*, Cambridge, MA: Harvard University Press.

Christian, David, (2005), *Maps of Time: An Introduction to Big History*, Berkeley, CA: University of California Press.

Coppinger, Raymond P. and Charles K. Smith, (1983), 'The domestication of evolution', *Environmental Conservation*, 10, 4: 283–92.

Daly, Herman E. and Joshua C. Farley, (2004), *Ecological Economics: Principles and Applications*, Washington DC: Island Press.

Diamond, Jared, (2006), *Collapse: How Societies Choose to Fail or Survive*, Harmondsworth: Penguin.

Despommier, Dickson, (2008), 'The Vertical Farm Essay, Parts I & II', available online at http://www.verticalfarm.com/VfEssays2.aspx. Accessed 1 May 2009.

Downton, Paul F., (2009), *Ecopolis: Architecture and Cities for a Changing Climate*, London: Springer.

Duncan, Richard C., (1989), 'Evolution, technology, and the natural environment: a unified theory of human history', Proceedings of the St. Lawrence Section ASEE Annual Meeting, Binghamton, NY. 14B1–11 to 14B1–20.

Duncan, Richard C., (2007), 'The Olduvai theory: terminal decline imminent', *The Social Contract* 17, 3: 141–51.

Eisenberg, Evan, (2000), *The Ecology of Eden*, London: Picador.

Elias, Norbert, (1978 [1970]), *What is Sociology?* London: Hutchinson. [Collected Works, Vol. 5, Dublin: UCD Press, forthcoming].

Elias, Norbert, (2000 [1939]), *The Civilizing Process*, rev. edn, Oxford: Blackwell. [*On the Process of Civilisation*, Dublin: UCD Press, forthcoming].

Elias, Norbert, (2007 [1987]), *Involvement and Detachment*, Collected Works, Vol. 8, Dublin: University College Dublin Press.

Elias, Norbert, (2011 [1991]), *The Symbol Theory*, rev. edn, Collected Works, Vol. 13, Dublin: UCD Press.

Fischer-Kowalski, Marina and Helmut Haberl, (2007), *Socioecological Transitions and Global Change: Trajectories of Social Metabolism and Land Use*, Cheltenham: Edward Elgar.

Goudsblom, Johan, (1977), *Sociology in the Balance: A Critical Essay*, Oxford: Blackwell.

Goudsblom, Johan, (1992), *Fire and Civilization*, London: Allen Lane.

Goudsblom, Johan, (2002), 'Introductory overview: the expanding anthroposphere', in Bert de Vries and Johan Goudsblom, *Mappae Mundi: Humans and their Habitats in Long-Term Ecological Perspective*, Amsterdam: Amsterdam University Press.

Goudsblom, Johan, (2003a), 'A four-stage model of photosynthetic appropriation', paper presented at a 'The culture and history of eating habits' workshop, hosted by Stichting Praemium Erasmianum, Amsterdam, Netherlands, 5–6 November 2003.

Goudsblom, Johan, (2003b), 'The Anthroposphere: expansion and transformations,' paper presented to the International Symposium on World System History and Global Environmental Change, Human Ecology Division, Lund University, Sweden, 19–22 September, 2003.

Grover, Sami, (2009), 'Vertical Farm at UK Zoo: 20-Fold Increase in Yield Per Acre', available online at http://www.treehugger.com/files/2009/08/vertical_farm_a.php. Accessed 20 January 2010.

Hansen, Jim, (2007), 'Climate catastrophe', *New Scientist*, 195, 2614 (July 28): 30–34.

Hayes, David and Andrew Dobson, (2008), 'A politics of crisis: low-energy cosmopolitanism', *Open Democracy* 26 October, available online at http://www.opendemocracy.net/print/46561. Accessed 1 January 2010.

Heinberg, Richard, (1995), 'The primitivist critique of civilization', available online at http://www.primitivism.com/primitivist-critique.htm. Accessed 20 January 2009.

Heinberg, Richard, (2005), *The Party's Over: Oil War and the Fate of Industrial Societies*, 2nd edn, Forest Row: Clairview.

Homer-Dixon, Thomas, (2006), *The Upside of Down. Catastrophe, Creativity and the Renewal of Civilization*, London: Souvenir Press.

Hopkins, Rob, (2008), *The Transition Handbook: From Oil Dependency to Local Resilience*, Totnes: Green Books.

Jablonka, Eva and Marion J. Lamb, (2005), *Evolution in Four Dimensions: Genetic, Epigenetic, Behavioural, and Symbolic Variation in the History of Life*, Cambridge, MA: MIT Press.

Jensen, Derrick, (2002), *A Language Older than Words*, London: Souvenir Press.

Jensen, Derrick, (2006), *Endgame*, Vol. 1, *The Problem of Civilization*; Vol. 2 *Resistance*, New York: Seven Stories Press.

Kaufman, Stuart, (1995), *At Home in the Universe: The Search for Laws of Complexity and Self-Organization*, Oxford: Oxford University Press.

Kaufman, Stuart, (2000), *Investigations*, New York: Oxford University Press.

Kunstler, James Howard, (2005), *The Long Emergency. Surviving the Converging Catastrophes of the 21st Century*, London: Atlantic Books.

Kunstler, James Howard, (2008), *A World Made by Hand*, New York: Atlantic Monthly Press.

Lash, Scott and John Urry, (1993), *Economies of Signs and Space*. London: Sage.

Lotka, Alfred J., (1922), 'Contribution to the energetics of evolution', *Proceedings of the National Academy of Sciences* 8, 6: 147–51.

Lotka, Alfred J. and A. James, (1925), *Elements of Physical Biology*, Baltimore, MD: Williams & Wilkins.

Lovelock, James, (2007), *The Revenge of Gaia*. London: Penguin.

Lovelock, James, (2009), *The Vanishing Face of Gaia: A Final Warning*, London: Allen Lane.

Loyal, Steven and Stephen Quilley, (2005), 'Eliasian sociology as a "central theory" for the human sciences', *Current Sociology*, 53, 5: 807–28.

Lynas, Mark, (2007), *Six Degrees: Our Future on a Hotter Planet*, New York: Harper.

McCarthy, Cormac, (2007), *The Road*. London: Picador.

Margulis, Lynn, (1992), *Symbiosis in Cell Evolution: Microbial Communities in the Archean and Proterozoic Eons*, New York: W. H. Freeman.

Margulis, Lynn, (1998), *Symbiotic Planet: A New Look at Evolution*, New York: Basic Books.

Marsh, Stefanie, (2007), 'The names that will get your baby into Oxbridge', *The Times*, 31 July.

Martin, James, (2007), *The Meaning of the Twenty-First Century*, London: Eden Project.

Marx, Karl and Friedrich Engels, (1998 [1848]), The Communist Manifesto: A Modern Edition, London and New York: Verso.

Mennell, Stephen, (1998), *Norbert Elias: An Introduction*, Dublin: UCD Press.

Mennell, Stephen, (1990), 'Decivilizing processes: theoretical significance and some lines of research', *International Sociology*, 5, 2: 205–23.

Needham, Joseph, (1937), *Integrative Levels: A Re-evaluation of the Idea of Progress*, Oxford: Clarendon Press.

Pearce, Fred, (2007), *The Last Generation: How Nature will take her Revenge for Climate Change*, London: Eden Project.

Pettersson, Max, (1996), *Complexity and Evolution*, Cambridge: Cambridge University Press.

Prigogine, Ilya and Grégoire Nicolis, (1977), *Self-Organization in Non-Equilibrium Systems*, London: Wiley.

Prigogine, Ilya and Isabelle Stengers, (1984), *Order out of Chaos: Man's New Dialogue with Nature*, London: Flamingo.

Quilley, Stephen, (2004a), 'Ecology, "human nature" and civilizing processes: biology and sociology in the work of Norbert Elias', in Steven Loyal and Stephen Quilley, (eds), *The Sociology of Norbert Elias*, Cambridge: Cambridge University Press: 42–58.

Quilley, Stephen, (2004b), 'Social development as trophic expansion: food systems, prosthetic ecology and the arrow of history', *Amsterdam Sociologisch Tijdschrift* 31, 3: 321–48.

Quilley, Stephen, (2009a), 'Transition skills: skills for transition to a post fossil-fuel age', in Arran Stibbe, (ed.), *The Handbook of Sustainability Literacy: Skills for a Changing World*, Totnes: Green Books

Quilley, Stephen, (2009b), 'The land ethic as an ecological civilizing process: Aldo Leopold, Norbert Elias and environmental philosophy', *Environmental Ethics* 31, 2: 115–34.

Quilley, Stephen, (2010), 'Integrative levels and the "great evolution": organicist biology and the sociology of Norbert Elias', *Journal of Classical Sociology*, 10, 4: 1–19.

Quilley, Stephen and Steven Loyal, (2004), 'Towards a central theory: the scope and relevance of Norbert Elias', in Steven Loyal and Stephen Quilley, (eds), *The Sociology of Norbert Elias*, Cambridge: Cambridge University Press: 1–22.

Quilley, Stephen and Steven Loyal, (2005), 'Science, cumulative knowledge, secondary involvement and synthesis: a reply to our critics', *Current Sociology*, 53, 5: 843–50.

Quinn, Daniel, (1995), *Ishmael*, New York: Doubleday.

Rawles, James Wesley, (2009a), *Patriots: A Novel of Survival in the Coming Collapse*, Berkeley, CA: Ulysses Press.

Rawles, James Wesley, (2009b), *How to Survive the End of the World as We Know It: Tactics, Techniques, and Technologies for Uncertain Times*, New York: Plume.

Rees, Martin, (2004), *Our Final Century: Will The Human Race Survive the Twenty-First Century?* London: Arrow.

Rees, William E., (1992), 'Ecological footprints and appropriated carrying capacity: what urban economics leaves out', *Environment and Urbanisation* 4, 2: 121–30.

Register, Richard, (2006), *Ecocities*, Gabriola, BC: New Society.

Sampson, Paul R. and David Pitt, (1999), *The Biosphere and Noosphere Reader: Global Society Environment and Change*, London: Routledge.

Scarrow, Alex, (2007), *Last Light*, London: Orion.

Schrödinger, Erwin, (1944), *What is Life?* Cambridge: Cambridge University Press.

Smil, Vaclav, (2008), *Energy in Nature and Society: General Energetics of Complex Systems*, Cambridge, MA: MIT Press.

Smith, Hamilton O., Robert Friedman and John, C. Venter, (2003), 'Biological solutions to renewable energy', *The Bridge*, 33, 2: 36–40.

Soleri, Paolo, (1969), *Arcology: The City in the Image of Man*, Cambridge, MA: MIT Press.

Tainter, Joseph A., (1990), *The Collapse of Complex Societies*, Cambridge: Cambridge University Press.

Teilhard de Chardin, Pierre, (1966), *Man's Place in Nature: The Human Zoological Group*, London: Collins.

Teilhard de Chardin, Pierre, (1959), *The Phenomenon of Man*, London: Collins.

Theroux, Paul, (2009), *Far North*, London: Faber.

Tönnies, Ferdinand, (2002 [1887]), Community and Society Gemeinschaft and Gesellschaft. Newton Abbot: David and Charles.

Tudge, Colin, (1998), *Neanderthals, Bandits, and Farmers: How Agriculture Really Began*, London: Weidenfeld & Nicolson.

Vernadsky, Vladimir I., (1944), 'Problems of Biochemistry II', *Transactions of the Connecticut Academy of Arts and Sciences*, 36: 483–517.

Vernadsky, Vladimir I., (1998 [1926]), *The Biosphere*, New York: Copernicus.

Waddington, Conrad H., (1957), *The Strategy of Genes*, London: George Allen & Unwin.

Wilson, Robert Charles, (2009), *Julian Comstock: A Story of Twenty-Second-Century America*, New York: Tom Doherty Associates.

White, Leslie A., (1943), 'Energy and the Evolution of Culture', *American Anthropologist*, 45, 3: 335–56

Wills, Christopher, (1998), *Children of Prometheus*, Reading, MA: Perseus Books.

Youngquist, Walter, (1997), *GeoDestinies: The Inevitable Control of Earth Resources over Nations and Individuals*, Portland, OR: National Book Company.

Zerzan, John, (ed.), (2005), *Against Civilization*, enlarged edn, Los Angeles, CA: Feral House.

Zerzan, John, (2009a), 'Why Primitivism?', available online at http://johnzerzan.net/articles/why-primitivism.html. Accessed 20 January 2009.

Zerzan, John, (2009b), 'No way out', available online at http://johnzerzan.net/articles/no-way-out.html. Accessed 20 January 2009.

Norbert Elias's post-philosophical sociology: from 'critique' to relative detachment

Richard Kilminster

Away, haunt thou me not,
Thou vain philosophy!
Little hast thou bestead,
Save to perplex the head,
And leave the spirit dead.
(Arthur Hugh Clough, 'In a Lecture Room', 1849)

Abstract: This paper argues that Elias's work presupposes a radical abandonment of philosophy as a vestige of magical–mythical thinking that has been rendered obsolete by the rise of sociology. For Elias, attempts by philosophers to claim a continuing non-empirical area of investigation are spurious and reflect only professional interests. The origins of Elias's position are traced to his rejection of neo-Kantianism and his partici-pation in the *Wissenssoziologie* of Karl Mannheim in Weimar Germany. Focusing on the traditional ethical or normative questions, the paper shows how Elias's conception of the 'detour via detachment' enabled him to transcribe these issues (as well as tradi-tional epistemological and ontological questions) into sociologically manageable terms. His strategy is further clarified through a comparison with the all-pervasive Critical Sociology approach to these matters, which emerges as severely handicapped by its reliance upon quasi-metaphysical, transcendental arguments. Also, its attribu-tions of social blame generate fear images that reinforce conflict and its negative over-statements strengthen anxiety and frustration, thereby bolstering precisely what it is trying to change. The paper reveals the tacit function as a leftist code-word that the term 'critical' performs for many sociologists. Neo-Marxist 'critique' is shown to be a profoundly flawed attempt to deal with issues of theory and practice.

Introduction

Norbert Elias's work constitutes a radical rejection of many of the common assumptions of twentieth-century sociology, particularly the trends dominant since 1945. For example, contrary to the widely held view of the discipline, he did not conceive of sociology as the study solely of advanced societies within the foreshortened timescale of 'modernity'. Rather, he saw it as including the study of long-term processes over the whole course of the development of human society. In opposition to the orthodox sociology of 'modernity', Elias's work represented a sociology of the human condition (Kilminster, 2007a: 5). This conception of sociology went back a long way in Elias's intellectual development. In a conference response in 1928 on primitive art (Elias, 2006a [1929]: 75) he said that 'if one wishes to understand man, if one wishes to understand oneself – every period of history is equally relevant to us'. Later in his life he also explicitly opposed several of the major paradigms of sociology, including structural functionalism, Marxism, phenomenology and systems theory. He typically found them to be, in various combinations: individualistic, rationalistic, ideological, economistic, abstract, static, over-analytic at the expense of synthesis, or lacking a developed sociological psychology.

Elias also censured other disciplines, notably history and psychology, for their individualism and narrowness of scope. But it was on the question of the relationship between sociology and philosophy that he was at his most trenchant, uncompromising and controversial. The strident and total rejection of philosophy that we find in Elias is rare in sociology. In the twentieth century, sociologists gradually established themselves institutionally in various countries. Central to this was their perception of the autonomy of a range of regularities *sui generis* ('society', 'sociation', 'the social', 'sociality', or whatever word it was given) and their scientific and professional claim to the investigation of this field. It became clear to many sociologists[1] that the arrival of the social sciences, including sociology, was of great significance for the intellectual authority of philosophy. Not only was philosophy no longer competent to investigate – theoretically or empirically – complex social processes, but also the sociological perspective promised to take over much of what had been traditionally the competence of philosophers, particularly in the time-honoured areas of epistemology, ontology and ethics. Naturally the philosophers responded, asserting their claim to competence and expertise in conceptual work, logic, clarification or other *non-*empirical, 'second-order' matters in order to legitimate their changing professional existence (Kilminster, 1998, chapter 1).

Subsequently, many sociologists have conceded to philosophers this range of non-empirical or 'transcendental' problems, usually to do with 'truth claims', *a priori* suppositions or the question of validity. This is part of an intellectual *modus vivendi* in the context of professional disciplinary relations in academic institutions. However, in this ethos, the longer-term cognitive issues raised by Elias about the subject matter and fate of philosophy are for the most part suppressed. Even Karl Mannheim – whose work in the 1920s on the sociology of knowledge was widely regarded as a challenge to philosophy – conceded 'the structural autonomy of the philosophical level of problems' (quoted by Meja and Stehr, 1990: 295). Elias refused to make even this concession. He was utterly opposed to the hegemony of philosophy and the subtle intrusion of philosophical modes of thought into sociology. He advised his fellow sociologists, whose discipline is of lower status than philosophy, not to defer automatically to philosophers' guidance in the task of building up a sociological research programme. Elias's own sociological work is grounded in a *sociological* theory of knowledge and the sciences, rather than in the traditional assumptions of conventional philosophical epistemology and philosophy of science. This is one of the main ways in which he differs from contemporary sociologists and from 'social theorists' in particular, who are generally far more deferential towards philosophy. Indeed, as I have argued elsewhere, 'social theory', as it is practised today, is effectively philosophizing by another name (Kilminster, 1998: 127–9; 176–8).

At the core of Elias's 'figurational' or 'process' sociology, then, is a rejection of philosophy as a superseded, pre-modern form of transcendental thinking. In view of the high prestige and virtually unquestioned intellectual authority of philosophy in academic circles and beyond, Elias's position on this subject will seem to stretch his credibility to the limit. In my view, though, taking Elias's argument seriously and following it through is part and parcel of the challenge that his work as a whole represents. This paper first traces the origins of Elias's rationale for the historical supersession of philosophy. Secondly, it explores its implications in relation to the place of sociologists' moral and political values (or what are commonly referred to as 'normative' questions) in the framing of their research. The focus will be on the shortcomings of the dominant 'critical' perspective on this issue. Let us now turn to the origins of Elias's thinking on this subject.

The sociological mission

Elias wrote his doctoral thesis at Breslau under the neo-Kantian philosopher Richard Hönigswald, from whom he acknowledged that he learned a great deal, even though the relationship ended in their estrangement. The thesis was entitled 'Idea and Individual: a critical investigation of the concept of history' (Elias, 2006b [1922]: 23–53) and was eventually accepted in January 1924, after a delay of more than a year occasioned by a dispute between student and supervisor. Their dispute concerned an issue fundamental for the whole neo-Kantian movement: whether there are any grounds for postulating a notion of truth that is transcendental, *a priori* to and independent of, human experience and human history. At stake here was the whole problematic of *Geltung* (validity) as a realm of valid knowledge held by some philosophers to be timeless and effectively absolute. Elias could not accept that in a time-bound world there could be anything timeless. The philosophers' insistence on this alerted him to its role as part of a professional ideology (Elias, 1994: 153).

In arguing against the vaunted principle of *Geltung*, Elias was part of an intellectual and generational movement which challenged the relevance of the neo-Kantianism of the older generation of philosophers that dominated philosophy departments in German universities. This challenge was predicated upon the charge that neo-Kantianism was incapable of dealing with the real and serious problems of society thrown into relief by the carnage of the First

World War and the economic crises and political violence of the post-War years. That philosophy was an idealistic, individualistic, philosophy of consciousness, which, in its preoccupation with epistemology, *Geltung* and methodology, ignored or implicitly devalued the real world. As Michael Zank (2002: 17) has put it, this younger generation (which included Elias) was 'nauseated by the sanctimonious cultivation of vast theoretical solutions to concrete practical problems'. They emphatically turned away from the philosophical systems and values that they saw as having led to the war and contributed to sustaining it. At the time, the philosopher Margarete Sussman spoke of an 'exodus out of philosophy' (quoted in Zank, 2002: 17).

The movement that challenged these priorities has been called the 'onto-hermeneutic turn' (Crowell, 1999: 186) in twentieth-century German academic philosophy. This consisted of a widespread incredulity towards the Kantian notions of the thing-in-itself, the knowing subject, fixed *a priori* categories and the idea of 'pure knowing' in general, as well as an acute awareness of the cul-de-sac of solipsism. Many of these objections and problems appeared in various combinations in Elias's doctoral dissertation (Elias, 2006b [1922]). They resurfaced in the context of sociological polemics in Elias's later programmatic writings and lectures on the sociology of knowledge (for example, Elias, 2009a [1971]; 2009b [1982]; 1984). In these later writings and lectures, in the course of a robust sociological re-evaluation of them, Elias showed a fluent familiarity with the philosophical controversies of his youth.

After his dispute with Hönigswald, Elias transferred into sociology under Alfred Weber in Heidelberg and from 1929 to 1933 became Karl Mannheim's first assistant (Hans Gerth was the second) in Frankfurt. Over time Elias developed a broader thesis: that the whole central tradition of modern Western epistemology, from Descartes through Kant to twentieth-century phenomenology, was misconceived. It was based on asking how a single, *adult*, human mind can know what it knows. Elias called this the model of *homo clausus*, the 'closed person', and found it lurking in much of modern sociology as well (Elias, 2000 [1969]: 470–9; 1978 [1970]: 119 ff.; Mennell, 1998: 188–93; Kilminster, 1998: 57–92). He argued that we must instead think in terms of *homines aperti*, 'open people', and in particular of 'long lines of generations of people' building up the stock of human knowledge. This should be our working assumption, not how an individual can come to know something or make moral judgements through the application of Reason. The crucial point, however, which he developed in *The Civilizing Process* and other later works, was that the image of *homo clausus* corresponded to a *mode of self-experience* that was *not* a human universal but was a social product, particularly associated with developments within and between European societies from the Renaissance onwards.[2]

For an adequate understanding of Elias, then, it is essential to appreciate how his sociology developed out of the desire to transcribe philosophical discussions of knowledge, society, culture and the human condition into a form amenable to empirical sociological investigation. These questions included those traditionally grouped under epistemology, ontology and ethics (that is, 'evaluative' or 'normative' questions), which reappear in Elias's works transcribed into a sociological idiom. One cannot overemphasize the robustly sociological character of Elias's world-view. He considered that his work presupposed the supersession of philosophy and he persistently questioned the authority of philosophers, refusing to enter into discussions conducted in philosophical categories (Elias, 2009b [1982]; 2009c [1985]; Kilminster, 1998: 3–26). In the reception of his work in recent years, the significance of its 'post-philosophical' character has not always been fully understood (Kilminster, 2007a).

On the subject of *epistemology*, from as early in his career as when he was a doctoral student under Hönigswald, there were indications in Elias's doctoral dissertation that he was moving in the direction of developing a sociological epistemology to replace the traditional philosophical one (Kilminster and Wouters, 1995). He could not have put it that way at the time, but this interpretation can be plausibly applied with hindsight. This transformed epistemology would relate ways of knowing to the patterned ways in which human beings live together, and remodel the traditional issue of *Geltung*. This realization gathers momentum in his work to a point where he makes a complete *break* with philosophy, decisively turning his back on the tradition. The failure to grasp this feature of his thinking has sometimes led some commentators to try to pull Elias back into the philosophy from which his life's work was a sustained attempt at emancipation (for example Maso, 1995); or to criticize him from philosophical positions that he regarded himself as already having moved beyond (Sathaye, 1973). As far as Elias was concerned, 'Traditional philosophical epistemology, in its transcendental form . . . [had] come to the end of its road' (Elias, 2009b [1982]: 135).

The neo-Kantian philosophy in which Elias was initially schooled did, however, alert him to key areas of enquiry, including the problems of the historical adequacy of knowledge, the origins and status of 'universal' categories of thought, and the prevalence of the model of the individual knowing subject in epistemology. The classical German philosophical tradition generally, and neo-Kantianism in particular, thus constituted a *point of departure* for Elias's transfer of his intellectual energies into a dynamic and historical sociology, which he believed could provide a more inclusive and adequate framework for the solution of those problems. Once Elias had made this break, I would argue, his sociological enquiries became *structurally different* from philosophy. In his work, the philosophical residues form at best trace elements or transformed distant presuppositions (see Kilminster, 1998: chapter 1, 2007a: 34–35).

What philosophers have discussed under the heading of *ontology*, for example Heidegger's abstract notion of the historicity of human beings and the bond between present and past involved in historical research, reappears in a transformed guise in Elias and is given an empirical inflection (Kilminster, 2007a: 93 ff). They are reflected very clearly in the complex structure of *The Civilizing Process*, in which 'present events illuminate the understanding of the past, and immersion in the past illuminates the present' as he puts it (Elias, 2000 [1939]: 436). Metaphysical speculations by various philosophical realists about the 'objects' of the different sciences, or the so-called 'modes of being' postulated by fundamental ontologists such as Heidegger, provided the stimulus for Elias to develop a *testable* theory of the levels of integration (physical, chemical, biological, social, and so on) of the social and natural worlds investigated by the different sciences (Elias, 2007a [1956], 2009d [1974]). By so doing, Elias subverted the fundamental ontologists' distinction between the *ontic* and the *ontological*. He had implicitly rejected the whole transcendental–theological underpinning of a distinction that had been framed by the ontologists and which justified their professional status as the guardians of the abstract question of Being itself (Goldmann, 1977: 105; Steiner, 1978: 86–7; Kilminster, 1979: 226–9; Kilminster, 1998: chapter 1).

Similarly, discussions of *values*, value-relevance and value-freedom in Rickert and Max Weber are recast by Elias as the theory of involvement and detachment, in which the conceptions of 'autonomous' and 'heteronomous' evaluations play a central role (Elias, 2007a [1956]; Kilminster, 2007a: chapter 5; more on this below). One finds in Elias, therefore, a principled avoidance of philosophical concepts and the consistent substitution of sociological alternatives that are more amenable to empirical reference. More examples include: 'truth' is recast as 'reality congruence'; 'part/whole' becomes 'unit and part-unit'; 'modes of being' are reframed as levels of integration; and 'abstractions' are transformed into 'symbols at a high level of synthesis'.

On the subject of *'evaluative'* or *'normative'* matters, or 'ought' questions, as philosophers call them, Elias commented very early in his career that 'ethical questions are always, and quite wrongly, separated from other scientific questions' (Elias, 2006c [1921]: 15). Furthermore, Elias's total commitment to sociology as a 'mission', which comes out clearly in his autobiographical *Reflections on a Life* (Elias, 1994) embraced an intense human commitment. He saw sociology as potentially able to assist human beings to orientate themselves in the figurations they form together and to help them to control the unintended social entanglements that threaten to escalate into destructive sequences such as mass killings and wars. The figurational view of society, and Elias's theories of civilizing processes and established–outsiders relations, are implicitly underpinned by the imperative of generating knowledge to help groups to achieve greater 'mutual identification' and thus to live in controlled antagonism with each other (de Swaan, 1995; 1997; Mennell, 1994). By implication, the level and type of abstraction of the transcendental inquiries of philosophers cannot generate the vivid, multi-faceted, concrete and *relational* knowledge required for this vital human task. Writers who have failed to grasp this aspect of Elias's work have tended, in their criticisms of him, to confuse the technical and normative dimensions of some of his concepts, for example, 'civilization' and 'civilizing processes' (for instance Leach, 1986; Bauman, 1989: 107). Elias was, however, aware of the 'normative' issue right from the start and had already, to his own satisfaction anyway, transformed the question and the relevant concepts into a sociological form amenable to empirical investigation (Fletcher, 1997: chapter 8).

The strong commitment of Elias (and the later sociologists working on extending his research programme) to empirical research can all too easily lead to a misunderstanding of the 'moral' dimension of his work, and to its being wrongly assimilated into the mode of 'value-free' sociological empiricism or even positivism (for example, Pels, 2003: 94–5). This matter can be clarified through briefly examining the links between Elias's thinking and Karl Mannheim's sociological programme from the 1920s and 1930s, in the development of which Elias participated (Kettler *et al.*, 2008). He shared the spirit, if not the last letter, of this intellectual venture. In addition to advocating a 'relational' or 'perspectival' view of society (echoes of which we find in Elias – see Kilminster, 1998: 47–51), Mannheim's programme was at the same time intended to deal with questions normally gathered together under the umbrella of 'ethics', 'politics' or 'evaluative' and 'existential' questions. These pertained to the ways in which humankind might achieve greater happiness and fulfilment individually and socially within what Mannheim called 'the forms of living together of man' (Mannheim, 1957 [1935]: 43).

In Mannheim's scheme of things, when considering evaluative matters the investigator makes a theoretical move sideways, the intention of this method being to redefine the scope and limits of assertions by politicians, philosophers and others about the possibilities of human freedom, democracy and happiness, by showing them to be coming inevitably from differing ideological perspectives. It was only through these one-sided perspectives ('involvements' as Elias later called them) that access was even possible to knowledge of society, all knowledge being existentially bounded and perspectival. For Mannheim, objectivity is sought by 'the translation of perspectives into the terms of another' (1936: 270–1). Having made these moves, the investigator is then potentially better able to evaluate the feasibility or soundness of 'ethical' or 'political' issues in the form in which they were originally raised by the particular politician, party, or ideology. Mannheim refers to this theoretical journey as attaining a new form of 'objectivity . . . in a roundabout fashion' (1936: 270). These analytic steps then reach a point where the process 'becomes a critique' (1936: 256). (Mannheim probably meant critique (*Kritik*) here in a broadly Kantian epistemological sense, but with a possible simultaneous evaluative inflection – see later.)

Elias's version of the journey specifies that it is only by a 'detour via detachment' that sociologists can hope to gain more adequate knowledge of the structure of social events in which they themselves are also emotionally caught up (Elias, 2007b [1987]: 169–70). He shared Mannheim's ambition to transcribe so-called ethical and evaluative matters into sociologically manageable terms and thus to put the questions raised philosophically or ideologically on to another level. This position constitutes the pith and marrow of Elias's whole sociological programme.

This 'evaluative' intention also pervades the empirical–theoretical pre-sentations that are laid out in *The Civilizing Process*. Elias opens the first volume with a sociogenetic inquiry, typical of the sociology of knowledge, into the origins of the concepts of *Kultur* and *Zivilization*, which were both redolent of the covert ideological dimension of Alfred Weber's sociology and other highly charged ideological conflicts at the time over whether civilized behaviour was the acme or the nadir of human social achievement. Amongst other things, the tacit task of *The Civilizing Process* is to reframe the range, applicability and realistic usefulness of these two key terms via sociological enquiry into their genesis in the European civilizing process in general. Significantly, Elias returns to the concepts in the final part of his book (2000 [1939]: 363–447) at a new level and *re-poses* the questions about human satisfaction, fulfilment and constraint embodied more ideologically in the antithesis which partly provided the starting point (Kilminster, 2007a: chapter 4).

Finally, it is important to point out that Elias had made a decision very early on in his career *not* to transform the discredited neo-Kantian philosophy by restructuring it in a *new* philosophical direction, say towards fundamental ontology or existentialism, or a *new* form of Kantian apriorism on the lines of Ernst Cassirer. But rather, his decision was to *abandon*[3] it altogether. Elias had been profoundly touched by another thorny debate in Weimar Germany. In an era of fundamental questioning, many philosophers and others even questioned the autonomy of philosophy itself or declared the 'end' of philosophy (Crowell, 1999: 186; Kilminster, 1998: 25–6). Agonised debates went on about the subject in Weimar Germany and many feared that sociology – and the sociology of knowledge in particular – represented a dangerous threat to philosophy (Arendt, 1990 [1930]; see also Kilminster, 2007a: 24). The autonomy of philosophy was usually justified in the final analysis by transcendental arguments of one kind or another. Out of these conflicts a division of labour emerged. Philosophers conceded that socio-historical study was the task of the empirical social sciences, including sociology. The province of philosophy, however, was reclaimed by the philosophers as 'systematics', that is, non-empirical, 'second-order', transcendental reflection arising out of the empirical sciences. This dualism appeared in different guises, according to the school of philosophy concerned, and continues to shape the perception of the two subject areas to the present day (for a detailed tabulation see Kilminster, 1998: 16–17). The Heideggerian distinction between the *ontic* (the objects of the sciences) and the *ontological* (the Being of the world) referred to earlier, follows the same pattern. Elias did not accept this division of labour between the two disciplines, instead turning his back on the various arguments from 'transcendence' involved in its construction (Kilminster, 2010).

Furthermore, this rejection cannot be reduced to an idiosyncratic whim on Elias's part. My point is that it is in fact an organic and principled part of his perspective as a whole. It was based on a scientific conviction that the entire tradition of philosophy is historically defunct and cognitively deficient. For him, it would be scientifically and intellectually dishonest to argue otherwise. Philosophy is revealed as a superseded and potentially disorienting form of human orientation related to theology and magical mythical thought (van

Benthem van den Bergh, 1986: 110).[4] Its demise was part of a social transformation in which the questions posed by the philosophers were continually being transposed on to another level as sociology, as part of a longer-term process that I have called elsewhere the 'Sociological Revolution' (Kilminster, 1998). This process had left the practitioners of philosophy historically defunctionalized, so driving them as a defence of their profession into creating their own fields of inquiry and expertise and laying claim to them (Elias, 2009b [1982]; Kilminster, 1998: chapter 1). From their superior position in the academic pecking order, philosophers have arrogated to themselves the authority to dictate to other fields what their methods and forms of explanation should be. But this authority is purely a product of the institutional power advantage and prestige of the philosophy establishment. That is no guarantee in itself of the cognitive weight or value of the justifications that underpin it. Elias's stance is the strong and final one that philosophy is based on an archaic form of non-empirical (transcendental) speculation that produces abstract reflections of little cognitive value. Hence, to continue with it is self-evidently pointless. Put in these terms, Elias's position – taken to its furthest conclusions – clearly poses a challenge for sociologists and philosophers, most of whom partake in the mythical aura surrounding philosophy. As he remarked, with some understatement, 'It is not easy to abandon work of such intellectual grandeur and prestige' (Elias, 2009a [1971]: 35).

On being 'critical' in sociology

Judging by the frequency with which sociologists today remind us of their 'critical' credentials, the issue of how political and moral commitments should or should not play themselves out in the everyday professional life of social scientists, is clearly one of the abiding concerns of the discipline. The distinctiveness of Elias's 'post-philosophical' sociology can be conveyed most compellingly in relation to these questions. (Rather, that is, than in relation to the more rarefied areas of philosophical epistemology and ontology, even though Elias's work has much to contribute also to the sociological transformation of these traditional subject areas; see Kilminster, 1998: chapter 1, 2007a: chapters 2 & 3, and 2010). As we have seen, these matters have traditionally been gathered together under the umbrella of 'ethics', 'politics' or 'evaluative', 'normative' and 'political' questions. At the present time, the 'critical theory' perspective is probably the most adopted (but by no means the most cogent) solution to the perceived problem of what should be the relationship between sociological research and political and moral convictions as to how society 'ought' to be organised.

The 'critical' viewpoint is one side of a polarization of opinion on the issue of the role of 'values' in sociological research. (a) One view accepts that research can be 'value-free' in Max Weber's sense, in which matters of moral values, political ideology or 'ought' questions generally are suspended for the sake of dispassionate inquiry. On this viewpoint, sociology works towards value-freedom, as an ideal, or this is employed as a regulative principle, in Kantian language. (b) Another view is the probably more dominant 'critical' perspective, based on contemporary variants of the Critical Theory of the Frankfurt School.[5] Proponents of this perspective argue that the pursuit of 'value-freedom' in sociology is undesirable because it does not put eliminating social inequality and domination at the centre of research. It should be substituted by social scientists placing values and normative concerns (typically referred to by high-level abstractions such as freedom, emancipation, equality, social justice, social transformation, self-determination, and so on) at the centre of research, shaping its focus and priorities.

This kind of 'critical' thinking is very pervasive in sociology and books about it are legion. Sociologists embracing it often describe what they are doing as 'critical' sociology or 'critical' social theory, always contrasted with and in opposition to, the 'value-free', mainstream orthodoxy. It is a position derived ultimately from Marxism and is presented as the fusion of social science and politics or theory and practice. As we will shortly see, Elias's theory of involvement and detachment goes beyond *both* of these two typical positions.

The word 'critical', as one of a family of words including critique, critiquing, and criticism, is ubiquitous at the present time in sociological writings and in the milieus of teaching, research, publishing and abstracts of conference papers. The word appears in the titles of countless books as well as journals, for example, *Critical* Discourse Studies; *Critical* Social Work; *Critical* Psychology in Action, *Critical* Sociology, Journal of *Critical* Social Policy and Theory, Culture and Society: Explorations in *Critical* Social Science, to name but a few. The obligatory adjective 'critical' has developed an almost magical aura, although it is often used carelessly. Sometimes it is used indiscriminately in the same piece of writing with different meanings, such as 'crucial' or 'fault-finding', without explanation, causing confusion. Important Kantian, Hegelian and Marxian meanings are often conflated, elided, or not mentioned at all.

In the traditional subject of literary criticism, 'critical' means involving careful, skilful, accurate, judgement, as part of the art of estimating the qualities of works of literature. Critical in that sense has been imperceptibly transferred into sociology to describe evaluations of theories or theorists. This might involve, say, showing in relation to sociological texts any inconsistencies, ideological inflections, hidden values, omissions or explanatory limits. Sociologists commonly provide a 'critical' review of the literature in a given specialism or topic area, or criticize this or that theory on various grounds. In doing so, they will be providing a 'critique' or will be 'critiquing' various theories or authors. It will also involve, as in literary criticism, judgements of the status or quality of a work or the intellectual standing of an author. Hence, very many sociological writings will be 'critical' in this legitimate but ultimately unexceptionable, sense. In the sociological usage, judgements are being made about cognitive or explanatory value rather than aesthetic quality in the literary version.

As all these meanings are separated and clarified, it becomes clear that the word critical has become almost desperately equivocal in contemporary usage in the social sciences and humanities. In one sense or another, particularly bearing in mind that in the humanities virtually any kind of theorizing is described as critical (Buchanan, 2010, in note 5 above) all sociologists and analysts in adjacent areas of study such as gender, film or literature are, without exception, 'critical' inquirers. Yet sociologists and others in the social sciences continue self-consciously to commit themselves to a sociology that is avowedly 'critical'. This conclusion only serves to underscore another implicit meaning of 'critical' in sociology that is the most widespread and significant – that is, its use as a code word. It is aimed at initiates who know what meaning is intended. It is difficult for the uninitiated to guess what is meant, the more so in view of the plethora of meanings of the word.

The meaning of 'critical' as a code word I would summarize as 'left-wing, actively committed to reducing inequality, oppression and injustice in unspecified and generalized ways'. Within these broad parameters, the code word encompasses a wide range of political positions and moral viewpoints, largely on the Left of the political spectrum. It functions for many sociologists and others as a talisman, conveying broad moral or political leanings. It satisfies the writer's conscience as well as signalling to others a broad commitment or allegiance. They will, in turn, recognise that the author is 'one of us'. As a code word, 'critical' signifies a potential, imagined or wished-for We-identity, in Elias's language. It bespeaks an imagined grouping that shares the same convictions as to what is wrong with society and how it can be remedied. It is part and parcel of what van Benthem van den Bergh (1986: 110) described as the tendency to look for individuals or groups to blame for unplanned social developments that thwart our pursuit of happiness; or for 'guilt-causes' in ever more abstract and personified categories. Writing about the sometimes threatening international and intra-societal conflicts in our time he continues:

> The lesser the degree of controllability of such problems and the greater the uncertainty and fear, the stronger the tendency to blame somebody or something will become. In such cases the basic categories and questions of a mythical-magical way of thinking, though they have become more abstract (not God or the Devil, but 'capitalism or 'communism' and the like) still largely determine the way in which people orient themselves. They will attempt either to blame specific individuals or groups, or to look for what I shall call 'guilt causes' in more abstract categories, which are often personified and endowed with consciousness, intent will and purpose, in the same way as mountains or rivers in former days. (van Benthem van den Bergh, 1986: 110–11)

Writers who self-consciously describe their inquiries as 'critical', frequently also refer to 'capitalism', 'communism' or 'consumerism' in the terms described above. At the time of writing, the personified concept of 'modernity' appears to be performing a similar function of 'guilt-cause' for many sociologists struggling to come to terms with conflicting political allegiances after the collapse of Soviet communism in 1989. In political discussions in the present period what has been superseded since that time has been the view that in assessing social ills, capitalism is the problem and socialism the solution. Many contemporary sociologists assume either that (a) there is now effectively only one global, capitalist 'modernity' associated with the bloc of wealthy nations led by the USA; or (b) the so-called 'socialist' societies of the former Soviet Union, as well as the capitalist ones outside the former Eastern bloc, are *both* part of the wider phenomenon of 'modernity' and that *this* is the source of their *common* problems (Bauman, 1992: 222). The new geo-political figuration has created a situation in which the previously time-honoured, clear-cut targets for blame have become confused and ambiguous. 'Modernity' steps into the vacuum. Modernity, in other words, is now to blame.

Examples of the personification of 'modernity' in contemporary social criticism abound. Scott Lash writes: 'What happens, analysts like Beck and Giddens ask, when modernity begins to reflect on *itself*? What happens when modernization, understanding *its* own excesses and vicious spiral of destructive subjugation (of inner, outer and social nature) begins to take *itself* as object of reflection?' (Lash, 1994: 112; my emphases). Austin Harrington writes: 'Only modernity *could have thought of applying* a scientific conception to the making and shaping of *its own* world' (Harrington, 2005: 315; my emphases). In the influential writings of Zygmunt Bauman we find that modernity 'is coming of age' and is now 'consciously abandoning what . . . it was unconsciously doing' (Bauman, 1990: 23). In another place he writes: 'Postmodernity may be conceived of as modernity conscious of its true nature – *modernity for itself*' (Bauman, 1992: 187; emphasis in original).

Let us now turn to some of the technical meanings of the term 'critical' in philosophy and sociology, which are tacitly implicated when it is being used as a code word. Here the origins of 'critical' inquiries in the German philosophical traditions of Kant and Hegel and their legacy in sociology and in Marxism will come to the fore. The intention behind this discussion will be to show not only the Hegelian–Marxian assumptions of the style of thinking hidden behind the code word, but also the Kantian 'critical' themes underlying much of classical and mainstream sociology, even though that sociological tradition would never be routinely referred to as 'critical'. This will pave the way for clarifying how Elias's theory of involvement and detachment can help us to move beyond the negative consequences of the legacy of *both* Kantianism and Hegelian–Marxism in sociology.

'Critical' inquiries in Kant and Hegel

1. In the *Kantian* tradition, 'critical' means showing presuppositions, that which 'makes possible X or Y', in knowledge and culture. The focus is on the limits of what can be known or envisaged. Kant's philosophy was known as The Critical Philosophy. His Categories of the Understanding were the *a priori* universals (for instance time, space, number) presupposed in knowledge and the process of knowing. He was trying to shed light on the true nature of reality

and what could and could not be known by establishing the conditions of possibility of experience. Later, in the work of Habermas (1970) and Apel (1980) the approach was extended into the transcendental importance of language and language communities. Here the 'ideal speech situation' has been posited as a regulative principle and yardstick for social criticism. Against the ideal speech situation, it is possible to point to 'distorted communication' as the result of the intrusion of hierarchy and inequality and power differentials into communications between groups of people.

The Kantian tradition has been very influential in classical sociology and beyond. Kantianism in various forms has probably been the single most influential philosophy in shaping the contours of sociology. This much is very well known, and it is hardly a striking observation. The work of Durkheim, Simmel, Weber, Parsons, Giddens, Lévi-Strauss and Foucault (not an exhaustive list by any means) was founded on Kantian philosophy or transcendental principles inspired by it. Parsons, for example, was interested mainly in the conditions that make social action *possible*, not in people acting, as such (Kilminster, 1998: chapters 2, 4 & 5, 2010). A Kantian approach to social science tends to be analytic, breaking up social reality into analytically conceived, abstract aspects – say Parsons's cybernetic hierarchy, Weber's ideal types, Simmel's forms of sociation or the social categories in Giddens's structuration theory (Kilminster 1998: chapter 7).[6] Despite the fact of Kantianism pervading much of twentieth-century sociology, no one would ever think of calling this tradition 'critical' sociology – which, in a certain sense, it is.

2. In the *Hegelian* philosophical tradition 'critical' refers to comparing a particular institution or other object with its universal ideal form. So, for the Hegelian, that which is finite is a particular determination of its embeddedness in what the nineteenth-century British Hegelians (Bradley, Bosanquet *et al.*) glossed as the *concrete universal* (Stern, 2007). 'Critique' here means relating the finite appearance of the object with its Universal quality or essence, which it also *is*. (Marx's 'critique' of political economy, in trying to demonstrate the reality or essence of exploited labour lying beneath the surface appearance of prices and profits, reproduces this basic metaphysical distinction.) So, in this scheme of things, what is perfect and universal has already been partially realized in the imperfect, finite, concrete world. For example, if one compared a given particular judicial system with the pure concept of Justice then it will always be found empirically to be falling short of what it could ideally be. This method gave the Left Hegelians of the 1840s the means to become merciless critics of society. Society in every aspect never matches the perfection of the idealizations; it could always 'do better'. Herein lies the origins of the contemporary attitude of Critical Theorists who criticize society relentlessly as not matching up to an idealized utopia of equality, democracy and solidarity (Kilminster, 1998: 53–4).

The writings of Marx and later Marxists are essentially secularized, politicized, social-scientific versions of this kind of thinking. Here we find the deeper significance of the code word. In Hegel, to repeat, universals such as pure freedom or the 'Absolute ethical life', are seen as actually embedded in the finite and imperfect world, or 'relative ethical life'. In the *Theses on Feuerbach* Marx advocates 'practical-critical' activity – that is, making society become what it could ideally be *in practice*, not just criticizing it purely verbally in the name of the idealized utopia. The whole structure of this way of thinking leads to the characteristic contrast in later Marxist work between society as it *is* and society as it *ought* to be (freedom, community, communism, etc.). The latter stage of human society was said to be embedded in the present society as its *telos*, or potential, yet to be realized by the victory of the proletariat (Kilminster, 1998: chapter 3).[7]

Once the possibility of proletarian revolution faded in the 1930s with National Socialism and fascism, the Frankfurt School (Adorno, Horkheimer, Marcuse and others) sought with its Critical Theory to preserve as a possibility the transcendental truth of communism and freedom in theory (Kilminster, 1979). This effectively meant a return to Hegelian dialectics, since the practical agent for the realization of the Ought, the proletariat, had apparently deserted its historical mission and the chance to realize the new world in practice had been missed. Adorno and others talked of the 'utopian moment of the object' or 'utopian horizon'. Later, theorists such as Habermas, Apel and Bauman have looked for new models of the as yet unrealized utopia to provide a defensible yardstick for social criticism of inequality and injustice in the present. These analyses have mixed together transcendental arguments from both Kant and Hegel in the service of remaining loyal to the 'idea of a future society as the community of free men . . . and to it there must be fidelity amid all change', as Horkheimer put it (Horkheimer, 1972 [1937]: 217). They have taken the form of Habermas's and Apel's ideas about distorted communication and the presupposed 'ideal speech situation' or 'speech community' (Habermas, 1970; Apel, 1980), which are argued in a Kantian fashion in the service of a Hegelian–Marxian critique.

In addition to the archaic philosophical and metaphysical hangovers pervading this kind of ultimately needless argumentation, there is another drawback. It is by no means the case that 'critique' in this sense always has a positive outcome. It is a common but erroneous assumption that Critical Theory is life-affirming. It has been pointed out by Michael Zank (2002: 197) that *Kritik* in German can be translated as either critique or criticism, so contains either the intention to establish the true nature of reality ('critique') or to achieve a condemnation of it ('criticism'). In other words, it can take either or both of two connotations: positive or negative, constructive or destructive. In the contemporary code word 'critical', the second meaning (which coincides with the dictionary meaning in English of fault-finding[8] or censorious, carping, passing judgement) comes to the forefront, the 'critical' theorist finding only what is *wrong* with society – what must be morally condemned. This is usually conceptualized as various combinations of stark inequality, control, oppression, exploitation or domination, all of which prejudge as subjugation the complex, uneven balances of power between *inter*dependent groups. The theorist has passed judgement on them, as Horkheimer had insisted, in the name of fidelity to an unrealized, but ultimately *unattainable*, idealized state of perfect freedom, democracy, equality and authentic community. One serious problem with the relentless pursuit of idealized goals or the comparison of society with a pure or ideal yardstick, is that we are fated to experience unending frustration. We can never fully give ourselves credit for our achievements, because we know that against the perfect, but forever unattainable goal, our efforts will *always* fall short. Durkheim warned of this outcome a long time ago: 'To pursue a goal which is by definition unattainable is to condemn oneself to a state of perpetual unhappiness' (Durkheim, 1951 [1897]: 248).

Furthermore, Arpad Szakolczai (2008) has drawn attention to the broader negative consequences of this kind of 'critical' or utopian orientation in sociology (see also Kilminster, 1979: part 4). He sees its essential destructiveness, in theory and in practice, citing communist Eastern Europe under the Soviet Union and China. This relentless, fault-finding orientation towards society results not only in a 'politics of suffering' but can also serve to reinforce or *even to bring about* exactly the frustrations it is purporting to highlight through 'critique'.

> Criticism . . . is a very old concern, safely located at the heart of modern disciplinary traditions, just as critical theory, in most of the social, political and human sciences, has become fully integrated within the mainstream. But . . . the oldest and clearest traditions – doubt, suspicion, critique, denouncing, looking for whatever is bad, ugly, questionable, or, that which shows suffering, pain, frustration, is *not*, after all, a nice thing to do. Bad things, of course, do happen, and they should not be ignored; they should be analysed, with due serenity, instead of continuously shown up, in a repetitive, quasi-incantatory way. After all, as the political, economic, social and cultural history of the past century has amply demonstrated, criticism and critical theory in all its varieties managed to produce one certain effect: to render things worse by magically and contagiously reproducing exactly those aspects of life it wanted to 'criticize' . . . (Szakolczai, 2008: 277–8)

Notice that the dictionary definition of the word 'uncritical' means the opposite of the kind of critique referred to above – that is, lacking in judgement, complacently accepting. For the 'critical' sociologist, any inquiry that is not self-described or vaunted as critical must be indifferent to or complicit in, the inequalities and injustices of the society being criticized. But, as Boland (2007: 123) has rightly said, 'it is hubristic and naive to imagine that one's own position has a monopoly on critique and that the discourse of all others is "uncritical".' The essentially political character of the commitment to a self-consciously 'critical' approach in sociology, and its function for relatively privileged intellectuals, is evident. Complacent acceptance runs counter to the self-image of the 'critical' sociologists and drives them to pursue the 'guilt-causes' of today's social ills in such personified entities as 'capitalism' and 'modernity'. Reinhart Koselleck has remarked on how the state of absolute freedom implied in utopian thought functions for the critic: 'A truth that will not appear until tomorrow absolves the critic of all guilt today' (Koselleck, 1988 [1959]: 110).

Zygmunt Bauman's conception of the contemporary globalized society as a condition of 'liquid modernity' (Bauman, 2001) presented in a series of books with titles employing the same metaphor of liquidity, is widely accepted by sociologists at the time of writing. Whatever the durability of this work proves to be in the future, it illustrates for present purposes the pitfalls of the metaphysical and transcendental hangovers still persisting in sociology. As a direct result of these presuppositions, Bauman one-sidedly undervalues the present society as producing and reproducing nothing but unremitting anxiety and uncertainty. This gloomy diagnosis is made by comparison with an ideal state of democracy, freedom, equality and solidarity, which exists as a persistent possibility, 'nagging' the theorist, as he sometimes tellingly puts it. In his influential book, *Postmodern Ethics* (Bauman, 1993, reprinted four times), Bauman develops a transcendental argument (Bauman, 1993: 69–81) inspired by the philosopher Emmanuel Lévinas, to the effect that a person's moral responsibility for another person is 'unconditional and infinite' (Bauman, 1993: 250) but is channelled in various ways in concrete societies and often obscured. The depth and extent of his unquestioned philosophical–theological commitments is clear: 'Morality is a *transcendence* of being; morality is, more precisely, the *chance* of such transcendence' (1993: 72; emphasis in original). This idea constitutes, he argues in a Kantian vein echoing Simmel, a new sociological *a priori*. Empirically, people can choose whether to exercise that responsibility and hence the moral self is '*always haunted by the suspicion that it is not moral enough*' (1993: 80; italics in original). Moral responsibility is thus ambivalent because it contains the sense of a standard that can never be reached. A person knows when they are in the realm of moral choice, says Bauman, when they feel 'moral anxiety' (1993: 80), 'constant anguish', 'conscience' (1993: 250) and 'guilt' (1993: 81).

From this guilt-driven view of the world, it is very difficult to conceptualize a notion of progress. Hence it is difficult to assemble a balance sheet of the longer-term social and scientific achievements accumulated unintendedly by humankind which must praised and preserved. Elsewhere I have referred to this tendency as 'overcritique' (Kilminster, 1979: 240 ff). To the critical mind, social praise is dangerous because to laud what is good in society blinds us to what is wrong, so playing into the hands of the advantaged power holders who can then claim that we live in the Leibnizian 'best of all possible worlds' as satirized by Voltaire in *Candide*.

Let us draw together the threads of the argument so far. Having its origins in the 'exodus from philosophy' in Weimar Germany at the end of the First World War, there is at the core of Elias's 'process sociology' a bald and uncompromising rejection of all forms of philosophy, including the utility of all arguments from 'transcendence'. Philosophy is regarded as a hangover of a pre-modern form of human orientation related to theology and magical–mythical thought that is unfettered by the continuous interplay with empirical evidence. Not only is philosophy no longer proficient to investigate empirically complex social processes, but also the emerging sociological perspective promised to take over much of what had been traditionally the competence of philosophers. Elias's work is thus founded in a *sociological* theory of knowledge in which he transformed ontological speculations about 'modes of being' into a theory of sciences based on the levels of integration in the natural and social realms they investigated. The evaluative and normative discussions dealt with as 'ethics', including the relation between sociological research and the political views of its practitioners, were reframed as part of a theory of involvement and detachment and rendered amenable to empirical inquiry. 'Critical' theorists in sociology have taken a different road, creating hybrids of social science and philosophy. They have used transcendental arguments as a matter of course in order to justify the legitimacy of a 'critical' kind of inquiry that can be used to condemn disparities of power and control in the name of unattainable idealized states of collective social life.

Because of the pervasiveness of traces of the Kantian critical philosophy in the classical tradition of sociology (Kilminster, 1998) most of this tradition could in fact accurately be described as 'critical' sociology. But no one would do so, because the term 'critical' in the Hegelian and Marxian usages has already been appropriated by a tradition of theory that runs counter to the 'value-freedom' principle and its variants that underpins the mainstream sociology tradition. From the 'critical' Marxian–Hegelian point of view, the mainstream of sociology (which is critical in a Kantian sense) emerges as 'uncritical'. So the only significant sense in which the word 'critical' is operative to describe an orientation or moral and political commitment in sociology is when it is being used as a code word. In this sense it means left-wing, actively committed to reducing inequality, oppression and injustice. In present usage its implicit but unexplained meaning endows it with the magical ring of an incantation. It functions as a talisman for many sociologists, who feel compelled by their conscience to reveal their 'critical' credentials or to justify those credentials with ever more elaborate, quasi-metaphysical constructions. All the other everyday meanings of the word 'critical' are either irrelevant or commonplace descriptions of various activities of all reputable sociologists.

There is also a problem with the high level of abstraction, and hence vagueness, of the principles to which the code word is said to commit the initiates – such as freedom, emancipation, liberation and social transformation. Because of its Marxian provenance, the code word is thus subject to many of the well-known shortcomings of that tradition. 'Critical' sociology or a 'critical' attitude towards research (however vaguely formulated) is underpinned mainly by Hegel, not Kant, although Habermas sometimes uses Kantian argumentation, as does Bauman. In the code-word sense, the 'critical' attitude is subject to the objection that it is trying to keep alive and work towards the abstract possibility of a utopian society that is, to repeat the point, *sociologically infeasible* and unattainable. Like all critique and criticism of this kind, critical sociology is destructive in a double sense. On the one hand, the knowing pursuit of the inherently unattainable generates nihilism and persistent discontent in the habitus of its adherents. On the other, the cataloguing of all that is wrong in society, at the expense of a more balanced picture involving achievements and benign compulsions, not only contributes to gloom and pessimism but also reproduces, through a kind of contagion, exactly the bad things it relentlessly denounces. Without careful specification of what can, cannot, and should not be changed, the statement that society could always 'be other than it is', becomes a vacuous slogan.

Furthermore, as we will see in the next section, the whole enterprise of critique and the elaborate philosophical trappings that go along with it, are unnecessary if one wants to ensure that sociology has a practical and beneficial impact on human social relations. *One could say that getting lost in the abstractions of 'critique', and 'critical' metatheory generally, are part of the problem of modern society, not part of the solution.* As we will see in the concluding section, Elias's resolute work on involvement and detachment suggests that sociology, properly done, can be 'evaluative' or 'critical' in a more inclusive and more constructive, sense.

Concluding remarks: critical theory or 'detour via detachment'?

Elias's 'post-philosophical' sociology gives us another perspective on transcendental hangovers in sociology, and a keen awareness of the role of guilt and blaming in our orientation towards the interdependencies in which, as sociologists, we find ourselves. It suggests that we do not need all the transcendental paraphernalia and the enchanted self-description 'critical', to affirm that sociology can potentially 'make a difference' in the world, as it is often expressed. The apparently positive overtones of the unremitting practice of systematic 'critique' are illusory; on the contrary, it emerges as socially iatrogenic, destructive, disorientating and unnecessary. My point is that Elias has provided the most constructive, useful, but challenging, alternative to deal with the issues of human bonding and orientation that are hidden beneath the sweeping 'critical' calls for emancipation, freedom and liberation.

Elias does not use the word critical to describe his sociology. Nor does he use transcendental arguments to try to build from philosophical components a moral or epistemological basis for a special kind of inquiry or activity devoted solely to condemning aspects of society. It is consistent with his approach that the issue of how to calibrate what is 'wrong' with society, so as to pass judgement on how society could be made 'better', is bound up with a continuous struggle in sociology to achieve *relative* detachment from social values and political ideologies which would help to provide a reliable factual basis for value judgements of that kind. For Elias, social forces continually combine to thwart or divert sociology from being able consistently to produce reliable knowledge of this kind (Kilminster, 2007a: chapter 5). Political ideologies (involvements in Elias's language) in particular colour the ways in which 'better' and 'progress' are evaluated. The whole problem of evaluation can be taken on to a different level to avoid the excesses and overstatements of 'critique'. Involvement and detachment are descriptive of relations between people (social forces), with objects (non-human nature, as studied by the natural sciences) and with the self (self-control). These three levels develop unevenly in societies. For Elias, sociology awaits the breakthrough to greater detachment, to help people control their interdependent relations (social forces) with others, which are often experienced as opaque or as an external force. It is in this arena, in particular, that the struggle for detachment manifests itself in modern societies.

In *Quest for Excitement* (2008 [1971]), Elias says that many people in the twentieth century took for granted that they had become 'morally better' and took pride in being less savage than their forebears. Hence the mass slaughter carried out by the Nazis came as a terrible shock. People had never faced the problem of how their feeling of moral superiority came about, thus this episode was a kind of warning. The civilizing process that had made this possible – a specific type of social development and a corresponding conscience-formation which resulted in a more differentiated and stable social control of the means of violence – had long been forgotten. The genocide perpetrated by the Nazis showed graphically that that process could clearly be *reversed*.

The point Elias is making is, I think, that the shock of those events should not deter us from trying to explain how the social processes that enabled more 'civilizing' forms of social conduct came about and how and why they went into reverse. The episodes of mass killing in themselves do not necessarily mean that twentieth century people could not be shown *sociologically* to have achieved a less savage level of social behaviour than their forebears. His remarks are essentially a plea, even in the face of such horrors, not to leap to value-judgements, for example about human nature (say that humans are basically savage because of their animal heritage) but to continue to pursue further sociological understanding of these matters through the 'detour via detachment'. In this spirit, Elias argues that it was the long forgotten internal pacification of states that partly provided the social conditions enabling 'less savage' social conduct. Hence, when the monopolization of violence by the state began to unravel in Germany in the twentieth century, this provided the insecure social conditions that made a 'decivilizing process' more likely, resulting in the rise of violence in the public sphere and culminating in war and genocides. On the question of whether modern behaviour may or may not be considered to be 'morally better', Elias broadens the issue:

> This [Nazi episode] does not necessarily imply that there are no grounds for evaluating the results of this [modern, more restrained] development in human behaviour and feelings as 'better' than the corresponding manifestations of earlier developmental stages. Wider understanding of the nexus of facts provides a much better basis – provides indeed the only secure basis – for value judgements of this type. Without it, we cannot know, for example, whether our manner of building up individual self-controls against physical violence is not associated with psychological malformations which, themselves, might appear highly barbaric to an age more civilized than ours. Moreover, if one evaluates a more civilized form of conduct and feeling as 'better' than less civilized forms, if one considers that humankind has made progress by

arriving at one's own standards of revulsion and repugnance against forms of violence that were common in former days, one is confronted by the problem of why an unplanned development has resulted in something which is evaluated as 'progress'. (Elias, 2008 [1971]: 125)

The tenor of this passage points to (a) the importance of the 'wider understanding of the nexus of facts' for providing a basis for value judgements. Elias is taking the whole problem of 'evaluation' on to another level through the 'detour via detachment'. A more vivid, all-round, broader and realistic *empirical–theoretical* picture of human societies needs to be developed. This would enable researchers to correct for the evaluative overstatements about social relations and interdependencies that arise from one-sided 'involvements', including systematic blaming, intruding into the research process. Developing social scientific knowledge of this specific and broader kind requires an institutionalized research programme committed to research principles of fact orientation and detachment (*autonomous evaluations* in Elias's language) and insulated from the intrusion of ideological evaluations coming from the wider society which would skew the inquiries more towards magical–mythical and wishful thinking (*heteronomous evaluations*).

The passage quoted above also points to (b) the importance of facing up to the fact that some social developments which we ideologically interpret as 'progress' (for example, the longer-term lessening of power differentials between groups that Elias (1978 [1970]: 69) calls 'functional democratization') were the result of *unplanned* development. In other words, these changes do not represent the inevitable march of freedom, nor are they the result of the application of liberal or socialist principles, as the ideologists would claim. To try to change these *relatively* more levelled power balances between interdependent groups whilst evaluatively exaggerating the power balances as subjugation or harsh oppression – or to work unrealistically towards the elimination of power itself in a utopian society – are to court disaster. The application of an inadequate theory of power relations will inevitably end in the failure of practice, resulting in disillusionment. And the fantasy expectations of a utopia of free citizens living harmoniously in communities will inevitably be dashed by the reality. As Elias warned: 'The whole of history has so far amounted to no more than a graveyard of human dreams' (Elias, 1978 [1970]: 28).

It is necessary to forestall the temptation to categorize Elias's 'detour via detachment' as another form of cold and passionless positivism. To describe the pleasure viewers derive from the aesthetic qualities of perspective paintings created through the painter's detachment, Elias developed the concept of *secondary involvement* (Elias, 2007c [1987]: 40–1). It can profitably be transferred on to the process of deriving pleasure from detached scientific research. In contrast to Romantic notions of science as always being cold and rational, Elias's argument is that for sciences to become established and institutionally self-perpetuating, many preconditions have to be fulfilled, one of which is the *sustained transfer of controlled affect into 'autonomous evaluations'* through a process of institutionalization. The practitioners of an emerging science (in this case a renewed sociology) in the developing institutional practices in which they participate, gradually begin to be emotionally moved by specifically scientific activities and values. They come to experience excitement and pleasure in relation to activities in which they are habitually applying a standard of detachment and an orientation to factual research and to discovery, thereby developing a very strong, emotionally reinforced, commitment to the science concerned.

It is compatible with Elias's conception of sociology (as I have argued elsewhere [Kilminster, 1998: 178]) that at the present stage in the development of societies and of the discipline itself, sociologists committed to autonomous evaluations should conduct themselves in the following way: they should apply in their practice of sociology the criteria of cognitive evaluation and the standard of detachment which *would* be widely taken for granted if the discipline, as a special science, had achieved a higher degree of self-perpetuating, institutional autonomy, and a corresponding intellectual authority, than at present. In applying these criteria and the standard of detachment, we *anticipate* their future embodiment in a stronger institutionalization of the discipline and, hopefully, help to bring it about.

This orientation constitutes the *anticipatory motif* in Elias's work. This motif is of a different character from other conceptions, coming from transcendental assumptions, of the regulative character of idealized states of affairs (for example, the ideal speech situation of Apel and Habermas, or the 'utopian moment of the object' in Adorno (Kilminster, 1998: 50–4)). Elias does not lapse into the teleological assumption that the renewed sociology *will* be consolidated in the future, nor does he endow the controlling principle of greater detachment with either an absolute metaphysical status or with a logical necessity. The implication of Elias's model is that although the battles for sociology are well worth fighting, the war could in the end be lost. There are no guarantees because of the vicious circle mechanism. Conflicts and tensions fuel fears that make people feel insecure; which in turn generates involvements (who is to blame?) and fear images. Hence, detachment in relation to social events is more difficult because people cannot control their strong feelings when their ability to control those events is small.

The promise of an institutionalized and self-perpetuating sociology of the human condition is that, with greater detachment and accumulating research data, evaluating becomes possible. The researchers execute a 'detour via detachment', whereby they suspend moral and political convictions but *return to them in a new form* after theoretical–empirical inquiry. Or, to put it another way, one puts Ought questions, hopes, desires, utopian fantasies, ideological convictions, wishful and egocentric thinking, and so forth on to the back burner. The philosophically or politically-posed questions (for example, free will–determinism, freedom–dependency) are broken down into specific relationships amenable to empirical work. After a sociological reframing of the problem through comparative research, one returns to the issue better armed for seeing the partiality of the philosophical or political formulation as it is absorbed into a wider explanatory framework. (I explained in an earlier section the way in which in *The Civilizing Process* Elias does this with the ideas of culture and civilization, returning to them at the end of the study and re-posing the questions from which he started out.) The exclusively philosophical mode of elaboration then falls away as simply untenable in its own terms. This way of working is present in Elias even in what seem to be largely empirical studies. Consider, for example, the following statement in *The Court Society* on the historians' fear that sociological research threatens to extinguish human freedom and individuality:

> If one is prepared to approach such problems through two-pronged investigations on the theoretical and empirical planes in closest touch with one another, rather than on the basis of preconceived dogmatic positions, the question one is aiming at with words such as 'freedom' and 'determinacy' *poses itself in a different way*. (Elias, 2006d [1969]: 33; my emphasis)

It is consistent with the tenor of Elias's theory of involvement and detachment that people can be expected to have strongly held views about politics, religion and morals, but these views are not to be regarded as shabby or of low calibre. It is only that these convictions should not one-sidedly be allowed *to shape research*. If you do this you may be contributing to the problems you are trying to solve, because the balance of involvement and detachment embodied in your inquiries is tilted more towards involvements. This is likely to strengthen 'we-images' as well as fear images and contribute to the intensification of conflicts between groups rather than their mitigation. Furthermore, in the course of research during the 'detour via detachment' you might find evidence that runs counter to your values or utopian vision and have to be prepared to face its implications. Clearly, working this way is emotionally very challenging. As researchers return to the original moral, value-related questions that may have prompted their inquiries they may find that the problem as originally posed, *now looks different*. And this, then, may affect our conception of the value issues that prompted the original investigation. This possibility of questioning often cherished values and hopes can be painful and frightening, and for many people more than they can bear.

Finally, carrying out more detached inquiries in the sense argued here can also affect *our relations with* other sociologists, philosophers, colleagues in other disciplines, political associates and friends. Writing about group we-images, Elias pointed out that it is asking a great deal of people in interdependent groups (including disciplinary and political groups) competing with each other to see in perspective the structure and functioning of their relationships with each other. Such a multi-perspectival grasp of their mutual interrelatedness could weaken the cohesion and solidarity of the group and its capacity to survive. He summarized the challenge:

> There is, in fact, in all these groups a point beyond which none of its members can go in his or her detachment without appearing – and, so far as their group is

concerned, without becoming – a dangerous heretic, however consistent their ideas or their theories may be in themselves and with observed facts, however much they may approximate to what we call the 'truth'. (Elias, 2007a [1956]: 83)

Notes

1 Some philosophers, too, have perceived the difficulty in justifying the autonomy of the subject matter and authority of philosophy in the light of the scope of sociology. For example, Richard Rorty commented: '[T]ranscendental arguments seem the only hope for philosophy as an autonomous critical discipline, the only way to say something about human knowledge which is clearly distinguishable from psychophysics on the one hand and from history and sociology of knowledge on the other' (Rorty, 1979: 77). I have explored further the character of transcendental thinking in the sociology of identity and in Critical Theory in Kilminster, 2010.

2 Elias's finding has been corroborated by later anthropological evidence. It has been shown (Westen, 1986) that people in simpler tribal societies in Africa and North America do not experience themselves as possessing a bounded, unitary centre, set against society or nature. Rather, they believe not in *one* soul residing in each person, but in multiple souls that are not coextensive with an individual; or they regard the 'self' as a substance which *all* share. Sometimes, in response to questions from Western researchers, people in these societies had difficulty in formulating statements about themselves or their biography using the personal pronoun 'I'. One woman, when referring to herself, used the locution 'that which came from my mother's womb' (ibid: 252–3).

3 Elias's active participation in the Zionist youth movement *Blau–Weiss* until its dissolution in 1926 probably played a role in shaping his uncompromising rejection of the neo-Kantianism of the assimilated Jewish philosophers of the earlier generation and by extension, of philosophy as a whole. See Kilminster, 2007a: 26 ff. As the young Leo Strauss, who was also associated with *Blau–Weiss* for a short period, put it in 1925: 'As Jews, we are radical; we do not like compromises. Let's bell the cat!' (in Zank, 2002: 133).

4 Sigmund Freud took a similar view: 'Philosophy has preserved essential traits of animistic modes of thought such as the over-estimation of the magic of words and the belief that real processes in the external world follow the lines laid down by our thoughts' (Freud, 1957 [1933]: 212).

5 Today, however, the term Critical Theory is no longer synonymous with the work of the Frankfurt School. Ian Buchanan, in his book *A Dictionary of Critical Theory* (2010) points out that a new interdisciplinary field has also taken the name Critical Theory. It has evolved in recent years as 'a hybrid of history, philosophy, psychoanalysis and sociology' (2010: vii) This field, he suggests, has 'leakier borders than most disciplines' (ibid). The book is intended for students of literary, cultural, film and gender studies, amongst other subjects. Sociologically speaking, the publication of a dictionary codifying various terms and listing key authors marks the professional recognition of this loosely defined 'field'. But its arrival has inadvertently added to the confusion already surrounding the epithet 'critical'. Buchanan disarmingly describes the new Critical Theory thus: 'Today the term is also used to refer – very loosely, it has to be said – to any form of theorizing in the humanities and social sciences, even when this isn't politically consistent with the outlook of the original Frankfurt School. This has tended to empty the term of any meaning and rendered both its political and methodological concerns invisible' (Buchanan, 2010: 101). The upshot of this comment is that everyone, without exception, working in sociology and the humanities today who uses concepts or ventures a 'theoretical' observation, could be accurately described as a 'critical' theorist. It also confirms that the term critical has become hopelessly equivocal in contemporary usage.

6 Whilst not Kantian as such in inspiration, the social phenomenology of Alfred Schutz (1972 [1932]) and the 'proto-sociology' of Berger and Luckmann in their celebrated book *The Social Construction of Reality* (1967) display the familiar transcendental–empirical contrast,

corresponding to the conventional division of labour between philosophy and sociology. This is because behind them is Husserlian philosophical phenomenology which – like all major twentieth-century European philosophies – carries this dualism at its core. The social phenomenologists attempted to describe the basic parameters of the historical process, whereby objective social reality, institutionally sedimented over generations, comes to be confronted by later individual human subjects who endow it with meaning. These parameters were held to be non-empirical, universal structures, *a priori*, not a description of any specific society. The structures were social *forms* said to find expression in human history and were to be given *content* in empirical inquiries into particular, concrete societies carried out by sociologists. (See Kilminster, 2007b and 2010 for further clarification of this dualism in phenomenological sociology.)

7 Georg Lukács's distinction in *History and Class Consciousness* (1971 [1923]) between the actual consciousness and imputed consciousness (embodying the *telos*) of the proletariat was a classical piece of sophisticated transcendental reasoning of this kind. The imputed consciousness (imputed, that is, by the theorist) was said to exist on a higher plane scientifically from the actual consciousness that could be established empirically (Kilminster, 1979: chapter 6).

8 In addition to 'crucial' and 'fault-finding', the Oxford English Dictionary also mentions the meaning of where one state passes over into another, as in the crisis of a disease ('the patient's condition is critical'); or in physics, in the concept of 'critical mass'. On the relation between 'crisis' and 'critique' in the Enlightenment, see Koselleck, 1988 [1959].

References

Dates given in square brackets are those of first publication.

Apel, Karl-Otto, (1980), *Towards a Transformation of Philosophy*, trans. Glyn Adey and David Frisby, London: Routledge & Kegan Paul.

Arendt, Hannah, (1990 [1930]), 'Philosophy and sociology', in Volker Meja and Nico Stehr, (eds), *Knowledge and Politics: The Sociology of Knowledge Dispute*, London: Routledge.

Bauman, Zygmunt, (1989), *Modernity and the Holocaust*, Cambridge: Polity Press.

Bauman, Zygmunt, (1990), 'From Pillars to Post', *Marxism Today*, February: 20–5.

Bauman, Zygmunt, (1992), *Intimations of Postmodernity*, London: Routledge.

Bauman, Zygmunt, (1993), *Postmodern Ethics*, Oxford: Basil Blackwell.

Bauman, Zygmunt, (2001), *Liquid Modernity*, Cambridge: Polity Press.

van Benthem van den Bergh, Godfried, (1986), 'The Improvement of Human Means of Orientation: Towards Synthesis in the Social Sciences', in Raymond Apthorpe and Andreás Kráhl, (eds), *Development Studies: Critique and Renewal*, Leiden: E. J. Brill.

Berger, Peter and Thomas Luckmann, (1967), *The Social Construction of Reality*, London: Allen & Unwin.

Boland, Tom, (2007), 'Critical Subjectivity: Towards a Gnomonic Model of Subject Constitution', *Culture, Theory & Critique*, 48, 2: 123–38.

Buchanan, Ian, (2010), *A Dictionary of Critical Theory*, Oxford: Oxford University Press.

Crowell, Steven Galt, (1999), 'Neo-Kantianism', in Simon Critchley and William R. Schroeder, (eds), *A Companion to Continental Philosophy*, Oxford: Blackwell.

Durkheim, Émile, (1951 [1897]), *Suicide: A Study in Sociology*, London: Routledge.

Elias, Norbert, (1978 [1970]), *What is Sociology?* London: Hutchinson.

Elias, Norbert, (1984), 'Knowledge and power: an interview by Peter Ludes', in Nico Stehr and Volker Meja, (eds), *Society and Knowledge: Contemporary Perspectives on the Sociology of Knowledge*. New Brunswick, NJ: Transaction Books: 251–91.

Elias, Norbert, (1994), *Reflections on a Life*, Cambridge: Polity.

Elias, Norbert, (2000 [1939]), *The Civilizing Process: Sociogenetic and Psychogenetic Investigations*, rev. edn, Oxford: Blackwell. [*On the Process of Civilisation*, Collected Works, Vol. 3, Dublin: UCD Press, forthcoming].

Elias, Norbert, (2000 [1969]), 'Postscript (1968)', in The Civilizing Process, revised edn, Oxford: Blackwell: 449–83.

Elias, Norbert, (2006a [1929]), 'On primitive art', Contribution to the debate on paper of that title by Richard Thurnwald, in *Early Writings*, Collected Works, Vol. 1, Dublin: UCD Press: 71–6.

Elias, Norbert, (2006b [1922]), 'Idea and individual: a critical investigation of the concept of history', DPhil thesis, Philosophy Faculty of the Friedrich-Wilhelms University, Breslau, in *Early Writings*, Collected Works, Vol. 1, Dublin: UCD Press: 23–54.

Elias, Norbert, (2006c [1921]), 'On seeing in nature', in *Early Writings*, Collected Works, Vol. 1, Dublin: UCD Press: 5–22.

Elias, Norbert, (2006d [1969]), *The Court Society*, Collected Works, Vol. 2, Dublin: UCD Press.

Elias, Norbert, (2007a [1956]), 'Problems of involvement and detachment', in *Involvement and Detachment*, Collected Works, Vol. 8, Dublin: UCD Press: 68–104.

Elias, Norbert, (2007b [1987]), 'The fishermen in the maelstrom', in *Involvement and Detachment*, Collected Works, Vol. 8, Dublin: UCD Press: 105–78.

Elias, Norbert, (2007c [1987]), 'Introduction', in *Involvement and Detachment*, Collected Works, Vol. 8, Dublin: UCD Press: 3–67.

Elias, Norbert, (2008 [1971]), 'The genesis of sport as a sociological problem [part I]', in Elias, N. and Eric Dunning, *Quest for Excitement: Sport and Leisure in the Civilizing Process*, Collected Works, Vol. 7, Dublin: UCD Press: 107–33.

Elias, Norbert, (2009a [1971]), 'Sociology of knowledge: new perspectives', in *Essays I: On the Sociology of Knowledge and the Sciences*, Collected Works, Vol. 2, Dublin: UCD Press: 1–41.

Elias, Norbert, (2009b [1982]), 'Scientific establishments', in *Essays I: On the Sociology of Knowledge and the Sciences*, Collected Works, Vol. 14, Dublin: UCD Press: 107–60.

Elias, Norbert, (2009c [1985]), 'On the creed of a nominalist: observations on Popper's *The Logic of Scientific Discovery*', in *Essays I: On the Sociology of Knowledge and the Sciences*, Collected Works, Vol. 14, Dublin: UCD Press: 161–90.

Elias, Norbert, (2009d [1974]), 'The sciences: towards a theory', in *Essays I: On the Sociology of Knowledge and the Sciences*, Collected Works, Vol. 14, Dublin: UCD Press: 66–84.

Fletcher, Jonathan, (1997), *Violence and Civilization: An Introduction to the Work of Norbert Elias*, Cambridge: Polity Press.

Freud, Sigmund, (1957 [1933]), *New Introductory Lectures on Psychoanalysis*, London: Hogarth Press.

Goldmann, Lucien, (1977), *Lukács and Heidegger: Towards a New Philosophy*, London: Routledge & Kegan Paul.

Habermas, Jürgen, (1970), 'On Systematically Distorted Communication', *Inquiry*, 13, 1: 205–18.

Harrington, Austin, (2005), 'Conclusion: social theory in the twenty-first century', in Austin Harrington, (ed.), *Modern Social Theory: An Introduction*. Oxford: Oxford University Press.

Horkheimer, Max, (1972 [1937]), 'Traditional and critical theory', in *Critical Theory: Selected Essays: Max Horkheimer*, New York: Seabury Press: 188–243.

Kettler, David, Colin Loader and Volker Meja, (2008), *Karl Mannheim and the Legacy of Max Weber: Retrieving a Research Programme*, Aldershot: Ashgate.

Kilminster, Richard, (1979), *Praxis and Method: A Sociological Dialogue with Lukács, Gramsci and the Early Frankfurt School*, London: Routledge.

Kilminster, Richard, (1998), *The Sociological Revolution: From The Enlightenment to the Global Age*, London: Routledge.

Kilminster, Richard, (2006), 'Note on the text', in *Early Writings*, Collected Works, Vol. 1, Dublin: UCD Press: xi–xx.

Kilminster, Richard, (2007a), *Norbert Elias: Post-philosophical Sociology*. London: Routledge.

Kilminster, Richard, (2007b), 'Berger and Luckmann', in Austin Harrington, Barbara L. Marshall and Hans-Peter Muller, (eds), *Encyclopaedia of Social Theory*. London: Sage: 36–37.

Kilminster, Richard, (2010), 'Transcendentalism and Identity', in Ronald L. Jackson, (ed.), *The Encyclopedia of Identity*, Vol. 2, London: Sage Publications: 838–841.

Kilminster, Richard and Cas Wouters, (1995), 'From philosophy to sociology: Elias and the neo-Kantians: a response to Benjo Maso', *Theory, Culture and Society*, 12, 3: 81–120.

Koselleck, Reinhart, (1988 [1959]), *Critique and Crisis: Enlightenment and the Pathogenesis of Modern Society*, Cambridge, MA: MIT Press.

Lash, Scott, (1994), 'Reflexivity and its doubles: structure, aesthetics, community', in Ulrich Beck, Anthony Giddens and Scott Lash, (eds), *Reflexive Modernization: Politics, Tradition and Aesthetics in the Modern Social Order*, Cambridge: Polity.

Leach, Edmund, (1986), 'Violence', *London Review of Books*, 23 October: 13–14.

Lukács, Georg, (1971 [1923]), *History and Class Consciousness: Studies in Marxist Dialectics*, London: Merlin Press.

Mannheim, Karl, (1936), *Ideology and Utopia*, London: Routledge & Kegan Paul.

Mannheim, Karl, (1957 [1935]), *Systematic Sociology: An Introduction to the Study of Society*, London: Routledge & Kegan Paul.

Maso, Benjo, (1995), 'Elias and the neo-Kantians: intellectual backgrounds of *The Civilizing Process*', *Theory, Culture and Society*, 12, 3: 43–79.

Meja, Volker and Nico Stehr, (eds), (1990), *Knowledge and Politics: The Sociology of Knowledge Dispute*, London: Routledge.

Mennell, Stephen, (1994), 'The formation of we-images: a process theory', in Craig Calhoun, (ed.), *Social Theory and the Politics of Identity*, Oxford, Blackwell: 175–97.

Mennell, Stephen, (1998), *Norbert Elias: An Introduction*. Dublin: UCD Press.

Pels, Dick, (2003), *The Unhastening Science: Autonomy and Reflexivity in the Social Theory of Knowledge*, Liverpool: Liverpool University Press.

Rorty, Richard, (1979), 'Transcendental arguments, self-reference and pragmatism', in Peter Bieri, Rolf-Peter Horstmann and Lorenz Krüger, (eds), *Transcendental Arguments and Science*, Dordrecht: D. Reidel.

Sathaye, Shriniwas G., (1973), 'On Norbert Elias's developmental paradigm', *Sociology*, 7, 1: 117–23.

Schutz, Alfred, (1972 [1932]), *The Phenomenology of the Social World*, London: Heinemann.

Steiner, George, (1978), *Heidegger*, London: Fontana.

Stern, Robert, (2007), 'Hegel, British idealism, and the curious case of the concrete universal', *British Journal for the History of Philosophy*, 15, 1: 115–53.

de Swaan, Abram, (1995), 'Widening circles of social identification: emotional concerns in sociogenetic perspective', *Theory, Culture and Society*, 12, 2: 25–39.

de Swaan, Abram, (1997), 'Widening circles of disidentification: on the psycho- and sociogenesis of the hatred of distant strangers – reflections on Rwanda', *Theory, Culture and Society*, 4, 2: 105–122.

Szakolczai, Arpad, (2008), 'What kind of political anthropology?: An external insider view', *International Political Anthropology*, 1, 2: 275–282.

Westen, Drew, (1986), *Self and Society: Narcissism, Collectivism, and the Development of Morals*, Cambridge: Cambridge University Press.

Zank, Michael, (ed. and trans.), (2002), *Leo Strauss: The Early Writings (1921–1932)*, Albany, NY: State University of New York Press.

Towards a process-oriented methodology: modern social science research methods and Norbert Elias's figurational sociology

Nina Baur and Stefanie Ernst

Abstract: This paper suggests that Norbert Elias's conception of process-oriented methodology consists of four stages: (1) explicating the researcher's theoretical and personal perspectivity; (2) reconstructing the figuration's rules and social structure using standardized data; (3) analysing the individual's placement within, perception of and ability to change the figuration, using open-ended data, and; (4) exploring the figuration's sociogenesis, using process-produced data. Having explicated this figurational methodological approach we will demonstrate how it can be used to illuminate contemporary discussions of: (a) the relationship between theory and data; (b) mixed methods research; (c) multi-level analysis; (d) process-produced data; (e) longitudinal research; and (f) methods of historical research.

Introduction

Purely empirical investigations – that is, investigations without a theoretical framework – are like sea voyages without a map or a compass. One sometimes chances on a harbour, but the risk of shipwreck is high. Theoretical investigations without an empirical base are usually, at bottom, elaborations of preconceived dogmatic notions; the dogmas are enshrined as a matter of faith, and cannot be refuted or corrected by any empirical proofs or detailed investigations. At most, an attempt is made to buttress them *a posteriori* with a few empirically related arguments. (Norbert Elias, 2009b [1978]: 130)

Norbert Elias is generally known for his process or 'figurational' sociology (Dunning, 1999; Ernst, 2003; 2010; Goudsblom and Mennell, 1997; Mennell, 1998: 251–70; Treibel, 2008; Wouters, 2004). In contrast, his methods are usually either rarely discussed or are criticized for their inadequacy. During the 1980s and 1990s, for example, there were many voices claiming that Elias's theory of the civilising process failed to live up to his own methodological guidelines (Gleichmann *et al.*, 1979; Duerr, 1988; 1990; 1993). According to Schröter (1997: 241),[1] Elias 'failed any longer to carry out a major empirical–theoretical study' in the time span from the 1940s to the 1960s, and produced only 'sociological miniatures' (Schröter, 1997: 245) based on his own observations in a casual and occasionally infinite process of association. At the same time, a relational approach, characteristic of Elias's process theory, seems to make any attempt at 'pinning down' his findings (Schröter, 1997: 249) an almost futile endeavour, much to the regret not only of his assistants but also of his colleagues.

However, Norbert Elias's remark quoted above implies that – in opposition to later critics' opinions – social research was in fact very important to him, because in his opinion sociological theory had to be empirically grounded. He conceived of himself as a 'theoretically and empirically orientated' scholar (Elias, 2009d [1983]: 99). If one looks at his complete works, it is obvious that his process theory goes beyond the well-known analysis of literature on manners and etiquette (Elias, 2000 [1939]). We shall illustrate in this chapter that, in consequence, methods of social research were also important to him, as they are the basis for sound research practice. Nevertheless, only very few explicit comments on explicit methodology and methods can be found in Elias's work, the most important in this regard being: *The Established and the Outsiders* (Elias and Scotson, 2008 [1965]), 'The retreat of sociologists into the present' (Elias, 2009c [1987]), 'The concept of everyday life' (Elias, 2009b [1978]), *What is Sociology?* (Elias, 1978 [1970]) and 'Towards a theory of social processes' (Elias, 2009a [1977]).

We believe that there are several reasons for this stark difference between Elias's interest in sound methodology and his failing to write methodological papers. Like most classical sociologists (for example, Karl Marx, Max Weber and Robert E. Park), Elias did not write about methods of social research – instead, he conducted actual social research, thus giving examples of good practice.[2] For a start, sociology had not yet been established as a university discipline when Norbert Elias started his academic career in Germany before World War II. Most German social scientists then were either originally trained in historical sciences (*Geschichtswissenschaft*), economics (*Nationalökonomie*) or public administration (*Verwaltungswissenschaft*). This meant, first, that sociology tried to establish itself as a new *theoretical* approach, implying that most academic discussion within German sociology addressed theoretical questions and tried to mask methodological considerations (as well as avoiding empirical research based on classical historical and economic methods such as documentary research and statistical analysis) in order to avoid competition with already established disciplines. In other words, neither a genuine sociological methodological debate nor sociological research on methods yet existed.

Secondly, due to their academic origins, early German sociologists (including Norbert Elias) were methodologically trained (a) in documentary research (*Historische Quellenkunde*) – that is, in the art of reading and interpreting historical documents – and/or (b) in analysing official statistics. These methods of social research dominating German sociology before World War II were (as a result of knowledge transfer from the USA to Germany) replaced after World

War II by cross-sectional survey research as the main means of data collection and statistical analysis as the main means of data analysis (Baur, 2005: 24–56). How strong was the effect of redefining methods of social research as methods of survey research can be deduced from a statement by one of Norbert Elias's close research assistants: Elias remained a 'master of narrative sociology and qualitative methodology' (Schröter, 1997: 245) and had always used a wide body of empirical data (for example, ethnography, literature, documents, maps). Still, when he first handled survey data in the 1960s, he self-ironically stated that he had now become an empiricist, an *Empiriker*.[3]

Not all methods, however, are suited for all theoretical questions, and while survey research corresponded well with the new theoretical interest in explaining individuals' intentional social action (Scheuch, 1977), it is not sufficient for answering the theoretical questions Norbert Elias posed. As he put it, 'The task of social scientists is to explore, and to make people understand, the patterns they form together, the nature and the changing configuration of all that binds them to each other' (Elias, 2007 [1987]: 79).

Elias thus openly criticized survey research as a formalistic effort by social scientists aimed at imitating the exact methods of physical measurement and transferring assumptions of causality from the realm of the natural to the social and anthropological sciences, leading to invalid generalizations and mechanistic models of explanation. The idea of explaining social phenomena 'by means of measurements' (Elias, 2007 [1987]: 91) has not only led to the 'neglect ... of wide problem-areas' but the neglect also of questions of 'greater significance' (Elias, 2007 [1987]: 87). Moreover, they are 'induced to cut their problems so as to suit their method' (Elias, 2007 [1987]: 87). In other words, Elias made a strong claim that methods should serve theory, not vice versa.

If methodology and methods were important to Elias and if survey research is not sufficient for figurational and process sociology, what methodology and methods *are* adequate? In order to answer this question, we have as a first step reconstructed Norbert Elias's methodological concepts from both (1) re-reading the explicit statements on methodology mentioned above and (2) reconstructing the methodology implicitly underlying his empirical studies, using *The Civilizing Process* (Elias, 2000 [1939]), *The Court Society* (Elias, 2006a [1969]) and *The Established and the Outsiders* (Elias and Scotson, 2008 [1965]) as examples. We will show that although Elias is more generally thought of as a sociological theorist, although he never conceived himself as a methodologist, and although many of his concrete methods and modes of analysis may be considered outdated from today's point of view, he had very clear ideas of what kind of methodology is best suited for figurational and process sociology.

Norbert Elias believed sociology should be an open-ended project. Therefore, because methodological research has advanced greatly in the decades since Elias conducted his empirical studies, we try to link Elias's methodological precepts with modern methodological discussion, namely mixed methods research (MMR), grounded theory, ethnography, multi-level analysis, social network analysis (SNA), cluster analysis, methods of longitudinal and historical research and research on process-produced data. Using these links, we will first discuss the relationship between theory and data as seen by both Elias and modern methodologists. We will then develop a framework for a process-oriented methodology. At the same time, we will show how Elias's ideas could inspire methodological debates even today.

The relationship between social theory and methods of social research

Involvement, detachment and the need for perspectivity

One point of discussion in modern methodological discourse is whether there can be 'objective facts' that speak for themselves (the positivist approach) or whether subjectivity distorts facts (the constructivist approach) (Bryman, 1988, 2007). Norbert Elias considered this 'static subject–object relationship . . . completely unusable' since 'in the process of gaining knowledge, knowledge changes; the subject itself changes; and the human being also changes as more knowledge is acquired over the generations' (2009d [1983]: 104). Like other early German sociologists (such as Max Weber) and later generations of German historians, Norbert Elias took an interpretative stance[4] and reframed this question: the problem is not *whether* subjectivity influences perception – it does – but *how* it frames perception (Baur, 2008a). In other words, one can distinguish between reflected and non-reflected or – in Elias's (2007 [1987]) terminology – detached and involved subjectivity. Three forms of subjectivity have to be distinguished (Koselleck, 1979; Baur, 2008a):

1. *Verstehen*: Subjectivity is necessary to understand the meaning of human action (and data in general), so in this sense it is an important resource for social science research. Using the terminology of modern ethnographic research (Fetterman, 1998; Atkinson and Hammersley, 2006), this is the 'insider-perspective'.
2. Partiality (*Parteilichkeit*): Subjectivity can also distort research, because researchers are so entangled in their own value system that they systematically misinterpret or even forge data. This kind of subjectivity has to be avoided at all costs.
3. Perspectivity (*Perspektivität*): Subjectivity is a prerequisite for grasping reality. The first important steps in social science research are framing a research question as 'relevant' and 'interesting', addressing this question from a certain theoretical stance and selecting data appropriate for answering that question. From an ethnographic point of view, this is the 'outsider-perspective'.

The basic tension between these three forms of subjectivity is reflected in Elias's discussion on the tension between involvement and detachment, which reminds us of Habermas's (1972) concern with unearthing the interests that inform the pursuit of knowledge in research.

On the one hand, Elias, who conceives himself as a challenger of myth (1978 [1970]: 50–70), makes a strong point against partiality: he categorically rejects the theoretical concepts of action research and systems theory for their ideological content and for ultimately obscuring their biases by employing inflated levels of abstraction, preconceived assumptions and secret codes. According to Elias, the systems-theoretical aspiration fails 'because its possible applications in practice are relatively limited, if not non-existent' (Elias, 2009d [1983]: 101), while efforts inspired by Marxism suffer from 'political partisanship' (Elias, 2009d [1983]: 101).

However, Elias observes that in a way all social research is partial, as researchers themselves are always part of figurations and social processes: 'More involved forms of thinking, in short, continue to form an integral part of our experience of nature' (Elias, 2007 [1987]: 74) and are dependent on human figurations. Individuals are 'not able to visualize themselves as part of these large patterns, being hemmed in and moved uncomprehendingly hither and thither in ways which none of them intended' (Elias, 2007 [1987]: 77). If one strips off 'philosophical encrustations', one can find out 'in what way perceived data are connected with each other' (Elias, 2007 [1987]: 79).

Social researchers face a dilemma in this respect: they are required to avoid partiality by adopting a specific theoretical perspective and disclosing their perspectivity. In order to achieve sound results, and if their premises and analyses are to be of any use for the understanding of social processes, they must adopt an analytically detached outsider-perspective and refrain as much as possible from being affected by the constraints and struggles for position that mark wider society. At the same time, they need insider knowledge and must fully participate and involve themselves in the research process (*Verstehen*). In the process, factual questions are rarely distinguished and detached from 'political questions' (Elias, 2007 [1987]: 100). In other words, partiality and *Verstehen* are typically entwined in the actual research process.

Still, Elias believed that a rich, experience-based science could be achieved methodically and systematically by making constructive use of the tense balance between commitment to the object of research and detached analysis (Schröter, 1997: 249). As the vicious circle of dispassionate observation and actively taking sides can never be completely overcome, it is the researcher's utmost responsibility to make her partiality and perspectivity as clear as possible. Firstly, therefore, Elias (1994) reflected on his own biography in a way that enabled him to identify his involvement in and detachment from the issues he researched over his lifetime.

The mutual relation of different types of theory

The second measure that one can take in order to mitigate the effects of partiality is using theory to guide empirical research and explaining one's theoretical perspective (Baur, 2008a). According to the interpretative paradigm, theory and data are closely linked in social research: data are the main source for building and testing theories, and without theoretical focus it is impossible to select and interpret data (Knoblauch, 2008). Without having a concept of how theory and data are linked, it is impossible to assess the validity of research (Baur, 2008b, 2009a). Accordingly, Elias strongly criticized the fact that although sociology is abundant in theoretical approaches and has accumulated a wealth of empirical sociological studies, the excessively strong focus on the present has fostered the division of sociology into an empirical and a theoretical strand. Elias (2009a [1977]: 22–8) goes on to argue that in consequence social scientists lack a grand social theory that provides a framework for the special fields of sociology, a theory that enables connections to be made to applied sociology in practice.

In contrast, Elias as a 'theoretically and empirically orientated' scholar, argued for *real* instead of *ideal* types, dynamic research based on figurations and process sociology instead of static descriptions of the status quo. These aspects define the empirical–theoretical research programme that Elias pursued in the sociological community study reported in *The Established and the Outsiders* (Elias and Scotson, 2008 [1965]), his theory of civilizing processes (Elias, 2000 [1939]), his studies of *The Court Society* (Elias, 2006a [1969]), and, not least, his thoughts toward a theory of power (Elias, 1978 [1970]). Therefore, Elias (2009c [1987]: 108–9) advocated that sociological theory should be constructed in such a way that it guides empirical research.

In order to establish how theory and empirical research should be linked, one first has to define what theory actually is (Kalthoff, 2008). This is important, as theories differ in their level of abstraction and at least three types of theories can be distinguished (Lindemann, 2008):

1 *Social theories* (*Sozialtheorien*) contain general concepts about what society is, what concepts are central to analysis, what the nature of reality is and what assumptions have to be made in order to grasp this reality (Lindemann, 2008). The social theory Elias relied on was a process-oriented figurational sociology. Social theory is a prerequisite for social research, because it helps researchers decide which data they need and which procedure is appropriate for answering their research questions (Baur, 2005, 2008a). Social theory thus allows researchers to link middle-range theories and theories of society with both methodology and research practice, since not all theories can make use of all research methods and data types (Baur, 2008a). For example, rational choice theory needs data on individuals' thoughts and behaviour; symbolic interactionism needs data on interactions – what is going on between individuals.[5]

2 *Middle-range theories* concentrate on a specific thematic field, a historical period and a geographical region. They model social processes solely for this socio-historical context (Lindemann, 2008). Similar to grounded theory (Glaser and Strauss, 1999 [1967]; Corbin and Strauss, 2008), Elias advocated the alteration of inductive, deductive and abductive procedures, meaning that (within a given framework of social theory) researchers should build middle-

range theories from data and test these theories again using data. For example, in *The Court Society*, Elias (2006a [1969]) analyses how Louis XIV was able to change French society in the seventeenth century by cleverly exploiting the power to act given to him by his position within a specific figuration. In a case study of a town in the British Midlands in the 1960s, Elias and Scotson (2008 [1965]) illustrate how two social groups of the same social class (the working class) are differentiated as 'the established' and 'the outsiders' on the basis of neighbourhood and lifestyle and how a group of people can monopolize power chances and use them to exclude and stigmatize members of another very similar group.

3 *Theories of societies* (*Gesellschaftstheorien*) try to characterize complete societies by integrating results from various studies to a larger theoretical picture (Lindemann, 2008) as Elias (2000 [1939]) did in *The Civilizing Process*. In other words, they build on middle-range theories and abstract further from them. Middle-range theories and theories of society are closely entwined as an analysis of social reality and thus demand 'constant guiding of detailed empirical investigations by comprehensive, integrating theories and a constant testing of these theories by detailed empirical investigations' (Elias, 2007 [1987]: 88). The objective is to focus and advance sociological hypotheses and syntheses of isolated findings for the development of a 'theory of increasing social differentiation' (Elias, 2009a [1977]: 25), of planned and unplanned social processes, and of integration and functional differentiation.

Elias's process-oriented methodology

So far, we have discussed how Elias thought that sociological theory was necessary in order to choose a suitable research design and to guide social research. As a consequence, the first two steps of social research should be reconstructing a researcher's perspective as stated above (see Figure 1 below). This means explicating why a researcher is asking a specific kind of question (partiality) and which general social theory the researcher is using (perspectivity). During the research process, the researcher should always consider how this influences the way data is interpreted or even distorted.

Elias's own theoretical perspective came to be known as 'figurational sociology', although he later came to prefer the term 'process sociology'. If one focuses on how the different parts of Elias's work link together, it becomes clear that for Elias, a process-oriented methodology consisted of three steps, illustrated in Figure 1.

1 Reconstructing the macro-level: the rules and social structure of the figuration

A figuration is a social structure consisting of a set of individuals who are linked by a set of positions, rules, norms and values (Elias, 2009e [1986]). The figuration

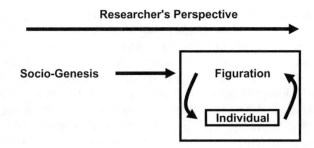

Figure 1: *Aspects to be considered in process-oriented methodology.*

is a framework for group and individual action, regulating and orientating their behaviour and communication. Figurations differ in their degree of formalization and informalization and how much they expect self-regulation from individuals with regard to the means for satisfying basic physical and social needs. Specific types of people (or groups of people) have different access to the positions within the figuration, and each position facilitates certain kinds of behaviour and inhibits others. Within a given figuration, each individual thus has – depending on her position within the figuration – certain constraints and options to act (Elias, 2009e [1986]). For example, in the French court society, the king had completely different life chances from a peasant, and there were rules about who could become king and who was likely to become a peasant (Elias, 2006a [1969]). Additionally, from the point of view of the figuration, individuals are involved in relationships that are usually characterized by tensions and conflicts. Thus, a first task of figurational sociology is to reconstruct the rules and social structure of the figuration.

2 Reconstructing the micro-level: the individual's placement within, perception of and ability to change the figuration

The figuration sets the frame of action for individuals: depending on their position within the figuration, they have more or less power to act (Elias, 2009e [1986]). However, the ability to act does not mean that individuals actually do act. Still, using the example of Louis XIV, Elias (2006a [1969]) shows that individuals can influence the figuration, thus not only changing their position within the figuration, but also changing the figuration itself (both concerning its rules and social structure). Thus, it is important for figurational sociologists to analyse how individuals perceive their figuration and their own position within it, how individuals' actions are embedded with other members in the figuration, how and why they enter or leave the figuration, how and why their position within the figuration changes during their life-course and how and why they manage or fail to change the figuration.

3 Reconstructing the Sociogenesis of the Figuration

So far, we have discussed the macro-level (figuration) and micro-level (individuals) as if they do not change or develop. However, according to Elias's process sociology, both individuals and their figurations are changing all the time and at the same time interweaving with each other. As society is ever-changing, there is no use for abstract theories such as systems theory and structural functionalism (Elias, 2009d [1983]). Instead, from the point of view of figurational analysis, a sound sociological analysis always has to be process-oriented, focusing on an explanation of social processes. In this context, while Elias recognises the limited benefits of sociology's focus on the present, he is also keenly aware of its limitations. In terms of its benefits:

> The narrowing of the sociologists' focus of attention and interest to the immediate present, in some respects undoubtedly represents progress in the development of the discipline. Sociologists are now much better able than before to study and in some cases solve short-term problems of their own society in a reasonably reliable manner. Concentration on present issues has found a striking expression in an almost explosive profusion of empirical sociological investigations, partly but by no means only of the statistical variety. (Elias, 2009c [1987]: 107)

'The weakness' of many theoretical and empirical studies confined in their temporal focus, however, lies in the fact 'that they have lost their connection with the past as well as with the future' (Elias, 2006b: 401). Instead, sociologists should also look at the past – and not only because it is interesting in itself:

> Long-term syntheses, even if they only provide a rough outline, are by no means limited to shedding more light on the problems of past societies only. They also help to create a greater awareness of contemporary problems and especially of potential futures. (Elias, 2006b: 407)

Only when looking at the past can one analyse the relation between the macro- and micro-level, the long-term evolution of contemporary processes, the changes in the balances of power and functional equivalents as well as 'the play and counter-play of long-term dominant trends and their counter-trends' (Elias, 2009a [1977]: 27; Treibel, 2008). This is also necessary as social entities like figurations may not only newly arise but also end. Additionally, individuals may join or exit the figuration or may change their position within the figuration (Abbott, 2001: 129–60, 261–79). By empirically analysing social processes, Elias aimed to develop middle-range theories and theories of societies that do not 'abstract from the diachronic as well as from the dynamic character of societies' (Elias, 2009a [1977]: 27). Elias (2009d [1983]: 104) thus intended to pioneer social sciences that go beyond the historical sciences and a static sociology limited to mere descriptions of the status quo. However, in seeking to achieve this goal, Elias was constrained by methods known at the time: in order to analyse social processes properly, one would need methods of studying how macro and micro-phenomena are intertwined in time. Neither during Elias's lifetime nor today are such methods available (Baur, 2005). As temporality was such a central aspect of Elias's theory, he analysed instead the sociogenesis of a figuration – that is to say the 'long-term development of social and personality structures . . . without pre-emptive dogmatism' (Elias, 2009a [1977]: 18) – a figuration's becoming, change and ending, which usually unfolds over several centuries.

Data and analysis procedures for a process-oriented methodology

So which kind of concrete data and analytical methods are best suited for a process-oriented methodology?

Typically, if Elias is not classified as a social theorist, he is typified as a qualitative methodologist or historical sociologist. Yet Elias (2009c [1987]: 108*n*) himself denied that he was an 'historical sociologist' (if that meant that historical sociology was just one empirical or methodological sub-field among so many), and thought that 'qualitative' research was not the 'proper' term, demanding that researchers should 'do figurational or process-sociological research instead' (Elias, 2006b: 390).

In contrast to the stark distinction between qualitative and quantitative research that is often made today (Schreier and Fielding, 2001; Bryman, 1988, 2006; Baur, 2008b), Elias can be seen as an early proponent of mixed method research (MMR).[6] If one views Elias's work, it becomes obvious that he used and triangulated various data, ranging: (1) from research-elicited data (such as interviews, surveys, ethnography) to process-produced data[7] (such as documents, literature, maps); (2) from visual data (like maps, buildings, landscapes) to verbal data (that is, texts); and (3) from open-ended qualitative data (for example, ethnography, literature) to standardized quantitative data (for example surveys, social bookkeeping data). When choosing a data source and procedure for analysis, Elias considers neither 'true–false' nor 'appropriate–inappropriate' (Elias, 2007 [1987]: 88) to be viable codes for the relationship between theory and data. The issue is rather which methods and data are 'comparatively more or less true or, more precisely, more adequate' since knowledge is 'relatively open-ended' (Elias, 2007 [1987]: 89*n*).

This does not mean that the choice of data and methods is arbitrary. Instead, as discussed above, when analysing figurations, researchers have to take into account at least three different aspects of a figuration: the macro-level (figuration), micro-level (individuals) and the figuration's sociogenesis.[8] For analysing each of these aspects of a process-oriented methodology, certain data and procedures of analysis are better suited than others. In other words, there is an affinity between certain theoretical problems and certain methods.

Data and methods for reconstructing the macro-level

A first task of a methodology suitable for process sociology consists of studying figurations as a whole – at the macro-level, so to speak, though Elias did not like the term.[9] Elias himself used two main data sources for reconstructing figurations in their totality.

First, similar to the early Chicago School (Palmer, 1928), Pierre Bourdieu (1992: 271–84) and historians like Fernand Braudel (1996) and Georges Duby (1981), Norbert Elias analysed what landscapes, buildings and maps can tell us about social structures and hidden rules. The most explicit example is his analysis of the floor plan of a noble household in *The Court Society* (Elias, 2006a [1969]): the idea underlying the use of the built environment as a data source is that humans construct buildings and change their natural environment in order to facilitate daily routines. In other words, we only build and make things we find useful at the time of production, and the more expensive a building is, the more important to us it needs to be. So, when seeing an old building, the researcher needs to ask why did they build it like this? For which kinds of social practices does this building make sense? For example, in a modern apartment building, husband and wife would share a bedroom. In contrast, in sixteenth-century France, aristocratic couples not only had separate bedrooms but also separate living quarters. In *The Court Society*, Elias discusses the kind of lifestyles which would be an adequate living arrangement for this specific building and concludes that – in contrast to the modern family – aristocratic couples had completely separate daily routines (including lovers) and usually only met on formal occasions. Whenever Elias uses maps, buildings and landscapes as a data source, he triangulates them with other data sources, including historical documents, diaries and letters. In using these types of documents, Elias is still innovative today, as he can be regarded as a pioneer of spatial methods.[10]

Second, Elias warned against overestimating and overusing standardised data (Elias, 2007 [1987]: 87 ff.). We believe that there are three reasons why Elias was not overly fond of standardized data:

1 Elias did not believe that they were sufficient as the only data source (Elias, 2007 [1987]: 81–2).
2 These data – like any data – are prone to measurement errors and need to be interpreted (Baur, 2008b; 2009b; 2009c), but due to their nature there is an inherent danger that researchers will believe that these data are 'objective'. Elias therefore distinguished his process sociology from quantitative longitudinal analysis and argued that process sociology in many cases cannot make do with 'the traditional, philosophically sanctified categories that for the most part accommodate the needs of natural scientists' (Elias, 2005: 189).[11]
3 The methodology for using standardised data was not much advanced in the 1950s and 1960s: it was both difficult to collect or gain access to standardized data and procedures for analysis were limited and time-consuming.

However, Elias's scepticism towards standardized data did not prevent him from using them in his own research. On the contrary, Elias made use of both surveys and social bookkeeping data.[12] Examples are his community study *The*

Established and the Outsiders (Elias and Scotson, 2008 [1965]), his writings on 'Technisation and Civilization' (Elias, 2008 [1995]), or the 'Young Workers Project' (Goodwin and O'Connor, 2006), which was discontinued owing to methodological differences. For instance, in 'Technisation and Civilization', Elias employs transport statistics from various countries as indicators for different levels of advancement in terms of the 'effectiveness of social standards of self-regulation' (Elias, 2008 [1995]: 73). Moreover, in the 'Young Workers Project', Elias conducted – although he was sceptical about overusing statistics and numbers – an 'interview-based survey of the school-to-work-transition experience of nearly 900 young adults in Leicester, UK' and developed the shock thesis (Goodwin and O'Connor, 2006: 161). In *The Established and the Outsiders*, Elias and Scotson (2008 [1965]) aimed at understanding problems of deviance, social control and the mechanics of stigmatization in a workers' district in a town in the Midlands in 1959–60, using a mixed-methods approach. They started by triangulating documentary analysis, analysing criminal statistics and conducting a preliminary survey analysis.

If Elias made use of standardized data, so can modern figurational sociologists, and they can benefit from methodological innovations in the last 50 years: in comparison to Elias's lifetime, today the social science infrastructure has much improved. Therefore, both survey data and public administrational data are easily accessible for a broad range of researchers. At the same time, there are many new multivariate statistical analysis procedures (Baur and Lamnek, 2007) that we believe could be helpful for analysing the structure of a figuration, especially cluster analysis, structural network analysis (SNA) and multi-level analysis.

As stated above, there are usually different positions and sub-groups within a figuration. Depending on the sub-group an individual belongs to, his or her power to act may differ. It thus could be interesting to identify the number and size of sub-groups within a figuration. This could be done using *cluster analysis* (Aldenderfer and Blashfield, 1984; Fromm, 2010) or other statistical procedures identifying latent classes. For example, Figure 2 shows three figurations. Each figuration consists of *n* individual members of the respective figuration. As can be seen, figuration A consists of seven sub-groups in contrast to figurations B and C. Although five sub-groups can be identified for figurations B and C, the social structure of the figuration is still distinct, as groups 1, 4 and 5 are larger in figuration B than in C, while groups 2 and 3 are larger in figuration C than in B.

As Elias (1978 [1970]) points out, modern societies consist of long chains of interdependence: an individual can interact with some individuals face to face and is at the same time part of the wider figuration of interdependent people. For example, figuration D in Figure 3 consists of several small subgroups. Most actors do only interact with one or two other actors. One actor is central to the network, as he links the different sub-networks. In contrast, interaction chains in network E are much denser: most actors have contact with many other actors. The actor in the corresponding position within the figuration is thus not as

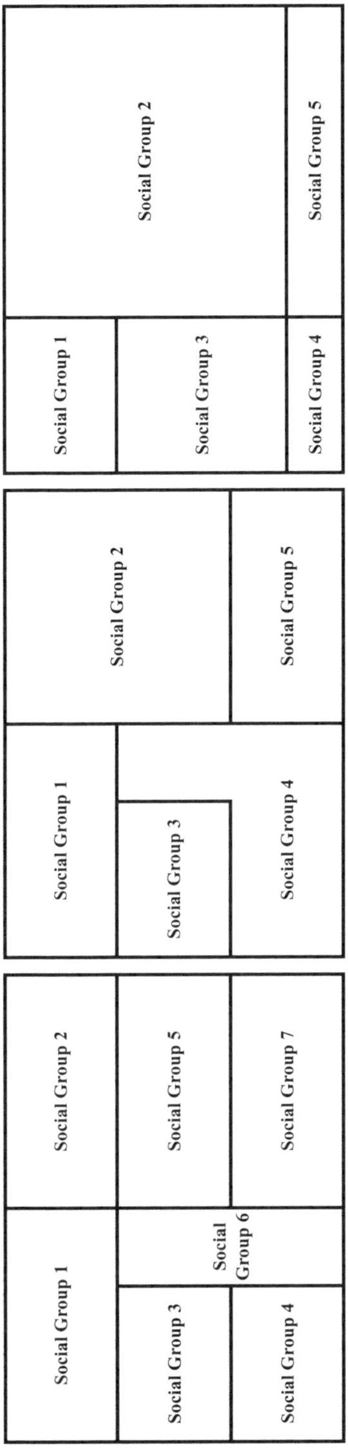

Figuration A:
Figuration Consisting of 7 Sub-Groups

Figuration B:
Figuration Consisting of 5 Sub-Groups,
with Groups 1, 4 and 5 being larger than in Figuration C

Figuration C:
Figuration Consisting of 5 Sub-Groups,
with Groups 2 and 3 being larger than in Figuration B

Figure 2: *Identifying sub-groups within a figuration using cluster analysis.*

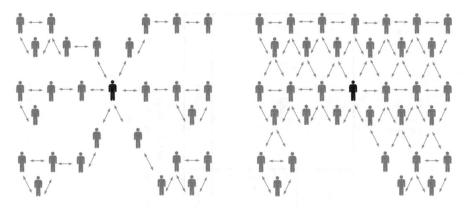

Figuration D: *Relatively Loose Network*   **Figuration E**: *Relatively Dense Network*

Figure 3: *Identifying relations between individuals within the structure using structural network analysis (SNA).*

central, as there are other interaction chains linking the actors. Such relationships between individuals can thus be used to characterize the figuration as a whole. This is exactly what *structural network analysis* (SNA) does (Wasserman and Faust, 1994; Scott, 2000; Carrington and Scott, 2005). It can be used either to characterise the figuration as a whole (for example, the density of the networks or typical patterns within the network) or to analyse the effects of an actor's position within the network.

Finally, *multi-level analysis* – for example, hierarchical linear modelling (HLM) (Snijders and Bosker, 1999; Hox, 2002) – can help to analyse the effects of the macro-level on the micro-level: an actor's way of thinking and willingness and power to act within these figurations may depend: (1) on her individual biography; (2) on the social group to which she belongs within the figuration; and (3) the characteristics of the figuration as a whole. Multi-level analysis can help to distinguish which of these aspects is how important and how these factors interact (see Figure 4).

Data and methods for reconstructing the micro-level

As stated above, it is important to analyse on the micro-level how individuals perceive the figuration, how they interact with others, how and why they enter or leave the figuration, how and why their position within the figuration changes during their life-course, and how and why they manage or fail to change the figuration. In order to tackle these questions, Elias generally used more open-ended data as a data source.

When reconstructing past individual action (as in *The Court Society*), Elias – like historians – interpreted *historical sources and life documents* such as

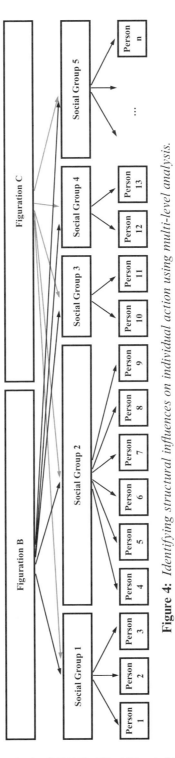

Figure 4: *Identifying structural influences on individual action using multi-level analysis.*

131

autobiographies and letters. In *The Civilizing Process* (2000 [1939]) we can also find literary examples, behavioural advice given in etiquette books from the Middle Ages and the age of the absolutist courts about table manners, dressing and undressing in the bedroom, the relations between men and women, and between parents and children.

When analysing current individuals' actions, Elias made use of *ethnographies*:[13] *The Established and the Outsiders* (Elias and Scotson, 2008 [1965]) methodologically resembles the Chicago School (Palmer, 1928) and the famous *Marienthal* study of Jahoda *et al.* (2002 [1933]). As mentioned above, in this sociographic community study, Elias and Scotson analysed the historical development of an industrial town through documents and crime statistics as well as through a preliminary survey. In addition, they analysed interaction, using participant observation. Moreover, they interviewed people at their workplaces and their homes and made a spatial analysis of the zones and districts the inhabitants lived and worked in. As a result they discovered so-called 'Mother-centred families' (2008 [1965]: 81–7)[14] as part of old and new families and the indicator 'duration of residence' in the interdependent figuration of blame and praise gossip.

Data and methods for reconstructing the figuration's sociogenesis

So far, we have discussed only methods suited to grasping a figuration (macro-level) and the behaviour and interaction of individuals within these figurations (micro-level) at a given point in time. However, a process-orientation is central to figurational sociology, meaning that researchers have to analyse the sociogenesis of a figuration, a figuration's *becoming*, *change* and *ending*. Ideally, this would mean that the relation of figuration and individuals is reconstructed at several points in time and linked.

While modern sociologists have focused their methodological discussion on research-elicited data and neglected process-generated data, especially interviews (Schulze, 2001; Baur, 2008b; 2010), Elias made extensive use of *process-produced data*. The reason why Elias used process-produced data is that, for each epoch, certain data types exist that supply extensive information. Qualitative interviews and surveys enable researchers to study only phenomena of medium duration (Elias, 2009a [1977]): medium-term social processes are more or less present in each individual's memory. Experiences gathered during that period influence her way of thinking and acting. If she is still alive, her memories may be obtained in an interview. If she is dead, they can be reconstructed from written testimonies. In contrast, people are usually unaware of change occurring more slowly than a single human being's lifespan. They perceive such patterns either as static or not at all (Vovelle, 1994). Consequently, in order to analyse very long-term processes (like the sociogenesis of a figuration), researchers have to select other data types.

Empirically reconstructing the sociogenesis of figurations by using process-generated data is what Elias is best known for, and his methodology for analysing these data is a field that can still inspire modern methodological debate. Elias not only showed with his empirical analyses that basically anything human beings left behind can be used as a data source, but he also gave guidelines in how to use these data for a process-oriented analysis. For example, in *The Civilizing Process*, Elias (2000 [1939]) uses literature and books of etiquette in order to reconstruct the sociogenesis of manners. In order to do so, he again uses social theory to guide empirical analysis:

1. Elias divides the period of analysis (Middle Ages through to the twentieth century) into sub-periods.

2. He selects for each sub-period central documents on manners. He picks etiquette books widely circulated, arguing that publishers can only afford high runs of copies if there is a demand for them. A high demand for books in turn is a sign that the topic the book is about and the way the topic is discussed within the book are important for the figuration at the time. Analysing these widely circulated documents thus enables researchers to reconstruct issues central to the figuration at the time.

3. In order to be able to trace how a figuration changed, one has to order the documents in a time-line and compare them (Figure 5). For example, in the Middle Ages (time period 1) it was common practice to relieve oneself in the presence of others, and no one was disturbed by this. This behaviour is also not mentioned in documents of the time (document 1). Later, it became an issue of power struggles (time period 2). Therefore, books of etiquette now mention that it is bad manners to defecate in view of others (document 2). Today (time period 3), controlling one's bodily functions is so well established within the figuration that small children learn this early during their socialization. Adults would find even the idea of relieving oneself in front of others absurd. Therefore, this aspect is no longer mentioned in books of etiquette (document 3) (Elias, 2000 [1939]: 109–21). All in all, by cross-reading process-produced data over several periods in time, Elias is able to reveal changes in a figuration's implicit rules and the unintentional consequences of human action.

Analysing the sociogenesis of a figuration has become easier in the last few decades, owing firstly to several methodological advances, and also to the fact

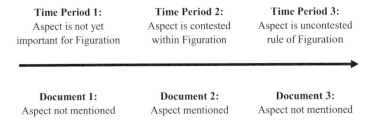

Figure 5: *Identifying change in a figuration by cross-reading process-produced data over different time periods.*

that public administration and other process-produced data are increasingly made available for a broad academic public (Baur, 2009b). Both qualitative methods (such as case studies research, grounded theory, biographical research, methods of path creation and development) and quantitative methods of longitudinal research (such as cohort analysis, time-series analysis, sequence analysis, event history analysis) have been developed and improved (Baur, 2005: 164–315).

Secondly, Elias's methodology has also been improved by later figurational sociologists. For example, Kuzmics (2009) explains how Elias's theoretical concepts can be operationalized for historical sources and how to find appropriate data such as diaries, letters and literature. He suggests a procedure for assessing the validity of this analysis.

Thirdly, using the example of popular literature, Ernst (2009) elaborates how data have to be sampled for a process-oriented analysis. She then explains how qualitative content analysis can be used for analysing long-term processes and how this data can be interpreted.

Conclusion: a suggestion for a framework for a process-oriented methodology

We have illustrated in this paper that – contrary to conventional wisdom – Norbert Elias was not only a theorist but also strongly methodologically and empirically minded. We have tried to reconstruct Elias's methodological concepts and to link them to modern methodological discourse. Finally, we have suggested that a process-oriented methodology inspired by Elias would consist of the following steps:

1 *Explicating the researcher's personal perspective* on the research topic in order to avoid partiality.
2 *Explicating the researcher's theoretical perspective*, which is necessary to decide on a research design and to link theory and data. In the case of Elias, the theoretical perspective was always figurational and process sociology. For this theoretical frame, we suggest that the following steps should be taken:
   • *Reconstructing the macro-level:* Elias tried to analyse the rules and social structure of a figuration using maps, buildings and landscapes, survey or social bookkeeping data. He triangulated them with other types of data.
   • *Reconstructing the micro-level:* Open-ended data (interviews, ethnography, and documents of life) are more suited for identifying the individual's placement within, perception of, and ability to change the figuration.
   • *Reconstructing the sociogenesis of the figuration:* Both individuals (micro-level) and their figurations (macro-level) are intertwined and changing all the time. Currently, there are no methods available to analyse these intertwined processes. As a substitute, the figuration's sociogenesis can be

analysed. Elias suggested using process-produced data such as literature and historical documents for this.

This outline strongly resembles the model for integrating qualitative and quantitative data suggested by Kelle (2008): an 'understanding of social structures as both stable over long periods of time and in unpredictable ways still capable of change due to being the product of social action, which although oriented by structures is not determined by them' (Kelle, 2008: 76). This makes an interpretive process theory a prime choice for empirically and theoretically rich analyses of contemporary sociological phenomena. As can be seen, some aspects of social processes can be analysed better today, using modern methodology (particularly the macro-level). For other aspects – namely the interaction between agency and structure – there is still a lack of appropriate methodologies. At the same time, Norbert Elias could even today inspire modern methodological discussion, as he used some data sources that have been long neglected and are only recently re-discovered, namely literature and spatial data.

Notes

1 All citations from German original texts have been translated by the authors.
2 This continues to be the practice of economists, who rarely write *about* 'methods' – instead they *use* methods.
3 Personal note from Hermann Korte.
4 On the difference between positivism, constructivism and interpretivism, see Kelle (2008).
5 For examples of how other process-oriented social theories, apart from Elias's social theory, influence social research and the link between theory and data, see Baur (2009f).
6 In addition to the qualitative and quantitative paradigm, today mixed methods research comprises a well-established third paradigm which can be defined as follows: 'Mixed methods research is the type of research in which a researcher or team of researchers combines elements of qualitative and quantitative approaches (e.g. use of qualitative and quantitative viewpoints, data collection, analysis, inference techniques) for the broad purposes of breadth and depth of understanding and corroboration' (Johnson *et al.*, 2007: 123). Mixed methods researchers generally agree that characteristics of mixed methods research are that qualitative and quantitative data are mixed and that mixing can take place at any stage of the research process (Johnson *et al.*, 2007: 118–22). MMR may be necessary to 'meet the aims of the research project' (Johnson *et al.*, 2007: 122), but specifically adds breadth and depth to the analysis (Hunter and Brewer, 2003: 587; Tashakkori and Teddlie, 2003b). For important methodological issues, see Tashakkori and Teddlie (2003a), Plano Clark and Creswell (2008), Creswell and Plano Clark (2006), Rieker and Seipel (2003) and Kelle (2008).
7 *Primary data* are collected by the researcher herself (for example, qualitative interviews, surveys, ethnography).
   Secondary data were also originally collected for social science research, but are later re-analysed, maybe even for different purposes.
   In contrast to these *research-elicited (primary and secondary) data*, *process-produced data* (or *process-generated data*) are data that are 'generated through the very *processes of living, working, interacting in the societies* . . . – from plain material evidence through all kinds of artefacts to the varieties of symbolic representations of ideas, activities, and events, whether drawings, tales, messages, or documents . . .' (Rokkan, 1966: 4–5). Process-generated data have in common with secondary data that they 'were originally recorded or "left behind" or collected at an earlier

time by a different person from the current researcher' (Johnson and Turner, 2003: 314). However, they differ from secondary data in being not originally intended for social research but being a by-product of social processes themselves. Baur (2010) discusses the respective advantages of qualitative and quantitative process-generated data compared with research-elicited data. On suggestions of how to handle methodologically process-produced data, see Baur (2009f; 2009g).

8 Note that this does not necessarily mean that researchers have to do empirical research on all these aspects at the same time but can either draw on other researchers' work or their own previous work.

9 Note that, according to Elias, both figurations as a whole (the macro-level) and individuals within the figuration (the micro-level) are continuously changing. In the following, we will focus on methods of analysing the figuration *at a given point in time* (1) due to lack of space and (2) as the methods described below are not currently developed far enough to analyse changing macro-levels properly. However, as this is one of the current issues in methodological debate, we expect that there will be methodological advances in this respect in the next few years.

10 On spatial methods, see Cromley (1999) and Rogerson and Fotheringham (2009).

11 Translated from the German, from a paragraph that is omitted from the published English translation.

12 On survey methodology see Groves *et al.* (2009), Bulmer (2004) and De Vaus (2002; 2007). On methodological problems of social bookkeeping data see Bick *et al.* (1984) and Baur (2009b, 2009e).

13 On the methodology of ethnography, see Palmer (1928), Fetterman (1998) and Atkinson and Hammersley (2006).

14 The mother-centred family had been 'discovered' in the East End of London and famously discussed a few years earlier by Michael Young and Peter Willmott (1957).

References

Dates given in square brackets are those of first publication.

Abbott, Andrew, (2001), *Time Matters*, Chicago: Chicago University Press.

Aldenderfer, Mark, S. and Roger K. Blashfield, (1984), *Cluster Analysis*, Newbury Park, CA: Sage.

Atkinson, Paul and Martyn Hammersley, (2006), *Ethnography*, London: Routledge.

Baur, Nina, (2005), *Verlaufsmusteranalyse*, Wiesbaden: VS-Verlag.

Baur, Nina, (2008a), 'Taking Perspectivity Seriously', *Historical Social Research/Historische Sozialforschung*, 33, 4: 191–213.

Baur, Nina, (2008b), 'Was kann die Soziologie methodisch von der Geschichtswissenschaft lernen?' *Historical Social Research/Historische Sozialforschung*, 33, 3: 217–48.

Baur, Nina, (2009a), 'Problems of linking theory and data in historical sociology and longitudinal research', *Historical Social Research/Historische Sozialforschung*, 34, 1: 7–21.

Baur, Nina, (2009b), 'Measurement and selection bias in longitudinal data', *Historical Social Research/Historische Sozialforschung*, 34, 3: 9–50.

Baur, Nina, (2009c), 'Memory and data', in Noel Packard, (ed.), *Sociology of Memory*, Newcastle: Cambridge Scholars Publishing: 289–312.

Baur, Nina, (ed.), (2009e), 'Characteristics of mass data, *Historical Social Research/Historische Sozialforschung* – Transition 22. Zentrum für Historische Sozialforschung, Cologne. URL: http://hsr-trans.zhsf.uni-koeln.de/volumes/vol22/HSRtrans_vol22.pdf. Accessed 13 March 2011.

Baur, Nina, (ed.), (2009f), *Linking Theory and Data*: Special Issue of *Historical Social Research/Historische Sozialforschung*, 34, 1.

Baur, Nina, (ed.), (2009g), *Social Bookkeeping Data*: Special Issue of *Historical Social Research/Historische Sozialforschung*, 34, 3.

Baur, Nina, (2010), 'Mixing process-generated data in market sociology', *Quality and Quantity*, 19, 1.

Baur, Nina and Siegfried Lamnek, (2007), 'Multivariate Analysis', in George Ritzer, (ed.), *The Blackwell Encyclopedia of Sociology*, Oxford: Blackwell: 5176–79.

Bick, Wolfgang, Reinhard Mann and Paul J. Müller, (eds), (1984), *Sozialforschung und Verwaltungsdaten*, Stuttgart: Klett-Cotta.

Bourdieu, Pierre, (1992), *The Logic of Practice*, Cambridge: Polity.

Bourdieu, Pierre, (2007), *Sketch for a Self-Analysis*, Cambridge: Polity.

Braudel, Fernand, (1996), *The Mediterranean and the Mediterranean World in the Age of Philip II*, Volume I. Berkeley: University of California Press.

Bryman, Alan, (1988), *Quantity and Quality in Social Research*, London: Unwin Hyman.

Bryman, Alan, (ed.), (2006), *Mixed Methods*, 4 vols, London: Sage.

Bryman, Alan, (2007), 'Barriers to integrating quantitative and qualitative research', *Journal of Mixed Methods Research*, 1, 1: 8–22.

Bulmer, Martin, (ed.), (2004), *Questionnaires*, 4 vols, London: Sage.

Carrington, Peter J. and John Scott, (eds.), (2005), *Models and Methods in Social Network Analysis*, Cambridge: Cambridge University Press.

Corbin, Juliet and Anselm L. Strauss, (2008), *Basics of Qualitative Research*, London: Sage.

Creswell, John W. and Vicki L. Plano Clark, (2006), *Designing and Conducting Mixed Methods Research*, London: Sage.

Cromley, Ellen K., (1999), 'Mapping spatial data', in Jean Schensul and Margaret D. LeCompte, (eds.), *Ethnographer's Toolkit 4*, Walnut Creek: Altamira Press: 51–124.

De Vaus, David, (ed.), (2002 and 2007), *Social Surveys 1 and 2*, 4 vols each, London: Sage.

Duby, Georges, (1981), *The Age of Cathedrals*, Chicago: University of Chicago Press.

Duerr, Hans Peter, (1988), *Nacktheit und Scham*, Frankfurt am Main: Suhrkamp.

Duerr, Hans Peter, (1990), *Intimität*, Frankfurt am Main: Suhrkamp.

Duerr, Hans Peter, (1993), *Obszönität und Gewalt*, Frankfurt am Main: Suhrkamp.

Dunning, Eric, (1999), *Sport Matters*, London: Routledge.

Elias, Norbert, (1978 [1970]), *What is Sociology?* London: Hutchinson. [Collected Works, Vol. 5, Dublin: UCD Press, forthcoming].

Elias, Norbert, (1994), *Reflections on a Life*, Cambridge: Polity Press. [in *Interviews and Autobiographical Reflections*, Collected Works, Vol. 17, Dublin: UCD Press, forthcoming].

Elias, Norbert, (2000 [1939]), *The Civilizing Process*, rev. edn, Oxford: Blackwell [*On the Process of Civilisation*, Collected Works, Vol. 3, Dublin: UCD Press, forthcoming].

Elias, Norbert, (2005), 'Technisierung und Zivilisation', in *Aufsätze und andere Schriften II*, Gesammelte Schriften, Vol. 16, Frankfurt am Main: Suhrkamp: 182–235.

Elias, Norbert, (2006a [1969]), *The Court Society*, Collected Works, Vol. 2, Dublin: UCD Press.

Elias, Norbert, (2006b), 'Über den Rückzug der Soziologen auf die Gegenwart', in *Aufsätze und andere Schriften II*, Gesammelte Schriften, Vol. 15, Frankfurt am Main: Suhrkamp: 389–408.

Elias, Norbert, (2007 [1987]), *Involvement and Detachment*, Collected Works, Vol. 8, Dublin: UCD Press.

Elias, Norbert, (2008 [1995]), 'Technisation and civilisation', in *Essays II: On Civilising Processes, State Formation and National Identity*, Collected Works, Vol. 15, Dublin: UCD Press: 57–92.

Elias, Norbert, (2009a [1977]), 'Towards a theory of social processes', in *Essays III: On Sociology and the Humanities*, Collected Works, Vol. 16, Dublin: UCD Press: 9–39.

Elias, Norbert, (2009b [1978]), 'The concept of everyday life', in *Essays III: On Sociology and the Humanities*, Collected Works, Vol. 16, Dublin: UCD Press: 127–34.

Elias, Norbert, (2009c [1987]), 'The retreat of sociologists into the present', in *Essays III: On Sociology and the Humanities*, Collected Works, Vol. 16, Dublin: UCD Press: 107–26.

Elias, Norbert, (2009d [1983]), 'A diagnosis of present-day sociology', in *Essays III: On Sociology and the Humanities*, Collected Works, Vol. 16, Dublin: UCD Press: 99–106.

Elias, Norbert, (2009e [1986]), 'Figuration', in *Essays III: On Sociology and the Humanities*, Collected Works, Vol. 16, Dublin: UCD Press: 1–3.

Elias, Norbert, (2009f [1977]), 'Towards a Theory of Social Processes', in *Essays III: On Sociology and the Humanities*, Collected Works, Vol. 16, Dublin: UCD Press: 9–39.

Elias, Norbert and John L. Scotson, (2008 [1965]), *The Established and the Outsiders*, Collected Works, Vol. 4, Dublin: UCD Press.

Ernst, Stefanie, (2003), 'From Blame Gossip to Praise Gossip?', *European Journal of Women's Studies*, 10, 3: 277–99.

Ernst, Stefanie, (2009), 'Using qualitative content analysis of popular literature for uncovering long-term social processes', *Historical Social Research/Historische Sozialforschung*, 34, 1: 252–69.

Ernst, Stefanie, (2010), *Prozessorientierte Methoden in der Arbeits – und Organisationsforschung*, Wiesbaden: VS-Verlag.

Fetterman, David M., (1998), 'Ethnography', in Leonard Bickman and Debra J. Rog, (eds), *Handbook of Applied Social Research Methods*, London: Sage: 473–504.

Fromm, Sabine, (2010), 'Clusteranalyse', in Sabine Fromm, (ed.), *Datenanalyse mit SPSS (PASW) für Fortgeschrittene: Multivariate Verfahren für Querschnittsdaten*, Wiesbaden: VS-Verlag.

Glaser, Barney G. and Anselm L. Strauss, (1999 [1967]), *The Discovery of Grounded Theory*, New Brunswick, NJ: Aldine.

Gleichmann, Peter, Johan Goudsblom and Hermann Korte, (eds), (1979), *Materialien zu Norbert Elias' Zivilisationstheorie*, Frankfurt am Main: Suhrkamp.

Goodwin, John and Henrietta O' Connor, (2006), 'Norbert Elias and the lost Young Worker's Project', *Journal of Youth Studies*, 9, 2: 161–76.

Goudsblom, Johan and Stephen Mennell, (eds), (1997), *The Norbert Elias Reader*, Oxford: Blackwell.

Groves, Robert M., Floyd J. Fowler and Mick P. Couper, (2009), *Survey Methodology*, New York: Wiley.

Habermas, Jürgen, (1972), *Knowledge and Human Interests*, London: Heinemann.

Hox, Joop J., (2002), *Multilevel Analysis: Techniques and Applications*, Mahwah, NJ: Lawrence Erlbaum.

Hunter, Albert and John Brewer, (2003), 'Multimethod research in sociology', in Abbas Tashakkori, and Charles Teddlie, (eds), *Handbook of Mixed Methods in Social and Behavioral Research*, Thousand Oaks, CA: Sage: 577–94.

Jahoda, Marie, Paul F. Lazarsfeld and Hans Zeisel, (2002 [1933]), *Marienthal*, New Brunswick, NJ: Transaction.

Johnson, R. Burke, Anthony J. Onwuegbuzie and Lisa A. Turner, (2007), 'Toward a definition of mixed methods research', *Journal of Mixed Methods Research*, 1, 2: 112–33.

Johnson, R. Burke and Lisa A. Turner, (2003), 'Data collection strategies in mixed methods research', in Abbas Tashakkori and Charles Teddlie, (eds), *Handbook of Mixed Methods in Social and Behavioral Research*, London: Sage: 297–320.

Kalthoff, Herbert, (2008), 'Zur Dialektik von qualitativer Forschung und soziologischer Theoriebildung', in Herbert Kalthoff, Stefan Hirschauer and Gesa Lindemann, (eds), *Theoretische Empirie*, Frankfurt am Main: Suhrkamp: 8–34.

Kelle, Udo, (2008), *Die Integration qualitativer und quantitativer Methoden in der empirischen Sozialforschung*, Wiesbaden: VS-Verlag.

Knoblauch, Hubert, (2008), 'Sinn und Subjektivität in der qualitativen Sozialforschung', in Herbert Kalthoff, Stefan Hirschauer and Gesa Lindemann, (eds), *Theoretische Empirie*, Frankfurt am Main: Suhrkamp: 210–33.

Koselleck, Reinhart, (1979), 'Standortbindung und Zeitlichkeit', in Reinhart Koselleck, (ed.), *Vergangene Zukunft*, Frankfurt am Main: Suhrkamp: 176–207.

Kuzmics, Helmut, (2009), Concept for validating the theoretical potential of historical sources, *Historical Social Research/Historische Sozialforschung*, 34,1: 270–305.

Lindemann, Gesa, (2008), 'Theoriekonstruktion und empirische Forschung', in Herbert Kalthoff, Stefan Hirschauer and Gesa Lindemann, (eds), *Theoretische Empirie*, Frankfurt am Main: Suhrkamp: 165–87.

Mennell, Stephen, (1998), *Norbert Elias: An Introduction*, rev. edn, Dublin: UCD Press.

Palmer, Vivien M., (1928), *Field Studies in Sociology*, Chicago: University of Chicago Press.

Plano Clark, Vicki L. and John W. Creswell, (eds), (2008), *The Mixed Methods Reader*, London: Sage.

Rieker, Peter and Christian Seipel, (2003), *Integrative Sozialforschung*, Weinheim: Juventa.

Rogerson, Peter A. and Stewart Fotheringham, (eds), (2009), *The Sage Handbook of Spatial Analysis*, London: Sage.

Rokkan, Stein, (1966), 'Comparative Cross-National Research', in Richard L. Merritt and Stein Rokkan, (eds), *Comparing Nations*, New Haven, CT: Yale University Press: 3–25.

Scheuch, Erwin K., (1977), 'Die wechselnde Datenbasis der Soziologie Zur Interaktion Zwischen Theorie und Empirie', in Müller, Pau J., (ed.), *Die Analyze prozeß-produzierter Daten. Historisch-Sozialwissenschaftliche Forschungen*, Volume 2, Stuttgart: Klenn-Cotta: 5–41.

Schreier, Margrit and Nigel Fielding, (eds), (2001), Qualitative and Quantitative Research, *Forum Qualitative Sozialforschung*, 2, 1. URL: www.qualitative-Research.net/index.php/fqs/issue/view/26. Accessed 13 March 2011.

Schröter, Michael, (1997), *Erfahrungen mit Norbert Elias*, Frankfurt am Main: Suhrkamp.

Schulze, Gerhard, (2001), 'Welche Daten braucht die Soziologie?' Paper 1 for the seminar 'Forschung und soziologische Theorie I' at Otto-Friedrich-University Bamberg, winter 2001–2.

Scott, John, (ed.), (2000), *Social Network Analysis*, London: Sage.

Snijders, Tom A.B. and Roel J. Bosker, (1999), *Multilevel Analysis*, London: Sage.

Tashakkori, Abbas and Charles Teddlie, (2003a), *Handbook of Mixed Methods in Social/Behavioral Research*, London: Sage.

Tashakkori, Abbas and Charles Teddlie, (2003b), 'The past and future of mixed methods research', in *Handbook of Mixed Methods in Social and Behavioral Research*, London: Sage: 671–701.

Treibel, Annette, (2008), *Die Soziologie von Norbert Elias*, Wiesbaden: VS-Verlag.

Vovelle, Michel, (1994), 'Geschichtswissenschaft und die "longue durée"', in Jacques L. Goff, Roger Chartier and Jacques Revel, (eds), *Die Rückeroberung des historischen Denkens*, Frankfurt am Main: Fischer: 103–36.

Wasserman, Stanley and Katherine Faust, (1994), *Social Network Analysis*, Cambridge: Cambridge University Press.

Wouters, Cas, (2004), *Sex and Manners: Female Emancipation in the West, 1890–2000*, London: Sage.

Young, Michael and Peter Willmott, (1957), *Family and Kinship in East London*, London: Routledge & Kegan Paul.

How civilizing processes continued: towards an informalization of manners and a third nature personality

Cas Wouters

Abstract: Based on an analysis of manners books in four Western countries since 1890, this paper describes how 'civilizing processes' have continued in the nineteenth and twentieth centuries. The paper first focuses on three central functions of a 'good society' and its code of manners, and then describes how, in a long-term phase of formalizing manners and disciplining people, 'dangerous' emotions such as those related to physical (including sexual) violence came to be controlled in increasingly automatic ways. Thus, a second-nature or conscience-dominated type of personality became dominant. The twentieth century saw rising social constraints towards being unconstrained, and yet reflective, flexible, and alert. These pressures coincided with an informalization of manners and an *emancipation of emotions*: emotions that had been denied and repressed regained access to consciousness and wider acceptance in social codes. Yet it has been only since the 'Expressive Revolution' of the 1960s that standards of self-control have increasingly enabled people to admit, to themselves and others, to having 'dangerous' emotions without provoking shame, particularly the shame-fear of losing control and face. To the extent that it has become 'natural' to perceive the pulls and pushes of both 'first nature' and 'second nature', as well as the dangers and chances, short-term and long-term, of any particular situation or relation, a 'third nature' type of personality has been developing. Examples illustrating this trend also help us to understand it as a process of psychic integration triggered by continued social integration.

Introduction

The major trends observed by Norbert Elias in his *The Civilizing Process* (2000 [1939]) arguably continued until the end of the nineteenth century. They represent a long-term phase of formalizing manners and disciplining people, in which 'dangerous' emotions such as those related to physical (including sexual) violence came to be avoided, repressed and denied in increasingly automatic ways – that is, by the inner fears of a rather rigid and authoritarian conscience. Driven by the disciplinary forces of expanding interdependency networks, in particular by state formation and market expansion, a 'second-nature' – that is, a conscience-dominated – type of personality was in the making, and became dominant. This process accelerated in the period in which bourgeois classes entered and came to dominate the centres of power and their 'good society'. It was discontinued in the twentieth century, when long-term processes of informalization of manners and 'emancipation of emotions' became dominant: emotions that had been denied and repressed regained access to consciousness and wider acceptance in social codes.[1] The following examples will provide an initial glimpse of this process.

During the 1990–91 Gulf War, fighter pilots, interviewed for TV in their planes before taking off, admitted to being afraid. They did this in a matter-of-fact way. This would have been almost unthinkable in the Second World War, when such behaviour would have been equated almost automatically with being fear-ridden, a condition in which it was thought to be impossible to perform well. Admitting to being afraid was to step on a slippery slope: one automatically had to act upon the emotion. The dominant response at that time, in answer to the problem of how to prevent soldiers from giving in to fear, may be summarized in a quotation from a 1943 manual for American officers: it is the soldier's 'desire to retain the good opinion of his friends and associates . . . his pride smothers his fear' (Stearns and Haggerty, 1991). Precisely the same pride kept soldiers from admitting they were afraid, especially before an operation. At the time of the Gulf War, all this had obviously changed. Today, admitting that one is afraid no longer means that one has automatically to act upon the emotion.

In the process of informalization and emancipation of emotions it has become quite common to admit feeling this or that, hate or lust, anger or envy, and yet to act quite differently, in a playful and subtle way. This implies a rise in the level of demands on self-regulation, a change that can perhaps be most clearly seen in changes in the relationship between the dying and those who live on. Here, the traditional rule that dying patients were to be kept under the delusion that there was a fair chance of recovery – doctors conducting a regime of silence and sacred lies, hardly ever informing the dying of their terminal situation – has changed to the expectation and, for doctors even the judicial obligation, to be open and inform them (Wouters, 2002). The norms for divorced couples have also swung round by 180 degrees: the traditional expectation that they would stop seeing each other is gradually being replaced by the expectation of having a 'good after-marriage' relationship: the ex-couple maintain a friendship, or work towards being on friendly terms again (Veeninga, 2008).

Informalization processes have continued into the twenty-first century. My analysis of them in this paper is based upon a longer-term research project, the purpose of which was to find, compare and interpret changes in American, Dutch, English and German manners books published since the 1880s. The project has resulted in two books: the first, *Sex and Manners* was published in 2004 and the second, *Informalization* in 2007. In these books general trends are reported, as well as national variations. Among the overall trends reported were a declining social and psychic distance between social classes, sexes and generations; a mixing of codes and ideals; increasing interdependencies;

an informalization of manners; expanding mutual identifications; and an 'emancipation of emotions'. All in all, these interrelated trends amounted to an informalization of manners, rising demands on emotion regulation, and increasing social and national integration.

Here, I aim to show how overall trends in Western regimes of manners in the twentieth century, and in earlier centuries, have been connected with general trends in self-regulation. These trends are the outcome of answering the question of what overall changes in social codes can be interpreted as involving specific changes in the balance of controls – that is, between external social controls and internal social controls or self-controls. I will first concentrate on continued social constraints towards self-constraints in the nineteenth century, particularly via an expanding entrepreneurial and professional bourgeoisie and an expanding market. Then I will focus on the last decades of that century, when the long-term phase of formalizing manners and disciplining people, as described by Elias, turned into a long-term phase of informalization of manners and an emancipation of emotions. I will try to interpret these changes by connecting them on the one hand to social integration processes that involved the successive ascent of larger and larger groups and their representation in national centres of power and their 'good societies', and on the other hand to changes in the balance of controls. The 'slippery slope' serves as a running example.

In addition, I will explore connections between social integration and psychic integration. In order to capture the observed changes in demands on self-regulation and in personality structure, the sensitizing concept of a 'third nature' is introduced: there was a change from a 'second nature' to a 'third nature'. The history of the corset is presented as a didactic example.[2] The final sections of this contribution focus on how social integration and the development of a third nature personality are connected to changes in the experience and control of feelings of superiority and inferiority. The latter will be illuminated by focusing on how changes in the social and individual regulation of these feelings can be specified for changes in the meaning and experience of guilt and shame. I start with a few remarks, stepping stones to sketch an empirical–theoretical framework.

On good societies and regimes of manners and emotions

As Elias has shown, changes in manners open a window on to changes in the relations *between* people, as well as onto changes *in* people, that is, in their demands for emotional regulation. Therefore the study of any regime of manners can reveal a corresponding regime of emotions. As a rule, within each society, the dominant code of manners and emotion regulation is derived from sociability within the centres of power and their 'good society' – that is, the circles of social acquaintance among people of families who belong to the centres of power, and who take part in their sociable gatherings. These codes of a good society have three functions: 1) a modelling function, 2) a representational function, and 3) a function of regulating social mobility and status competition. These three functions are also operative in good societies further down the social ladder, or in the country or provinces.

1) As the codes of good society were decisive in making acquaintances and friends, for winning a desirable spouse, and for gaining influence and recognition, they serve as an example or model for all socially aspiring people – they have a *modelling function*. Until the nineteenth century, courts had this function. In comparison with court circles, later circles of good society were larger, and sociability in them was more *private*, which made the modelling function of good society less visible. However, the dominant social definition of proper ways to establish and maintain relations was constructed in these circles.

2) At any time, the manners prevalent in good society will reflect the balance of power and dependence between established groups and outsider groups in society as a whole. As increasing layers of society became emancipated and more socially integrated, the social codes of good societies came to represent these layers – they have a *representational function*. In order to avoid social conflict and maintain their elevated position, the people in the centres of power and good society had increasingly to take the presence of rising groups into account. As part of this, the established had to show more respect for the ideals, sentiments, morals, and manners of the rising groups. Therefore the code of a good society tends to spare the sensibilities of all groups represented in them; it reflects *and* represents the power balance between all those groups and strata that are integrated in society at large.

3) In the nineteenth century, an elaborate and increasingly formalized regime of manners emerged. It consisted of a complicated system of introductions, invitations, calls, leaving calling cards, 'at homes', receptions, dinners, and so on. Entrance into good society (or its functional equivalent among other social strata) was impossible without an introduction, and, particularly in England, any introduction required the previous permission of both parties. This regime of manners not only regulated sociability, but also functioned as a relatively refined system of inclusion and exclusion, an instrument to screen newcomers seeking entry into social circles, thus helping to identify and exclude undesirables and ensuring that the newly introduced would assimilate to the prevailing regime of manners and self-regulation. Thus the codes of good society also *function to regulate social mobility and status competition*.

The modelling function of good society operates only partly through the medium of social codes or rational individual choice, because differences in manners and sensibilities become ingrained into the personality of individuals – their *habitus* – as they grow up. The same goes for many external social constraints as they are transformed into habitual self-restraints. In this context, Norbert Elias described important connections between the formation of good societies, status motives, and the transformation of constraints by others into self-restraints: 'fear of loss or reduction of social prestige is one of the most powerful motive forces in the transformation of constraints by others into self-restraints' (Elias, 2000 [1939]: 395–6). Once these external social constraints have been transformed into habitual, second-nature self-restraints, the social constraints from which they originated and which continue to back them up, are no longer experienced or perceived as such, nor are the powerful status motivations involved in their transformation.

In contrast to individual social ascent, the ascent of an entire social group involves some form of mixing of the codes and ideals of the rising group with those of the previously superior groups. In the twentieth century, the successive social ascent of larger and larger groups has been reflected in the dominant codes and habitus (a shorthand expression for the mentality, the whole distinctive emotional make-up of the people who are thus bonded together). The sediments of this mixing process can be found in manners books: the patterns of self-regulation of increasingly wider social groups come to be reflected in the codes of manners. They can be perceived in such changes as in the ways in which authors of manners books address their readers, how they draw social dividing lines such as between public and private, formal and informal, and what they have written about social introductions and forms of address. As a rule, any regime of manners and emotions symbolizes and reinforces ranking hierarchy and other social dividing lines, while the same rule has it that changes in these regimes reflect changes in social dividing lines and in balances of power. This helps one to understand why the nineteenth century witnessed an *aristocratization* of the bourgeoisie alongside an *embourgeoisement* of nobility, to be partly succeeded and partly supplemented in the twentieth century by an *embourgeoisement* of the working classes and a *proletarianization* of the bourgeoisie: *informalization*.

The disciplinary forces of state formation and market expansion

The life and career of the bourgeois classes both in business and in the professions depended heavily on keeping promises, and on the rather punctual and minute regulation of social traffic and behaviour. Accordingly, nineteenth-century manners books placed great emphasis on acquiring the self-discipline necessary for living a 'rational life'; they emphasized time-keeping and ordering activities routinely in a fixed sequence, and at a set pace. Thomas Haskell has pointed to the significance of the 'disciplinary force of the market' in connection with the rising norm of promise keeping and the ascendancy of conscience. This 'force of the market provided the intricate blend of ceaseless change, on the one hand, and predictability, on the other, in which a preoccupation with remote consequences paid off most handsomely' (Haskell, 1985: 561). An overall change in sensibility occurred via the expansion of the market, the intensification of market discipline, and the penetration of that discipline into spheres of life previously untouched by it. The expectation that everyone would live up to promises – as comprised in contracts made on 'the market' – became a mutually expected self-restraint, which eventually became taken for granted to the extent that it came to function as part of people's conscience.

This type of conscience-formation presupposes state formation in the sense that the monopolization of the use of violence by the state, and ensuing pacification of larger territories, provided a necessary condition for the expectation of promise-keeping and living up to contracts to become taken for granted, and engrained in the personality as conscience (Elias, 2000 [1939]). Taking the development of these conditions into consideration helps us to understand why it was not until the eighteenth century, in Western Europe, England, and North America, that societies first appeared whose economic systems 'depended on the expectation that most people, most of the time, were sufficiently conscience-ridden (and certain of retribution) that they could be trusted to keep their promises. In other words, only then did promise keeping become so widespread that it could be elevated into a general social norm' (Haskell, 1985: 353).

This argument adds to the one put forward by Durkheim in his writing about the order behind the contract: 'For everything in the contract is not contractual'. The order behind the contract, 'in current parlance, is designated by the name, state' (1964 [1893]: 211, 219). It was in the process of state formation that the commitment to live up to a contract came to be increasingly taken for granted and internalized. This internalization ran in tandem with, and depended upon, rising levels of mutually expected protection of people and their property.

The entrepreneurial bourgeoisie largely took this protection by the state, the order behind the contract, for granted. It was their point of departure. Their whole social existence heavily depended upon contracts, contracts regulating the conditions of such activities as buying, producing, transporting and selling. In turn, the making of these contracts, as well as the conditions stipulated in them, depended upon an individual's reputation for being financially solvent and morally solid. To a large extent this reputation was formed in the gossip channels of good society.

Building trust and moral solidity in nineteenth-century bourgeois circles

A reputation for moral solidity referred to the self-discipline of orderliness, thrift, and responsibility, as the qualities needed for a firm grip on the proceedings of business transactions. Moral solidity also pertained to the social and sexual sphere: without demonstrable control over their wives and families, working bourgeois men would fail to create a solid impression of reliability, and ability to live up to the terms of their contracts. Therefore, bourgeois means of controlling potentially dangerous social and sexual competition depended to a substantial degree on the support of a wife for her husband. Her support and social charm could make a crucial difference, as is implied in the opinion that 'nothing makes a man look more ridiculous in the eyes of the world than a socially helpless wife' (Klickmann, 1902: 25).

At the same time, these pressures offered specific opportunities for women. Whereas men dominated the eighteenth-century courtesy genre of manners books, in the nineteenth-century etiquette genre women gained a prominent position, both as authors and as readers (Curtin, 1987). As the social weight of the bourgeoisie increased, middle-class women enjoyed a widening sphere of opportunities. Although confined to the domain of their home and good society, upper- and middle-class women came, more or less, to run and organize the social sphere of good society. The workings of this social formation took place, in large part, in women's private drawing rooms. To some extent, women came to function as the gatekeepers of good society.

In developing the level of trust and respect within a relationship necessary for signing a contract, an invitation into the world of sociability was (and remains) an appreciated strategy. In their relations with friends and acquaintances, with women in general, and with their own wife in particular, men could demonstrate and prove their respectability and trustworthiness. They could show this to a potential client by inviting him and his wife into their home and into the rest of their secluded good society world. Hence, to be introduced, accepted and entertained in the drawing rooms and parlours of the respectable or, in other words, to be successful in the good society, was an important and sometimes even a necessary condition for success in business.

A basic rule of manners among those acknowledged as belonging to the circle was to treat each other on the basis of equality. Quite often this was expressed in what became known as the Golden Rule of manners: do unto others as you would have them do unto you. Some were treated with relative intimacy. Others were treated with reserve, and were thus kept at a social distance. The questions who was properly introduced or introducible, and who was not, were therefore equally important. To spot undesirables and to keep one's distance from strangers was a matter of great concern (Curtin, 1987). The prototypical stranger was someone who might have the manners of the respectable, but not the morals. Strangers personified the bad company that would endanger the self-control of the respectable, prompting loss of composure in response to repulsive behaviour or, worse, the succumbing to temptation (Lofland, 1973; Wouters, 2007).

The fear of the slippery slope: the rise of a second-nature type of personality

In the nineteenth century, authors of advisory books came to describe the fall of innocent young men as being instructive of lessons in moral virtue and vigilance. Their repeated warnings against strangers expressed a strong moral appeal, revealing a fear of the slippery slope towards giving in to immoral pleasures. As women were guarded by chaperones, these warnings were directed at young men. A study of a number of such American stories reports that 'these anecdotal dramas encompass many pitfalls – from seemingly harmless pleasures like dancing to the mortal dangers posed by alcohol – for conduct writers see young men's mistakes not just as individual dangers, but as part of a web of dangerous activity: one slip inevitably leads to the next' (Newton, 1994: 58). Playing a single game of cards with strangers, for example, would 'always end in trouble, often in despair, and sometimes in suicide' (Loosjes, 1809: 98), an early nineteenth-century advice book warned. Van Tilburg, in her study of Dutch books of this genre, concluded that, by its nature, any careless indulgence in pleasure would lead to 'a lethal fall' (van Tilburg, 1998: 67). Stuart Blumin also reports on a whole genre of

> purportedly true stories of individual drunkards, nearly all of whom were identified as wealthy, educated, or respectable before they took to drink. Moderate drinking invariably led to heavy drinking and drunkenness, and drunkenness to financial ruin and the destruction of family life. Often it led to the death of the drinker, his impoverished wife (the drunkard in these tales was almost always male), or his children. The loss of respectability, of the ability to pursue a respectable occupation, of wealth, and of family life in a well-appointed home (the forced sale of furniture is a common motif) was crucial to these tales, and spoke clearly and powerfully to the major preoccupations of the upper and middle classes. (1989: 200)

Newton concludes:

> Self-control, self-government, self-denial, self-restraint, and discipline of the will are all terms used repeatedly in the conduct book lexicon to reinforce the social construction of masculinity. The true man, then, is he who can discipline himself into qualities of character that lead to material and personal success. This discipline also extends to controlling and subjugating the passions as well. Control of anger, of sexual appetite, of impatience, even of emotion are instilled in the American male psyche as essential to the manly character. (1994: 58–9)

This strong moral advice was intended to teach young men the responsibilities needed not only for a successful career but also, because marriages were no longer arranged by parents, for choosing a marriage partner. The advice betrayed the fear that such choices would be determined mainly by sexual attraction.

Social censorship verged on psychic censorship: warnings expanded to the 'treacherous effects' of fantasy, itself a demonstration of the prevailing conviction that dangerous thoughts would almost automatically lead to dangerous action. The rigorous and violent censorship in stricter and more authoritarian regimes demonstrates the extent to which authorities and others believed in the danger of thoughts, imagination or fantasy. Because of this direct connection between thoughts and actions, warnings against having dangerous thoughts were formulated as powerfully as possible. This kind of high-pitched moral pressure signalled the development of rather rigid ways of avoiding anything defined as dangerous or unacceptable via the formation of a rigorous conscience. It stimulated the rise of conflict-avoiding persons, obsessed with self-discipline, punctuality, orderliness, and the importance of living a rational life. For them, the view of emotions came to be associated predominantly with dangers and weaknesses. Giving in to emotions and impulses would lead either to the dangers of physical and/or sexual violence, or to the weaknesses of devastating addictions and afflictions. Thus the successive ascent of large middle-class groups and their increasing status and power relative to other groups was reflected in the regimes of manners and emotions. From the pressures of these growing interdependencies and intensified status competition, a particular type of self-regulation originated (for details, see Wouters, 2007).

This type of personality was characterized by an 'inner compass' of reflexes and rather fixed habits (Riesman, 1950). Impulses and emotions came to be controlled increasingly via the more or less automatically functioning counter-impulses of a rigorous conscience with a strong penchant for order and regularity, cleanliness and neatness. Negligence in these matters indicated an inclination towards dissoluteness. Such inclinations were to be nipped in the bud, particularly in children. Without rigorous control, 'first nature' might run wild.[3] This old conviction expresses a fear of the slippery slope that is typical of rather authoritarian relations and social controls, as well as a relatively authoritarian conscience.

The long-term trend of formalization reached its peak in the Victorian era, from the mid-nineteenth century to its last decade; the metaphor of the stiff upper lip indicated ritualistic manners and a kind of ritualistic self-control, heavily based on a scrupulous conscience, and functioning more or less automatically as a 'second nature', that second-nature type of personality which Riesman (1950) called inner directed.

The longing for total belonging and control

It was particularly in the last decades of the nineteenth century, in the wake of expanding industrialization, that many new groups with new money demanded representation in the centres of power and their good societies. Facing mounting pressures arising from the necessities of social mixing, from increased interdependencies and its intensified competition and cooperation, the advantages of the stiff upper lip diminished. In that *fin de siècle* period, the 'domestication of nature', including one's own (first) nature, increasingly came to trigger both the experience of 'alienation from nature' (one's own nature included) and a new romanticized longing for nature. The more nature was exploited and controlled, the more the image of an unexploited nature was valued. There was a new interest in mountains and seaside scenery, satisfying many of the new emotional longings: 'The absolute stillness, the dying of the day, the open landscape, all gave a feeling of total belonging, of a quiet ecstasy'. The connection with the rise of a second-nature type of personality seems obvious, for 'the man who endures hardship and deprivations to conquer a mountain single-handed . . . masters both an inner and an outer nature'

(Frykman and Löfgren, 1987: 55, 52). These decades saw the genesis of sports as an important part of public life (Elias and Dunning, 2008 [1986]). It seems likely that most of them became fashionable and popular, at least partly, because practising them could bring this feeling of total belonging and control. The same feeling was also projected through the romanticizing of a past, with an old harmonious peasant society, where each person knew his or her station in life.

Sociologists Frykman and Löfgren describe a comparable development regarding 'our animal friends': when middle-class people 'had mastered the animal within' and had developed a moral superiority to 'the more bestial lower classes', they felt a growing intimacy with animals and at the same time distanced themselves from them. They developed 'an abhorrence for "natural ways" together with a longing and fascination for "the natural way of life"' (1987: 85–6). There was a quest for spontaneous, authentic, relaxed and informal conduct, which carried the spread of informalizing processes.

Throughout the twentieth century, however, that typical second-nature domestication of 'first nature' survived, despite increasingly losing adherents and vitality, particularly since the 1960s. An early twentieth-century example may show how the fear of the slippery slope mirrors the dream of total control:

> Each lie breeds new lies; there is no end to it. Let no one begin to lie to members of the household or to cheat with customers, for no escape is possible: one has to continue! . . .
> Therefore, beware of beginning.
> Do not take that first step.
> And if you have already turned into the wrong path, possibly have walked it a long way already – then turn around at once, avert yourself . . . It is better to die than to be false! (Oort, 1904: 10, 14)

A similar rigidity in dividing the world into black and white, right and wrong, is captured in a popular (USA) song of the 1940s: 'you've got to accentuate the positive, eliminate the negative, . . . don't mess with Mister In-Between.' Mister In-Between is the personification of the slippery slope, of course. The first step on his path of vice is the point of no return: the slippery slope is an omnipresent bogey of the second-nature type of personality.

Social mixing and the rise of social and psychic control over superiority feelings

At the end of the nineteenth century and in the first decades of the twentieth, old ways of keeping a distance had to be abandoned as many groups of *nouveau riche* were allowed into the centres of power and their good societies. Further industrialization, including new forms of public transport, demanded more social mixing, at work as well as in trams and trains. Growing interdependency implied that social and psychic dividing lines were opening up, and the new levels of social mixing made it more necessary to achieve greater mastery over the fear of being provoked, pulled down by losing one's self-control, and degraded. Social mixing obliged increasing numbers of people to accelerate, steadily, 'down the slippery slope'. Thus, the fear of degrading contact with lower classes and/or with lower impulses had to be brought under more flexible social and psychic control. This was a major incentive to control expressions of superiority.

In the 1930s, some etiquette books, mainly Dutch and German, still contained separate sections on 'good behaviour' towards social superiors and inferiors. Later, these sections disappeared.

Ideals of good manners became dissociated from superior and inferior social position or rank. The trend tended towards drawing social dividing lines, less on the basis of people's belonging to certain groups – class, race, age, sex, or ethnicity – than on the basis of individual behaviour. An example of this process is the waning of references to 'the best people', 'best Society' or 'best sets'. An English manners book of the 1950s declared 'the old criterion of all etiquette writers . . . the best people' to be one of the casualties of a new and gentler code of manners (Edwards and Beyfus, 1956: x). In American manners books, these references had not been exceptional until the late 1930s. In the new edition of 1937, however, Emily Post had changed the title of her first chapter from 'What is Best Society?' to 'The True Meaning of Etiquette'. By formulating the latter mostly in terms of individual qualification – that is, in terms of personal qualities such as charm, tranquillity, taste, beauty, and so on – Mrs Post had turned the perspective away from the social level to the psychic, or even the biological level. Formulations such as 'the code of a thoroughbred . . . is the code of instinctive decency, ethical integrity, self-respect and loyalty' (1937: 2) are examples of social avoidance internalized: from avoiding lower-class people, to avoiding layers of superiority feelings.

These examples also indicate why displaying feelings of superiority would not only humiliate and provoke social inferiors, but also grate on the senses of anyone in good society. Superiority feelings had come to be considered as a lower class of feelings, and to display them as betraying a flaw of the personality. As subordinate social groups were emancipated, references to hierarchical group differences, and to 'better' and 'inferior' kinds of people, were increasingly tabooed. Whereas at one time people of inferior status were avoided, later in the twentieth century behaviour that betrayed feelings of superiority and inferiority came to be avoided: avoidance behaviour was internalized, turning tensions *between* people into tensions *within* people. In the process, the once automatic equation that superiority in power equals superiority as a human being declined to the point of inviting embarrassment. As many types of 'lofty grandeur' came to be viewed as insulting stiffness, a different pattern of self-control came to be demanded: a stronger and yet more flexible self-regulation in which these feelings of superiority were expected to be kept under control. This was a motor in the process of informalization.

The slippery slope rejuvenated

This process of informalization was observed by many authors of manners books. In 1899, for example, a German author wrote that 'social relations have gradually become much more informal – that is, more natural' and added that 'to strive after nature' was 'a general trend in art, science, and living' (quoted in Krumrey, 1984: 413). The trend was generally welcomed, until early in the twentieth century, when an English author also expressed a concern:

> The boy of early Victorian days was a ceremonious little creature. He called his parents 'Sir' and 'Madam', and would never have dreamed of starting a conversation at table, and scarcely in joining in it . . . One would not wish to see the ceremoniousness of those times revived, but it is possible that we . . . err in the opposite direction. (Armstrong, 1908: 187–8)

In this question 'Do we err in the wrong direction?', the old fear of the slippery slope was rejuvenated and has accompanied the whole twentieth-century process of informalization. No longer was it that first step which needed to be avoided, but where *did* solid ground and confidence stop, and the slippery slope become unstoppable? These questions became pressing each time young people had escaped further from under the wings of their parents, revived in particular by each flow of emancipation of young women and their sexuality.

Rising constraints to be unconstrained, and yet reflective, flexible, and alert

As interdependency networks expanded, status competition intensified, and the art of obliging and being obliged became more important as a power resource, demonstrations of being intimately trustworthy while perfectly at ease also gained importance. In this sense, processes of democratization, social integration, and informalization have run parallel with increasing constraints towards developing 'smooth manners'. The expression 'a constraint to be unconstrained' seems to capture this paradoxical development.

This expression resembles that used by Norbert Elias: 'the social constraint towards self-constraint' (2000 [1939]: 365–79). Indeed, in the process of informalization the two constraints have become hardly distinguishable: the constraint towards becoming accustomed to self-constraint is at the same time a constraint to be unconstrained, to be confident and at ease. Almost every etiquette book contains passages that emphasize the importance of tactful behaviour, rather than demonstrative deference, and of 'natural' rather than mannered behaviour. However, in processes of emancipation and informalization, some ways of behaving that had previously been experienced as tactful deference came to be seen as too hierarchical and demonstrative, in the same way that what had once been defined and recommended as natural came to be experienced as more or less stiff and phony, and branded as mannered. It then became so obviously a cliché-ridden 'role', in which so many traces of constraint could be 'discovered', that 'playing' this role would provoke embarrassment. People who stuck to these old ways of relating were running the risk of being seen as bores, as lacking any talent for 'the jazz of human exchange' (Hochschild, 1983). Hence, new forms of relaxed, 'loose', and 'natural' behaviours were developed.

All of this also helps one to understand changes in the practices and ideals in raising children. In the old and new middle classes, parents who themselves had learned to behave in a rather reserved, inhibited and indirect manner, and to conceal their 'innermost feelings behind a restrained observance of conventional forms' (Goudsblom, 1968: 30), became charmed and fascinated by the more outright, spontaneous, straightforward and direct behaviour of children. This attractiveness of the (more) 'natural' functioned as a catalyst to the emancipation of emotions.

As 'ease' and 'naturalness' gained importance, and demands for individual authenticity and a socially more meaningful personal identity rose, to behave according to a set of fixed rules of manners increasingly came to be experienced as rigid and stiff, and their performance as too obvious and predictable, as 'insincere', even as 'fraudulent' or as 'deceit'. In its wake, for example, the mourning ritual was minimized (Wouters, 2002: 7). This means that traditional ways of behaving and regulating emotions have been losing part of their 'defensive' or 'protective' function. The former formal codes had functioned as a defence against dangers and fears which were now diminished, or could be avoided or controlled in more varied and subtle ways – ways in which both social superiority and inferiority were less explicitly and less extremely expressed. Increasing numbers of people pressured each other to develop more differentiated and flexible patterns of self-regulation, triggering a further impetus towards higher levels of social knowledge, self-knowledge and reflectivity.

Emancipation of emotions – rise of a 'third-nature' personality

As most social codes have been becoming more flexible and differentiated, manners and emotion regulation have also been becoming more decisive criteria for status or reputation. People have been pressurizing each other to become less stiff but more cautious, that is, more conscious of social and individual options and restrictions, and this has been putting social and self-knowledge in greater demand. The same goes for the ability to empathize and to take on others' roles. Respect and respectable behaviour have been becoming more dependent upon self-regulation.

Between the 1950s and 1980s, these processes of social and psychic emancipation and integration accelerated dramatically. Together with the old conviction that being open to such 'dangerous' emotions would almost irrevocably be followed by acting upon them, many varieties of the fear of the slippery slope were destroyed. The dominant mode of self-regulation had reached a strength and scope that increasingly enabled people to admit to themselves and to others to having 'dangerous' emotions, without provoking shame, particularly the shame-fear of losing control, and having to 'give in to' and act upon these feelings. This kind of self-regulation implies that emotions, even those which could provoke physical and sexual violence, have become more easily accessible, while their control is less strongly based upon a commanding conscience, functioning more or less automatically as a 'second nature'.

In the course of the integration of 'lower' social groups within Western societies and the subsequent emancipation and integration of 'lower' impulses and emotions in personality, both psychic and social censorship declined. The fear and awe of fantasy or dissident imagination diminished together with the fear and awe of the authorities of state and conscience. There was a significant spread of more and more unconcealed expressions of insubordination, sex and violence, particularly in the realms of imagination and amusement. Ego functions came to dominate conscience or superego functions, and a more ego-dominated pattern of self-regulation spread. To the extent that it has become 'natural' to perceive the pulls and pushes both of 'first nature' and 'second nature', as well as the dangers and chances, short-term and long-term, of any particular situation or relation, a 'third nature' has been developing. Increasing numbers of people have become aware of emotions and temptations in circumstances where shame-fears and dangers had been dominant before.

Obviously, this emancipation of emotion involves an attempt at reaching back to 'first nature' without losing any of the control that was provided by 'second nature'. Thus, the rise of a 'third-nature personality' demands and depends on an emancipation of 'first nature' as well as 'second nature'. Of this development, the history of the corset may serve as a didactic example.

Wearing a corset spread from Spanish aristocratic women in the sixteenth century to other strata and other countries, and it flourished in the nineteenth century. The spread of the corset symbolizes the spread of increasing control over the body – loose clothes came to indicate loose morals. Towards the end of the nineteenth century, as for instance in the movement for reform of clothing, ideals of naturalness amalgamated with ideals of beauty. From that time onwards until the 1960s, the boned corset came to be used only as an orthopaedic gadget for female bodies gone out of control, ones that burst the bounds of the prevailing standard of beauty. This standard increasingly contained ideals of naturalness, but not without control: much female flesh that was not quantitatively excessive remained controlled by corset-like underwear, girdles, straps, corselets, and bras. Only at the end of the 1960s did women succeed in liberating their bodies from this kind of control. However, it was not a full liberation. It was clearly a controlled decontrolling, while the control of the corset over the body was continued as self-control: women turned heavily to diets, sports, aerobics, fitness, home trainers, and other forms of 'working the body' such as plastic surgery (Steele, 2001). Since the 1980s, a stylized visible corset has reappeared as a playfully provocative form of erotic display, but as it is taken for granted that the women who wear one do not need such a corset for controlling their bodies, the visible corset can also be taken as a symbol of how ideals of beauty, naturalness, and self-control have merged with each other – another indication of the spread of a third-nature personality.

Sociogenesis and psychogenesis of a third-nature personality

The spread of 'third nature' was embedded in national, continental, and global integration processes, exerting pressure towards increasingly differentiated regimes of manners, and also towards increasingly reflective and flexible regimes of self-regulation. These trends accelerated in the period after the Second World War in processes of global emancipation (including decolonization) and diminishing power differences. Expanding networks of interdependence incited rising levels of mutual identification: ideals of equality and mutual consent spread and gained strength. It was on this basis that in the 1950s and 1960s avoidance behaviour came to be less and less rigidly directed at 'lower-class' people and 'lower' emotions, that behavioural and emotional alternatives expanded, and that there was a spurt in the emancipation of emotions, accompanied by a shift from conscience to consciousness (to use this shorthand expression). In this way, the social processes in which relations and manners between social groups became less rigid and hierarchical are connected with psychic processes in which relations between the psychic functions of people's emotions and impulses became more open and fluent. A self-regulation via the rather automatically functioning counter-emotions and counter-impulses of conscience was losing out to a regulation via consciousness. As social and psychic dividing lines opened up, social groups as well as psychic functions became more integrated – that is, the communications and connections between both social groups and psychic functions have become more flowing and flexible. Lo and behold: the sociogenesis and psychogenesis of a third-nature personality!

There was, however, one important exception to the expansion of behavioural and emotional alternatives: the social codes increasingly came to dictate that overt expression of inferiority and superiority feelings be avoided. The avoidance of these feelings and of behaviour that expressed them was a confirmation of social equalization and a necessary condition for informalization to occur. Thus, there was a further curbing of emotions in relation to the display of arrogance or self-aggrandizement, and 'self-humiliation'. These displays were either banished to the realm of imagination, games and sports, or compartmentalized behind the social and psychic scenes. The latter leads to hiding superiority and inferiority feelings, and this process can be interpreted as a countertrend or, at least partly, as a reversal of the direction of the main process.

From this perspective arises a question of major social and psychic importance: will processes of an *emancipation of emotions* and *controlled decontrolling of emotional controls* continue and eventually come to include more feelings of superiority and inferiority? Will feelings of inferiority and superiority be further admitted into consciousness, while, at the same time, they come under a stronger, a more comprehensive, more stable and subtle internal (ego) control, one that is sharply scrutinized and thus backed up by external social controls? The answer to these questions strongly depends, of course, on the future of integration processes and their inherent integration conflicts. Will these integration conflicts remain sufficiently controlled and contained? The opposite, however, is true also: the control and containment of social integration conflicts depends to a large extent on the degree of control over superiority feelings in the societies of the established: on their degree of informalization.

Again and again, from the suicide bomber to the 'war president', superiority and inferiority feelings appear to be directly and highly significant for understanding why social and psychic conflicts erupt in violence. From this perspective, it seems highly relevant to analyse and interpret the emotions connected with longings and triumphs, humiliations and defeats, and focus on the regulation of emotions and impulses connected with the struggle for power, status and human value, particularly feelings of inferiority and superiority. Within the sociology of emotions, few sociologists study these feelings and hardly any psychologist takes this type of study to the level of power and status competition between groups and societies. At this point, nearing the end of this contribution, it must suffice to sketch a few significant changes in the social and individual regulation of a specific type of inferiority feelings: shame and guilt. The focus is on broad changes in the meaning and experience of guilt and shame, and in the practice of shaming.

A shift from guilt to shame and shaming

In the 1960s and 1970s, the acceleration in the shift from a second-nature towards a third-nature personality involved a different function for, and appreciation of guilt. In comparing the three types of persons that he distinguished – tradition-directed, inner-directed, and other-directed – Riesman wrote about the inner-directed type: 'He goes through life less independent than he seems, obeying his inner piloting. Getting off course, whether in response to inner impulses or to the fluctuating voices of contemporaries, may lead to the feeling of guilt.' In contrast, 'the other-directed person, must be able to receive signals from far and near; the sources are many, the changes rapid. . . . As against guilt-and-shame controls, though of course these survive, one prime psychological lever of the other-directed person is a diffuse anxiety' (1950: 24–5). These words can be read as a harbinger of the widespread attack on guilt and guilt feelings in the 1960s and 1970s, expressed through the widely used words 'guilt trip' in exclamations like 'Don't lay that guilt trip on me!'. Ralph Turner observed that 'guilt becomes an evil thing. It becomes the impediment to individual autonomy and to an individual sense of worth. Guilt is the invasion of the self by arbitrary and external standards' (1969: 402). This social movement was mirrored in changing opinions about guilt in criminal law and punishment, as well as in a critique of the attribution of blame as a means of orientation (van Benthem van den Bergh, 1986), and in the 'self psychology' of Kohut (1977).

Guilt feelings came to be experienced more strongly as indicative of a conscience-ridden personality make-up and, therefore, as an anxiety to be mastered. They came to be seen as a symbol and a symptom of a commanding and rather automatically functioning conscience. Thus, in fact, guilt was rejected for being an internalized form of shame that functions as a form of rigid self-constraint. In comparison, shame feelings that have been less internalized and which, therefore, function less rigidly and automatically than do guilt feelings, are more strongly experienced as external constraints. They refer more directly to other people and also, of course, to the fact that one's conscience is at least partly in agreement with these others. This perspective opens a window on to the reasons why the shift from a superego-dominated personality in the direction of an ego-dominated personality has coincided with a decline in the status of guilt, both as a feeling and as a concept.

This trend seems to be a reversal of the direction of development from a shame-culture to a guilt-culture, as it has been represented in an extensive body of literature, especially in the 'culture and personality' school of anthropology, of which Ruth Benedict's *The Chrysanthemum and the Sword* (1946) is a classic example. In the informalization process of the twentieth century, this development from a shame-culture to a guilt-culture seems to have been reversed: from a guilt-culture to a shame-culture. It would be absurd, however, to equate the pattern of shame in what has been described as shame-cultures with the pattern of shame in informalized societies. Obviously, a distinction between two types of shame mechanisms – or better, shaming mechanisms – corresponding to (at least) two types of external constraints is needed (see Schröter, 1997: 102–4), just as much as is a distinction between two types of shame-culture.

Traditional shame-cultures, inner-directed guilt-cultures, other-directed shame-cultures

In traditional shame-cultures, shaming is a form of external social control exercised mainly to prevent people from engaging with opportunities to go against the codes. If they had done so anyway, shaming techniques such as the pillory functioned to punish them. Continued shaming processes fuelled these external social controls to become transformed into habitual self-controls, resulting in the making of a guilt-ridden second-nature type of personality. In people with this inner-directed type of personality, the shame-fear of being unable to control affects in accordance with the prevailing regimes of manners and emotions was internalized, placed under the authority of a rigorous conscience, and experienced as guilt. Johan Goudsblom has argued that the authorities of state and church were at the cradle of this process. Seen from a developmental sociological perspective, he writes,

> a process of differentiation has taken place, in the course of which a number of causes for shame were gradually brought under the control of more centralized institutions, the state and the church. Part of the burden of shame was converted into guilt by virtue of those institutions which developed special branches for meting out punishment. Other institutions, especially the family, adjusted to this penal pattern. In society at large, it was the state and the church that created guilt-generating forms of punishment. In doing so, both state and church have strengthened the processes of conscience formation. The confessional and the courtroom were the material reflections of the effort to replace shaming rituals by more rational forms of accusation, allowing the victims (be they 'culprits' or 'sinners') the possibility of appeal according to written rules. (2007: 15)

From this perspective, in which guilt appears mainly as the product of new forms of shaming, to conceptualize more recent changes as a transformation from a guilt-culture to a new shame-culture may not seem very illuminating. Yet doing so might add to the meaningfulness of Riesman's concept 'other-directedness'. It draws attention to a change in the pattern of self-regulation in the direction of less inner-directedness – in the sense of bowing to the rules of a rigorous conscience – and greater awareness of others and of the pressures they exercise, or have exercised in the past. For the *emancipation of emotions* also implied that more and more people increasingly became conscious of emotions that, as a rule in the past, had been either ignored or concealed for fear of parents and others on whom they were dependent. In the informalization spurt of the 1960s and 1970s, many people discovered that self-restraints of all kinds were in fact constraints by others, or at least based upon such external constraints (Wouters, 1990: 53). Thus, processes of psychologization and sociologization were tightly interwoven.

As the range of behavioural and emotional alternatives expanded in processes of informalization, avoiding shame and shaming became increasingly dependent upon the ways in which individuals control and regulate their manners and emotions. Self-regulation increasingly became both the focus *and* the locus of external social controls. The implied reading of the two shame cultures shows a markedly different balance of controls. The same goes for balances of power and also for two other balances. Whereas the regime of emotions in the old shame-culture was characterized by a we–I balance (Elias, 2010 [1987]) that is strongly tilted to the side of the we, the we–I balance in the regime of the recent shame-culture is strongly tilted to the I. Likewise there is a commensurably strong tilting in the balance of involvement and detachment: emotion regulation in the old shame-culture was characterized by relatively low levels of detachment, while the new shame-culture has relatively high levels. Yet, no matter how the controlling of shame-fears in new shame-cultures of other-directed persons may differ from that of the old shame-culture of tradition-directed persons, their concern has remained the same: status degradation, loss of human value, respect and self-respect. The comparison of old and new forms of shaming and shame-cultures reveals a trend towards developing increasingly reflexive and flexible regimes of self-regulation, demonstrating a rising level of reflexive 'civilizing' of social and psychic authorities. This development has triggered and strengthened informalization processes and the rise of a 'third-nature' type of personality. If continued, feelings of inferiority and superiority will be further admitted into consciousness, while, at the same time, they come under a stronger, a more comprehensive, more stable and subtle internal (self-)control, one that is sharply scrutinised and thus backed up by external social controls. From a perspective on a lower level of reflexive 'civilizing' of social and psychic authorities, this may seem like dancing on a slippery slope.

Notes

1 The word 'regained' cannot be taken literally, of course, as emotions that find more or less direct expression in behaviour differ from emotions that find access into a type of consciousness that allows for processing them into a large variety of ways of expressing and/or repressing them.
2 In this example, reaching back to 'first nature' refers to regulating the naked body – which clearly demonstrates that I do not believe we can ever get to 'first nature'. But I do believe we shall continue with attempts at authenticity – that perfect balance of first, second and third nature.
3 The term 'first nature' refers to the needs and affects that stem from the 'animalic nature' that human beings share with many other animals. Human 'first nature' has a very high degree of plasticity and is always subjected to external and internal controls. It is 'nature', yet never without regulation.

References

Dates given in square brackets are those of first publication.

Armstrong, Lucie Heaton, (1908), *Etiquette up-to-date*, London: Werner Laurie.
Benedict, Ruth, (1946), *The Chrysanthemum and the Sword*, Boston: Houghton Mifflin.
van Benthem van den Bergh, Godfried (1986), 'The improvement of human means of orientation: towards synthesis in the social sciences', in Apthorpe, Raymond and Andreás Kráhl, (eds), *Development Studies: Critique and Renewal*, Leiden: Brill: 109–36. [For the original full English version dating from 1977, see http://www.norberteliasfoundation.nl/network/essays.php]
Blumin, Stuart M., (1989), *The Emergence of the Middle Class: Social Experience in the American City, 1760–1900*, Cambridge University Press.
Curtin, Michael, (1987), *Propriety and Position*, New York: Garland.
Durkheim, Émile, (1964 [1893]), *The Division of Labour in Society*, Glencoe, IL: Free Press.
Edwards, Anne and Drusilla Beyfus, (1956), *Lady Behave*, London: Cassell.
Elias, Norbert, (2000 [1939]), *The Civilizing Process*, rev. edn. Oxford: Blackwell. [*On the Process of Civilisation*, Collected Works, Vol. 3, Dublin: UCD Press, forthcoming].
Elias, Norbert, (2010 [1987]), *The Society of Individuals*, Collected Works, Vol. 10, Dublin: UCD Press.
Elias, Norbert and Eric Dunning, (2008 [1986]), *Quest for Excitement: Sport and Leisure in the Civilizing Process*, Collected Works, Vol. 7, rev. edn. Dublin: UCD Press.
Frykman, Jonas, and Orvar Löfgren, (1987), *Culture Builders: A Historical Anthropology of Middle-Class Life*, New Brunswick, NJ: Rutgers University Press.

Goudsblom, Johan, (1968), *Dutch Society*, New York: Random House.

Goudsblom, Johan, (2007), 'Shame as Social Pain', *Sociology of Emotions Newsletter*, 21, 1: 6 and 10–15.

Haskell, Thomas, (1985), 'Capitalism and the Humanitarian Sensibility', *American Historical Review* 90, 2–3: 339–61 and 547–66.

Hochschild, Arlie Russell, (1983), *The Managed Heart: Commercialization of Human Feeling*, Berkeley, CA: University of California Press.

Klickmann, Flora, (1902), *The Etiquette of To-day*, London: R. S. Cartwright.

Kohut, Heinz, (1977), *The Restoration of the Self*, New York: International Universities Press.

Krumrey, Horst-Volker, (1984), *Entwicklungsstrukturen von Verhaltensstandarden*, Frankfurt am Main: Suhrkamp.

Lofland, Lyn H., (1973), *A World of Strangers*. New York: Basic Books.

Loosjes, Adriaan Pz., (1809), De Man in de vier Tijdperken Zijns Levens, Haarlem: A. Loosjes Pz.

Newton, Sarah E., (1994), *Learning to Behave*, Westport, CT: Greenwood Press.

Oort, H.L., Dr. (1904), *Goede Raad aan de jonge mannen en jonge meisjes der XXste eeuw*, Utrecht: Broese.

Post, Emily, (1937), *Etiquette in Society, in Business, in Politics and at Home*, New York: Funk and Wagnalls.

Riesman, David, Nathan Glazer and Reuel Denney, (1950), *The Lonely Crowd*, New Haven, CT: Yale University Press.

Schröter, Michael, (1997), *Erfahrungen mit Norbert Elias*, Frankfurt am Main: Suhrkamp.

Stearns, Peter N. and Timothy Haggerty, (1991), 'The Role of Fear: Transitions in American Emotional Standards for Children, 1850–1950', *The American Historical Review*, 96, 1: 63–94.

Steele, Valerie, (2001), *The Corset: A Cultural history*, New Haven, CT: Yale University Press.

van Tilburg, Marja, (1998), *Hoe hoorde het?* Amsterdam: Het Spinhuis.

Turner, Ralph H., (1969), 'The Theme of Contemporary Social Movements', *British Journal of Sociology*, 20, 4: 390–405.

Veeninga, Djoeke, (2008), *Het nahuwelijk*, Amsterdam: Augustus.

Wouters, Cas, (1990), *Van minnen en sterven: Informalizering van de omgangsvormen rond seks en dood*, Amsterdam: Bert Bakker.

Wouters, Cas, (2002), 'The Quest for New Rituals in Dying and Mourning: Changes in the We–I Balance', *Body & Society*, 8, 1: 1–27.

Wouters, Cas, (2004), *Sex and Manners: Female Emancipation in the West since 1890*, London: Sage.

Wouters, Cas, (2007), *Informalization: Manners and Emotions since 1890*, London: Sage.

Sport and leisure

Katie Liston

Abstract: This paper explores the main contributions of the figurational sociological tradition to the sociology of sport. It also charts the development of this work since the pioneering text, *Quest for Excitement*, by Norbert Elias and Eric Dunning, as well as offering a brief overview of some of the debates and disagreements that have arisen within the area.

Introduction

In the mid 1990s Mouzelis argued that the kinds of debates between figurational sociologists and their critics would be of significance not only to 'those interested in the sociology of sport and leisure' but also, more widely, to 'all those interested in the present state and future prospects of sociological theory' (1993: 252). This observation was prescient in light of subsequent developments in figurational studies of sport and leisure and the rich intellectual contributions made by proponents of this theoretical paradigm. Such has been the significance of these contributions that any social scientific textbook on sport and leisure necessarily includes engagement with the figurational tradition. Tomlinson (2006), for example, includes two excerpts from Elias and Dunning's *Quest for Excitement* (1986) in *The Sports Studies Reader* and Coakley and Pike (2009) make reference to figurational research on sport on theoretical and empirical grounds. Equally, the *Handbook of Sports Studies* (Coakley and Dunning, 2000) and *Sport and Modern Social Theorists* (Giulianotti, 2004) incorporate separate theoretical chapters on the figurational sociology of sport tradition. Figurational research on sport has become, therefore, a well established and prominent paradigm in the sociology of sport and leisure since the 1970s for a number of reasons, not least of which is its explicit commitment to furthering continuity in the theoretical and empirical testing and extension of Elias's work.

Contrary to those academics who more or less eschew theoretical frames of understanding – Giulianotti, for example, has criticized the Leicester School's work on football hooliganism and his self stated intellectual predilection is 'to disassociate the investigation of sport from particular perspectives' (2005:

210)[1] – figurational sociologists of sport have, over the past 40 years or so, attained a distinctive degree of intergenerational continuity which diverges from the wider pattern of non-cumulative sociological thought and the associated tendency to 'reinvent the wheel'.[2] Part of the explanation for this continuity can be found in the belated publication of Elias's work, most of which was written far earlier than its relatively recent publication, and the associated belated rise in the popularity and acceptance of his work in the late twentieth century, thus enabling recent generations to engage meaningfully with the richness of the figurational sociological approach.[3] It was also assisted by Elias's willingness to acknowledge that his central theory – civilizing processes and their variants – had nothing more than the status of a working hypothesis, requiring sustained empirical investigation across a range of social contexts and time periods, to test, refute, refine or extend its explanatory power.[4]

Norbert Elias's intellectual ambition was wide ranging, and Mennell (1998: 140) notes that Elias 'came to sport as a topic for sociological investigation relatively late in his career'. In the 1960s and 1970s Elias published with Eric Dunning 'Dynamics of sport groups with special reference to football' (1966). Three years later there followed 'The quest for excitement in leisure' (1969) and, in 1971, 'Folk football in medieval and early modern Britain' and 'Leisure in the spare-time spectrum'. All four papers were subsequently reprinted or extended in what many would describe as the landmark text for figurational studies of sport and leisure – *Quest for Excitement: Sport and Leisure in the Civilizing Process* – published first in 1986 and more recently in 2008 as Volume 7 of the Collected Works of Elias. Interestingly, these four pioneering papers with sport and leisure as their focal point were published prior to the English language edition of *The Civilizing Process*, which has become synonymous with Elias's figurational sociology. In this connection, some of the early and continued criticism of figurational studies of sport and leisure arises from the misunderstanding that Elias's aforementioned *magnum opus*, and its investigation of long-term structured processes of development at the social and individual levels, was tantamount to an analysis merely of violence and aggression to the relative exclusion of other important areas of research (see Stokvis, 1992; related responses from Dunning, 1992; Murphy *et al.*, 2000; Malcolm, 2002; and a commentary by Green *et al.*, 2005).[5]

Such is the 'intellectual force' (Rojek, 2008: 173) forged by figurational sociologists of sport and by work 'so closely associated with Dunning and the Leicester School' that Bairner describes them as having 'attracted admirers and critics in almost equal measure' (2008: 82) within the sociology of sport. This intellectual force within sport, allied to the breadth of figurational-informed research outside the sub-discipline, has also meant that some protagonists of other sociological paradigms or theoretical traditions in sport assume figurational sociology to have far greater dominance in sociology more generally. Yet, although 'sociologists in general have shown a growing interest in the figurational or process-sociological approach in recent years . . . it is nevertheless clearly the case that figurational sociology remains a much more influential theoretical framework within the sociology of sport than within the broader discipline of sociology more generally' (Waddington and Malcolm, 2008: 4). In particular, the work of the Leicester School in the 1980s played a key role in this, though this corpus of work has not been without its critics.

Perhaps one of the explanations for what has been described as the 'jaundiced', 'misplaced and ultimately unhelpful' criticism (Bairner, 2008: 94/82) aimed at the Leicester School's work on football hooliganism in the 1980s and 1990s comes from the fact that Dunning, his fellow members of the Leicester School, graduates and subsequent generations of figurational sociologists elsewhere have embodied an estimable commitment to 'the epistemological trajectory that . . . links their theoretical upbringing and their sociological interventions' (Bairner, 2008: 94). There is also the fact that, as is demonstrated throughout this monograph, the scope of the theory of civilizing processes was immense. In extending the trajectory of figurational-informed work over time, process sociologists have sought to demonstrate the applicability and differential explanatory role of the scientific (as opposed to the evaluative or moral) concept of civilization to a variety of seemingly unrelated and separate phenomena such as patterns of hygiene, gender relations, work, leisure, play, sport, celebrities, state formation, food and eating, globalization, national identities, nuclear war, drug use including tobacco, informalization processes, sex, race relations, criminology and manners amongst others. Be that as it may, the tempering of violence and aggression within societies, together with a long-term decline in most people's capacity for obtaining pleasure from inflicting pain on others and engaging in and witnessing violent acts, is the theme most commonly associated with figurational research. Perhaps, not surprisingly, this was a pivotal subject matter in *Quest for Excitement* (2008 [1986]).[6] However, the sub-title, *Sport and Leisure in the Civilizing Process*, hints much more at the extensive sociological groundwork that was laid by Elias and Dunning for the figurational study of sport and leisure beyond the themes of violence and aggression.[7]

Using sport as the medium through which to examine longer-term social processes, Elias and Dunning argue that in highly constrained, relatively highly 'civilized' societies, sports – as well as a range of other cultural and leisure activities – are to be understood not just in terms of 'relaxation' or a dualistic conception of *either* work *or* non-work (also described loosely as leisure). Rather, sports in their modern form are to be understood processually: that is, modern sports are by no means 'complete' in form or function, nor can they be viewed in isolation. Modern sports are also to be understood in developmental terms for their role in the socially generated need for pleasurable excitement and its pleasurable resolution. Here, the conceptual links to *The Civilizing Process* are apparent, most specifically in the social constraint towards self-restraint – that is, in an increase in the social pressure on people to exercise stricter, more continuous and more even self-control over their feelings and behaviour. In *Quest for Excitement*, Elias and Dunning established the case for understanding sport as a thoroughly social *and* sociological phenomenon – one that cannot be understood without reference to the overall social standards of 'conduct and sentiment' (2008 [1986]: 5) in which an increasing sensitivity to violence was one component. Elias himself noted that 'when we [he and Dunning] started on this work, the sociology of sport was still in its infancy' (2008 [1986]: 3). Certainly, Elias and Dunning were at the forefront in seeking to establish sport and leisure as 'serious' academic subjects in the 1960s and 1970s and they, along with a small group of similarly motivated sociologists at that time, faced intellectual ridicule arising from their contention that 'knowledge about sport was knowledge about society' (2008 [1986]: 3).[8]

Perhaps what set Elias and Dunning apart from their peers (most notably historians, Marxists, feminists and functionalists) in the 'early' academic study of sport was their prioritization of social scientific knowledge about sport and leisure that was of a particular kind – that which was characterized by the desire for a greater degree of detachment and which served a primary purpose of generating reality-congruent knowledge about the problems under investigation. In other words, their work did not have a prior political or moral objective other than to understand sport. Their passion came in the first instance from the pursuit of knowledge.[9] This primary scientific purpose involved 'a species of detour behaviour' that Elias terms the 'detour via detachment'. As Mennell noted, 'one of the results of a successful detour via detachment is greater human control of the forces – physical, biological or social – it is sought to understand' (1998: 163). In the UK and Western Europe, the rising concern at football hooliganism in the 1980s, the increasing globalization and politicization of 'mega' sporting events such as the Olympics amidst the 'frozen clinch'[10] (Elias, 2010 [1985]: 131–2, 153–7) between the United States, the Soviet Union and their various allies following the Cold War, led to the sociology of sport being recognized as having academic and practical application. In part response to this, Elias and Dunning and the emerging Leicester School were acutely concerned to maintain a relatively detached approach to the sociological study of sport, one that sought to maintain some distance from dominant ideologies and behaviour of the time and which amalgamated comparative as well as developmental perspectives into their analysis. In Dunning's words, it was:

> Norbert's conviction that the crying need for human beings is the production of a solid body of reliable knowledge about themselves, the complex societies that they form and why people recurrently drift into crisis after crisis, including war . . . Elias's view was that . . . programmes of action . . . were ideological and were continuing to produce the sort of unintended consequences that lay at the heart of the problem. (in Rojek, 2004: 339, 342–3)

For these reasons, *Quest for Excitement* was an intellectual departure from the then populist, often empiricist and ideologically driven functionalist, historical, Marxist and feminist analyses of sport and leisure. In it, Elias and Dunning established the distinction between the more culturally universal and less stipulative definition of sport and leisure in use by some writers at that time – one in which sport was used very generally to refer to physical activities beyond the work sphere (with or without the element of competition) – and the sociological and relational concept of sport to be 'used more concretely to refer to a group of competitive physical activities which are specifically modern in key respects and which first began to emerge in England, Scotland, Wales and Ireland – 'the Atlantic Isles' – in the eighteenth and nineteenth centuries' (Dunning *et al.*, 2004a: 8–9). Elias coined the term 'sportization' to refer to:

> a process in the course of which the rules of sports came more and more to be written down, nationally (subsequently internationally) standardized, more explicit, more precise, more comprehensive, orientated around an ethos of 'fair play' and providing equal chances for all participants to win, and with reducing and/or more strictly controlling opportunities for violent physical conduct (Dunning *et al.*, 2004a: 9).

Conceivably it might be said that, with some exceptions,[11] since the 1980s, figurational studies of the emergence and development of modern sport and leisure forms have focused far more on sport. Coincidentally, governments have come increasingly to view modern sport as a social, economic and political tool by which to achieve non-sporting objectives. The range of sports that have been studied within the figurational paradigm thus far includes Japanese martial arts, Gaelic sports, motor sports, gymnastics, baseball, basketball, cricket, soccer, American football, boxing, tennis, rugby union and league, rowing, cycling, horse racing, swimming, ice hockey, gymnastics, bird-watching, and shooting.

By way of contrast, 'questions of culture and consumption' (Rojek, 2008: 174) and studies of leisure have been comparably less developed by figurational sociologists since the 1980s. In 'Leisure in the sparetime spectrum' (2008 [1986], chapter 3),[12] Elias and Dunning argue that the balance between routinization and deroutinization is a feature of all sports and leisure activities. More particularly, the cathartic function of sport and leisure activities is evident in the generation *and* dissipation of tensions and pleasurable excitement.[13] As Dunning clarified, some 13 years after the first edition of *Quest for Excitement*, 'different sports, arts and leisure forms generate different levels of tension and they generate them differently' (1999a: 32). Crucially, the mimetic functions of leisure activities mean that 'all leisure activities are sparetime activities but not all sparetime activities are leisure activities' (Elias and Dunning, 2008 [1986]: 77). Some sparetime activities have a work-like character to them (such as household, family or personal routines) while deroutinization and decreasing social compulsion go farthest in leisure activities that are mainly sociable in function and in which individuals' own emotional satisfaction takes precedence over all other concerns, for example, pub, family and party gatherings, watching football or going to a play. The full significance of the conceptual category of the sparetime spectrum can be seen in the bypassing of the polarized concepts of work and leisure and the misconception that leisure is pure freedom (Maguire, 1992; Garrigou, 2008). More accurately, the character of sparetime (including leisure) activities changes in the course of civilizing processes in tandem with the balance between external constraints and self-restraint. Leisure activities 'provide chances for experiencing a pleasurable stirring-up of emotions, an enjoyable excitement which can be experienced in public and shared with others and which can be enjoyed with social approval and in good conscience' (Elias and Dunning, 2008 [1986]: 81). In this connection, the tension-bound balance between routinization and deroutinization within sparetime and leisure activities is an equally primary and enjoyable basis of their dynamics as is the risk of 'going to the brink' (2008 [1986]: 81).

Sport (which first acquired its modern connotation in eighteenth-century England) is also one such example of the risk of going to the brink within which 'a flexible balance also began to be established between the possibility of obtaining a high level of pleasurable combat or contest tension and what was regarded as reasonable protection against the chances of injury' (Dunning *et al.*, 2004a: 9).[14] Elias and Dunning argued that the sportization of pastimes occurred in two main waves – in the eighteenth and nineteenth centuries – in which the aristocracy and bourgeoisie respectively were mainly responsible for developments. Using this framework as a starting point, Maguire (1999) extended the work on sportization to include three more waves up to and including the late twentieth century. The third sportization phase began around 1870 and lasted until the 1920s and was associated with the 'take off' or 'differential diffusion of "English" sport forms' (1999: 83). In the fourth global sportization phase (1920s to the 1960s), the 'American version of the achievement sport ethos' (1999: 84) gained ascendancy over the amateur ethos associated with English and British sports in the first two waves. In this phase, 'English*men* were being increasingly beaten . . . by fellow occidentals at games that they felt they had, by birthright, a "God-given" right to be winners' (1999: 86, emphasis in original). This process was intensified in the fifth phase of sportization (from the 1960s onwards) in which Anglo/Euro and American control of sport began to wane on and off the playing field. 'This fifth phase of global sportization involves a degree of creolization of sport cultures – increasing varieties are evident' (1999: 87). For Elias and Dunning, and following them Maguire, modern sport fulfilled both mimetic and cathartic functions in that it involved a:

> greater emphasis on the enjoyable tension-excitement of the forepleasure, the human attempt to prolong the point-like pleasure of victory in the mock-battle of sport (and it) was symptomatic of a far-reaching change in the personality structure of human beings. (Elias and Dunning, 2008 [1986]: 9)

Conceived in these terms, *Quest for Excitement* was a pioneering text, and the authors' developmental interest in wider and more fundamental issues, above and beyond a series of apparently unconnected social and psychological data, was palpable. So too was their desire, as Elias expressed it much earlier, to pass on knowledge 'to younger men and women understanding and able enough to take it up and use it in their own way' (1952, cited in *Figurations*, No. 22, 2004). It is this developmental focus which has, perhaps, exercised earlier generations of figurational sociologists more, while younger generations have certainly strengthened the present-centred focus and applicability of the paradigm, though not to the detriment of maintaining developmental sensitivities – that is, without ignoring the impact of 'the past' on 'the present'. In this connection, figurational studies in the sociology of sport and leisure (at least in the Atlantic Isles) have so far been mainly concerned with the problem areas of the social aspects of sports injuries (for instance Roderick *et al.*, 2000; Sheard, 2006; Liston *et al.*, 2006; Pike and Maguire, 2003); sport, health and drugs (e.g., Waddington, 2000; Waddington and Smith, 2009); sport and race (Dunning, 1999b; Jarvie, 1992); sport, leisure and gender relations (e.g., Colwell, 1999; Mansfield, 2007; 2008; Liston, 2005; 2007; 2008; Velija and Malcolm, 2009); young people's sporting and leisure lives (for instance Smith and Green, 2005; Smith *et al.*, 2007); physical education (Green, 2002; 2008a; Green *et al.*, 2009; Smith and Parr, 2007); the globalization of sports, national identities and the migration of players and athletes (e.g., Bloyce, 2004; Liston and Moreland, 2009; Maguire, 1999; 2005; Maguire and Poulton, 1999; Maguire and Tuck, 2005; Molnar and Maguire, 2008); football hooliganism, spectator and player violence in sport (Dunning *et al.*, 1988; Dunning *et al.*, 2002); the development of modern sports in civilizing processes, not all of which are necessarily team or contact-based sports (e.g., Sheard, 2004; White, 2004; Malcolm, 2004; Smith, 2004; Lake, 2009); and the growing commercialization and professionalization of sport particularly at the elite levels (e.g., Dunning and Sheard, 2005 [1979]; Maguire, 1999).

Given the breadth and intellectual ambition of the figurational sociological approach, it is not possible here to delineate in any great detail the respective contributions of this inter-generational and singular corpus of work. More useful for present purposes might be a brief sketch of some of the key features therein, followed by a short commentary on the main controversies and critical debates that have arisen in and around figurational research on sport and leisure.

The 40-year corpus of figurational research on sport has, as we noted previously, spanned developmental and present-centred axes in studies of sport and leisure. It has also used and applied the theory of the civilizing processes in various ways to sports and leisure forms throughout the world. For example, Ohira's (2009) edited collection exemplifies Japanese applications of the figurational tradition in research on long distance relay running (*ekiden*) and baseball (*yakya*) while, in Norway, Skille and Waddington (2006) have investigated the success of 'alternative' sport and physical activities provided by the Sports City Programme. The Lusophone world has also begun to utilize the figurational approach (see, for example, Pinheiro, 2006; Gebara, 2004). Figurational sociologists have examined the sociogenesis and psychogenesis of identity formation as exemplified at national and individual levels (and through gendered and athletic identities) and, at one and the same time, they have also demonstrated the variable centrality of violence to an understanding of contact, non-contact, team and individual sports (see, for example, Dunning *et al.*, 2004a;

2004b). Beyond the confines of this research across time and space, there is also the careful application of particular figurational concepts as sensitizing tools in the sociology of sport. In other words, within the totality of Elias's work, there are a number of key heuristic tools that have yielded fruitful knowledge in their application. For instance, in building on 'civilizing *and* decivilizing processes' (Elias, 2000 [1939]), there is Malcolm's (2004) examination of decivilizing processes in imperial cricket and exemplifying the pursuit of an appropriate balance between 'involvement and detachment' (Elias, 2007 [1987]), there are Green's (2008a) circumspect comments on the role of ideology in physical education. Waddington and Smith (2009) discuss fantasy-laden thinking in the context of drug use in sport, while Maguire's lifelong scrutiny of aspects of the global–local nexus in sport (see for example Maguire, 1999) illustrates his appropriation of 'diminishing contrasts and increasing varieties' (Elias, 2000 [1939]: 382–7). Finally, 'games models' (Elias, 1978 [1970]: 71–103) form the conceptual basis for Hanstad, Smith and Waddington's (2008) study of the management of organizational change and unplanned outcomes within the World Anti-Doping Agency. Further illustrations of figurational sensitizing concepts include Liston's (2005) utilization of established–outsider relations and, connected to this, Velija and Malcolm's (2009) employment of habitus (including I-, we- and they- images) in research on sport and gender relations. Principally, however, this body of inter-generational work rests on the key process-sociology concepts of figuration and power,[15] and an appreciation of the ways in which the outcomes of social action – that is, of people, bound together in invisible chains of interdependence in which not all of them will necessarily know, or be aware of, each other – always and inevitably generate consequences which are both predictable and unplanned. Unintended consequences are an inevitable outcome of 'complex social processes involving the interweaving of the more-or-less goal-directed actions of large numbers of people' and which 'includes outcomes that no one has designed and no one has chosen' (Dunning *et al.*, 2004b: 200). In this connection, Maguire (1999: 209–10), for instance, outlines some of the intended and unintended outcomes of globalization processes in sport such as the ways in which the French 'now use soccer, in the form of the French Cup, to maintain links between their former colonies (Outre-Mer) and metropolitan France'. This was despite their earlier resistance to the import of so-called 'English' sports. The globalization of sport has also led, unintentionally, to the challenging of the dominant achievement model in the West and this is reflected in the emergence of snowboarding, extreme sports and the spread of martial arts to the West. Similarly, 'legacy gigantism' (Bloyce and Smith, 2010: 186) is 'a broad unintended consequence of the increasing competition to host the [Olympic] Games between cities and governments . . . where each bidding city competes with the others to host an Olympic Games with the "best legacies ever".'

Such precise application of theoretical concepts has widened and deepened the scope of figurational studies of sport. Yet, at the same time, this precision has generated some controversy for critics because it has apparently contributed to theoretical isolationism and reflected an almost singleminded adherence to the figurational paradigm. These controversies arise from the confusion which currently surrounds the ways in which sociologists and academics more generally seek to engage in 'critique' and 'criticism' (see Kilminster's essay in this monograph) – that is to say, making explicit the hitherto implicit idea that figurational sociologists must in the end come to disagree with Elias's work and that, if they do not, they are failing to engage in a critique of that work. It is a regrettable fact that, while the scientific process involves careful examination and revision of theories, the term 'critique' has acquired an almost theological sense. In this regard, progress in the field does not necessarily mean a demolition of one's own or others' theoretical foundations while robust critique and counter-critique such as that between Collins (2005) and Curry, Dunning and Sheard (2006), for example, are crucial to the advancement of knowledge about sport. It is to these and other controversies that we now turn.

Claims about the alleged tendency of figurational sociologists to 'worship' the work of Elias (see Giulianotti, 2004: 151, for example) and, in so doing, to exaggerate the explanatory power of civilizing processes and violence control in particular, stem, in part, from the refusal of figurational sociologists to accept misinterpretations of Elias's work based on a limited reading of his work or the isolation of aspects of this work from the totality of his arguments. Conversely, figurational sociologists have advanced criticisms of Elias's work, none more so than in the field of sport. For example, Dunning (1999a) has suggested that Elias's concept of violence is too general, and he is also critical of Elias's discussion on 'stress tensions' in sport and leisure activities, while Bloyce and Murphy (2007) have engaged in a critique of the reliability of Elias's work on established–outsider relations. Figurational sociologists have also gained much from 'thinking in conjunction with, and in opposition to' (Mansfield, 2002: 331) various theoretical approaches, as is demonstrated by: Dunning *et al.*'s (1988) use of Suttles's (1968) theory of ordered segmentation and defended neighbourhoods as a building block for their explanations of football hooliganism; Mansfield's claim to synthesize aspects of figurational and feminist work in studies of leisure and fitness cultures; Roderick's (2006) employment of the work of Goffman alongside Elias to investigate professional footballers' experiences of pain and injury; Maguire's (1999: 215) identification of 'common ground with other sociological approaches', such as that of Robertson and Featherstone, in his work on the globalization of sport; and Malcolm's (2009) combining of notions of medical uncertainty with the figurational concept of interdependence.[16] There have also been instances where, as has been noted, figurational perspectives on the development of sport have benefited from focusing attention elsewhere than merely on civilizing processes (Murphy, Sheard and Waddington, 2000). Of course, sociologists from other discrete theoretical backgrounds like Marxism and feminisms have also been criticized for their so-called 'isolationism'. This criticism is a consequence of the ways in which sociology (with its sub-disciplines like the sociology of sport) is at present a multi-paradigmatic discipline and one which, like many other academic disciplines, is characterized by relations of tension and conflict. As Dunning and Mennell have suggested:

> Arguably both symptomatic of and contributing to this state of affairs is the fact that practitioners of the subject have not yet managed to establish a degree of inter-generational continuity in concept-formation, theory-building and research that is anywhere near comparable with what has been achieved in the considerably more advanced natural sciences. (2003: ix)

Be that as it may, figurational sociologists have, it is suggested, attained a degree of inter-generational continuity which has, paradoxically, led to criticisms of isolationism on the one hand and over-adherence to a theoretical framework on the other. Maguire (1999) also highlights the problems identified by critics of the figurational paradigm who argue that multidirectionality and multicausality (two hallmarks of figurational or process sociology) lead to the downplaying of particular explanatory concepts and processes such as class or gender. It was this issue of theoretical primacy accorded to class relations, and to class-based domination in particular, that has been at the heart of a debate between figurational sociologists and Marxists/neo-Marxists.

Given the totality of Elias's work and its sensitivity to multi-causal and multidirectional processes at work in social life, it is perhaps not surprising that Elias's polymorphous conception of power relations was the focus of criticisms by Marxists such as Rigauer (1981), and neo-Marxists (using hegemony theory) such as John Hargreaves (1986) and Gruneau (1983). Put simply, they were concerned with the apparent downplaying by figurational sociologists of class-based domination in sport. For them sport is always (and inevitably) involved in the process of maintaining class hegemony and the political power of the bourgeoisie in particular. In Hargreaves's own words, 'we are concerned with the relation between sports and working-class culture, and the extent to which sport has played a role in accommodating the British working class to the social order' (1986: 2). In responding to this charge, as the contributors to *Sport Histories* (Dunning *et al.*, 2004c) attest, for figurational sociologists class-based domination is but one important form of domination that plays a central role in understanding the development of modern sport.[17] Taken together, the significance of the contributions to *Sport Histories* is that they challenge the theoretical *primacy* accorded to class relations by neo-Marxists. They also demonstrate very clearly the role of other forms of domination and power including, for example, changing power relations within and between English public schools in the eighteenth and nineteenth centuries, civilizing processes in boxing, and technical developments in gymnastics – the latter being a response to concerns of physical safety in particular. As has been acknowledged by Elias himself and others such as Dunning *et al.* (2004c), an exclusive focus on the explanatory power of class relations or gender, for example, would most likely generate an inadequate understanding of modern sport. In this connection, it was the charge of gender- (if not political) neutrality that similarly led feminists such as Jennifer Hargreaves (1992, 1996) to criticize Elias and Dunning's, and later Dunning's sole-authored, work on the sociology of sport.[18] Her criticism was twofold and centred on Elias's notion of involvement–detachment, alleging that this concept claimed complete detachment and 'objectivity' as the hallmark of figurational research, and on Dunning's failure to investigate gender relations, as if to suggest that research on women (and not men) was analogous to research on gender. In other words, feminists eschewed the concept of involvement–detachment for its perceived connotations of intellectual superiority, objectivity and value-neutrality and, perhaps, for its apparent promotion of men's view of science and traditional notions of a scientific method (Liston, 2007). For feminists, 'theory is only useful if it *informs* political action and practice and it is also *developed* out of these' (Scraton and Flintoff, 2002: 3, emphasis in original). Consequently, feminists (including the second and third waves) maintain that facts are not apolitical.

Putting the figurational sociological position on gender relations succinctly, sensitivity to the variable functional interdependence of the sexes means that, for them, gender relations can be equally, or more, or less, important than other dimensions of social relations. The same can be said of class or race relations of course. A commitment to changing class, race-based or gender inequalities might be one outcome of figurational research, but not the only one.

> Process sociologists still believe that the task of a sociologist entails being both a hunter and destroyer of myths and the provider of relatively adequate reality-congruent knowledge. What better form of empowerment is there than to provide citizens with such knowledge? (Maguire, 1999: 215)

The types of knowledge espoused by figurational sociologists and their critics were at the heart of the exchange between figurational sociologists and feminists in the 1990s, including Dunning's (1999a) chapter on gender relations in sport. As was argued by Liston (2007), the exchange was less than fruitful because of the ideological differences displayed by adherents of the two approaches concerning the role of theory and the related misconception that the involvement–detachment balance was equivalent to value-neutrality and objectivity. Subsequent to this, there has been a discussion amongst younger generations of sociologists with varying degrees of commitment to feminist and figurational sociology concerning the potential for theoretical synthesis between these two theoretical paradigms (see Colwell, 1999; Liston, 2008; Mansfield, 2007, 2008), though this debate has not been without some discord. Colwell in particular drew what she saw as the boundaries between feminist and figurational work on gender which are, for her, characterized primarily by the latter's commitment to an ideology-banishing scientific model. Building on this, she maintained allegiance to the figurational scientific model and discriminated between this and other work which could lay claim to being *informed* by (but not necessarily fully committed to) this ideology-banishing model such as that of Mansfield (2007, 2008). In so doing, she reinvigorated a longstanding debate concerning the differing approaches taken to the challenges associated with the scientific status of sociology, the use of the sociological imagination and the ubiquitous problem of values.

In the desire for theoretical, conceptual and linguistic precision, 'scholars introduce concepts and ideas that are often distinctive to their theoretical positions' (Liston, 2008: 127). This desire for precision has been at the heart of synthesizing developments in feminist and figurational sociological work on sport and leisure (Liston, 2008), as it has been at the core of the inter-generational body of work within the figurational paradigm over the past 40 years or so. By way of extension, this desire for intergenerational precision by figurational sociologists might also explain the spurious criticism that they adhere apparently single-mindedly to the figurational paradigm (see, for example, Giulianotti, 1999; 2004; 2005 and a related commentary by Bairner, 2008). While there is a characteristic linguistic specificity associated with figurational sociology, to criticise its development and consistent use on grounds of single-mindedness would be to fail to understand the desire by Elias and figurational sociologists to develop language and concepts that were, for them, a necessary requirement to bypassing various conceptual problems associated with *homo clausus* approaches to understanding the individual–society relationship and avoiding the hodiecentric trap. Hence, Elias's use of the grounding concept of figuration was a deliberate attempt to bypass and reconceptualize the parameters of *homo clausus* sociological approaches (such as agency–structure, action–structure, or 'individual' and 'society') and to denote the complex webs of interdependent relationships between people (which he conceptualizes as *homines aperti*). As Goudsblom puts it, 'It makes sense, therefore, to state quite explicitly that we are concerned with *people*, bonded together in dynamic constellations which, because of their specific nature, may best be designated by a specific generic name: figurations' (1977: 6–7). The commitment by figurational sociologists to this particular epistemological trajectory is built upon Elias's work on the sociology of knowledge (2007 [1987], 2009) and his view of wider problems in the discipline of sociology such as the fallacy of treating mankind in the singular (Goudsblom, 1977), itself reflected in the emergence of reflexive and dialogic approaches (and, of late, action research). The second fallacy 'is that of treating man and society as static givens . . . our whole conceptual apparatus is attuned to permanence rather than change . . . In all of us is a deeply-rooted tendency towards hodiecentrism or today-centred thinking, towards taking as immutable the world as it is now' (Goudsblom, 1977: 7). These fallacies, one variant of which includes latterly postmodernist and poststructuralist turns, have led many sociologists to shun the perils that can arise in the devising of 'theories of a wide scope, one of the chief perils . . . being the exposure of an ideological viewpoint' (Goudsblom, 1977: 169). The immense scope of figurational sociology leaves this paradigm open to criticism on these grounds but, 'if any conclusion can be drawn, it is . . . that sociological ideals reflect a balance between 'knowledge' and 'fantasy', the ratio of which has to be investigated in each instance' (Goudsblom, 1977: 172). This does not mean that theorists must always challenge systems of ideological belief that serve to maintain the dominant positions held by various social groups or that they self-consciously adopt their own viewpoints. This would be to fall foul of the hodiecentrist trap. By the same token, in the sport–gender controversy, the limits to a potentially successful synthesis between the two theoretical approaches were evident in the dissonance between the guiding principle of feminisms – to evaluate and challenge the status quo of gender/sex relations – and Elias's active minimizing of the intrusion of evaluation and idealized pictures of particular sports or sports people, at least in the process of conducting sociological research (Colwell, 1999; Liston, 2007). In point of fact, Elias never excluded the possibility that evaluation might indeed be one outcome of research. As Quilley and Loyal put it:

> The development of a scientific sociology depends not upon the eradication of passion or a deep sense of 'involvement' on the part of social scientists. Rather it requires the emergence of forms of 'secondary involvement' in the process of sociological investigation itself (as opposed to immediate politico-ethical attachment), and a 'passion for detachment'. (2004: 44)

This having been said, 'it is true that process sociologists are more circumspect with regard to predicting the future' (Maguire, 1999: 215) or, perhaps more specifically, their *preferred* future. Of course, the fact that social processes are in a constant state of flux makes prediction very difficult indeed.[19] Nonetheless, some figurational writers are more explicit than others in terms of, for example, declaring their detour via detachment and being against the intrusion of political ideologies into their research. Fewer are explicit about the ways in which, through a process of secondary involvement, they use this reality-congruent knowledge to formulate more effective, more realistic and more reliable ways for dealing with the problem at hand. Some exceptions might be Waddington and Smith's (2009) consideration of the future possibility of differentiating anti-doping policy on a sport by sport basis, as well as the relative effectiveness of harm minimization/reduction policy over the more punitive 'detect and punish' approach currently adopted by the World Anti-Doping Agency (WADA).[20] Green (2008b) tentatively predicts an examinable if not 'academic' basis for the future of physical education in the UK.[21] Similarly, Bloyce and Smith (2010: 78) tender a note of caution that the continued championing of the wider (and non-sporting) social benefits of school sports partnerships by those working in school-based youth sports development schemes 'could be viewed as less of an opportunity and more of a threat to the future of PE (physical education) and sport in schools'. This more explicit commentary might go some way towards silencing those critics who perceive figurational sociology as being politically quiet, theoretically obscure and having little practical relevance.

Today, of course, Elias's work is equally noted for his critique of the atheoretical approach to history and of the related tendency of sociologists to research 'structures without history'.[22] Put differently, Elias argues against the idea of 'history without structure, a collation of details determined more by traditions and transient fashions than by systematic cross-fertilization with any consistent theory' (2008: 138). It was in this context that figurational sociologists and historians of sport demonstrated their respective differing commitments to sociological versus empiricist history (see, for example, Collins, 2005; Curry *et al.*, 2006). Briefly, Collins charged Dunning and Sheard (2005 [1979]) with exaggerating levels of violence in their seminal work on rugby union, presenting long-term change as linear progress and projecting the present into the past. In their robust response, Curry *et al.* (2006) accepted the charge of exaggerating levels of violence in Northern (English) rugby but strongly rebutted Collins's criticism of the status-rivalry hypothesis for the bifurcation of soccer and rugby as well as his accusations of teleological thinking. In this connection, they also clarified the differences between a 'retrospective judgement about a factually observable sequence [and] a statement about an inevitable progressive trend' (Curry *et al.*, 2006: 117), the latter criticism arising from the misconception that the application of a wide ranging theory of scope and depth, such as that of figurational sociology, equates to a form of linear if not evolutionary thinking.

The predilection for atheoretical work – that is, to dissociate theory from empirical research where the latter exists in isolation from any theoretical model within which the data are analysed, explained and interpreted, thus becoming little more than a 'synthesis of scattered notions and facts' (Goudsblom, 1977: 19) – may be one outcome of the bifurcation of history and sociology into apparently unrelated (if not competing) disciplines. It is also a reflection, perhaps more recently, of that generation of academics whose attitudes to sociology and history are shaped by the wider trend towards non-cumulative knowledge, the related tendency to 'slay the master', and to practise process reduction. These practitioners who are more wedded to the more reflexive contemporary kinds of sociological and historical academic activities may view the figurational pursuit of 'the methodological imperative of greater detachment and suspension of value-judgements, pursued rigorously and *in its pure form alone*, [as] . . . simply inflexible and even authoritarian' (Kilminster, 2004: 38).[23] Indeed, if Bairner (2008) is correct, then the figurational emphasis on scope and greater detachment has engendered tensions within the academic study of sport such that it has attracted almost equal numbers of admirers and critics.

The kinds of debates briefly reviewed here are certainly more than a sideshow to readers of the sociology of sport. Indeed, the role played by figurational researchers of sport in challenging the differentiation and proliferation of this sub-discipline is a principal example of what we might regard as 'good theoretical practice'. Without taking refuge in impenetrable and theoretical obliqueness, they have sought a 'bold scale of ambition' in their theoretical enterprise while at the same time always acknowledging that 'their work should be judged as no more than an early stage in the scientific understanding of the sports process' (Rojek, 2008: 173) – that is to say, this corpus of work should be viewed as a 'preliminary phase of long-term inter-generational labour' (Rojek, 2008: 174). Perhaps the most enduring legacy of the corpus of work conducted by figurational sociologists of sport is that, above all, it has enhanced Elias and Dunning's refutation of the claim that 'physical' phenomena like sport and leisure were of lower value than intellectual activities. In actual fact, Elias's conceptualization of human beings 'in the round' – that is, in terms of human movement, emotions, thought and rationality – laid the basis for the development of a theoretical paradigm which has attained notable prominence in the sociology of sport and leisure. Elias's work can be (and has been) empirically tested, modified and expanded in a number of ways, especially in relation to the overall direction of European civilizing process (though the use of the term 'European' here should not be taken as support for the misinformed suggestion that his work was Anglo- or Euro-centric), in the civilizing consequences of decivilizing developments in Britain, France and elsewhere, and in the timeframe that Elias himself used. Elias was, for example, always fully aware of the problems that loss of empire was raising for Britain, France and the other European colonial powers (Elias, 1996 [1989]: 4). His work can also be tested in relation to the adequacy of his theoretical perspective *vis-à-vis* processes of state formation, pacification and functional democratization in other countries – that is, by the applicability of his work on the sociogenesis and psychogenesis of civilizing processes in hitherto unexplored countries and the ways in which these processes are related to behavioural and normative developments at the levels of manners and habitus. Within this paradigm, the figurational sociology of sport tradition is well placed to continue to engage in meaningful and knowledge-based dialogue with fellow sociologists in order to demonstrate that knowledge about sport is undeniably central to knowledge about society and *vice versa* because, 'for sociologists, the Socratic imperative implies a quest for understanding ourselves as social individuals, as interdependent human beings' (Goudsblom, 1977: 203).

Notes

1 More specifically, he resists 'explanations that presuppose the overweening, deterministic might of social structures or the pure agency of individualistic voluntarism. Anthropological and historical strains within sociology ensure that I am hostile to the evolutionism of structural-functionalists like Parsons and (less nakedly) the cross-cultural conservatism of Elias' (Giulianotti, 2005: 210).

2 Following the debates centred on explanations of football hooliganism in the 1990s, Maguire, (2008: 111), for instance, points to lessons regarding process thinking and the fallacy of false dichotomies which he claimed 'were lost on a new generation of researchers'.

3 'Indeed, if sociology were a sport, Elias would win the "comeback of the century award"' (Gordon, 2002: 68).

4 Rojek (2008: 173) puts it as follows: 'Theirs [figurational sociologists'] is a holistic approach to the phenomenon of sports which paradoxically, recognizes the 'partiality' of their own perspective in the sense of acknowledging that their work should be judged as no more than an early stage in the scientific understanding of the sports process'.

5 Subsequently, this misunderstanding, as well as the singular corpus of thinking that has emerged within figurational studies of sport, also laid the basis in part for the associated misplaced criticism that figurational sociologists adopt an unquestioning and almost single-minded

adherence to the theoretical paradigm (see Giulianotti, 1999, 2005, and a commentary by Bairner, 2008).

6 Elias (2000 [1939]: 161–72) referred in this regard to a dampening of *Angrifflust* – literally, 'joy in attacking'.

7 Only two of Elias's books were co-authored, the first with John Scotson (of which established–outsider relations was the focus (see Elias and Scotson, 2008 [1965]), and the second, *Quest for Excitement*, with Eric Dunning, first published in 1986 and now available as an enlarged and revised edition in the Collected Works (2008, Volume 7). Following Eric Dunning's (1961) MA thesis, entitled 'Early Stages in the Development of Football as an Organised Game', which was co-supervised by Elias, the collaboration between them culminated in *Quest for Excitement*, which is, at one and the same time, a groundbreaking text for the sociology of sport and leisure and, more importantly, it is a principal contribution to sociology more generally. Eric Dunning, who is now widely regarded as one of the 'founding fathers' of the sociology of sport, concentrated on football through most of his career. The 2008 edition of *Quest for Excitement* includes the addition of a previously unpublished discussion (chapter 5) by Elias entitled 'The genesis of sport as a sociological problem, part 2', and the updating by Dunning of chapter 12 on 'Football hooliganism as an emergent global idiom'. There is also an added postscript by Dunning on gender (chapter 11).

8 Mennell (1998: 140) describes the sociology of sport in the 1960s as 'an unfashionable backwater' while Rojek (2008: 174) describes it as having been seen as 'peripheral, even "trivial" by the upper echelons within the sociological community' in the 1970s and early 1980s. Dunning (1992: 224) himself noted 'a contemptuous dismissal of sport as an area of sociological enquiry'.

9 In this connection, Curry, Dunning and Sheard (2006) describe Elias as a hardheaded realist.

10 In later writings, Elias more often used the related term 'double bind', which he borrowed from Gregory Bateson.

11 See, for example, Maguire and Mansfield's work on fitness cultures (1998), Rojek's discussion of the consumption of leisure (1995) and, Smith *et al.* (2007) study of young people's sports *and* leisure lives.

12 This was a metaphor for conceptual categories named after the colour spectrum in which colours usually blend into or intersect with one another.

13 Elias and Dunning argue that sport and leisure did not have a simple cathartic function as traditionally understood – that is, sport and leisure did not simply provide a release valve for pressures built up elsewhere (for example at work). Rather, sport and leisure firstly generate (pleasurable) tensions before providing a release for these tensions.

14 Elias and Dunning (2008 [1986]) differentiate between sports, games and sport-games in which the latter can involve physical competition but be played (e.g., baseball, rugby union or soccer) while the former always involve physical competition (e.g., athletics or boxing). Games usually involve non-physical competition between players (e.g., chess).

15 Power is polymorphous in form and an aspect of all interdependent social relations, because all relationships of interdependence involve a balance of power – or, better expressed (because the 'balance' is by no means always equal), a more or less unequal 'power ratio'. Elias also argues that power 'is not an amulet possessed by one person and not by another; it is a structural characteristic of human relationships – of *all* human relationships' (1978 [1970]: 74).

16 The associated risk here is an eclectic use of Eliasian concepts that may, unintentionally or otherwise, reproduce and reinforce some of the problematic practices in contemporary sociological theory.

17 Dunning (2008: 283) contends that figurational sociologists were, in fact, 'among the first sociologists to recognize that football hooliganism is not and probably never has been solely working-class'.

18 Dunning's postscript to 'Sport as a male preserve: notes on the social sources of masculine identity and its transformations', in the new edition of *Quest for Excitement* (2008 [1986]: 257–9) is a revealing insight into the difficulties of practising the balance between involvement and detachment, not least in terms of grappling with the 'rational and emotional dimensions' of his involvement with his wife, from whom he was divorcing at the time of writing the original

chapter and, related to this, what he describes as 'the painful realization that a substantial amount of exploitation and taking for granted of females has always undergirded male participation in sport' (p. 258). Given the less than fruitful exchange that took place subsequently between Dunning (with Sheard, and later Maguire) and feminist writers on sport, this is a remarkable admission. So too is the short account of his socialization of the idea that men should not strike women. If our understanding of the sport–gender nexus is to be extended, then this postscript will prompt some reactions in feminist and figurational academic communities, for his relational and processual work on gender has run counter to the now-dominant trend in which most of the empirical research on women's sports has been conducted by women on women and a similar pattern is evident in research on men in sport. It is as if the structural imbalances in sport (differential rates of participation and organizational capacity between the sexes) have found an almost opposite expression in research on gender and sport: today, we arguably know far more, empirically at least, about women's gendered experiences in sport than we do men's, and this is almost certainly the case in Western Europe. Dunning's approach to the relationship between sport and patriarchy is exemplified best in the three case studies in this chapter: the development of modern combat sport; the emergence and relative decline of the macho subculture in rugby union; and the phenomenon of football hooliganism in Britain.

19 This is somewhat ironic, given that Rojek (2004: 346) highlighted the prescience of Elias's work.

20 'We have also suggested that WADA policy is likely to be ineffective in terms of protecting the health of athletes and that, if this is indeed one of WADA's policy objectives – as WADA publicly claims – then it is perhaps time for WADA seriously to consider alternative approaches to the problems associated with the use of performance-enhancing drugs, with harm reduction policies perhaps being amongst the more useful and realistic policy options to be considered' (Waddington and Smith, 2009: 230).

21 'The upshot of a configuration of the twin processes of sportization and academicization could well be that the term "physical *education*" becomes increasingly associated with, and reserved for, examinable (and especially academic) forms of the subject, while "traditional" PE – rebranded as "school sport" – is moved to the margins of the curriculum (that is, to extra-curricular PE and sports clubs)' (Green, 2008a: 232–33).

22 'What is of enduring value in the work of Elias is his insistence that we recognise the value of slow, unfolding processes of history for understanding the present' (Scambler, 2005: 157).

23 Figurational sociologists of sport are an exemplar of 'sociologists still wedded (more or less) exclusively to the greater detachment, fantasy-control, ideology-banishing model of scientific activity' (Kilminster, 2004: 38).

References

Dates given in square brackets are those of first publication.

Bairner, Alan, (2008), 'The Leicester School and the study of football hooliganism', in Dominic Malcolm and Ivan Waddington, (eds), *Matters of Sport: Essays in Honour of Eric Dunning*. London: Routledge: 81–96.

Bloyce, Daniel, (2004), 'Baseball: myths and modernization', in Eric Dunning, Dominic Malcolm and Ivan Waddington, (eds), *Sport Histories: Figurational Studies of the Development of Modern Sports*. London: Routledge: 88–103.

Bloyce, Daniel and Patrick Murphy, (2007), 'Involvement and detachment, from principles to practice: A critical reassessment of *The Established and the Outsiders*', *Irish Journal of Sociology*, 16, 1: 3–21.

Bloyce, Daniel and Andy Smith, (2010), *Sport Policy and Development: An Introduction*. London: Routledge.

Coakley, Jay and Eric Dunning, (eds), (2000), *Handbook of Sports Studies*, London: Sage.

Coakley, Jay and Elizabeth Pike, (2009), *Sports in Society: Issues and Controversies*, London: Open University Press/McGraw Hill.

Collins, Tony, (2005), 'History, sociology and the "civilizing process"', *Sport in History*, 25, 2: 289–306.

Colwell, Sharon, (1999), 'Feminisms and figurational sociology: contributions to understandings of sport, physical education and sex/gender', *European Physical Education Review*, 5, 3: 219–40.

Curry, Graham, Eric Dunning and Kenneth Sheard, (2006), 'Sociological versus empiricist history: some comments on Tony Collins's 'History, theory and the "civilizing process"', *Sport in History*, 26, 1: 110–23.

Dunning, Eric, (1992), 'Figurational sociology and the sociology of sport: some concluding remarks', in Eric Dunning and Chris Rojek, (eds), *Sport and Leisure in the Civilizing Process*. London: Macmillan: 221–84.

Dunning, Eric, (1999a), *Sport Matters: Sociological Studies of Sport, Violence and Civilization*. London: Routledge.

Dunning, Eric, (1999b), 'Sport in the process of racial stratification: the case of the USA', in *Sport Matters*, London: Routledge: 179–218.

Dunning, Eric, (2008), 'Football hooliganism as an emergent idiom', in Norbert Elias and Eric Dunning, *Quest for Excitement: Sport and Leisure in the Civilizing Process*, Collected Works, Vol. 7, Dublin: UCD Press: 260–90.

Dunning, Eric and Stephen Mennell, (2003), 'Editors' Introduction', in *Norbert Elias*, 4 vols, London: Sage: ix–xxxvii.

Dunning, Eric and Kenneth Sheard, (2005 [1979]), *Barbarians, Gentlemen and Players: A Sociological Study of the Development of Rugby Football*, 2nd edn., London: Routledge.

Dunning, Eric, Dominic Malcolm and Ivan Waddington, (2004a), 'Introduction: history, sociology and the sociology of sport: the work of Norbert Elias', in Eric Dunning, Dominic Malcolm and Ivan Waddington, (eds), *Sport Histories: Figurational Studies of the Development of Modern Sports*, London: Routledge: 1–14.

Dunning, Eric, Dominic Malcolm and Ivan Waddington, (2004b), 'Conclusion: figurational sociology and the development of modern sport', in Eric Dunning, Dominic Malcolm and Ivan Waddington, (eds), *Sport Histories: Figurational Studies of the Development of Modern Sports*, London: Routledge: 191–206.

Dunning, Eric, Dominic Malcolm and Ivan Waddington, (eds), (2004c), *Sport Histories: Figurational Studies of the Development of Modern Sports*, London: Routledge.

Dunning, Eric, Patrick Murphy and John Williams, (1988), *The Roots of Football Hooliganism*, London: Routledge.

Dunning, Eric, Patrick Murphy, Ivan Waddington and Antonios Astrinakis, (eds), (2002), *Fighting Fans: Football Hooliganism as a World Problem*, Dublin: UCD Press.

Elias, Norbert, (1978 [1970]), *What is Sociology?* London: Hutchinson. [*Studies on the Genmans*, Collected Works, Vol. 5, forthcoming].

Elias, Norbert, (1996 [1989]), *The Germans: Power Struggles and the Development of Habitus in the Nineteenth and Twentieth Centuries*, Cambridge: Polity. [Revised and enlarged edition, Collected Works, Vol. 11, forthcoming].

Elias, Norbert, (2000 [1939]), *The Civilizing Process*, rev. edn, Oxford: Blackwell. [Revised edition, *On the Process of Civilization*, Collected Works, Vol. 3, forthcoming].

Elias, Norbert, (2006 [1969]), *The Court Society*, Collected Works, Vol. 2, Dublin: UCD Press.

Elias, Norbert, (2007 [1987]), *Involvement and Detachment*, Collected Works, Vol. 8, Dublin: UCD Press.

Elias, Norbert, (2008), 'The genesis of sport as a sociological problem, part 2', in Norbert Elias and Eric Dunning, *Quest for Excitement: Sport and Leisure in the Civilizing Process*, Collected Works, Vol. 2, Dublin: UCD Press: 134–49. [This essay did not appear in the original 1986 edition of *Quest for Excitement*].

Elias, Norbert, (2009), *Essays I: On the Sociology of Knowledge and the Sciences*, Collected Works, Vol. 8, Dublin: UCD Press.

Elias, Norbert, (2010 [1985]), *Humana Conditio*, in *The Loneliness of the Dying and Humana Conditio*, Collected Works, Vol. 6, Dublin: UCD Press.

Elias, Norbert and Eric Dunning, (2008 [1986]) *Quest for Excitement: Sport and Leisure in the Civilizing Process*, rev. and enlarged edn., Collected Works, Vol. 7, Dublin: UCD Press.

Elias, Norbert and John Scotson, (2008 [1965]), *The Established and the Outsiders*, rev. and enlarged edn., Collected Works, Vol. 4, Dublin: UCD Press.

Figurations: Newsletter of the Norbert Elias Foundation, (2004), 22: 20, available at http://www.norberteliasfoundation.nl/figurations.php. Accessed 30 March 2011.

Garrigou, Alain, (2008), 'Illusio' in Sport', in Malcolm, Dominic and Ivan Waddington, (eds), *Matters of Sport: Essays in Honour of Eric Dunning*, London: Routledge: 163–71.

Gebara, Ademir, (2004), 'Education and leisure in the theory of the civilizing process: first contacts between Portuguese and Brazilians', *Journal of the Second Week in History*, 2: 134–44 (in Portuguese).

Giulianotti, Richard, (1999), *Football: A Sociology of the Global Game*, Cambridge: Polity Press.

Giulianotti, Richard, (2004), *Sport and Modern Social Theorists*, London: Palgrave Macmillan.

Giulianotti, Richard, (2005), *Sport: A Critical Sociology*. London: Polity Press.

Gordon, Daniel, (2002), 'The canonization of Norbert Elias in France: a critical perspective'. *French Politics, Culture & Society*, 20: 68–94.

Goudsblom, Johan, (1977), *Sociology in the Balance*. Oxford: Basil Blackwell.

Green, Ken, (2002), 'Physical education teachers in their figurations: a sociological analysis of everyday "philosophies" in physical education', *Sport, Education and Society*, 7, 1: 65–83.

Green, Ken, (2008a), 'Physical education and figurational sociology: an appreciation of the work of Eric Dunning', *Sport and Society*, 9, 4: 650–64.

Green, Ken, (2008b), *Understanding Physical Education*, London: Sage.

Green, Ken, Katie Liston, Andy Smith and Daniel Bloyce, (2005), 'Violence, competition and the development and emergence of modern sports; reflections on the Stokvis–Malcolm debate', *International Review for the Sociology of Sport*, 40, 1: 119–23.

Green, Ken, Andy Smith and Miranda Thurston, (2009), 'Busy doing nothing? Physical education teachers' perceptions of young people's participation in leisure-sport', *Sport, Education and Society*, 14, 4: 401–20.

Gruneau, Richard, (1983), *Class, Sports, and Social Development*, Amherst, MA: University of Massachusetts Press.

Hanstad, Dag Vidar, Andy Smith and Ivan Waddington, (2008), 'The establishment of the World Anti-Doping Agency: a study of the management of organizational change and unplanned outcomes', *International Review for the Sociology of Sport*, 43, 3: 227–49.

Hargreaves, John, (1986), *Sport, Power and Culture*, Oxford: Polity.

Hargreaves, John, (1992), 'Sex, gender and the body in sport and leisure: has there been a civilizing process?', in Eric Dunning and Chris Rojek, (eds), *Sport and Leisure in the Civilizing Process*, London: Macmillan: 161–83.

Hargreaves, John, (1996), *Sporting Females: Critical issues in the history and sociology of women's sports*, London: Routledge.

Jarvie, Grant, (1992), 'Sport, power and dependency in Southern Africa', in Eric Dunning and Chris Rojek, (eds), *Sport and Leisure in the Civilizing Process*, London: Macmillan: 183–200.

Jarvie, Grant and Joseph Maguire, (eds), (1994), *Sport and Leisure in Social Thought*, London: Routledge.

Kilminster, Richard, (2004), 'From distance to detachment: knowledge and self-knowledge in Elias's theory of involvement and detachment', in Steve Loyal and Stephe Quilley, (eds), *The Sociology of Norbert Elias*, Cambridge: Cambridge University Press: 25–41.

Lake, Robert J., (2009), 'Real Tennis and the Civilizing Process', *Sport in History*, 29, 4: 553–76.

Liston, Katie, (2005), 'Established–outsider relations between males and females in sports in Ireland', *Irish Journal of Sociology*, 14, 1: 66–85.

Liston, Katie, (2007), 'Revisiting the feminist-figurational sociology exchange', *Sport in Society*, 10, 4: 623–645.

Liston, Katie, (2008), 'The problem of ideology in making sense of physical education and sport: Reflections on the Colwell-Mansfield debate', *European Physical Education Review*, 14, 1: 123–33.

Liston, Katie and Elizabeth Moreland, (2009), 'Hockey and habitus: sport and national identity in Northern Ireland', *New Hibernia Review*, 13, 4: 127–40.

Liston, Katie, Dean Reacher, Andy Smith and Ivan Waddington, (2006), 'Managing pain and injury in non-elite Rugby Union and Rugby League: a case study of players at a British university', *Sport in Society*, 9, 3: 388–402.

Loyal, Steve and Stephen Quilley (eds), (2004), *The Sociology of Norbert Elias*, Cambridge: Cambridge University Press.

Maguire, Joseph, (1992), 'Towards a sociological theory of sport and the emotions: a process-sociological perspective', in Eric Dunning and Chris Rojek, (eds), *Sport and Leisure in the Civilizing Process*, London: Macmillan: 96–120.

Maguire, Joseph, (1999), *Global Sport: Identities, Societies, Civilizations*, Cambridge: Polity.

Maguire, Joseph, (2005), *Power and Global Sport: Zones of Prestige, Emulation and Resistance*, London: Routledge.

Maguire, Joseph, (2008), 'Millwall and the making of football's folk devils: revisiting the Leicester period', in Dominic Malcolm and Ivan Waddington, (eds), *Matters of Sport: Essays in Honour of Eric Dunning*, London: Routledge: 97–113.

Maguire, Joseph and Louise Mansfield, (1998), 'Nobody's perfect: women, aerobics and the body beautiful', *Sociology of Sport Journal*, 15, 2: 109–37.

Maguire, Joseph and Emma Poulton, (1999), 'European identity politics in Euro 96: Invented traditions, imagined communities and national habitus codes', *International Review for the Sociology of Sport*, 34, 1: 17–29.

Maguire, Joseph and Jason Tuck, (2005), '"A world in union"?: rugby, globalisation, and Irish identity', in Joseph Maguire, (ed.), *Power and Global Sport: Zones of Prestige, Emulation and Resistance*, London: Routledge: 109–29.

Malcolm, Dominic, (2002), 'Cricket and civilizing processes: a response to Stokvis', *International Review for the Sociology of Sport*, 31, 1: 37–57.

Malcolm, Dominic, (2004), 'Cricket: civilizing and de-civilizing processes in the imperial game', in Eric Dunning, Dominic Malcolm and Ivan Waddington, (eds), *Sport Histories: Figurational Studies of the Development of Modern Sport*, London: Routledge: 71–87.

Malcolm, Dominic, (2009), 'Medical uncertainty and clinician-athlete relations: the management of concussion injuries in Rugby Union', *Sociology of Sport Journal*, 26, 2: 191–210.

Mansfield, Louise, (2002), 'Feminist and figurational sociology: dialogue and potential synthesis', in Joseph Maguire and Kevin Young, (eds), *Theory, Sport and Society*, London: JAI Elsevier Science: 317–35.

Mansfield, Louise, (2007), 'Involved-detachment: a balance of passion and reason in feminisms and gender-related research on sport, tourism and sports tourism', *Journal of Sport and Tourism*, 12, 2: 115–41.

Mansfield, Louise, (2008), 'Reconsidering the relationships between feminisms and the work of Norbert Elias for understanding gender, sport and sport-related activities', *European Physical Education Review*, 14, 1: 93–121.

Mennell, Stephen, (1998), *Norbert Elias: An Introduction*, Dublin: UCD Press.

Molnar, Gyozo and Joseph Maguire, (2008), 'Hungarian footballers on the move: Issues of and observations on the first migratory phase', *Sport in Society*, 11, 1: 74–89.

Mouzelis, Nicos, (1993), 'On Figurational Sociology', *Theory, Culture and Society*, 10: 239–253.

Murphy, Patrick, Ken Sheard and Ivan Waddington, (2000), 'Figurational sociology and its application to sport', in Jay Coakley and Eric Dunning, (eds), *Handbook of Sports Studies*, London: Sage: 92–105.

Ohira, Akira, (ed.), (2009), *Norbert Elias and Globalization: Sport, Culture and Society*, Tokyo: DTP.

Pike, Elizabeth and Joseph Maguire, (2003), 'Injury in women's sport: classifying key elements of "risk encounters",' *Sociology of Sport Journal*, 2: 232–51.

Pinheiro, Maria C., (2006), *The development of sport in Portugal with reference to women's participation in sport from the Salazar regime to the democratic period*, Unpublished PhD thesis, University of Leicester.

Rigauer, Bero, (1981), *Sport and Work*, New York: Columbia University Press.

Roderick, Martin, (2006), *The Work of Professional Football: A Labour of Love?* London: Routledge.

Roderick, Martin, Ivan Waddington and Graham Parker, (2000), 'Playing hurt: managing injuries in English professional football', *International Review for the Sociology of Sport*, 35, 2: 165–80.

Rojek, Chris, (1995), *Decentring Leisure: Rethinking Leisure Theory*, London: Sage.

Rojek, Chris, (2004), 'An anatomy of the Leicester School of sociology: an interview with Eric Dunning', *Journal of Classical Sociology*, 4, 3: 337–59.

Rojek, Chris, (2008), 'Sports Celebrity and the civilizing process', in Dominic Malcolm and Ivan Waddington, (eds), *Matters of Sport: Essays in Honour of Eric Dunning*, London: Routledge: 172–88.

Scambler, Graham, (2005), *Sport and Society: History, Power and Culture*, Maidenhead: Open University Press.

Scraton, Sheila and Anne Flintoff, (eds), (2002), *Gender and Sport: A Reader*, London: Routledge.

Sheard, Kenneth, (2004), 'Boxing in the western civilizing process', in Eric Dunning, Dominic Malcolm and Ivan Waddington, (eds), *Sport Histories: Figurational Studies of the Development of Modern Sports*, London: Routledge: 15–30.

Sheard, Kenneth, (2006), 'Pain and injury in boxing: the medical profession divided', in Sigmund Loland, Berit Skirstad and Ivan Waddington, (eds), *Pain and Injury in Sport*, London: Routledge: 127–43.

Skille, Eivind and Ivan Waddington, (2006), 'Alternative sport programmes and social inclusion in Norway', *European Physical Education Review*, 12, 3: 251–72.

Smith, Stuart, (2004), 'Clay shooting: civilization in the line of fire', in Eric Dunning, Dominic Malcolm and Ivan Waddington, (eds), *Sport Histories: Figurational Studies of the Development of Modern Sports*, London: Routledge: 137–52.

Smith, Andy and Ken Green, (2005), 'The place of sport and physical activity in young people's lives and its implications for health: Some sociological comments', *Journal of Youth Studies*, 8, 2: 241–53.

Smith, Andy and Michael Parr, (2007), 'Young people's views on the nature and purpose of physical education: a sociological analysis', *Sport, Education and Society*, 12, 1: 37–58.

Smith, Andy, Michael Thurston, Ken Green and Kevin Lamb, (2007), 'Young people's participation in extra-curricular physical education: a study of 15–16 year olds in North-West England and North-East Wales', *European Physical Education Review*, 13, 3: 339–68.

Stokvis, Ruud, (1992), 'Sports and civilization: is violence the central problem?', in Eric Dunning and Chris Rojek, (eds), *Sport and Leisure in the Civilizing Process*, London: Macmillan: 121–36.

Suttles, Gerald D., (1968), *The Social Order of the Slum: Ethnicity and Territory in the Inner City*. Chicago: University of Chicago Press.

Tomlinson, Alan, (ed.), (2006), *The Sports Studies Reader*, London: Routledge.

Velija, Philippa and Dominic Malcolm, (2009), 'Look it's a girl: cricket and gender relations in the UK', *Sport in Society*, 12, 4: 613–26.

Waddington, Ivan, (2000), *Sport, Health and Drugs: A Critical Sociological Perspective*, London: E & F. N. Spon.

Waddington, Ivan and Dominic Malcolm, (2008), 'Eric Dunning: this sporting life', in Dominic Malcolm and Ivan Waddington, (eds), *Matters of Sport: Essays in Honour of Eric Dunning*, London: Routledge: 1–11.

Waddington, Ivan and Andy Smith, (2009), *An Introduction to Drugs in Sport: Addicted to Winning?* London: Routledge.

White, Andrew, (2004), 'Rugby Union football in England: civilizing processes and the de-institutionalization of amateurism', in Eric Dunning, Dominic Malcolm and Ivan Waddington, (eds), *Sport Histories: Figurational Studies of the Development of Modern Sports*. London: Routledge: 53–70.

A land of a hundred thousand welcomes? Understanding established and outsiders relations in Ireland

Steven Loyal

Abstract: This paper examines the discriminatory and exclusionary treatment experienced by migrants in Ireland. After outlining the tremendous socio-economic changes that have taken place in the country, it discusses the rise of ethno-racial discrimination in Ireland before examining how these discriminatory and exclusionary practices have so far been interpreted largely within a post-structuralist frame of reference. After outlining the problems inherent in this literature, the paper examines how applicable an Eliasian established–outsider framework is for explaining these exclusionary processes whilst simultaneously noting the differences between Elias's Winston Parva study and the Irish situation.

Over the last fifteen years, high and sustained levels of immigration have transformed Irish society. Between 1999 and 2008 the population increased by 18 per cent – the highest rate in the 27 countries comprising the European Union. Increasingly multi ethnic and cosmopolitan, the emerging pattern of cultural heterogeneity and diversity – with immigrants from 188 countries – is unprecedented. From a nation defined previously by large-scale emigration, Ireland has now become a country of entrenched immigration. In the 'new' Ireland, Islam constitutes the third-largest religion in the State. As well as the scale of this transformation, the pace of change is breathtaking. The 2002 census recorded that just under six per cent of the population was composed of non-Irish nationals. By 2006, this had increased to over ten per cent – a rise of one percentage point each year.

These socio-cultural changes have, in varying ways and at different levels of intensity transformed a number of sociological aspects of Irish society: the operation of labour markets; the state regulation of political and civic rights; cultural issues concerning diversity, citizenship, multiculturalism, integration, and ethno-racial domination. They have also reframed a number of socio-economic issues concerning class, poverty, unemployment, social welfare, social exclusion, housing, political representation, trade union membership, national belonging and membership, and equality in Ireland (Loyal, 2011).

Despite Ireland's tourist-orientated national self-image as a welcoming, hospitable country, varying levels of racism directed towards migrants undoubtedly exist. In a survey carried out in 2000, almost 80 per cent of individuals from black or ethnic minority groups living in Ireland claimed they had experienced some form of racism or discrimination while living here (O'Mahony *et al.*, 2001). Many of these discriminatory attacks were not one-off or incidental occurrences. Rather, they constituted a feature of everyday life occurring in a multiplicity of social situations: in pubs, from neighbours, in banks, on buses and taxis, with regard to housing, at school and even at the cinema. More recent reports have suggested that this level of discrimination has not diminished.[1] A study carried out by the EU's Fundamental Rights Agency in 2009 found that Ireland was among the worst five countries in the EU when it came to racial discrimination and abuse.

It is also likely that there is a significant degree of underreporting of racism. A Europe-wide survey found that 82 per cent of respondents who said they had been discriminated against did not report their experience, offering varied reasons for not doing so. These included: a feeling that nothing would happen or change by reporting the incidents; a belief that it was too trivial and happened so often that it was normal; a fear of negative consequences of reporting; the bureaucratic inconvenience involved; language impediments; insecurities, including having an undocumented status; and not knowing how or where to report racist incidents (O'Connell *et al.*, 2008).[2] In Ireland, there are, indeed, few formal mechanisms in place for reporting such experiences.

Migrant workers have also suffered from high levels of exploitation. According to Quinn and Hughes (2004), work permit holders earn up to 14 per cent less than indigenous workers, despite the fact that they are on the whole better qualified. The number of cases that the Labour Relations Commission Rights Commissioner Service has processed involving foreign workers has continually increased. In 2002, of the 5,692 cases processed, only 2 per cent involved migrant workers. By 2003, the proportion of cases had risen to 3.5 per cent of 4,737 processed, and in the first eight months of 2004 migrant workers brought 8 per cent of all cases processed by the Labour Relations Commission (Labour Relations Commission, 2005: 12). In 2002, over 80 per cent of these claims were settled in favour of the claimants. There has also been a steady increase in the number of cases dealt with by the Equality Tribunal on employment equality grounds. More particularly they rose from two in 2000 to 71 in 2004. In 2003, 85 cases related solely to racial discrimination with an unspecified number also falling within the 76 undertaken on multiple grounds. Similarly, in that year, 43 cases relating to racial discrimination took place under the equal status criterion in relation to access to goods and services, with again an unspecified number within the 202 that took place under multiple grounds. Investigations into employment violations included a variety of offences: the employment of migrant workers with unequal pay and conditions in comparison with other Irish or EEA staff; failure by employers to pay workers pre-arranged wage rates; paying workers below the minimum wage;

workers being subject to excessive working hours; illegal pay deductions, with recruitment costs to be borne by the prospective employee; and the non-payment of overtime or holiday pay. Large-scale cases included the Irish Ferries dispute and the Gama controversy in which Latvian and Turkish workers, respectively, were sometimes receiving just over €2 an hour when the minimum wage stood at over €7. All this was broadly illustrative of the multifaceted nature of employment violations against migrant workers (Loyal, 2011).

Migrant workers have also been hindered from accessing employment and certain occupations because of prejudice and discrimination. Non-Irish nationals are three times more likely to experience discrimination while looking for work, while it is estimated that black people are seven times more likely. Moreover, once in the workplace, non-Irish nationals are twice as likely to experience discrimination than Irish nationals (ibid.). Thirty-two percent of work permit holders reported experiencing harassment and insults in the work place, constituting the second most common form of discrimination (McGinnity *et al.*, 2006).

The report-based evidence cited above portrays a one-sided and extreme picture of discrimination in Ireland that is in reality more complex and needs to be qualified in two ways. First, a far right anti-immigrant party has yet to emerge in Ireland, where a longstanding centre-right populism instead remains dominant. Second, unlike nearly all other European and North American states, Ireland has not been strongly affected by post-2001 anti-Muslim hysteria.

Explaining ethno-racial domination in Ireland

Studying racism and ethno-racial domination is a complex and contested endeavour. There are perhaps few areas in the social sciences where the degree of emotive political and ethical involvement is as high as it is on the issues of racism and discrimination. This means that the sociological approach undertaken can often be framed by preconceived, heteronomous evaluations that are extraneous to the subject matter. The result is a perspective that ends up praising or blaming one side or the other rather than explaining social processes regardless of their relative 'goodness' or 'badness'.[3] In addition, the concept of racism has become increasingly expansive and contested. Historically 'racism' has accrued more and more meanings and inflections, so that its use has become indistinguishable from 'prejudice', 'discrimination', 'ethnocentrism' and 'xenophobia'.

Academic discussions of ethno-racial domination and discrimination in Ireland have generally been dominated by questions of culture, subjective identity and representation. This reflects broader patterns that characterize the field of sociological theory more generally in which 'cultural studies' and 'post-structuralism' have recently become paradigmatic explanatory frameworks. The use of French models of 'race and racism' as the basis for understanding and explaining Irish variants of ethno-racial domination has been particularly popular, while the new writing on racism and immigration in Ireland has borrowed especially from abstract French post-structuralist philosophy. The concept of Otherness, for example, has its intellectual roots in Husserl's discussion on the impossibility of gaining access to another's consciousness in the fifth Cartesian Meditation (1960 [1931]), before being developed by Levinas in *Totality and Infinity* (1969), later to be incorporated within Derrida's (1981) discussion of 'violent hierarchies', which was itself influenced by the Algerian War. Rather than adopting a sociological reflexivity towards these concepts (as opposed to the self-reflexivity involved in acknowledging one's social position and location in the social world in terms of gender, ethnicity and so on), writers and migration experts in Ireland have uncritically adopted this framework in their analyses of racism and immigration. Consequently, a large number of the articles and chapters in a variety of major edited works on racism and immigration in Ireland have focused too restrictively on the discursive construction of a narrow sense of Irishness and Identity, and its concomitant engendering of Otherness (Cullen, 2000; Gillespie, 1999; Gray, 1999; Lentin, 1999; Lentin and McVeigh, 2002; McDonagh, 2002; O'Toole, 2000; Sinha, 1999; White, 2002). Such analyses have tended to concentrate on interrogating the homogenous and exclusionary construction of national discourses of Irish identity as white, settled and Catholic. Such a restrictive notion of identity, these writers argue, militates against the construction of a more inclusive and encompassing notion of a multi-ethnic Ireland by stigmatizing or racializing an 'out-group' or 'Other'. The apparent solution to such exclusionary definitions and processes is to celebrate diversity, difference, and hybridity.

More specifically, the majority of the various theoretical frameworks contained in these edited books can be accommodated within two broad positions: first, those post-modern positions which rightly emphasize power (conceived in a zero-sum manner) and racialization (Lentin, 2000; Lentin and McVeigh, 2002; Gray, 1999; O'Toole, 2000; Sinha, 1999; White, 2002); and, second, those liberal positions which focus on the importance of celebrating diversity, multiculturalism, and pluralism (Farrell and Watt, 2001; MacLachlan and O'Connell, 2000; Monshengwo, 2001; Tannam *et al.*, 1998). Notwithstanding their divergent conceptual frameworks in relation to power, both of these broad positions share an emphasis on difference and diversity and also an analytic framework which approaches racism through a Self–Other, Us–Them dynamic. Thus, typically, it is suggested that

> Othering – denying equal legitimacy to individuals and cultures that do not conform to one's own arbitrary, ever shifting criteria of normality – is a two-sided coin. On the one hand it creates a clearly defined undifferentiated 'them' . . . On the other, it forges a bond of solidarity. (Ní Shuinear, 2002: 177)

Or that,

> we cannot understand Irish racism, or the Irish racialization of the Other, without understanding the racialization of the Irish self. (Lentin, 1999; 3)

It is my view that the singular emphasis on the construction of Irish identity, Otherness and diversity is problematic for a number of reasons. First, such an analysis fails to explain why these self–other or Us–Them processes emerge in the first place. Accordingly, it therefore remains at the level of description rather than explanation. Although questions of racialization as a subset of themes of Othering are insightfully discussed, there seems to be little analysis of the rationale underlying these processes of group-making and the socio-historical triggers that engender this. Some exceptions are to be found in the most interesting of the available works, but these rationalizations for group formation are pitched at a very high level of generality and point to endemic tendencies in the broad abstraction of 'modernity' to exclude Others (Lentin, 1999: 8; Gray, 1999: 66), or to restrictive forms of ethnic nationalism (Fanning, 2002). Second, the historical specificity of Irish national ethno-racial social dynamics is submerged under an imported theoretical model in which all European societies construct 'Others' in order to construct an in-group identity. All European societies, as modern societies that need to 'Other', are painted as racist without examining the different racial inequalities within and between these societies and the concrete socio-economic mechanisms that explain them. Processes of racialization and stigmatization are, however, uneven, complex, and historically determined. Earlier processes of ethno-racial discrimination had a significant class dimension so that disempowered groups or those on the lower rungs of the social ladder, including peasants and workers, were racialized as an inferior race or a 'breed apart' by middle-class and aristocratic groups in their construction of racial typologies. Whether and which groups are racialized, and the intensity and extent of negative evaluative judgments associated with race, vary and have shifted historically. The post-modern and liberal standpoints that have been drawn on by Irish sociology have disarticulated the social and economic conditions of the emergence of forms of signification and racialization. As Hall himself noted in his earlier writings:

> the question is not whether men-in-general make perceptual distinctions between groups with different racial or ethnic characteristics, but rather, what are the specific conditions which make this form of distinction socially pertinent, historically active. (1980: 338)

The signification of 'Otherness' as a basis for racialization and racism, can have effect and meaning only within determinate historical, economic and political relations of social domination. Such perceptual and cognitive distinctions are made by embedded individuals in the real world, in their practices and in their struggles over symbolic and material resources. Language as a practice, as Wittgenstein rightly notes, is always embedded in other, broader practices or forms of life (Wittgenstein, 1958).

Third, the exclusive focus on difference and Otherness in these analyses ignores the contradictory attitudes – or what Gramsci called 'contradictory common sense' (Gramsci, 1971: 323–43) – which many in the indigenous population have towards immigrants. Far from a general fear about difference, these include more specific concerns about competition for scarce resources, maintaining status and distinction, jobs and pay levels. But these can often co-exist with feelings of mutual identification and humanitarian concern towards asylum seekers and migrants and their social conditions in other social contexts. Moreover, the generalized identification of immigrants as 'spongers' – rather than, say, tax-avoiding entrepreneurs or establishment politicians – is itself a function of specific political conjunctures. The crucial point here is to avoid analytically transmuting the complex and contradictory attitudes of the indigenous population into a flattened metaphysical formula about a 'fear or dislike of the Other' – but rather to analyse these responses empirically within their specific social contexts.

Fourth, there is also often a prevalent and unwarranted idealism in the focus on racism conceived as a 'discourse' or 'narrative', rather than seeing ethno-racial discrimination as a manifestation of material and symbolic practices embedded simultaneously in institutions and bodies as habitus (Wacquant, 1997). That is, there is a failure to look at social relations, networks, figurations and the interdependencies between individuals.

There are also specific problems with each of these positions. In terms of the post-modern standpoint and resistance, power is seen as de-centred into a host of social spaces. As a result, there appears to be little common ground from which to develop a strategy to oppose racism that involves the majority of the indigenous population. With reference to the standard liberal policy oriented positions that utilize psychological frameworks of prejudice to explain discrimination, state, church and media discourses have emphasized the values of diversity and pluralism while packaging it within the framework of 'interculturalism'. Interculturalism was the National Consultative Committee on Racism and Interculturalism's preferred term for designating cultures that interact with one another. This body, predominantly funded by the Department of Justice, Equality and Law Reform before its very recent abolition, stressed the idea of a partnership between NGOs, employers, the unions and the state to challenge racism. There was, however, little recognition that some of these groups might actually benefit from racism. Thus an NCCRI publication on diversity at work simply assumes that the business 'community' has an automatic interest in eliminating racism. It is further assumed that a harmonious immigration policy can be created which takes into account, 'the long term (as opposed to event driven) national security concerns; the broad socio-economic concerns of migrants and broad human rights/equality concerns . . . and the medium to long term needs of the economy (as opposed to annual fluctuation)' (Watt, 2002: 14–45).

Established and outsiders

Poststructuralist approaches that rely on an abstract, idealist, and ultimately a speculative notion of Othering rooted in modernity are limited in their scope for explaining the diverse and differentiated causes underpinning the concrete social contexts within which ethnoracial forms of discrimination are expressed in Ireland. It will be argued below that Elias provides a more robust and powerful explanatory sociological framework. Although his established–outsider model is also, at one level, a broad model to the extent that it explains constructing an 'out-group' in terms of racial, ethnic, class and gender differences within a single general framework in the same way that the notion of Othering does, there are major differences. Elias's approach takes as its point of departure 'humans in the round', so to speak, who are at once material, social, and psychological beings motivated by economic forces, social interdependencies and mutual susceptibilities, as well as by emotions and drives rooted in their habitus. Such a framework allows us to understand and examine the multi-faceted ways in which ethnoracial discrimination in all its empirical manifestations takes place without forcing it into a singular theoretical straightjacket, be it a Marxist or Weberian emphasis on economic criteria tied to accessing scarce resources, or a psychological propensity to Other rooted in Western modernity as poststructuralists argue. As we shall see below economic factors certainly play a role in ethnoracial discrimination in Ireland, but so do socio-psychological processes entailing status distinction as expressed through verbal abuse directed at non-Irish nationals. In addition, it is grounded in a historically informed and concrete analysis of actual hierarchical social relations (or figurations) of power. Unlike the Othering framework which tends to have a dichotomous and in some ways essentialised understanding of fixed-frozen power relations grounded upon identities based on 'whiteness' or 'Irish-ness' standing opposed to non-White, or non-Irish marginalised groups, Elias posits a processual sociology in which power ratios may shift so that groups may lose their dominance to varying degrees. He also provides a multi-tiered relational framework within which power relations and forms of discrimination exist between subaltern migrant groups.

For Elias the material and socio-psychological dynamics underpinning discrimination are ultimately manifestations of a long-term conflict rooted in the struggles between survival units and the different levels of power that exist between them. That is, it refers to a universal process that is expressed through concrete communities linked to specific places and forms of life with their own histories. This is an anthropological rather than philosophical argument that is amenable to empirical investigation.

Elias and Scotson's theory of established–outsiders relations was based on a study in 1958–61 of a community on the outskirts of Leicester that was then ethnically homogeneous, white and working-class. But it has proven to be highly relevant and illuminating when applied to the effects of the mass migrations that have taken place since then. Indeed, it is symbolic that the city of Leicester is now on the brink of becoming the first city in the UK to have a majority in its population of people of recent migrant origin.

The Established and Outsiders (2008 [1965]) is a study of a small suburban community in Leicester (fictitiously) named Winston Parva. The book examines the dynamics between three distinct neighbourhoods or 'zones': zone 1 inhabited by a middle class population; zone 2 characterised by an 'old' established working class population; and zone 3 characterized by a newly arrived population which was working class. The old communities refused to have dealings with the new community other than those imposed by occupational ties. Elias and Scotson showed that, even without any visible ethnic markers, tension could arise between groups within a community simply on the basis of differences in their length of local residence. Elias and Scotson point to four major tendencies shared by established–outsider relationships. A tendency to see outsiders as anomic; for the established to judge outsiders according to the 'minority of the worst'; for outsiders to internalize their stigmatization and group disgrace; and for established groups to perceive outsiders as 'unclean' or polluting (Dunning, 2004: 82).

Although often mistakenly interpreted as separate from his *magnum opus*, *The Civilising Process*, the discussion of established–outsider relations in fact also forms a central part of that work, albeit in this case abstracted from a longer-term historical framework. Issues concerning the length of chains of interdependency, social cohesion, the self-restraint of drives and affects, adherence to behavioural codes, and claims of status superiority as – *more* 'civilised' – are all present in the study of Winston Parva. Elias's central point in this work is that it is the configuration of their social relationships, and not their characteristics *per se* that explains the relationship of domination between groups. Central to established–outsider relations, therefore, are not the characteristics of the groups themselves, whether 'race' as a physical marker or culture as a social factor is utilized. Given the wide range of differences and similarities, the selection of what is deemed similar or different is relatively arbitrary – although historically physical or normative–cultural differences have dominated. Rather, of fundamental explanatory importance is the *unequal power ratio* between these groups, itself determined by the way they are bonded together, their different degrees of organization and cohesion. A singular emphasis on race, racialization, nationality, religion, or ethnicity – whether the focus is on differences in skin colour or cultural values – draws attention away from what Elias considers a broader and more pertinent causal factor that explains the process of domination and discrimination: a differential in the power ratio between groups. *The Established and Outsiders* thus constitutes a small-scale investigation into the sociology of power underwritten by an analysis of the structure of social figurations. The discussion of power is prioritised over other conventional sociological taxonomies invoking class, race, religion, nationality etc. The latter are instead deployed as second-order categories that 'take on force' or explanatory significance when seen in relation to the former.

According to Elias, when established groups feel exposed to an attack against their monopolized power resources, they use stigmatization and exclusion as weapons to maintain their distinct identity, assert their superiority, and keep outsiders in their place. In Winston Parva, processes of group charisma and group disgrace involved maintaining a positive 'we-image' by the established residents and a negative 'they-image' through the stigmatization of outsiders and the propagation of collective fantasies (Elias, 2009 [1998]: 73–81). This, in turn, involved generalizing the worst characteristics from the 'anomic minority' of a group to the whole group – attributing to all those living in zone 3 negative characteristics that only pertain to a small 'minority of the worst', whilst simultaneously attributing the best 'most nomic' behaviour onto the established group – modelling the self-image of the dominant group in terms of characteristics held by the 'minority of the best'.

The established–outsider framework, according to Elias, serves as an empirical paradigm of a universal human theme involving power, exclusion, and inequality. It provides a standardized or exemplary model with which researchers 'can better come to grips with the similarities and differences of other cases' (Elias, 2008 [1990]: 213). In light of this claim, I will use the established–outsider model to examine the dominance–subordination relations that exist between Irish nationals and newly arrived immigrants, in order to show that it has greater explanatory force in explaining ethno-racial domination in Ireland than the heretofore dominant poststructuralist approaches. However, in the limits of this single paper, I can only offer a brief and impressionistic outline of the applicability of this framework to the Irish case.

In applying Elias's framework it is important to acknowledge the similarities and differences between his discussion of Winston Parva and the Irish case. Rather than examining the neighbourhood relations between groups following the arrival of white working-class immigrants from within the country, the sociological object concerns the social exclusion and discrimination faced by newly arrived white and non-white immigrants from outside the country. It therefore entails issues involving skin colour and ethnicity that were absent from Elias's study. Second, the Irish case not only involves a shift in the composition of the groups studied but also in scale. Rather than examining small, contiguous neighbourhood dynamics, I shall draw primarily on evidence gathered from a study that included 80 qualitative interviews, focus groups and 400 surveys of Chinese, Nigerian, Lithuanian and Indian migrants scattered ecologically across the country.[4] In addition, I shall also draw on data from other qualitative and quantitative studies and opinion polls undertaken in Ireland.

It may be useful to outline the demographic make-up of the newly arrived immigrants coming to Ireland. Unlike in many other developed countries experiencing mass immigration, the majority of non-Irish nationals come from the European Union and are, on the whole, well qualified. The census estimates that 275,775 individuals from the EU-25 were resident in Ireland in 2006, making up 66 percent of the non-Irish population. Almost 120,000 of these were from the accession states that joined the European Union in 2004. The European nationals who had migrated to Ireland, were followed by nationals from Asia (11 percent), Africa (6 percent), and North and South America (5 percent). Hence, although 188 different nationalities are estimated to be residing in Ireland, 82 percent of them are estimated to be from just ten countries.[5] According to the 2006 census, the largest, and paradoxically least discussed, group of non-Irish nationals was from the United Kingdom. They were followed by immigrants from Poland, Lithuania, Nigeria, Latvia, the US and China. Non-Irish nationals are also on the whole very well qualified. While they reported higher overall levels of education than the Irish population – 38 percent were thought to have had tertiary education, compared to 28 percent of Irish nationals[6] – the majority of immigrants have settled around Dublin and other major cities including Cork, Galway and Limerick. However, concentrations of immigrants are also found outside of these larger centres. In Dublin, about 15 per cent of residents are non-Irish nationals, with large numbers of Polish, Lithuanian, Chinese and Nigerian nationals resident in the greater Dublin area.

Despite their high levels of qualifications, many migrants in Ireland were forced into jobs for which they are over-qualified. Although 23 per cent of Lithuanians had a third level qualification, only two per cent of them are working as professionals. One study found that employers, faced with applications from candidates who were identical in all relevant characteristics other than their ethnic or national origin, were twice as likely to call Irish applicants for interview than they were minority nationals (McGinnity *et al.*, 2009). Other studies have demonstrated that non-Irish nationals are three times more likely to report having experienced discrimination whilst looking for work than Irish nationals, and blacks seven times more likely (O'Connell and McGinnity, 2008). Although this may point to different qualifications, the existence of discrimination as an explanatory factor appears to be significant and is supported by interview data from O'Connell and McGinnity's study. One Nigerian national who had a Masters degree in human resource management spoke of how he could only get a job as a delivery driver. He had made over 100 applications in the year but was only called to one interview. It was with a car rental company. He talked about his experiences with the business sector thus:

> If I think about it, it has to do with stereotyping. Because you say you're Nigerian, that's why you can't get that job. (Festus, Nigeria)

The above example illustrates the problems migrants have accessing work. Competition for economic chances of power plays a major role in many aspects of group conflicts and established–outsider relations, and Elias remains sensitive to issues of economic monopolisation in his analysis of established–outsider relations (Elias, 2008 [1990]: 211). As we can see from the above, such processes are also evident in Ireland. Immigrants have also been concentrated in specific economic sectors, particularly in low-pay occupations. Three-quarters of all nationals from the EU accession states, for example, were concentrated in four industries: manufacturing, construction, wholesale and retail trades, hotels, and restaurants (CSO, 2008). Nigerians have also been concentrated in 3-D (dirty, difficult and dangerous) occupations that indigenous Irish nationals have refused to take up (Immigrant Council of Ireland, 2008).

Social closure aimed at securing privileged access to material resources has played a vital role in discrimination against and exclusion of migrants. The greater social cohesion, solidarity and uniformity of norms and self-discipline that characterize Irish nationals as a result of living in the same country for a substantial period also allow them to hold positions of power, including positions of recruitment. In addition, length of residence allows Irish nationals to develop specific norms, standards and distinctive conduct, and to share forms of knowledge and 'know how'. These networks 'represent inheritable chances to exercise power in relation to others which, as a group, have only limited access to, or are excluded from, such chances' (Elias and Scotson, 2008 [1965]: 176–7). Irish nationals, though with some variations depending on class position, have been able to monopolize sources of power to a relatively high degree and this means that they are able to deny these chances and opportunities from immigrants. The transmission of standards runs parallel with the transmission of property and access to occupations.

Although acknowledging that economic processes play a central role in his analysis, Elias nevertheless regards Marxists' analysis of class and economic power as reductionist (Elias, 2008 [1990]: 211). Differences in the organisation of physical power, state-formation, and the development of self-value relationships based on pride and social distinction also play a part in different societies, although according to different degrees. Hence, in addition to materialist explanations, he rightly also points to the operation of non-economic factors relating to status and recognition playing a part in explaining the ostracism and discrimination perpetrated by native-born groups.

Social superiority engenders the gratifying euphoria and emotional rewards that go with the consciousness of belonging to a group of higher value or possessing a higher status. The need for self-enhancement and looking down on the members of other groups appears as a ubiquitous feature of all societies according to Elias. He notes: 'it is difficult to imagine a human society that has not developed a stigmatising technique in relation to a part group akin to that encountered in Winston Parva.' (Elias, 2008 [1990]: 227). However, although 'the value one attaches to oneself as a member of a group or as an individual person is . . . one of the most fundamental ingredients of one's existence as a human being' (Elias, 2008 [1990]: 229), struggles for the satisfaction of other human requirements may become more protracted when the certainty of material needs has been firmly established. Non-economic factors relating to status become increasingly important where power balances are less uneven, for example, between middle-class migrants and the indigenous working and middle-class elements of a host population. Here, struggles for the satisfaction of human requirements other than material resources and physical survival, relating to recognition and status, become more protracted. Social superiority engenders feelings of human superiority and contributes to the self-endowment of group charisma, which has as its correlate, group disgrace imposed on the less powerful group. Exclusion and stigmatization are powerful weapons for maintaining identity, asserting superiority, and for keeping others subordinate. According to Elias, the need for status distinctions has an important biological and historical rationale for human survival.[7]

The explicit discrimination many immigrants have faced from Irish nationals has certainly involved maintaining a status distinction between the latter and the former. It also follows from their social cohesion and social reproduction of values that have resulted in 'rigidities of outlook and conduct'. This means established groups 'have been brought up in the belief that everyone does, or ought to, feel and behave in the essentials as they themselves feel and behave . . . By and large the threshold of tolerance for forms of behaviour and belief that are different from one's own, if one has to live with the representatives in close contact, is still exceedingly low' (Elias and Scotson, 2008 [1965]: 183). Some of these 'rigidities of conduct' and status distinctions are expressed in the verbal abuse that immigrants have experienced from Irish nationals outside the economic sphere. As one immigrant from Nigeria noted: 'If they could find a means of hijacking you and sending you back to your country, they would have done it. Just imagine when we go for shopping, they will come and meet you. "You f**king black stupid thing, get out of this place, you go back to your f**king country"' (Abassi, Nigeria). Though a large amount of abuse is directed at Africans, immigrants from Asia, including Chinese and Indians, also noted significant levels of abuse: 'If I walk in O'Connell Street in the middle of the night, maybe some drunk man will shout at you "Chinese b******d"' (Ho, China). In another case a Sikh student from India, wearing a turban, reported experiencing abuse every day of the three years he had spent in Ireland.

It is important therefore not to oversimplify or homogenize the causes of ethno-racial domination in Irish society by reducing them to the fight for scarce material resources, as some Marxist analysts have done. Elias rightly points to the inadequacies of reductionist materialist accounts. Symbolic factors and status also appear to play a role. Socio-psychological processes involving transference, labelling, and a search for distinction and recognition are important, too. The nature of group fantasies and emotions, which can often slip through theoretical conceptual nets, need to be acknowledged: their logic is, however, not arbitrary but possesses a structure and discernible dynamic of its own. In addition, the hard distinction between material and symbolic processes is merely an analytical construct of the researcher. Depending on the empirical situation and the specific research topic, the two may overlap and reinforce one another. Alternatively, they may operate relatively independently. Elias's approach also points beyond the abstract and simplified discussions that reduce discrimination to an inherent tendency in modernity to think in terms of an 'Other'.

There are, however, some respects in which the Irish case diverges from Elias's Winston Parva and a later more extreme model of power and racial differences in the context of the US South that he calls the 'Maycomb model'.[8] The established and outsider groups are both differentiated by various internal strata. Established groups are stratified according to class, whilst outsider groups are hierarchically differentiated according to class and ethno-national characteristics. This means that we need to examine multiple established–outsider figurations, entailing groups that are established in some contexts and outsiders in others. Lower class Irish nationals are outsiders themselves in relation to higher ranking economic elites whose more secure socio-economic position, class codes and behavioural norms and restraints are expressions of their higher levels of economic and cultural capital. This means that the modality and form of discrimination expressed by established groups may differ according to their class position. Irish nationals in a higher social class, and therefore with a different habitus, may not express their verbal racist hostility as explicitly or openly as those in the lower social classes. They may discriminate more 'informally', so to speak – employers refusing to give job interviews to Nigerians. In other cases, where they have high levels of cultural capital as well as economic capital, and therefore a more cosmopolitan outlook, they may find acts of discrimination to be repulsive.

The existence of class-mediated racism is partly borne out in studies. In research carried out by the Irish Refugee Council, for example, many asylum seekers referred to the hostility they encountered from other excluded and marginalized groups (Fanning *et al.*, 2000). It was felt that such indigenous excluded groups often perceived asylum seekers and refugees as welfare scroungers, or as preventing them from receiving certain scarce social resources. As one of the respondents put it:

> I think Irish people . . . are racist people, but I think the racist people are from Ireland's cities, the people who are getting Social Welfare. I really think that educated people are not racist . . . even if in their roots they have some racism they learn to control it or they learn what it is to be racist. (quoted by Fanning *et al.*, 2000)

Another respondent added:

> In inner city areas these people think that refugees and asylum seekers are their competitors, or in competition with them. (Fanning *et al.*, 2000: 21)

Such explicit, potentially violent hostility shown towards migrants living in poor Irish communities concurs with 'popular' definitions of discrimination as well as with the definitions used by the media and government. But such a view occludes the more silent but equally pernicious forms of discrimination through employer recruitment, state practices, and state classifications. And, of course, asylum seekers (and immigrants generally) are more likely to encounter such overt racial hostility from inner-city working-class communities because of their similar social and geographical position.[9] In such a context, 'the established group feels compelled to repulse what they experience as a threat to both their power superiority (in terms of their cohesion and monopolization of local offices and amenities) and their human superiority, their group charisma, by means of a counter-attack, a continuous rejection and humiliation of the other group (Elias and Scotson, 2008 [1965]: 31).

However, although their social cohesion allows them to apply these characterisations of immigrants and make them stick, it is also important to see the role of state and media organisations in facilitating such negative discourses. Negative images and stereotypes of this kind that are reproduced and amplified through neighbourhood gossip, rarely emerge spontaneously and often arise from state and media discourses, given their monopoly over the powers of governance, diffusion and representation. Thus, refugees in Ireland, and Europe generally have been represented by the state and politicians as being responsible for a number of social and economic problems (which usually existed well before the refugees' arrival), such as housing shortages, unemployment and the general lack of adequate statutory provisions. For many disempowered sections of the population, embedded in atrophying housing estates, racist discourses often constitute a description of, and explanation for, the world they experience on a day-to-day basis. In a study carried out by Amnesty International (O'Mahony *et al.*, 2001), 44 per cent of respondents believed that asylum seekers were depriving indigenous Irish people of local authority housing, 95 per cent believed that some asylum seekers were in Ireland illegally, and 15 per cent believed that asylum seekers could obtain grants to buy cars, while ten per cent believed that they were given free mobile phones.[10] Many of these 'fantasy' beliefs were reproduced by local nationals in their neighbourhoods through blame-gossip.

In such a context, discriminatory ethno-racial discourses provide an ideological account of the social world which recognizes and offers an explanation for the housing crisis, for the lack of jobs, for the continuance of poverty – experiences which many marginalized groups face. As a correlate of radicalization, discrimination also serves to make a causal link between observed, material differences in Irish society and signified phenotypic and cultural differences of black and ethnic minorities. It helps to make sense of the economic and social changes accompanying poverty, urban decline and social exclusion, as they are experienced by sections of the working class within the context of a booming Celtic Tiger economy. In Ireland, a shift in media and political discourses concerning immigrants took place after 2004. Prior to that date, discourses centred on 'bogus' asylum seekers (primarily correlated with Nigerians in the public mind) coming to Ireland to exploit its generous welfare system predominated. Following 2004, when nationals from Eastern Europe arrived in the Republic the discourse became centred on issues of job displacement and immigrants reducing the wages of Irish nationals in a 'race to the bottom'.

Further to this, outsider, immigrant groups are differentiated through the existence of racial hierarchies. The interviews undertaken with immigrants tended to confirm this. Specific groups, who are perceived as phenotypically different from Irish nationals, especially in terms of skin colour (principally immigrants from Nigeria, and to a lesser extent Chinese and Indians from Asia), have been targets of explicit verbal abuse in a way that Lithuanians from Eastern Europe have not. The EU's Fundamental Rights Agency's report of 2009 reinforced the view that such hierarchies operated. Seventy-three per cent of those who were surveyed from sub-Saharan Africa stated they had experienced racism in Ireland, as opposed to 25 per cent of those from central and Eastern Europe (Fundamental Rights Agency, 2009: 6). Other studies have yielded similar results (O'Connell *et al.*, 2008; ESRI, 2006).

The proliferation of negative images and other negative characterisations of immigrants by established groups have sometimes become accepted by migrants themselves, according to their hierarchical treatment – thus further weakening their social position. The power differential allows the stigma to stick without counter-assertion, and the discrimination has the effect of 'biting into' the immigrants, so to speak. The internalization of negative or stigmatized self-images by less powerful groups – so much that those who are disempowered often see themselves through the eyes of the dominated – is also present in the inter-national and inter-ethnic hostility among migrants. Examples are hostility between Polish and Chinese nationals or Lithuanian and Nigerian nationals. Thus some Lithuanians in interviews talk about Nigerians as lazy or as here to 'sponge' off the welfare system and Chinese talk about the abuse they have received from Polish migrants when working in shops, for instance.

In addition, to fully understand the complex divisions between multi-player figurations, we need to look at different levels in society. This means that, in order to examine the variety of uneven power balances, we need to move from what Elias (1978 [1970]) would call a one-level game model to a multi-player game model played at different levels. An understanding of the hostilities and rivalries between established and outsider groups requires a conceptualisation in terms of multi-group constellations that are layered and variable. This entails not only examining the role of the media and politicians, together with business and economic elites, but also the state policy and state classification. State discourses have both individualized migrants and disempowered them in terms of rights and entitlement. Rather than providing all residents with the same civil and political rights, bureaucratic state classification schemes engender systematic patterns of discrimination. The legal and administrative immigrant categories of 'asylum seeker', 'refugee' and 'economic migrant' are important in that they confer different rights and entitlements to resources in contrast to Irish citizens. These rights and resources include: access to social welfare, to education, to fair treatment in the labour market and workplace, to social services including the health service, as well as the right of individuals to vote, to have family members live with them and to be treated equally and free from discrimination generally. The administrative categories and classifications used by the state also play an important role in defining processes of self-identification by Irish nationals and immigrants and this reinforces the immigrants' social exclusion. Both dominant and marginalised groups come to define themselves and each other through such categorisations. This is not simply an ideological or cognitive influence but about 'everything that native insertion into a nation and a state buries in the innermost depths of minds and bodies, in a quasi-natural state, or in other words far beyond the reach of consciousness' (Bourdieu, 2004: xiv). In other words, it involves a question of habituses.

Racism and recession

In the immediate context of the recession, the power difference between established Irish workers and immigrants has shifted slightly in favour of the former. It appears that racism is increasing as immigrants increasingly become scapegoated for the loss of Irish jobs. Such scapegoating has been led by the state and politicians supported by the media. The state initially responded to the recession by increasing restrictions both on the entry of work permit holders and on their rights and entitlements once they arrived here, claiming that Irish nationals needed to be prioritized for jobs. These new restrictions fed into a populist discourse that served to apportion blame for the lack of jobs to migrants. The call for a clampdown on work permits and the creation of tougher permit rules was led by a vociferous group of populist politicians. As Fianna Fáil, TD Noel O'Flynn remarked: 'What in the name of God are we doing bringing workers in when we haven't work for our own people?' (Molony, 2009). Such views were also echoed by local politicians. In November 2009, the Fine Gael Mayor of Limerick called for the cutting of social welfare payments and deportation of immigrants, including EU nationals, who were abusing Ireland's generous welfare system or who could not find work in Ireland. An *Irish Times* poll carried out at the end of 2009, found that 72 per cent of respondents wanted to see a reduction in the number of non-Irish migrants, and for some or all migrants to leave the country.

However, this shift may be seen as a short-term phenomenon. The nature of the uneven balance of power between the groups and the tensions between them are not fixed, but continually altered in changing conjunctural contexts. Processes of exclusion and stigmatization alter as power ratios between groups become less uneven. Over the long term, power differences may lessen between established natives and immigrant outsiders, the fantasy-laden collective 'we-images' of social superiority characteristic of the established may begin to diminish. The power to stigmatize through closing ranks diminishes when a group can no longer maintain a monopoly on the principal sources of power available. For Elias, economic changes and/or functional democratization tend towards equalizing power ratios. Outsider groups that had formerly accepted their inferiority and low position in the social hierarchy may come to challenge and contest their stigmatization, and to pursue a more equal access to various power resources in a dialectic of oppression and counter-oppression. As migrants begin to organize more effectively, to overlook their internal group differences, and to form alliances with other social actors such as trade unions so that the power balance in Ireland shifts, they will be in a better position to resist symbolic forms of violence and resort to counter-stigmatization. However, gratification derived from the self-endowed group charisma and feelings of status superiority may, because of the specific logic of emotions, mean that social prejudice may remain for a time even following a shift in the balance of power and the lessening of *de jure* and *de facto* discrimination.

Conclusion

Elias's established–outsider framework allows us to see that ethno-racial distinctions not only create symbolic and material barriers between groups but also emotional barriers which rigidify these antagonistic relations. The theory also allows us to transcend both a one-sided idealism and a similarly conceived one-sided materialism by denying the separation of the material and symbolic spheres in the first place, other than as an analytical device. Although Elias argues he is transcending Marxist reductionism, he nevertheless sees Marxism as an indispensable starting point for his analysis. He also examines social practices involving 'real individuals, their activity and the material conditions of their life [which] can be verified in a purely empirical way' (Marx and Engels, 1976 [1846]: 37). Moreover, rather than examining ethno-racial discrimination in order to assign blame and guilt, we need to try to understand the power mechanisms that engender it and the modalities through which it is expressed, utilizing more 'detached' scientific sociological accounts. This involves moving beyond imposing simple dichotomous labels of racist and anti-racist to divide and evaluate the moral standing of various groups in the population. The social dynamics underlying processes of social closure in which more powerful groups have a self-image of themselves as better – sometimes asserted as national group identity by members who define themselves as similar – have both a material and a symbolic dimension. In terms of the former, discrimination permits economic and occupational advantages and privileged access to the means of production. Superior job positions can be reserved for native members while excluding migrants, in turn reinforcing the established groups' cohesion and power. In terms of the latter, it provides a sense of social superiority, pride, and positive self-valuation.

Rather than looking specifically at ethno-racial domination, Elias used the term 'established–outsider relations' in order to emphasize exclusionary processes generally. Yet this concept has some limitations. The term is equally prone to reification. Moreover, because it is a generic concept more capacious than say race, ethnicity, or class distinctions which are say seen as manifestations of it, the term can by its very generality sometimes mean that the specific modalities and mechanisms of domination that distinguish, for example, racial domination as compared to say class stratification may be overlooked. However, the specificity of various forms of domination would have been accepted by Elias as something that was to be uncovered empirically in each instance, as long as it was within the context of different power ratios.

In Ireland, processes of immigration and ethno-racial domination need to be understood within a framework which includes such concepts as the social relations of capitalist accumulation, cultural nationalism, social closure and status, and state regulation and control. This entails a conceptual shift from looking at two-player game models, simply involving Irish citizens and immigrants, to multiple three- or four-player game models on different levels involving the state, capital, trade unions, and immigrants (Elias, 1978 [1970]: 71–103). Elias's approach not only allows us to move beyond accounts focusing singularly on identity (Brubaker and Cooper, 2000) but also beyond some of the inherent theoretical, empirical, and strategic limitations of the dominant post-modern and one-sided materialist understandings of ethno-racial and ethno-national processes of domination and discrimination in Ireland. Equally it provides a more solid conception of power and a more robust conception of social actors. Rather than talking of power in an abstract metaphysical sense, something that characterizes a number of the approaches adopted in the Irish analyses mentioned above, Elias's grounded, processual, and relational understanding of the concept provides a helpful tool for empirical analysis.[11] Elias also has a superior ontological starting point for his analysis when compared to these theorists, because he starts out from a plurality of individuals who are in one way or another interdependent with one another. Figurations are irreducible – they do not exist independently of individuals, nor do individuals exist independently of them.

Although there are differences between the Winston Parva study, the Maycomb model and the Irish case discussed above, there are also features that all three share: in all cases, the newcomers are bent on improving their position and the established groups are bent on maintaining theirs. The newcomers resent, and often try to rise from, the inferior status attributed to them; and the established try to preserve their superior status, which the newcomers appear to threaten. The newcomers cast in the role of outsiders are perceived by the established as people 'who do not know their place'; they offend the sensibilities of the established by behaving in a manner in which in their eyes clearly bears the stigma of social inferiority; and yet, in many cases, newcomer groups are apt quite innocently to behave, at least for a time, as if they were the equals of their new neighbours. The latter show the flag; they fight for their superiority, their status and power, their standards and beliefs, and almost everywhere in that situation they use the same weapons, among them humiliating gossip, stigmatizing beliefs about the whole group modelled on observations of its worst section, degrading code words and, as far as possible, exclusion from all chances of power – in short, the features that are abstracted from the figuration in which they occur under headings such as 'prejudice' and 'discrimination' (Elias and Scotson, 2008 [1965]: 182–3).

Because his sociological insights are at once theoretical and empirical, and apply both universally and to particular social situations, Elias allows us to move beyond the lacunae that characterize more fashionable post-structuralist approaches with their abstract notions of 'Othering' and power. The current structure of social figurations in Ireland, characterized by differential power balances and varying levels of social cohesion, allows us to see why Ireland is not yet 'a land of one hundred thousand welcomes'.

Notes

1 In a follow-up survey based on a different methodology (McGinnity *et al.*, 2006), an ESRI study found that reports of incidents of racism taking place in a variety of contexts had continued.

2 Thirty-six per cent indicated they did not report the incident because they did not know how to go about doing so or where to go.

3 Sociologists are people, and without their involvement in social life they would be neither motivated nor able to explain social processes. However, whilst distancing himself from the Weberian understanding of value-neutrality, Elias insisted on the need for the social sciences to engender a *relatively* greater degree of detachment in order to grasp longer-term figurational dynamics and developments (Goudsblom, 1977: 8). Without this they are more, not less, prone to images based upon fantasy thinking rather than on careful investigation. In *Involvement and Detachment* (2007 [1987]) Elias shows how increasingly reliable knowledge of non-human nature and an expanding techno-economic 'zone of safety', paradoxically, made human beings more dependent on social processes and vulnerable in relation to them. On the attribution of blame as a means of orientation in the social sciences, see also van Benthem van den Bergh, 1986.

4 In addition to participants located in Dublin, interviews were conducted with Chinese in Bray, Indians in Donegal, Lithuanians in Cork, and Nigerians in Navan, Drogheda and Kildare.

5 See CSO, 'Census 2006. Non-Irish Nationals Living in Ireland' (Dublin: CSO, June 2008), www. cso.ie/census/documents/NON%20IRISH%20NATONALS%20LIVING%20IN%20IRELAN D.pdf.

6 CSO, 'Census 2006 Volume 10 – Education and Qualifications. Table 31,' http://beyond2020. cso.ie/Census/TableViewer/tableView.aspx?ReportId=76961. Accessed 24 March 2010.

7 'In the last resort these techniques may have a survival value. Collective self-glorification may strengthen the integration of a group, and thus improve survival chances' (Elias, 2008 [1990]: 227). This quest for self-enhancement, of maintaining a differentiated and hierarchical status order is underpinned by what he deems to be the basic unit of sociological analysis – survival groups that fear each other. He adds 'The fear of each other built into the situation of human groups is one of the main causes of group hostilities, in the case of established and outsider groups as in many others' (ibid.: 230).

8 Elias compares the Winston Parva model with what he calls the 'Maycomb model' which represents a more extreme power imbalance between established and outsider groups. Elias's inspiration for his essay 'Further aspects of established–outsider relations: the Maycomb Model' (in Elias, 2008 [1990]: 209–31), which he wrote in the last few months of his life, was Harper Lee's celebrated novel *To Kill a Mockingbird* (1961). [This essay is to be found only in the Collected Works edition of *The Established and the Outsiders*].

9 There may be generational factors at play – one study highlighted young people, albeit from poor backgrounds, as a source of anti-migrant sentiment (O'Connell and McGinnity, 2008).

10 Opinion poll for Amnesty International, Lansdowne Marketing Research, Dublin, April 2002.

11 His definition of power is refreshingly straightforward. 'We depend upon others; others depend on us. Insofar as we are more dependent on others than they are on us, they have power over us, whether we have become dependent on them by their use of naked force or by our need to be loved, our need for money, healing, status, a career or simply for excitement. (Elias, 1978 [1970]: 93)

References

Dates given in square brackets are those of first publication.

Banton, Michael, (1977), *The Idea of Race*, London: Tavistock.

van Benthem van den Bergh, Godfried (1986), 'The improvement of human means of orientation: towards synthesis in the social sciences', in Raymond Apthorpe and Andreás Kráhl, (eds), *Development Studies: Critique and Renewal*, Leiden: Brill: 109–36. [For the original full English version dating from 1977, see http://www.norberteliasfoundation.nl/network/essays.php]

Bourdieu, Pierre, (2004), 'Preface', in Abdelmalek Sayad, *The Suffering of the Immigrant*, Cambridge: Polity.

Bourdieu, Pierre, (1984), *Distinction: A Social Critique of the Judgement of Taste*, London: Routledge & Kegan Paul.

Brubaker, Rogers and Frederick Cooper, (2000), 'Beyond "identity"', *Theory, Culture and Society* 29, 1: 1–47.

CSO (2008), 'Non-Irish nationals living in Ireland', Dublin: Government publications.

Cullen, Paul, (2000), 'Identity, emigration and the boomerang generation', in Ronit Lentin, (ed.), *Emerging Irish Identities*, Dublin: Ethnic and Racial Studies, Department of Sociology, Trinity College Dublin.

Derrida, Jacques, (1981), 'Positions', Chicago: University of Chicago Press.

Dunning, Eric, (2004), 'Aspects of the figurational dynamics of racial stratification: a conceptual discussion and developmental analysis of black-white relations in the United States', in Steven Loyal and Stephen Quilley, (eds), *The Sociology of Norbert Elias*, Cambridge: Cambridge University Press.

Elias, Norbert, (1978 [1970]), *What is Sociology?* London: Hutchinson. [Collected Works, Vol. 5, Dublin: UCD Press, forthcoming].

Elias, Norbert, (2007 [1987]), *Involvement and Detachment*, Collected Works, Vol. 8, Dublin: UCD Press.

Elias, Norbert, (2008 [1990]), 'Further aspects of established-outsider relations: the Maycomb model', in *The Established and the Outsiders*, Collected Works, Vol. 4, Dublin: UCD Press: 209–31.

Elias, Norbert, (2009 [1998]), 'Group charisma and group disgrace', in *Essays III: On Sociology and the Humanities*, Collected Works, Vol. 16, Dublin: UCD Press.

Elias, Norbert and John L. Scotson, (2008 [1965]), *The Established and the Outsiders*, Collected Works, Vol. 4, Dublin: UCD Press.

ESRI (2006), *Migrants' Experience of Racism and Discrimination in Ireland: Survey Report*, Dublin: Economic and Social Research Institute.

Fanning, Bryan, Steven Loyal and Ciaran Staunton, (2000), *Asylum Seekers and the Right to Work in Ireland*, Dublin: Irish Refugee Council.

Fanning, Bryan, (2002), *Racism and Social Change in the Republic of Ireland*, Manchester: Manchester University Press.

Farrell, Fintan and Philip Watt, (2001), 'Responding to racism in Ireland: an overview', in Fintan Farrell and Philip Watt, (eds), *Responding to Racism in Ireland*, Dublin: Veritas.

Fundamental Rights Agency, (2009), *European Union Minorities and Discrimination Report*. http://fra.europa.eu/fraWebsite/attachments/eumidis_mainreport_conference-edition_en_.pdf. Accessed 25 March 2010.

Gillespie, Paul, (1999), 'Multiple identities in Ireland and Europe', in Ronit Lentin, (ed.), *The Expanding Nation: Towards a Multi-Ethnic Ireland*, Dublin: Ethnic and Racial Studies, Department of Sociology, Trinity College Dublin.

Gilroy, Paul, (2000), *Against Race: Imagining Political Culture Beyond the Color Line*, Cambridge, MA: Belknap Press.

Goudsblom, Johan, (1977), *Sociology in the Balance*, Oxford: Blackwell.

Gramsci, Antonio, (1971), *Selections from the Prison Notebooks*, London: Lawrence & Wishart.

Gray, Breda, (1999), 'Steering a course somewhere between hegemonic discourses of Irishness', in Ronit Lentin, (ed.), *The Expanding Nation: Towards a Multi-Ethnic Ireland*, Dublin: Ethnic and Racial Studies, Department of Sociology: Trinity College Dublin.

Hall, Stuart, (1980), 'Race, articulation and societies structured in dominance', in *Sociological Theories: Race and Colonialism*, Paris: Unesco.

Hughes, Gerald and Emma Quinn, (2004), *The Impact of Immigration on Europe's Societies: Ireland*, Dublin: ESRI.

Husserl, Edmund, (1960 [1931]), *Cartesian Meditations*, Dordrecht: Kluwer.

Immigrant Council of Ireland (2008), *Getting On: from Migration to Integration. Chinese, Indian, Lithuanian, and Nigerian Migrants' Experiences in Ireland*, Dublin: Immigrant Council of Ireland.

Labour Relations Commission (2005), *Migrant Workers and Access to the Statutory Dispute Resolution Agencies*, Dublin: LRC.

Lee, Harper, (1961), *To Kill a Mockingbird*. Philadelphia: Lippincott.

Lentin, Ronit, (1999), *The Expanding Nation: Towards a Multi-Ethnic Ireland*, Dublin: Ethnic and Racial Studies, Department of Sociology, Trinity College Dublin.

Lentin, Ronit and Robbie McVeigh, (eds), (2002), *Racism and Antiracism in Ireland*, Belfast: Beyond the Pale.

Levinas, Emmanuel, (1969), *Totality and Infinity*, Pittsburgh: Duquesne University Press.

Loyal, Steven, (2011), *Understanding Immigration in Ireland: State, Labour and Capital in a Global Age*, Manchester: Manchester University Press.

MacLachlan, Malcolm and Michael O'Connell, (2000), *Cultivating Pluralism: Psychological, Social and Cultural Perspectives on a Changing Ireland.* Dublin: Oak Tree Press.

Marx, Karl and Friedrich Engels, (1976 [1846]), *The German Ideology*, Moscow: Progress Publishers.

McDonagh, Roseleen, (2002), 'The web of self-identity: racism, sexism and disablism', in Ronit Lentin and Robbie McVeigh, (eds), *Racism and Antiracism in Ireland*, Belfast: Beyond the Pale.

McGinnity, Frances, Jacqueline Nelson, Pete Lunn and Emma Quinn, (2009), *Discrimination in Recruitment – Evidence from a Field Experiment.* Dublin: Equality Authority.

McGinnity, Frances, Philip O'Connell, Emma Quinn and James Williams, (2006), *Migrants' Experience of Racism and Discrimination in Ireland: Survey Report.* Dublin: Economic and Social Research Institute.

Miles, Robert, (1989), *Racism*, London: Routledge.

Molony, S., (2009), 'Outspoken TD calls for work permit clampdown', *Irish Independent*, February 7.

Monshengwo, Kensika, (2001), 'The potential of public awareness programmes', in Fintan Farrell and Philip Watt, (eds), *Responding to Racism in Ireland*, Dublin: Veritas.

Ní Shuinear, Sinead, (2002), 'Othering the Irish (Travellers)', in Ronit Lentin and Robbie McVeigh, (eds), *Racism and Antiracism*, Belfast: Beyond the Pale.

O'Connell, Philip and Frances McGinnity, (2008), *Immigrants at Work: Ethnicity and Nationality in the Irish Labour Market,* Dublin: The Equality Authority and Economic and Social Research Institute.

O'Mahony, Eoin, Steven Loyal and Aogán Mulcahy, (2001), *Racism in Ireland: The Views of Black and Ethnic Minorities*, Dublin: Amnesty International.

O'Toole, Fintan, (2000), 'Green, white and black: Race and Irish Identity', in Ronit Lentin, (ed.), *Emerging Irish Identities*, Dublin: Ethnic and Racial Studies, Department of Sociology, Trinity College Dublin.

Omni, Michael and Howard Winant, (1986), *Racial Formation in the United States from the 1960s to the 1980s*, New York: Routledge & Kegan Paul.

Rattansi, Ali, (2007), *Racism*, Oxford: Oxford University Press.

Sinha, Shalini, (1999), 'The right to Irishness: implications of ethnicity, nation and state towards a truly multi-ethnic Ireland', in Ronit Lentin, (ed), *The Expanding Nation: Towards a Multi-Ethnic Ireland.*, Dublin: Ethnic and Racial Studies, Department of Sociology, Trinity College Dublin.

Stoler, Ann Laura, (1995), *Race and the Education of Desire*, Durham, NC: Duke University Press.

Tannam, Marian, Suzanne Smith and Suzie Flood, (1998), *Anti-Racism: An Irish Perspective*, Dublin: Harmony.

Wacquant, Loïc J. D., (1997), 'Towards an Analytic of Racial Domination', *Political Power and Social Theory*, 11: 221–34.

Watt, Philip, (2002), 'Introduction and Overview', in Migration Policy: Reform and Harmonisation, Dublin: NCCRI.

White, Elisa, (2002), 'The new Irish story-telling: media, representations and racialized identities', in Ronit Lentin and Robbie McVeigh, (eds), *Racism and Antiracism in Ireland*, Belfast: Beyond the Pale.

Whorf, Benjamin Lee, (1956), *Language, Thought and Reality*, Cambridge, MA: MIT Press.

Wittgenstein, Ludwig, (1958), *The Blue and Brown Books*, Oxford: Basil Blackwell.

Norbert Elias and developmental psychology

Norman Gabriel

Abstract: This paper looks at the important similarities between Norbert Elias and two of the most well-known developmental psychologists of childhood, John Bowlby and Lev Vygotsky. After discussing some of the connections in their approach to the social learning of young children, it argues that Elias's perspective is more suitable for integrating the affective and cognitive aspects of early development and comparing the many different types of language that humanity has developed. Long-term research of parent–child relations in different cultures can also illuminate some of the ways in which our ancestors developed a range of caring and protective arrangements for the survival of their offspring.

Introduction

In this paper I argue that one can illuminate the distinctive aspects of Norbert Elias's figurational sociology by exploring some of its intimate connections with influential psychological approaches that attempt to integrate the different levels of human interdependence. In his discussion of human interdependencies, Elias addresses the problem of what binds people together as human beings, how social bonds are formed with each other in interweaving social relations. Although he identifies various affective and sexual bonds as being important, he does not reduce human bonding to sexual or emotional needs. Instead he calls for an investigation of 'love and learning' relationships. This will be used as a starting point to explore some of the major assumptions made by two major developmental psychologists of childhood, Lev Vygotsky and John Bowlby, both of whom had a close affinity with some of the arguments that Elias made about the importance of finding new conceptual tools for understanding the relationship between biological and social processes. I also draw attention to some of the important differences between Elias's approach and the work of Bowlby and Vygotsky, arguing that we not only need to avoid biological determinism, but develop a better understanding of the relationship between biological evolution, culture and social development.

'Love and learning' processes

For Norbert Elias (2009a [1987], 1991), it was crucial for sociologists to determine the relation between nature, culture and society and the unique characteristics that distinguish human beings from other animal species. He made an important conceptual distinction between the term 'evolution' which refers to biological processes that are genetic and largely irreversible and social 'development', processes which are malleable and potentially subject to change. Elias (2009a [1987]) argued that one of the distinctive characteristics of the human species is the 'interlocking' of biological and social processes in the development of knowledge. In the evolutionary process, humans are the only type of living beings for whom unlearned forms of steering conduct became subordinate to learned forms. This biological propensity for learning is one of the main differences between animal and human societies, providing a framework for social development to take place without any biological changes. To identify the universal features of social life that makes society possible, the adaptation of a distinctive biological organization of human beings for learning needs to be understood. In terms of social-evolutionary development, the distinguishing, evolutionary breakthrough for human beings was that learned ways of steering behaviour became dominant in relation to unlearned forms. One important issue in the development of children is the relation between the biological basis of behaviour and the social conditions in which this activity takes place. For young children, there are 'natural human structures which remain dispositions and cannot fully function unless they are stimulated by a person's "love and learning" relationship with other persons' (Elias, 2009a [1987]: 147).

Elias argues here that this 'love and learning' relationship emphasizes that specific experiences must happen at 'the right time', mentioning in particular when children are ready to learn a language 'and, one may add though one cannot enlarge on it here in the "right manner"'. This relational integration of love and learning draws attention to the way in which children's development is both a cognitive and affective process, one in which biological and social processes are intimately woven together. It is also significantly an important critique of an 'academic' approach to psychology which separates areas into institutional divisions that treat individual psychology as a natural science and social psychology as a social science:

> Yet, although the psychological levels of a human person – whether conduct or feeling, conscience or drive – are invariably patterned by learning and thus have natural and social characteristics at the same time, quite a number of individual psychologists proceed in their research as if the persons they study were natural objects pure and simple, unaffected by their social language or any other social patterning. (Elias, 2007b [1992]: 116–17)

In one of the first attempts by John Bowlby (1979a) to integrate an ethological approach in child development with psychoanalysis, he emphasized the way in which sensitive phases of development are often found in species-specific patterns of behaviour. These sensitive phases of development are very similar to Elias's right-time hypothesis because they draw our attention to the way in which important areas of the development of young children have to be 'stimulated', 'activated' and patterned by social relationships if they are to develop at all. In a similar way to Elias, Bowlby is trying to steer a middle course between learning approaches that are solely dependent on learnt behaviour, excluding any 'built-in social responses', yet at the same time avoid a return to a naive version of biological determinism:

> In his equipment the balance has tipped far in favour of flexibility of behaviour, and therefore of learning, and away from in-built fixity. Yet it would be odd were the biological security which comes from fixed patterns to have been wholly abandoned. Crying, sucking and smiling I suspect are some of our many built-in motor patterns and represent nature's insurance against leaving everything to the hazard of learning. (Bowlby, 1979a: 40)

Smiling is a good illustration of the way the evolutionary process has facilitated human beings to live in groups, steering conduct towards the dominance of learned over unlearned forms of behaviour. According to Bowlby (1969), during the first year of life, an infant's smiling develops through four main phases: spontaneous and reflex smiling, unselective social smiling, selective social smiling and differential social responsiveness. Both Bowlby and Elias (2009a [1987]) agree that smiling develops from the spontaneous, more innate forms of smiling in the human infant to the more malleable, 'selective' and 'discriminating' repertoire that is available later in adulthood.

I now want to return to Elias's 'right manner hypothesis'[1] which, as he himself admits, requires the theoretical synthesis of a great deal of unorganized knowledge or evidence. This paper will focus on the way that Elias and Bowlby can be integrated to develop a better understanding of the bonds of early attachment or early childhood development. We can then begin to understand how these early structures help to shape 'the constitutional reliance of the human child on learning from other people' (Elias, 1978 [1970]: 110). Elias emphasises the importance of these bonds by referring to 'open valencies':

> each individual has open valencies ready to connect with those of other individuals according to a schema whose groundwork has already been laid by his early childhood experiences in the family, which have been further elaborated by his emotional experiences as a constituent of other configurations. (Elias, 2009b [1969]: 170)

For Bowlby, these 'open valencies' become connected in the very beginning of human relationships through the 'instinctual attachment' of infants to mothers. One of the most fundamental aspects of attachment theory is its focus on the biological bases of attachment. During the time when humans were evolving, when they lived in 'the environment of evolutionary adaptedness', genetic selection favoured attachment behaviours because they increased the likelihood of child-mother proximity, which increased protection and provided survival advantage (Cassidy, 1999).

Bowlby (1969) argued that there is an attachment behaviour system which is species-specific and leads to certain predictable and beneficial outcomes that result from the child's proximity to the parent, including feeding, learning about the environment and social interaction. But the most important survival advantage to the child is protection from predators. Infants who were more biologically predisposed to stay close to their mothers were less likely to be killed by predators. This is known as the biological function of attachment behaviour: without protection from predators, feeding and learning cannot take place.

The ethological turn?

Another important aspect to the affective and learning processes in Elias and Bowlby's approach to early parent–child relationships will now be explored by tracing the key influence of ethology on Bowlby's theory of attachment. Ethologists provide a biological framework for studies of social behaviour by emphasizing techniques of observation of animals in their natural habitat. This particular approach appealed to psychologists like Bowlby working with children, because of its roots in 'naturalistic' observation[2] and also because it provided a theoretical critique of psychoanalysis[3]. According to Holmes (1993: 132), 'attachment theory is perhaps seen as a variant of object-relations theory': in the traditional psychoanalytic view, human beings are driven by the impulse to express instinctual drives, and in order to do this successfully relationships with others are formed. In object-relations theory, the organism is not an isolated drive-driven creature in search of an object on whom to discharge accumulated tension, but a person relating to other persons. Freud's theory of instincts and drives is replaced by an assumption that humans are fundamentally relation-seeking creatures. Bowlby argued that the attachment system is not related to feeding, or the by-product of any more fundamental processes or 'secondary drives' proposed within the psychoanalytic tradition.[4]

> What I've been trying to do, really, is to rewrite psychoanalysis in the light of ethological principles ... I've always felt that traditional psychoanalytical metapsychology was out of date, grabbed from nineteenth-century physics. My main concern, right back from the thirties, has been to get psychoanalysis onto a decent scientific basis. (Bowlby, 1979b: 325)

Bowlby used this ethological approach to compare the different mechanisms involved in early parent–child relationships, focusing on some of the important differences between species, but also on some of the similarities in closely related primates. He was particularly attracted to the systematic observation and application of research methods derived from the European School of animal behaviour studies headed by Lorenz and Tinbergen. Lorenz's work (1957 [1935]) on imprinting was of special interest, because it showed that in some species of bird, strong bonds to an individual mother figure could develop without any reference to food. Imprinting is a rapid form of learning in which familiarity with the specific characteristics of the mother hen are learned in a few hours after hatching by the baby chick. This early experience of following the mother allowed geese to bond without feeding by learning the specific visual characteristics of the mother.

Harlow *et al.*'s (1963) experimental studies had shown that in the rearing of rhesus monkeys the infant's attachment behaviours (clasping and clinging) lead him to seek proximity and contact more often with an inanimate surrogate mother figure that is soft than with another which yields milk. Although the first attachment bond in humans is analogous to these monkeys, it is based on species-specific human behaviours. In human infants, because clinging is so poorly developed, crying and smiling become even more crucial for eliciting maternal caretaking in the early months.

From the end of the first year, children are increasingly able to represent the world in symbolic form – they can think about their attachment figures, about themselves and about the relationship between themselves and the other person:

> the model of himself that he builds reflects also the images that his parents have of him, images that are communicated not only by how each treats him but by what each *says* to him. These models then govern how he feels towards each parent and about himself, how he expects each of them to treat him, and how he plans his own behaviour towards them. They govern too both the fear and wishes expressed in his daydreams. (Bowlby, 2005: 146)

These initial models can then be generalized to other people and relationships: children viewing themselves as lovable are likely to expect positive relationships with others. But children who feel rejected might approach any new relationship with low expectations. So, according to Schaffer (2004), these models emphasize the fact that attachment is a lifelong process: they are representations of the past, but can also be used to guide behaviour in future close relationships. This perspective on human relationships from early childhood is remarkably similar to Elias's call for more research into the specific nature of valencies:

> Nor does one know much about the long-term development of an individual's configuration of valencies in its connection with the sequence of figurations which he socially forms with others from the simple, narrow, and relatively undifferentiated family configurations of early childhood, to the wider and more differentiated configurations of adolescence and childhood, and again to the shrinking configurations of old age. Thus a configurational approach, by extending attention to the whole profile of a person's valencies throughout his development, with its recurrent as well as its changing patterns of *affective attachment* and conflict, provides a theoretical scheme for the formulation and study of problems concerning the connections between the individual and the group level of human beings. (2009b [1969]: 171–2; my emphasis)

I now want to explore some of the problems that stem from adopting an ethological approach for explaining the development of children by drawing on several related critiques that Elias mentions in his work. A discussion of these problems emphasizes that even though there are important similarities in the biological characteristics of human beings and other animal species, it is important to focus on the distinctive, evolutionary breakthrough of humankind:

> The approach of ethologists and other specialists in animal psychology, which investigates all human behaviour with the same theoretical tools that have proved adequate and fruitful in studying sub-human organisms, can yield only limited results. It distracts attention from a decisive factor. In the biological species of man, structured qualities that humans share with animals and which, in other words, prove their undoubted descent from non-human organisms, are indissolubly interwoven with structural qualities which represent an evolutionary innovation. These features are uniquely, specifically human and are absent in the biological equipment of all other organisms on this earth, as far as is now known. (Elias, 2010 [1987]: 171)

Elsewhere, it is significant that Elias (2010 [1987]) describes the maturation process in the development of a language in terms of the child's organic equipment – a vocal and aural apparatus that is used and activated in communicating sound-patterns, gradually overlaid and patterned by the social process of learning a language. But to what extent does Bowlby ignore this evolutionary innovation or the unique 'biological endowment' of human beings? Although Bowlby (1969) does draw attention to 'forms of behaviour' that mediate attachment in young babies and infants (for example, crying, smiling and babbling) and to the behavioural equipment of the human neonate (see, in particular, Bowlby, 1969: 268–96), at other points in his argument, he does eventually return to a form of biological reductionism. He gives a good example (1969: 61–2) where, although he acknowledges that there are differences between 'man and sub-human species', 'their similarities are equally important, and perhaps more so than their differences'. Later in his book on attachment, in a sub-section entitled 'Differences from and similarities with that seen in sub-human primates', one would expect from the title some differences to be mentioned in attachment behaviour. But once again, although he points to the mother keeping in close contact with human infants, because they are less mobile than other primates, he is nevertheless keen to downplay these differences: 'Thus the difference in infant–mother relations in gorilla and in man is not so great' (Bowlby, 1969: 198–9).

Burman (1994) also shares similar concerns that attachment theorists and, more generally, developmental psychologists, in their attempt to overcome the division between the biological and the social by referring to the 'adaptedness' of the infant for social interaction, present an impoverished view of what it means to be social. The social is primarily represented by the mother–child relationship, which is further equated with communication and then finally seen as 'interpersonal'. Developmental psychologists like Bowlby lapse into a form of biological reductionism by dissolving the social into the biological, ignoring other significant relationships that involve infants and young children. Burman argues that, in the attempt to overcome the division between the 'social' and the 'cultural', an evolutionary perspective once again is reintroduced, one that fragments 'cultural variation into individual differences' (Burman, 1994: 43).

Burman, however, is also in danger of reproducing the division between 'biology' and 'society' and 'nature' and 'culture' by placing too much emphasis on the socially constructed aspects of child development.[5] Wood (2007) points to a more nuanced approach that can begin to integrate the different levels of the social and biological in the development of attachment bonds by arguing that it is mistaken to assume that evolutionary psychology must necessarily be deterministic or reductive. According to Wood (2007), an important point of contact between Elias and evolutionary psychology is human nature.

The work of Colwyn Trevarthen is a good starting point for developing this type of integration, because he synthesizes a great deal of recent neurological, biological and psychological research to highlight the unique biological equipment of human beings that prepares young babies and children to enjoy and share companionship with others. In a similar way to Elias, he emphasizes how the 'human body and brain' are adapted for communication: momentary shifts of gaze and 'gazing reverie' are made possible by the distinctive white sclera of human eyes and the versatility of human vocalization and sustained phonation achieved by the 'uniquely adapted human respiratory system' (Trevarthen, 2005: 60–1). He also offers an important critique of attachment theory for only including aspects of early human relationships that are solely based on 'protection' and a 'secure base'. Innate emotions of 'attachment for companionship', affective systems for testing the opportunity and value of shared activity and experience, are just as important as emotions of 'attachment for care'.[6] Similarly, Elias (1978 [1970]: 110) argues that what makes human societies possible is 'the adaptation of human biological organization for learning'. He identifies two features: language, 'the dominance of a society-specific form of learning', over 'the species form of communication' and the 'individualization of human faces' (Elias, 2009a [1987], 2009b [1969]).

So far, I have emphasised how the different strands of early learning and social development need to be integrated into a suitable theoretical framework, one that can be used to explain the distinctive, biological characteristics of human beings. The rest of this paper will now focus on one important, universal feature in society, the early development of language by young children, investigating the relationship between Elias and the Russian developmental psychologist, Lev Vygotsky.

Quest for synthesis

What can two very different biographical and intellectual careers have in common? Elias, a sociologist who productively worked and lived in various European countries until the age of 93; Vygotsky, a Russian developmental psychologist who was influenced by the Marxist ideas of the Soviet Revolution, dying at the young age of 37 from tuberculosis. First, what is significant is that both were not only attempting a broad intellectual synthesis from within their own subject areas, but were also trying to integrate disciplines that were usually considered separate and unrelated: biology, social anthropology, history and psychoanalysis, to name just a few. They argued that previous approaches in psychology or sociology had reduced social relationships to the investigation of isolated concepts, with little consideration of how factors relate to one another. For example, in studies of language development, academic specialists[7] have separated connected processes into independent areas of study; as a result of the application of this form of analysis to verbal thinking, meaning had been divorced from sound. To reflect complex psychological processes as activities, what was required was a significant reorientation of thought, one that would restore the dynamic and interrelated aspects of socio-psychological systems, capturing 'the movement from thought to word and from word to thought' (Vygotsky, 1987: 250). In a very similar way, Elias (1991: 65) emphasized that traditional academic specialists like philosophers have constructed theories of knowledge and language into separate human activities, three different worlds known as language, reason and knowledge. To replace the reduction of processes to static entities, Elias argued that these three different realms should be viewed as symbols whose function is to connect relationships between thinking, speaking and knowing.

Second, another key similarity between Elias and Vygotsky was their integration of a highly sophisticated developmental perspective. Their developmental approach not only attempted to understand the group moulding of individual childhood in existing societies, but also wished to place these within a wider framework that included the different stages of human development in history. Both emphasized that development is not linear, a straight path of quantitative accumulations, but a dynamic and uneven process that can give rise to new structures or qualitative changes at higher levels of organization. In the 1920s Vygotsky and his colleagues, Alexander Luria and Alexei Leontiev, proposed a human science of psychology to stand alongside the natural sciences. The central thesis of the Russian cultural-historical school was that the structure and development of human psychological processes emerge through culturally mediated, historically developing, practical activity. Crucial to this approach was the integration of individual, social and cultural-historical levels within the analytic unit of activity:

> The growth of the normal child into civilization usually involves a fusion with the processes of organic maturation. Both planes of development – the natural and the cultural – coincide and mingle with one another. The two lines of change interpenetrate one another and form what is essentially a single line of socio-biological formation of the child's personality. To the extent that development occurs in the cultural medium, it becomes transformed into a historically conditioned biological process. (Vygotsky, 1930: 47)

Within this perspective, Cole (1998) has argued that culture should be viewed as the species-specific medium of *Homo sapiens*. Human biology and human culture should not be juxtaposed with one another – the human brain and body co-evolved over a long period of time with the species' complex cultural environment. Cole (1996) summarizes the 'either/or' aspects of these scholarly debates by asking whether language is acquired through a process of culturally mediated learning, or is a specialized domain that needs to be triggered into action. Cole argues that both the natural and the cultural lines of development need to be present for language acquisition: not only are children born with the 'seeds' of language, they also have to participate in jointly organized activities that enable them to gain control over their environment. According to Resnick (1994: 479), the biological roots of development predominate in infancy and early childhood, while the sociocultural roots take 'increasing control . . . as each individual's personal history of situations grows and initial biologically prepared structures are successfully modified'.

Moreover, this cultural context should not be seen as something outside the process of development 'as that which surrounds' but an intrinsic part of 'that which weaves together' (Cole, 1996: 132–5). Patterns of nurturance and communication do not merely influence children's development, but are an intrinsic part of the developmental process. In Vygotsky and Luria's (1994) view, a developmental approach should be the main method used to analyse three lines of human behaviour – evolutionary, historical and ontogenetic. In each of these lines or genetic domains, different principles operate to produce a change in the type of development itself. Each stage in the formation of higher psychological processes is distinguished by a particular organization of psychological activity. For example, when speech begins to serve as a psychological instrument for the regulation of behaviour, children learn to use language that will enable them to plan future actions. From accompanying children's actions in chaotic problem solving, speech now acts as a guide to determine future behaviour (Vygotsky, 1978).

Significantly, Vygotsky argued that these higher processes such as language cannot be reduced to inferior ones: according to Van der Veer and Valsiner (1991), Vygotsky's consistently anti-reductionist perspective can be seen as a major contribution to psychology. He believed that human psychological functions are organized hierarchically, each level needing to be studied in its specifics. As human beings develop, the natural stage is not replaced by later cultural stages, but superimposed like scaffolding on top of the former, changing, restructuring and adapting these natural processes. The biological new-born grows up in an environment composed of cultural artefacts – as a result, two 'lines' of development, the natural and the cultural, merge into a specifically, unique form of human development. Within this framework, Vygotsky outlined a new general process of development:

> two qualitatively different lines of development, differing in origin, can be distinguished: the elementary processes, which are of biological origin, on the one hand, and the higher psychological functions, of socio-cultural origin, on the other. The history of child behaviour is born from the interweaving of these two lines. (1978: 46)

When Elias (2009a [1987]) discussed 'higher psychological functions' such as learning, he used concepts that were extraordinary similar in imagery to Vygotsky. For example, he considered learning as the 'reciprocal processes of the biological and the social' and the 'intimate interweaving of learned and unlearned processes'. Like Vygotsky, Elias argued that evolutionary biology needed to be interwoven into a long-term conception of human development. In his fragments on the 'Great Evolution' (2007a [1987]: 179–233), he outlined in a non-reductive way the different stages of integration from atoms to the most highly integrated of organisms – human beings. In trying to explain this developmental process, he emphasized that higher levels of integration must be explained in terms of their stage-specific behavioural and functional properties, which are not reducible to their lower component parts.[8] To explain more complex formations, one needed to know not only the structural properties of lower level units, but also how they are organized functionally.

Elias and Vygotsky were therefore both engaged with explaining the connection between nature and society, and more specifically, the biological framework that is necessary for children to learn a language. I shall now examine some of the concepts that were introduced by them to understand the development of young children as they move from communicating sound-patterns to learning and eventually mastering a language. It will be argued that both these perspectives can enrich one another in refining and elaborating a long-term socio-psychological perspective of children's development in societies.

Learning to speak a language

For Elias (2009a [1987]), the fundamental difference between human and animal societies is that in the steering of conduct a social means of communication becomes dominant over unlearned signals – young children must learn a language in order to survive. A child develops into a human being and is integrated into a particular society by learning a social language which involves his or her capacity to produce words and sentences as well as understanding sound patterns produced by others. As Elias argues, this blending of biological and social processes in learning reveals the hinge that connects human nature with culture and the development of an evolutionary advantage referred to as symbol emancipation:

> They [children] learn to regulate their own speech behaviour and, indeed, their own behaviour generally in accordance with the common code of producing and retrieving articulated sound-patterns as messages for and from other people which prevail in their society. This is the crucial aspect of the interlocking of nature and society in the structure of human languages. For the purposes of communication the production and reception of voice-sounds, a purely organic or physical event, is no longer subjected mainly or exclusively to the bondage of genetic fixating. Instead, the organic event of voice-production, to a large extent, can be patterned in accordance with a

211

learned social code of voice regulation which most members of a language society have made their own when young, and which makes it possible for them to understand the same sound-patterns as symbols of the same objects and functions of communication. (Elias, 1991: 53)

How do these 'voice sounds' in young children gradually become overlaid as a means of communication? According to Vygotsky (1987), a pre-intellectual stage in the development of children's speech can be primarily characterized by an emotional form of behaviour, one that is displayed through crying and babbling. During this stage, laughing, pointing and gesture emerge as a complex form of infant interaction with adults: when an infant cries or reaches for an object, adults attribute meaning to that behaviour.[9] Within this context, Vygotsky (1981) has discussed the emergence of indicative gestures – in the confusion that surrounds infants in the first few months of their lives, parents point and carry their children to objects and places of adaptive significance. Though infants have no communicative intent, these acts function to communicate their needs to caretakers – very young children are included in social activity even before they have the capacity to use or respond adequately to communicative devices.

Once young children have moved from vocalized reflexes and imitating sounds, the symbolic function of speech occurs: they discover the functional use of words as a means of naming objects, for expressing certain wishes and gaining control of their environment (Vygotsky, 1987; Vygotsky and Luria, 1994). In children's developing communicative activity, a stage of language acquisition is marked by a rapid accumulation of words, which children repeat and invent when they meet situations where previously heard words do not fit. Like Elias, Vygotsky argued that a most important aspect of this developmental change was the manner in which previously separate and elementary biological functions are integrated into new functional learning systems. For children to make any advancement in intellectual behaviour they must go beyond learned reactions that fail to overcome some difficulty or barrier. Mastering cultural knowledge, children can take a step towards emancipation from nature: whereas animals are almost fully dependent on the inheritance of genetically based traits, humans can transmit the products of culture by adapting and learning new skills. However, children not only acquire tools that have been transmitted from one generation to another, but create new ones – what Knox (1994) refers to as a 'Second Symbol System', words or signs that substitute for objects. This system is first used by human beings to communicate with or control each other and then internalized to regulate their own behaviour in new situations.

Vygotsky (1987) has argued that relatively early in speech development two planes of development move towards one another to merge: children become increasingly aware that the living process of meaningful speech is composed of auditory and semantic aspects. At the auditory level, children master vocal speech by progressing from single words to two word phrases and then to simple sentences.[10] During this early stage, the word is an 'oral indicative gesture', its function to designate or isolate one aspect of a situation from others. Like indicative gestures, words have no meaning outside the concrete contexts in which they are used. At the semiotic level, meanings which are inherent in children's utterances begin as full sentences and only gradually become differentiated to express phrases or single words. Newman and Holzman (1993) have argued that this process of 'meaning-making' is a crucial stage in adapting to society – children learn to use pre-determined tools of language to become more communicative and engage fully in societal behaviour.

As mentioned previously, for Elias (1991) an important conceptual distinction needs to be made between the term 'evolution', which should refer to biological processes that are genetic and relatively fixed, and 'development', social processes that are more malleable and subject to change. In his attempt to identify some of the distinguishing characteristics of human beings that 'animal psychologists' (ethologists) have ignored, Elias mentions a unique human capacity 'for controlling and modifying drives and affects in a great variety of ways as part of a learning process' (Elias, 2007b [1992]: 125). This capacity for developing forms of self-restraint is central to Elias's argument in *The Civilizing Process:* the increasing social constraint towards self-constraint is related to more demanding social standards of self-control. Social pressures lead to more self-control, with the behaviour of individual people being regulated 'in an increasingly differentiated, more even and more stable manner'. An integral aspect of civilizing processes is that young children should eventually grow up through their own self-regulation. Here is where we can directly compare the long-term movement from 'external control' to 'self-control' with Vygotsky's explanation of the central role of internalization processes in the acquisition of language. In order for children to regulate their own speech behaviour and understand the same symbols, speech is internalized, becoming a vital part of the higher psychological processes – it organizes, unifies and integrates disparate aspects of children's behaviour, such as perception, problem solving and memory:

> The greatest change in children's capacity to use language as a problem-solving tool takes place somewhat later in their development, when socialised speech is *turned inward*. Instead of appealing to the adult, children appeal to themselves; language thus takes on an *intrapersonal function* in addition to its *interpersonal use*. When children develop a method of behaviour for guiding themselves that had previously been used in relation to another person, when they organize their own activities according to a social form of behaviour, they succeed in applying a social attitude to themselves. (Vygotsky, 1978: 26)

How are these processes 'turned inward,' enabling children to develop their use of language? In this context, Vygotsky (1987) explained the important process of internalization for understanding the cultural evolution of children's thinking. According to Vygotsky (1987), inner speech is what makes thinking possible. It is a distinctive speech function, a form of verbal thinking that mediates between word and thought. Two important processes are interwoven in inner speech:

the transition from external communication to inner dialogue and the translation of intimate thoughts into a linguistic and communicative form. This concept of inner speech is a type of speech that is 'mute' and 'silent', involving no vocalization. In inner speech, word sense – which is dependent on the context of speech – develops and becomes predominant over meaning.

Once again, what is remarkable is Elias's similar use of imagery to discuss internalization. In *The Symbol Theory* Elias (1991) addresses the problem of understanding the connections between thinking and speaking by tracing the different developmental stages in the sending and receiving of sound-patterns. In language communication, one of the functions of the term 'thinking' is to refer to the capacity of human beings to put through their paces symbols anticipating a sequence of possible future actions without their performance in reality. At this level, thought is not easily recognizable as a flow of voicelessly produced sound-symbols, an abbreviated version of the audible use of language that can be converted into spoken language. These forms of abbreviated thinking are associated with the manipulation of stored memory images: according to him, these do not have to be set out step by step, but can be telescoped, recalled and used when the occasion demands.

But although there are important similarities in Elias's and Vygotsky's accounts of internalization, a distinctive emphasis can be identified. It is important to note that whereas Elias (1991: 78) discussed the conversion of spoken language into the voiceless language of thought as a 'most easily' convertible process, Vygotsky (1987: 267) viewed this process as much more gradual, emerging from the development of egocentric speech in children. There is 'no simple transition toward a telegraphic style', but a tendency toward a form of abbreviation where the predicate and related words are preserved. This distinction may be due to the fact that Elias is discussing a longer-term process that has already been mastered by adults, while Vygotsky, basing his results on experiments with children, is uncovering some of the complex layers that children have to learn before achieving similar capabilities. Given these differences, Vygotsky's concepts may provide a suitable framework for developing a more detailed refinement of the theory of civilizing processes – the learning processes in early childhood that lead to a greater degree of self-control.

Conclusion

This paper has argued that sociologists need to overcome some of their deepest fears and insecurities about the role of biology in the historical development of human beings. In the place of artificial barriers that have been constructed to prevent biologists, sociologists and psychologists from speaking and listening to one another (and perhaps even learning from one another), we need a flexible and dynamic approach, capable of investigating the various lines of child development. I have suggested that an important starting point is to examine closely the contributions made by two influential psychologists of child development, John Bowlby and Lev Vygotsky.

Bowlby and Elias were both concerned with the identification of a universal bond of attachment that bound people together in human societies, one that was distinctive, but related to sexual satisfaction. In their critique of psychoanalytic theory, especially of Freud and Melanie Klein, they were keen to investigate the different levels of individual and group interdependencies that enabled infants and young children to survive, to grow up safe and secure in their societies. Important points of connection can be made between Elias's concept of 'open valencies', which emphasizes the strong, affective ties that link people with one another, and the biological theory of attachment proposed by Bowlby: approach behaviours of the child and 'imprinting' from the stimulations from parents (eye contact, smiles, vocal signals of affection) were considered essential biological foundations for human relationships, and for the building of working models of a parent as a source of emotional strength and security. As adults, children would later use these early attachments to form relationships with others in society.

I then discussed the influence of Lorenz's ethological theory on Bowlby's theory of attachment by responding to some of the important criticisms that it is too deterministic and reductive, relegating social relationships to biology. By closely looking at Elias's critique of animal psychologists like Lorenz, I argued that he provides a much needed sociological explanation of the distinctive, biological characteristics of human beings that enable them to live with one another in societies. The development of language is the 'symbolic breakthrough', the developmental bridge between 'the seemingly unalterable divide between "nature" and "society"', and thus also between "nature" and "culture"' ' (Elias, 2007b [1992]: 125).

This article then turned to some of the innovative concepts that Elias and Vygotsky introduced to thinking about a universal process of humankind, the early development of language in young children. Both provide a sophisticated, developmental perspective that can follow the interweaving of biological and social processes as children learn to communicate in society. In trying to explain the complexity of children's learning, it becomes important to recognize that, though development may be a continuous process, new levels of communication emerge that cannot be reduced to previous stages of development. The development of these stage-specific levels or higher psychological processes are the 'symbolic' breakthrough that distinguishes newly born members of the human species from other animals and enables them to survive and continually learn from other human beings.

For Elias and Vygotsky, a central feature of this development is an explanation of the relationship between 'verbal thinking' and spoken language or how external communication becomes turned into silent or inner speech. Such internalization processes are crucial for understanding the ways in which young children become active learners and members of different language communities. In thinking about internalization, Elias and Vygotsky introduce innovative concepts that can enrich one another – both display a remarkable sensitivity to step-by-step processes that are involved in learning to speak. By deepening our understanding of children's development in learning a language, the 'civilizing process' can be further elaborated and refined – we may then be able to explain how each generation of children become members of a 'language society' and linked to the wider development of humanity.

I have argued that Elias overcomes traditional philosophical dualities by identifying the hinge that connects social and biological processes in the long-term development of humanity. From this viewpoint, all young children need to experience 'love and learning' relationships: they are not only biologically equipped at birth to communicate sound-patterns, but must learn a specific language from their elders to survive and grow in their societies. Moreover, Elias discusses these processes in newly constructed concepts that are deliberately sensitive and more suitable for integrating the affective and cognitive aspects of social learning processes and comparing the many different types of language that humanity has developed. Although members of scientific societies can sometimes use a superior 'we-image' to elevate their thinking above others, it is important to determine the direction of long-term processes by understanding the contribution of previous generations:

> Only through understanding and explaining the thought and experience of earlier-stage people in terms of their position in a sequential order can one even hope to arrive at an understanding of, and be able to explain, those of groups that represent a later stage. In order to explain such differences between earlier and later-stage societies, one needs, in other words, a developmental ordering of evidence which can only be brought to life by a testable process theory that shows how such processes as the development of knowledge and the closely related civilizing process fit into the wider development of human societies. (Elias, 2007a [1987]: 117*n*)

Our task ahead is to understand and explain how similarities in the natural potential of language development become overlaid with group and social processes of learning, forming the multitude of different languages spoken by children and adults throughout the world. Careful, long-term comparative research of parent–child relations in different cultures can also illuminate some of the ways in which our ancestors developed a range of caring and protective arrangements for the survival of their offspring.

Notes

1 This 'right manner hypothesis' is mentioned by Elias, but this time in the context of language development: 'Every child has to make an individual effort to reproduce the sound-patterns used by his or her elders in their various communications. The child has to remember what these sound-patterns symbolically represent . . . and to use the remembered sound symbols in the '*right*' way, the way standardized in the society of grown-ups' (Elias, 1991: 37–8).
2 According to Bronfenbrenner (1979), ecologically valid research must fulfil three conditions: (1) maintain the integrity of the real-life situations it is designed to investigate; (2) be faithful to the larger social and cultural contexts from which the subjects come; (3) be consistent with the participants' definition of the situation.

3 Significantly, Fonagay (1999: 596) argues that Bowlby's presentation of psychoanalysis was at times 'disingenuous', 'guilty of combating a psychoanalytic straw figure'. '. . . Bowlby consistently focused on the weakest facets of the psychoanalytic corpus, almost as if he wished to forestall a mutually corrective relationship.'

4 See Bowlby's very revealing review of the history of the psychoanalytic approach to attachment in his appendix in the first volume of *Attachment* (1969).

5 In the construction of a new paradigm for the sociological study of childhood, James and Prout (1990) have similarly challenged the universality of childhood as a biological fact by arguing for a wider definition of childhood that incorporates different social and cultural contexts. But important issues have tended to be overlooked or not directly addressed in their analysis, the traditional difficulties which emerge when sociologists are faced with trying to bridge the gap between the 'social', 'natural' and 'cultural' worlds of childhood.

6 Despite this step in the right direction, Trevarthen (2005: 71) still reproduces some of the static, philosophical divisions that Elias is keen to avoid. For example, the following quotation highlights the unhelpful dichotomies between 'bodies' and 'minds', 'actions and 'states': . . . 'human attachment is perhaps first to a *conversational partner* who reciprocates motive states, not to a caregiver. . . . Newborn infants show themselves sociable persons with minds of their own. The needs for sociability, even for a newborn, go beyond a seeking for regulation, care, protection, stress-regulation, etc., that the internal body needs.'

7 Vygotsky (1987: 49) observes that, 'traditional linguistics conceptualized sound as independent of meaning in speech; it conceptualized speech as a combination of these two isolated elements. The result was that the individual sound was considered to be the basic unit of analysis in the study of speech in sound. We have seen, however, that when sound is divorced from human thought it loses the characteristics that makes it unique as a sound of human speech: it is placed within the ranks of all other sounds existing in nature.'

8 Elias (2007a [1987]: 130) further argued that these higher levels of integration require different forms of thinking, 'To do justice to the peculiarity of combinations of these events on higher levels of organization, one finds oneself in need of stage-specific terms and context-models that are not applicable to lower levels. Expressions like "birth", "death" and "life" or, to mention stage-specific terms for structural properties of yet higher planes of integration, 'consciousness' or "mind", are examples of these.'

9 Vygotsky (1978: 55) further explains these developmental processes by tracing the emergence of pointing from the 'grasping movement': 'Initially, this gesture is nothing more than an unsuccessful attempt to grasp something, a movement aimed at a certain object which designates forthcoming activity. The child attempts to grasp an object beyond his reach; his hands, stretched towards that object, remain poised in the air. His fingers make grasping movements. . . . when the mother comes to the child's aid and realises his movement means something, the situation changes fundamentally. Pointing becomes a gesture for others. The child's unsuccessful attempt engenders a reaction not from the object he seeks but *from another person*.'

10 Vygotsky and Luria (1994: 202) provide a good example of how this process operates: 'The word *nanny* in no way means only nanny for the child: It means "Nanny, come here", or "Nanny, go away", or "Nanny, give me an apple". Depending on the circumstances, it may acquire different meanings, but always appears in its active form that expresses in a single combination of sounds the child's whole wish. The first period of meaningful speech is always a period of one word sentences. Words actively express the child's wish or singles out certain elements on which the child has focused. Other complex speech phenomena are differentiated precisely from this root.'

References

Dates given in square brackets are those of first publication.

Bowlby, John, (1969), *Attachment and Loss*, Vol. 1, *Attachment*, London: Hogarth Press.
Bowlby, John, (1979a), *The Making and Breaking of Affectional Bonds*, London: Tavistock.

Bowlby, John, (1979b), Interview in *New Society*, 10 May: 323–5.

Bowlby, John, (2005), *A secure base*, London: Routledge.

Bronfenbrenner, Urie, (1979), *The Ecology of Human Development*, Cambridge, MA: Harvard University Press.

Burman, Erica, (1994), *Deconstructing Developmental Psychology*, London: Routledge.

Butterworth, George and Margaret Harris, (1994), *Principles of Developmental Psychology*, Hove: Lawrence Erlbaum.

Cahan, Emily, Jay Mechling, Brian Sutton-Smith and Sheldon White, (1993), 'The elusive historical child', in Glen Elder, John Modell and Ross Parke, (eds), *Children in Time and Space: Developmental and Historical Insights*, Cambridge: Cambridge University Press.

Cassidy, Jude, (1999), 'The Nature of the Child's Ties' in Jude Cassidy and Phillip R. Shaver, (eds), *Handbook of Attachment: Theory, Research, and Clinical Applications*, London: Guilford.

Cole, Michael, (1996), *Cultural Psychology – A Once and Future Discipline*, Cambridge, MA: Harvard University Press.

Cole, Michael, (1998), 'Culture in Development', in Martin Woodhead, Dorothy Faulkner and Karen Littleton, (eds), *Cultural Worlds of Early Childhood*, London: Routledge.

Elias, Norbert, (1978 [1970]), *What is Sociology?*, London: Hutchinson. [Collected Works, Vol. 5, Dublin: UCD Press, forthcoming].

Elias, Norbert, (1991), *The Symbol Theory*, London: Sage. [Collected Works, Vol. 13, Dublin: UCD Press, 2011].

Elias, Norbert, (2007a [1987]), *Involvement and Detachment*, Collected Works, Vol. 8, Dublin: UCD Press.

Elias, Norbert, (2007b [1992]), *An Essay on Time*, Collected Works, Vol. 9, Dublin: UCD Press.

Elias, Norbert, (2009a [1987]), 'On Human Beings and Their Emotions: A Process-Sociological Essay', in *Essays III: On Sociology and the Humanities*. Collected Works, Vol. 16, Dublin: UCD Press: 141–58.

Elias, Norbert, (2009b [1969]), 'Sociology and Psychiatry', in *Essays III: On Sociology and the Humanities*, Press Collected Works, Vol. 16, Dublin: UCD: 159–79.

Elias, Norbert, (2010 [1987]), *The Society of Individuals*, Collected Works, Vol. 10, Dublin: UCD Press.

Fonagay, Peter, (1999), 'Psychoanalytic Theory from the Viewpoint of Attachment Theory and Research', in Jude Cassidy and Phillip R. Shaver, (eds), *Handbook of Attachment: Theory, Research, and Clinical Applications*, London: Guilford.

Harlow, Harry F., Margaret K. Harlow and Ernst W. Hansen, (1963), 'The maternal affectional system of rhesis monkeys', in Rheingold, Harriet R., (ed.), *Maternal Behaviour in Mammals*, New York: Wiley.

Holmes, Jeremy, (1993), *John Bowlby and Attachment Theory*, London: Routledge.

James, Allison and Alan Prout, (eds), (1990), *Constructing and Reconstructing Childhood*, Basingstoke: Falmer.

Kessel, Frank S. and Alexander W. Siegel, (eds), (1983), *The Child and Other Cultural Inventions*, New York: Praeger.

Knox, Jane E., (1994), 'Introduction', in Lev S. Vygotsky and Alexander R. Luria, *Studies on the History of Behaviour: Ape, Primitive, and Child*, London: Lawrence Erlbaum.

Lorenz, Konrad Z., (1957 [1935]), 'Companionship in Bird Life – Fellow Members of the species as Releasers of Social Behaviour', in Claire H. Schiller, (ed.), *Instinctive Behaviour*, New York: International Universities Press: 83–128.

Newman, Fred and Lois Holzman, (1993), *Lev Vygotsky: Revolutionary Scientist*, London: Routledge.

Resnick, Lauren B., (1994), 'Situated rationalism: biological and social preparation for learning', in Lawrence A. Hirschfield and Susan A. Gelman, (eds), *Mapping the Mind: Domain Specificity in Cognition and Culture*, New York: Cambridge University Press.

Richards, Martin P.M., (ed.), (1974), *The Integration of a Child into a Social World*, Cambridge: Cambridge University Press.

Schaffer, Heinz R., (2004), *Introducing Child Psychology*, Oxford: Blackwell.

Trevarthen, Colwyn, (2005), 'Stepping away from the mirror: pride and shame in adventures of companionship', in C. Sue Carter, Lieselotte Ahnert, Klaus E. Grossman, Sarah B. Hrdy, Stephen W. Porges and Norbert Sachser, (eds), *Attachment and Bonding: A New Synthesis*, Cambridge, MA: MIT Press.

Van der Veer, René and Jaan Valsiner, (1991), *Understanding Vygotsky: A Quest For Synthesis*, Oxford: Blackwell.

Vygotsky, Lev S., (1930), *The Genesis of Higher Psychological Functions* [in Russian], Moscow: Academy of Pedagogical Sciences.

Vygotsky, Lev S., (1978), *Mind in Society*, Cambridge, MA: Harvard University Press.

Vygotsky, Lev S., (1981), 'The development of the higher forms of attention in childhood', in James V. Wertsch, (ed.), *The Concept of Activity in Soviet Psychology*, Armonk, NY: M. E. Sharpe.

Vygotsky, Lev S., (1987), *The Collected Works of L. S. Vygotsky*, Vol. 1, *Problems of General Psychology*, New York: Plenum Press.

Vygotsky, Lev S. and Alexander R. Luria, (1994), *Studies On the History of Behaviour: Ape, Primitive, and Child*, London: Lawrence Erlbaum.

Wood, John C., (2007), 'The limits of culture: society, evolutionary psychology and the history of violence', *Cultural and Social History*, 4, 1: 95–114.

Norbert Elias, the civilizing process and penal development in modern society

John Pratt

Abstract: For much of the twentieth century the punishment of offenders in modern society came to be administered on a scientific, rational basis with policy driven largely by expert knowledge. The anonymity of the prison, as a place for reflection and rehabilitation, steadily replaced the pre-modern drama and spectacle of punishment to the human body. Recently, though, some modern societies (particularly those in the Anglophone world) have seen recourse to more expressive and severe penalties, driven more by public opinion than by expert knowledge. Other modern societies, however (particularly the Scandinavian countries) remain largely immune to these trends. This article outlines and explores these contrasting trends and developments and uses Norbert Elias's work on the civilizing process to explain them.

Introduction

Modern Western societies like to think of themselves as 'civilized.' One of the criteria for meeting this standard relates to the way in which offenders are punished for their crimes in such societies. As the then Home Secretary Winston Churchill explained in 1910, 'the mood and temper of the public in regard to the treatment of crime and criminals is one of the most unfailing tests of the civilisation of any country' ([British] Hansard, HC Deb 20 July 1910 c1354). This commonsense use of the term 'civilized' provides those societies that claim this status with a feeling of superiority, of moral censoriousness over those thought to belong in the 'uncivilized' world; but at the same time, this status also puts restraints on the deployment of any punishment practices that have resonances with those in the uncivilized. As the then Home Secretary David Blunkett explained when it was suggested that his decision to release two juvenile murderers after eight years of detention might spark vigilante reprisals against them, 'we are not in the Mid-West in the mid-nineteenth century, we are in Britain in the twenty-first century and we will deal with things effectively and we will deal with them in a civilized manner' (*The Weekly Telegraph*, 27 June–3 July 2001: 1). Of course, though, in sociology, the concept of 'civilization' has more than a normative meaning. For Norbert Elias (2000 [1939]), it did not refer to some innate quality that Western societies possessed as of right, which is how it has now come to be understood in a commonsense way. Instead, it was the product of a long-term historical *process* – from the Middle Ages onwards – representing the contingent outcome of socio-cultural and psychic change. As such, it is to be regretted that he made so little reference to the punishment of offenders in his *magnum opus*, as a way of illustrating its historical development. As David Garland (1990: 216) has pointed out, he offers some brief remarks about the place of the gallows in the medieval world of the knight and he notes, on the very first page, that 'the form of judicial punishment' is one of the social facts to which 'civilization' typically refers. Along the way he charts changes in attitudes to nose blowing, table manners, bedroom activities and so on, to establish the course of the civilizing process. In a similar way, a study of penal change over the same time span has the potential to provide a very rich tapestry.

The potential of such a study is illustrated by Pieter Spierenburg's (1984) analysis of changing attitudes towards the use of capital punishment and lesser punishments to the human body during the course of the seventeenth and eighteenth century in Amsterdam. In this period, many of the brutal excesses involved in the array of punishments at its start began to be toned down or disappeared altogether (it seems, for example, that tongue-piercing, blinding and the cutting off of ears and hands did not survive the seventeenth century); while execution, although it continued to be administered in public, began to take the form of a more solemn affair (for example, the execution dais was eventually draped in black; after execution, the corpses of the condemned were no longer put on display). Similar patterns are found in other European societies at this time. In England, the riotous march from Newgate Prison to Tyburn Gallows came to an end in 1783 and then took place outside the prison until the abolition of public executions in 1868. The 'bloody code' which had made the death penalty available for over 300 offences at that time was steadily reduced to the point where the death penalty, for all intents and purposes, was only available for murder after 1861. The last occasion when beheading the corpse of the condemned took place was in 1820. In 1832, gibbeting was abolished, as was the hanging of bodies in chains in 1834 (see Gatrell, 1994).

The reasons for such changes, Spierenburg argues, are due to a growing repugnance at such 'disturbing events', including these sights of brutal pain and suffering inflicted on powerless human beings. These sensitivities were initially manifested in social elites. They looked with increasing disdain at the vulgarity of the lower classes who raucously celebrated such spectacles (Gatrell, 1994). To a degree, these sensitivities percolated through the rest of society, although perhaps more importantly for our purposes here, changes in state formation also concentrated power in the middle classes in whom these sensitivities seem to have been most concentrated.[1] They were then able to put these sensitivities into legislation. The 'spectacle of suffering' that the punishment of crime had once represented had, by the late nineteenth century in most of the modern world, been turned into a bureaucratic accomplishment, with the public excluded from any participation.

What I want to do in this article is examine the *subsequent* history of punishment in modern society through an Eliasian prism. In terms of periodization, this means that we leave behind the world of gallows and gibbets, stocks and whips and move instead to one where, by the mid nineteenth century, prison had become the central response to crime. What we shall then find is that, thereafter, prison development, design and administration followed much the same course as the array of punishments on the human body that were once available. Its use declined and it came to be seen as too excessive a sanction for all but the most serious offenders. Its decline in use was paralleled by the steady amelioration of its conditions of confinement: at least, this was the route that was followed by most Western societies up to the 1980s. From that point, however, and particularly in the Anglophone world, we find both a resurgence of prison use and more emphasis placed on 'austere' conditions in the prisons themselves, as well as, to a degree, the reappearance of penal values and practices from the pre-modern world. As we shall see, though, the Scandinavian countries provide exceptions to these more general trends.[2] To understand these developments and contrasts, we need to be aware that the civilizing process is not formulaic. It does not proceed at a uniform pace across Western society. In addition, in periods of great social change or breakdown, it can be 'put into reverse' and decivilizing forces will then impact on individual and social development. Under these circumstances, 'the armour of civilized conduct crumbles very rapidly' with a concomitant weakening of central state authority and a decline in human capacity for rational action (Elias, 2000 [1939]: 532*n*). This makes possible the re-emergence of conduct and values more appropriate to previous eras. Mennell (1990) provides a very helpful contrast in the constituent elements of civilizing and decivilizing processes. These are reproduced as Table I and provide the structure for the rest of the article.

The civilizing process and modern penal development

Structural processes

After the phasing out of public punishments in the first half of the nineteenth-century, prison for the first time became a central feature of penal development.[3] In England, prior to the establishment of a central prison administration in 1877, there had been competing accounts from prison governors about the preferred prison 'model': how much religious instruction there should be; to what extent should the prisoners be kept in solitary confinement and to what extent should they be allowed to work with others in silence (Pratt, 2002)? At the same time, prison chaplains enjoyed equal status with governors (see Griffiths, 1875: 46): there had been no regard, it would appear, for the potential for conflict between these two professional groups that their shared status in

Table 1

EUROPEAN CIVILISING PROCESS	POSSIBLE SYMPTOMS OF DECIVILISING PROCESSES
STRUCTURAL PROCESSES	
↑ State-formation: Monopolization of means of violence and taxation	Breaking links, shorter chains of interdependence
↑ Division of Labour/Social functions/ Heterogeneity	
↑ Trade, towns, money, markets, population	↑ Homogeneity, cellular structure
All interweaving to produce longer chains, denser webs of interdependence, with consequences:	↑ danger level, incalculability
CHANGES IN MANNERS/CULTURE	
↑ Movement 'behind the scenes' (bodily functions etc., *and violence*)	↑ re-emergence of violence, etc., into public sphere
↑ Diminishing contrasts, increasing varieties	
↑ Mutual identification (inc. ↓ cruelty to humans, animals)	↓ mutual identification, ↑ cruelty
CHANGES IN SOCIAL HABITUS	
↑ Pressures towards foresight:	↓ Pressures restraining expression of impulses
– Psychologisation	
– Rationalisation	
– Advancing thresholds of shame and embarrassment	
↑ distance between child's and adult standards	↓ gap child/adult standards
No zero-point in self-constraint, but becomes	↑ reliance on external constraints
↑ more automatic	↑ impulsive
↑ more even and continuous	↓ uniformity
↑ more all-round, all-embracing	↑ exceptions
Taming of agressiveness	Freer expression of aggressiveness
CHANGES IN MODES OF KNOWLEDGE	
↑ Detachment, ↓ Involvement	↑ Involvement, ↓ Detachment
↓ fantasy content, ↑ 'reality-congruence'	↑ fantasy content, ↓ 'reality congruence'

Reproduced with the permission of the author, from Mennell, S. (1990), 'Decivilizing Processes: Theoretical significance and some lines for research,' *International Sociology*, 2: 205–23.

managing the prisons might bring. After centralization, however, the competing claims and counter claims, authority conflicts and discretionary powers came to an abrupt end. Thereafter, official commentaries on prison development were largely made in the annual report of the Prison Commission, which had Sir Edmund Du Cane as its first chairman. The individual reports of prison governors were now appended to the general summary of the Commissioners and became increasingly anodyne and routine. The autonomy of the other prison professionals was restricted and their status downgraded. Chaplains, for example, were often overseers of rudimentary teaching arrangements that were provided towards the end of the nineteenth century for some prisoners, or served a merely ornamental purpose: sitting with the governor on adjudications to provide dignity to what was taking place, but effectively powerless to intervene, as one cleric revealed to a prisoner after witnessing prison officers inflicting a beating: 'it's no good . . . there's nothing we can do' (Balfour, 1901: 224).

The increasingly monopolistic power of the penal bureaucracy had two important consequences in relation to the development of the civilizing process. First, it ensured that there would be longer chains and denser interdependencies *within* the penal bureaucracy itself. This was because the possibilities of disagreement in the development of prison policy, or the quixotic activities of individual doctors and chaplains in the exercise of their discretion, had been removed by centralization. The Prison Commissioners now decided how all prisons should be administered down to the last $1/16^{th}$ of a gramme of bread that prisoners should receive with their food – and the rest of the prison service had to fall in line with their dictats. If, at one level, this brought about greater consistency in training and regulations, it also meant, at another, that it would be increasingly difficult for those in the particular institutions to act as individuals, rather than bureaucratic representatives. Indeed, the way in which the British state made all its prison employees sign the Official Secrets Act cemented this reality and added to the increasing secrecy and regimentation associated with imprisonment. Second, the penal bureaucracy was able to shape and develop prison policy largely to suit its own interests, free from any public involvement. Du Cane, a former officer in the Royal Engineers, had ruthlessly implemented the 'hard bed, hard fare, hard labour' regime in British prisons, after complaints that these new institutions were too luxurious (Pratt, 2002). Following his forced retirement in 1895, however, the Prison Commission tended to take a more liberal approach, fending off periodic complaints about 'pampered prisoners'. As Chair of the Prison Commission, Sir Lionel Fox (1952: 137) later elliptically explained, 'one cannot be unaware that the body of assumptions underlying the common talk of common people and directing their praise and praise alone are not, in these matters, the assumptions on which contemporary prison administration is based'. In effect, the interests of the penal bureaucracies superseded those of the general public. The *Report of the Director of Penal Services* (1957: 8) condescendingly stated that 'the public should accept something less than one hundred per cent security . . . if the public wants to develop the positive and redemptive side of prison work, it must face the fact that the occasional prisoner may escape and do damage'.

The dissipation of the initial excitement and curiosity at the new prison buildings had contributed to this decline in public interest in these institutions. The more remote and exclusionary these institutions became, the more the general public became indifferent to what happened in them. This had already been noted by Du Cane (1875: 303) when he told a social science congress that 'I gladly accept the inference that the public interest has decreased [in prison matters]'. Indeed, other than public interest being provoked by scandals that emerged from time to time (whether this was in relation to prisoners being treated too leniently or too brutally), public knowledge and understanding of prison life had largely come to an end. Thus, while the bureaucratic structure of prison management had created longer and denser interdependencies within it, the chains between it and the general public had actually become much shorter.

Changes in manners and culture

In addition to the administrative veil that had been drawn across the punishment process, prison design and location increased the physical distance between punishment and the general public. Prison architecture quickly jettisoned the gothic designs characteristic of the first half of the nineteenth century in favour of an outward appearance that denoted 'functional austerity' rather than extravagance (Pratt, 2002). At the same time, the new prisons were more likely to be built away from city centres: up to this time, there had been no need to separate prisons from community life, as prints and paintings prior to the mid nineteenth century indicate (Evans, 1982; Brodie *et al.*, 1999). Growing public distaste at the sight of prisons and what they represented was extended to prisoners themselves. This led to them, first, being removed from public works beyond the walls of the prison. Thereafter the prison authorities steadily 'anonymized' the transport of prisoners, bringing to an end the parading of them as they moved from court to prison, or from prison to prison, in chains and uniform. By the early twentieth century in England they were transported in reserved railway carriages with blinds drawn. They were also allowed to wear civilian clothing to ease their shame during these increasingly fleeting public appearances. These sensibilities were later incorporated within the 1948 prison rules: '[prisoners] shall be exposed to public view as little as possible, and proper safeguards shall be adopted to protect them from insult and injury' (Fox, 1952: 164–5).

This general 'disappearance' of both prisons and prisoners from much of public life occurred in conjunction with *diminishing contrasts* (Elias, 2000 [1939]: 382–97) within the punishment spectrum. The contrasts were now between custodial and community sanctions, with increasing variations between them, rather than the more stark options of life or death, as in the pre-modern world. At the beginning of the twentieth century, special institutions began to be opened for 'inebriates', 'habitual offenders' and the mentally deficient, with borstals for young offenders. By the 1950s this differentiation had come to include open and closed prisons and psychiatric prisons. Outside the prison, there were variations in the conditions that could be imposed in probation orders; thereafter, from the 1960s, further varieties were added to this sector, such as suspended sentences, community service and deferred sentences. Within the prison figuration we find growing mutual identification between the prison authorities and the prisoners themselves (or at least on behalf of the management elites – prison officer culture seems to have been much more resistant to such sensibilities; see, for example, Thomas 1972). By the early twentieth century in England, prisoners were being addressed by their name rather than their number. The language of punishment reflected these changes in prison culture from the late nineteenth century. The term 'convict' was falling into disuse, to be replaced by 'prisoner', which in turn by the 1960s had been replaced by the less stigmatic 'inmate' or even 'trainee.'

In conjunction with this growing mutual identification and reduced social distance, prisoners came to be understood as more to be pitied than feared. As the prominent British psychiatrist Edwin Glover (1956: 267) explained, 'they have certainly injured their fellows but perhaps society has unwittingly injured them.' Indeed, for the prison authorities, it was as if there was little innate difference between those in prison and the public beyond it: 'between a hundred prisoners and a hundred persons chosen at random from the street outside, the resemblances are more noticeable than the differences' (Fox, 1952: 111).

Changes in social habitus

Du Cane (1875: 302–3) had written that prisoners had characteristics that were 'entirely those of the inferior races of mankind – wandering habits, utter laziness, absence of thought or provision [and] want of moral sense'. However, this moralizing that was characteristic of the late Victorian era steadily gave way to more objective, scientific understandings. Du Cane's successor, Sir Evelyn Ruggles-Brise (1985 [1921]: 194), argued for the need for 'criminal laboratories' as in the United States 'where science and humanity march hand in hand exploring prisons as places of punishment'. In addition, rather than simply leaving prisoners to their fate, he also recognized that it was the duty of the state at least to try to effect a 'cure' (1985 [1921]: 87) for their criminality. At the same time, the sight of cowed and broken prisoners had become repugnant as thresholds of shame and embarrassment advanced. On a visit to Dartmoor Prison, Prison Commissioner Sir Alexander Paterson noted with distaste that

> as [the prisoners] saw us coming, each man ran to the nearest wall and put his face against it, remaining in this servile position, till we had passed behind him . . . the men looked hard in body and in spirit, healthy enough in physique and colour, but cowed and listless in demeanour and response (quoted in Ruck 1951: 11).

Thereafter, it was recognized that 'the deterrent effect of imprisonment must finally be in the loss of personal liberty and all that this involves . . . *that effect is not reinforced if the period of loss of liberty is used in a mere repressive or punitive way'* (Home Office 1959: 13, my italics). Instead, 'we have found that the study of art, music and drama has for those in prison a particular appeal, and that these arts may bring for the first time to the lives of depressed and distorted men and women perceptions of beauty, goodness and truth' (*Report of the Commissioners of Prisons for the year 1951*, 1952: 52). Now the prison authorities expected that prison officers would share in these new ways of understanding prisoners. The Director of Penal Services, Victoria, Australia, thus claimed that 'group counselling [enables] closer relationships with inmates and allows guards to have an even greater impact in terms of changing inmate behaviour' (*Report of the Director of Penal Services, 1961*, 1963–4: 2).

Changes in modes of knowledge

Expert knowledge and research became increasingly influential on penal development, particularly in the post-1945 era. In England, the Advisory Council on the Treatment of Offenders was established in 1944. As Home Secretary R. A. Butler later explained, 'research may sound academic, but I am quite certain that in this field of crime it is the absolutely vital basis without which we cannot work' ([British] Hansard, HC Deb 31 October 1958 c505). For the elite groups undertaking research or developing policy, prisoners had become detached from the previous irredeemable moral culpability and incorrigibility that had been associated with them in the development of nineteenth century prison policy. Instead, they were understood as inadequates, living unfulfilled lives. They no longer constituted a menace to the rest of the community. Taylor (1960: 35), in his study of preventive detention prisoners, found that 'they were lonely men who had become inept in handling personal contacts and from their experiences had developed paranoid attitudes towards other people. In their view, the world was a threatening and frightening place.' The punishment that they had received was not only out of proportion to their wrongdoing but also magnified their sense of isolation from the rest of society. In these respects, to avoid such destructive excesses, prison was increasingly relegated to a 'last resort' penal option. From the 1960s to the 1980s increasing resources were used in the development of what were thought to be more humane community based alternative sanctions.

In such ways, and using England as our main example, we can demonstrate how the development of penal policy in much of Western society followed the course of the civilizing process. There are important points to note, however, from this brief historical overview. First, while we can illustrate sociologically the effects of the civilizing process at work, this does not then mean that the penal arrangements it produced were normatively 'civilized.' The accounts of the prison had certainly become more sanitized in official discourse, but, as prisoner biographies over about a century testified (Pratt, 2002), it was certainly not civilized in commonsense usage of the term. However, the civilizing process itself helped to ensure that these alternative accounts of prison life were usually ignored or discredited. Its structural processes had allowed the prison bureaucracy to grow stronger and become more deeply entrenched, with control over knowledge and information that was accessible to the public. At the same time, the physical and administrative distance between public and prisoners that the disappearance of prison had brought about meant that the latter came to be thought of as essentially 'different.' Their very status as prisoners *ipso facto* disqualified their own accounts. As Elias and Scotson (2008 [1965]) suggested in developing their 'established–outsiders' concept, the greater the social distance between these groups, in any particular figuration, the more predominant would be the world view of the established, and the more power, within the specifics of the figuration they would have, in relation to the outsider group.

Second, the civilizing process as it related to prison and penal development in Western society should be understood as a continuum rather than some uniform standard. There were variations within the Anglophone societies. The civilizing process had come much later to the Southern United States, for example, as was reflected, up to the 1950s, in their high rates of imprisonment, chain gang and vigilante traditions, fondness for the death penalty and slowness in instituting prison reform (Pratt, 2002):[4] features which are indicative of a weak central state authority and low thresholds of shame, embarrassment and self-restraint. In contrast, the Scandinavian countries stood at the opposite end of the civilizing continuum. Here, the death penalty in peacetime had effectively ceased (if not *de jure* then at least *de facto*) in the mid nineteenth century, as opposed to the mid twentieth century in most of the Anglophone world. These countries not only had some of the lowest levels of imprisonment in the West,[5] but (Sweden particularly) had also become renowned for humane, 'civilized' prison conditions. In an article titled 'Almost the best of everything', Tom Wicker (1975: 201) wrote that 'Sweden's prisons are models of decency and humanity . . . Although debate continues among socially aware Swedes as to whether prisons here are not still too harsh, most American inmates would regard . . . Sweden's maximum security penitentiary – as a country club.' At this time, Scandinavian countries were regarded by the liberal elites in control of policy development in the Anglophone world as 'the leaders' of the civilized world, setting the example for the rest to follow.

Why had the civilizing process become more advanced and intensified in this region? There was a long tradition of egalitarianism that reduced social distance and made interdependencies much longer throughout society (the extreme homogeneity of the region also contributed to this). Norway abolished its nobility in 1817, for example. Property was divided between descendants on the death of the owner rather than inherited by the first-born, thus preventing the build up of a landed gentry. By the early twentieth century, its egalitarianism had become one of its identifying characteristics: 'among civilised states, there is scarcely any that is so fortunate with regard to the equality of its social conditions as Norway. There is no nobility with political or economic privileges, no large estates, no capitalist class . . . The highest and lowest strata of society are on the whole no farther removed from one another than that there is constant reciprocal action between them, and transition from one to the other' (Berner, 1900: 202). In these respects, there were not the concerns about the 'dangerous classes' characteristic of the Anglophone societies in this period. Rather than being shut out of society, prisoners were to be re-educated, remoralized, later 'treated' in such ways that they could be reintegrated. In contrast, in the Anglophone world, prisoners were members of the dangerous classes, feared and shut out of society. They were right at the bottom of a long series of divisions that extended throughout British society: divisions which separated the social classes and then further divided them – the respectable poor, workhouse paupers, the mentally ill and finally prisoners.

Furthermore, penal institutions were small, often housing less than fifty prisoners, and remained in the centre of local community development. There seems to have been little public pressure to have them removed from view. They were not turned into threatening monstrosities, visible only in public fantasies and imaginings of them. The way in which 'prison' was imagined in Scandinavia was likely to have far less fantasy content, leading to much higher levels of tolerance. In the post-1945 period, prisoners themselves were more likely to be working outside the prison, or at least able to move more easily between prison and community. As a result there was a relatively short social distance between prisoners and the public. In Sweden, the literal translation of the term for prison officer is 'prison carer' (*fångvårdare*). Equally, the term 'client' is used for all prisoners in official correctional discourse.

The post 1945 development of the Scandinavian welfare state strengthened the powers of its bureaucratic organs of government. At the same time, because virtually the whole population materially benefited from its generous, universal benefits, there was comparatively little stigma attached to being a welfare beneficiary. Prisoners were usually regarded as just another group of welfare beneficiaries, no different from any others and of no particular interest. In addition, the Scandinavians placed a high value on education. In Norway and Finland, for example, the study of language and literature became a means of solidifying their nineteenth-century struggles for independence from Sweden and Russia respectively. The importance of education to the well-being and identity of the nation became another feature of the culture of these societies, and perhaps is another reason for the high levels of trust and status accorded to experts in these societies. This, then, allowed them to develop their aspirations for penal reform further than it was possible for their Anglophone counterparts to do. At the same time, the functional democratization of penal governance, whereby debate was conducted much more in public, between representatives of all 'stakeholders', ensured that the public at large had a better and more realistic understanding of penal affairs. In this region, these matters were not allowed to become the exclusive property of bureaucratic elites.

Again, though, we need to recognize that, even where, as in the Scandinavian countries, the civilizing process reached a very advanced stage, it can provide no guarantees against uncivilized outcomes. The high levels of trust in the Scandinavian 'protective state' allowed abuses of state power to develop: for example, an emphasis on indeterminate prison sentences (in Sweden especially), in the belief that crime was a form of mental illness (the time for release would be when each individual prisoner was cured), and the maintenance of a eugenics programme for deviants of various kinds from the 1930s to the 1970s (in the belief that the state could 'humanely' control those who could not control themselves) (Hagelund, 2003).

Decivilizing symptoms

The contours of the civilizing process across Western society had led to penal arrangements with three key characteristics at this point: a strong central state authority with monopolistic control of the power to punish; high levels of shame and embarrassment; and high levels of trust in the penal authorities that then allowed them to develop research driven policy. From the 1970s, economic and social reconstruction across much of the Anglophone world has meant that it has been impossible to sustain the unity of these characteristics of 'civilized' penal development. The ascendancy of neo-liberal polities has meant that the authority of the central state has fragmented. It now assumes a more residual role in everyday governance that is no longer privileged around the idea of a strong central state working as one with its bureaucracies. Recourse has been made to alternative modes of governance in the private and voluntary sectors. Indeed, with the shortcomings of state sector provision regularly highlighted in public discourse and political debate, the purchase of private security has become much more commonplace. But this has also meant that security has become commodified, rather than a state guarantee (Garland, 2001). At the same time, interdependencies have become much shorter. As Beck (1992), Fukuyama (1995) and Putnam (2000) have noted, many of the longstanding institutions and cultural expectations that had become deeply embedded in these societies in the twentieth century have declined: job security, the stability of family life, and membership of trade unions, churches and other organizations.

Furthermore, the deregulation of the news media and the introduction of new print technology since the 1980s is itself conducive to modes of knowledge that have high levels of fantasy content rather than detached, objective analysis. Newsmaking and reporting become more sensationalized as each paper or television channel competes with its rivals. It also becomes more simplified to attract the largest audience and secure advertising revenue. This has meant that crime and punishment issues are likely to receive greater coverage than used to be the case because of their interest to audiences: such matters became the most obvious symbols and representations of what Giddens (1991) has referred to as 'ontological insecurity'. In this way, crime and punishment have become regular features of public and political debate, rather than being determined 'behind the scenes' by elite experts.

As a result of these changes, we can discern decivilizing symptoms in each level of the civilizing process.

Structural processes

Since the 1980s, private prisons have been reintroduced to most of the Anglophone world, having previously disappeared during the course of the nineteenth century. These have a vested interest in high levels of imprisonment since their profits are dependent on fully occupied beds. Civil service restructuring along with political appointments at senior levels within it have considerably undermined its capacity to dilute more punitive political agendas and impose its own liberal imprint on policy (Loader, 2006). As this has happened, so single-issue law and order lobby groups, variously claiming to represent crime victims in particular and 'ordinary people' in general, have campaigned for more punitive sentences and more direct victim input to the punishment process (in the mistaken belief that all victims are vengeful). In some jurisdictions, these groups have taken advantage of the provision for plebiscites and referenda in the electoral process to provide the momentum for the introduction of particularly punitive legislation.[6] Governments have also indicated a readiness to acquiesce to the agendas of these groups while at the same time distancing themselves from the policy making establishment. For example, when introducing the Labour government's controversial Crime and Disorder Bill (which made provision for anti-social behaviour orders), the then Home Secretary Jack Straw proclaimed that '[it] represents a triumph of community politics over detached metropolitan elites' (*The Times*, 8 April 1998: 4).

In such ways, policy has become increasingly punitive and intolerant, with a reinvigoration of prison use. This has occurred in conjunction with the resurrection of a variety of other penal strategies and symbols from the past: stigmatic and highly visible public punishments such as 'community payback' orders in Britain (formerly community service) and chain gangs in some of the Southern states in the USA. We also find a deterioration in prison conditions, often the product of overcrowding but sometimes deliberately engineered by governments. Prison austerity, it is thought, symbolizes the new unity between government and the general public in relation to the punishment of crime. It not only manifests public outrage and anger towards criminals but will also ensure that those who experience such conditions will not choose to return to prison in the future (in contrast to the overwhelming body of research evidence which demonstrates exactly the opposite). This was the essence of the 'prison works' strategy, developed by the then British Home Secretary Michael Howard in 1993. He signalled his intention to reverse the long-held expectations of the penal establishment that policy must have a reduction of the prison population as its primary purpose, since high levels of imprisonment were *ipso facto* an unwelcome stain on the texture of any country that professed to belong to the 'civilized world.' Instead, Howard proclaimed that 'prison works' and that 'this may mean that more people will go to prison. I do not flinch from [this]. We shall no longer judge the success of our system of justice by a fall in the prison population,' (quoted in Cavadino and Dignan, 2002: 34). It was a policy that was then avidly followed by New Labour when it came to power in 1997 (see Tonry, 2004).

Changes in manners/culture

As the influence of criminal justice elites on policy has declined, so too has the culture of tolerance and forbearance that they were associated with. Instead of the restraints and moderation that this 'established group' were able to impose on penal culture, the angry and intolerant representations of the former 'outsiders' – the general public – have become more dominant influences. Governments have been eager to position themselves alongside these sentiments. Tony Blair, when British Prime Minister, thus made the point that

> crime, anti-social behaviour, racial intolerance, drug abuse, destroy families and communities. They destroy the very respect on which society is founded . . . Fail to confront this evil and we will never build a Britain where everyone can succeed . . . by acknowledging the duty to care, we earn the right to be tough on crime . . . it is time for zero tolerance of yob culture'. (*The Guardian*, 27 September 2006: 3)

The difference between law-breakers and the rest of society is thus re-emphasized. The Blair speech is also a reflection of the new language of punishment that now informs penal debate. Other examples include phrases such as 'Three Strikes and You're Out' and 'Life means Life – No Parole'. These all originated in the USA – the Western society which punishes the most and the most inhumanely, illustrative of the turnaround in the leadership of punishment in the civilized world from the time when Sweden was the example to follow. Now, however, instead of mutual identification with offenders what we find instead is a growing mutual identification with their victims. This is also reflected in attempts to 'bridge the justice gap' and to 'rebalance the criminal justice system'. Victims have been given a range of *representational* rights that can include opportunities to be heard at sentencing and parole adjudications through victim impact statements. This rebalancing simultaneously involves a reduction in the rights of offenders. For example, the state's control over prisoners *after* their sentence has finished can be extended. Electronic monitoring, introduced as a liberal and cost efficient way to reduce the prison population in the 1980s, is used in some jurisdictions to regulate sex offenders for upwards of ten years. Opportunities they might have to 'profit' from their crimes are removed. In New Zealand, the Prisoners and Victims Claims Act 2005 was backdated to prevent a payout to six prisoners (around $US100,000 in total) in 2004 after their ill-treatment by the Department of Corrections – they had been kept in conditions close to those in an American super-max prison,[7] for which there was no lawful authority. The legislation made provision for victims to be able to sue their offenders for any windfall they might receive (whether this be from a lotto ticket or damages from the government for mistreatment) for up to six years on leaving prison. In explaining the Bill, the Minister of Justice rejected the notion that criminals 'pay their debt to society' while in prison: 'it costs us $50,000 a year to keep someone in prison . . . that is the cost to society, not the repayment of a debt . . . you don't repay your debt to the victim by being in prison' (*The Dominion Post*, 25 January 2005: B5). In this new penal culture there is to be no redemption.

Changes in social habitus

Because of its weakened authority, the central state is now more likely to acquiesce to citizens' demands for greater involvement in the exercise of penal power. Community consultation regarding released sex offenders, in varying degrees depending on the jurisdiction,[8] is one example of this. Even so, when the external constraints it had previously been able to impose on citizens' involvement begin to breakdown, then such gestures are frequently not enough to hold back the tide of public anger and frustration that has been released. Instead, we are likely to find sporadic outbursts of aggression and vindictiveness and the return of vigilante activities (Johnston, 1996; Girling *et al.*, 1998). These have no reliable pattern or predictability, other than that they are likely to occur amongst those sectors of society where the state's authority is weakest, but a rumour or newspaper headline may be enough to ignite them. In probably the most well-known and wide-ranging outburst of vigilante activities in the aftermath of the rape and murder of a young child in England in 2000, the leaders of one local group claimed to possess a self-constructed self-styled 'list of power' – the names and addresses of local people whom they suspected of paedophile activities and whom they were intent on hunting down. One woman who was later interviewed about her participation in these activities explained that she had

> enjoyed walking up the street with a gang of women, all shouting to get the paedophiles out. 'I can't help it but this is how I felt. Walking the streets with all the noise, I got a buzz out of it. I know it sounds really childish. But when I came back [home] I thought, what have I done?' (*The Observer*, 13 August 2000: 12)

Participation in such activities seems more 'natural', more taken for granted, when thresholds of shame and embarrassment are lowered, thereby removing previous reticences and inhibitions against such involvement.

At the same time, policy-making has become more impulsive. Rather than the product of long-term planning and research, it is increasingly likely to be developed in response to exceptional cases that are then seen as 'the norm'. In Britain, there were 54 new criminal justice bills between 1997 and 2006 (Garside, 2006). This has been in addition to innumerable 'summits', 'initiatives' and 'proposals', that have included 'on the spot fines for louts', 'benefit cuts for truants' parents and 'on the spot fines for dropping chewing gum on the streets' (Tonry, 2004): all of which are again indicative of the way in which the response to social problems is framed around 'commonsense', 'what everybody knows' as a matter of course rather than around research-informed expert opinion. The way in which such initiatives are frequently targeted at the most minor crime is indicative of a habitus that now demands instant, commonsensical responses to social problems, as if these can no longer wait for more considered long-term solutions. The Home Office White Paper *Justice for All* (2002: 86) thus contains the statement that 'the people are sick and tired of a sentencing system that does not make sense'. It argues for the need to 'rebalance the [criminal justice] system in favour of victims, witnesses and communities', on the basis that 'the people of this country want a criminal justice system that works in the interests of justice'. Not only are such statements illustrative of the new configuration of penal power that directs policy, but they also reflect the taken-for-granted assumption that the interests of justice necessitate an enhanced role for victims with, again, a reduced focus on the well-being of offenders.

Changes in modes of knowledge

The spokesperson for the Sensible Sentencing Trust, a particularly influential law and order lobby group in New Zealand, proclaimed in 2007 that 'We do not need academics, criminologists or psychologists to tell us the simple truth that if you reward bad behaviour you will get more of it!' (Sensible Sentencing Rally for Safe NZ). This is symptomatic of regular claims in public discourse that this established group is 'out of touch', and 'living on another planet' (see Hough, 1996). The almost total absence of any interdependencies that previously existed between such elites and 'ordinary people' under the previous configuration of penal power has helped to produce these dramatic changes in modes of knowledge. The social distance that existed between the two only built up resentment and distrust. Criminal justice elites are thus now seen as responsible for rising crime because of their ineptitude, even though all the indications are that it has been falling right across Western society since the early 1990s: for example, in England, the 2010 British Crime Survey 'revealed that offences fell by nine per cent from 10.5 million to 9.6 million in 2009–10, the lowest since at least 1981' (*Daily Telegraph*, 15 July 2010: 1). And the same elites are associated with punishments that are too liberal, even though prison populations have been increasing: in England the rate of imprisonment increased from 88 per 100,000 of population in 1992 to 154 in 2010 (World Prison Brief).

The changing structure of the news media has contributed to these changes in modes of knowledge because of its preoccupation with crime and punishment issues. The media have fuelled perceptions that crime is increasing, giving added legitimacy to those law and order lobbyists who vividly draw attention to this menace, while detracting from that of academic commentators who discuss crime in a more detached, analytical fashion. The latter seem to play down its threat even though in the media, the main source of information about it for most people, it is ever-present and in need of immediate, punitive responses.

The end of civilization?

At various points, then, we can see that the contours of the civilizing process have been interrupted by these decivilizing symptoms in the Anglophone countries. However, their presence does not then act as some sort of time machine, reversing the entire course of penal development. Some of the reversals that have taken place are quite peripheral – indicative of new horizons and possibilities for punishment, perhaps, rather than cornerstone features of the penal system. Other than this, the most striking feature of contemporary penal arrangements is the enlarged presence of the prison in the Anglophone world especially to degrees that would have been unthinkable in the 1970s. But while this may reflect a reversal of those earlier political priorities aimed at reducing prison numbers, this has not been accompanied by a renaissance of punishments to the human body (outside the USA). Overall, it is more the case that the civilizing process has been rerouted rather than reversed as a consequence of the impact of these countervailing influences. At the same time, the civilizing process itself continues to produce 'uncivilized' consequences. The use of electronic monitoring, introduced as an efficient and humane way of reducing the prison population, can actually expand it. It leads to increasing numbers being sent back to prison, not because of further crimes but because of parole violations. Furthermore, the bureaucratic veil that has been drawn across the prison has allowed the authorities in the USA to devise 'supermax' prisons, institutions that provide the most extreme forms of segregation and sensory deprivation. However, it should also be noted that the retreat observed in the threshold of shame and embarrassment and the more emotive content that has been brought into criminal justice proceedings – decivilizing symptoms – has also given rise to the restorative justice movement. Here, outpourings of emotion – from both victim and offender – are actively encouraged but are designed to be used productively and reintegratively, leading to apologies, forgiveness and reconciliation (Braithwaite, 1989). It may thus be that, in just the same way that the civilizing process can lead to uncivilized consequences, so the decivilizing tendencies may have the potential to bring more civilized outcomes.

These themes are now common across much of the Anglophone world. They are, though, greatly exaggerated in the USA. Why should this be so? As Mennell (2007) has demonstrated, despite recent declines, incidents of violent crime are still higher in the USA than corresponding societies. As this type of crime usually carries more severe penalties than others, then, to some extent, this in itself will account for both the longer prison terms and the use of executions. One of the reasons for the high levels of violence in this country may relate to the way in which the central state was never really able to gain the monopolistic control of violence as was the case in Europe. As we have seen, its authority, particularly in the South, was always fragile. It may also be that, because the free market has been given greater licence here than in some European countries in the aftermath of social and economic reconstruction, interdependencies have been weakened. This then helps to generate deep feelings of suspicion, fear and intolerance that can be vented in plebiscites and citizens' 'propositions', opportunities provided by the constitutional structure of that country for more direct citizen involvement in the policy making process at state level. Much of its groundbreaking punitive legislation – three strikes, sexual predator and community notification laws – have come about through these mechanisms rather than originating at the level of state governments and their bureaucracies (see Zimring, 1996; Domanick, 2004).

Scandinavian exceptionalism

In contrast, the Scandinavian societies have remained largely untroubled by these decivilizing trends. Whilst there have been some increases in imprisonment in this region, Finland, the previous exception to the Scandinavian penal model,[9] has actually seen a dramatic decline in imprisonment from the 1970s, to the level where it is on a par with the other Scandinavian societies. At the same time, despite some tightening of maximum-security arrangements, prison conditions, if anything, have improved still further (Pratt, 2008). In these respects, there is now a massive gulf between Anglophone and Scandinavian societies in relation to prison levels and conditions. Yet, on the face of it, the foundations of the civilizing process have been shaken in this region as well. The high levels of mutual identification that its extreme homogeneity had provided have been eroded as immigration (to Sweden particularly) has increased.[10] There have been stirrings from right wing populist parties across these societies (indeed the Norwegian Progress Party is the second most numerous in parliament and in 2008 was actually leading in opinion polls). Their message is based on division and exclusion: anti-immigration, secure borders, welfare for Norwegians and no one else, longer prison sentences. Equally, in Sweden, expert opinion regarding drug use and drug control – with its connotations of Eastern menace to this most advanced Western society – has been largely ignored in favour of a more common-sense 'zero-tolerance' policy (Tham, 2001). We also find other modifications to everyday life that are indicative of changes in manners and culture. Stockholm bus drivers do not carry cash for fear of being robbed – (passengers must buy tickets in advance to board), and there were massive public outpourings of grief in relation to the funeral of ten-year-old Engla Hoglund, which was televised in full on state television (she had been murdered by a man with a history of violent crime).[11] One is also likely to see skinhead gangs wandering around Stockholm city centre, often threatening and harassing ethnic minorities, again indicative of previously high levels of restraint and tolerance breaking down.

It is not the case, then, that there are no discernible signs of decivilizing symptoms in such societies. As yet, however, these have made relatively little impact on penal development. For the most part, the strong Scandinavian central state authorities remain very much in place – there has been no recourse to private prisons, for example. Furthermore, the extensive Scandinavian welfare state remains largely intact. Its guarantees of security reduce danger levels and incalculable risk. Not only does this allow these societies to remain largely inclusive, but it also encourages high levels of trust between individuals and state authorities – including the criminal justice establishment, thereby allowing it to remain in control of much of policy development. Again, there was never the wide division between experts and the public that was allowed to develop in the Anglophone world. Thus lay people sit with judges in lower courts and decide sentencing as well as guilt or innocence. Victims of crime have not been shut out of criminal justice proceedings, and then allowed to proclaim the injustice of their exclusion to the popular media as in the Anglophone countries. Instead, as soon as guilt is pronounced they receive compensation from the state, which then tries to recover this from their offender. This also means that there are no emotive 'victim impact statements' read to the court. As such, most of the new initiatives we see in the Anglophone penal arrangements – community payback orders, naming and shaming practices – would be quite unthinkable in the Scandinavian penal world. And in just the same way, because of the different experience and pace of the civilizing process in these two clusters of societies, Scandinavian penal practices would be equally unthinkable in the Anglophone penal world. It remains to be seen whether their respective penal routes now drift further apart, or whether they move closer together. The civilizing process itself contains no predictive capabilities, nor has any endpoint in sight.

Notes

1 See, for example, Dickens (1846), Thackeray (1901–3 [1840]).
2 The Anglophone countries are at the top end of the Western imprisonment spectrum. The USA, the highest, has a rate of imprisonment of 760 per 100,000 of population; New Zealand, third highest after Mexico, has a rate of 191; England, fifth highest after Spain, has a rate of 152. In contrast, the rates of imprisonment in the Scandinavian countries are: Denmark 63, Finland 67, Norway 70, and Sweden 74. Prison rates are taken from the World Prison Brief website of the International Centre for Prison Studies, Kings College, London University, www.kcl.ac.uk.
3 Prior to this, prisons had been used mainly in a holding capacity prior to trial, transportation or execution.
4 The rate of imprisonment in Georgia in 1970 was 258 per 100,000 of population (the rate for the USA as a whole was then 110 [Waller and Chan, 1974]).
5 The rate of imprisonment in Norway in 1970 was 37 per 100,000 of population (Waller and Chan, 1974).
6 See Zimring (1996) in relation to California; Pratt and Clark (2005) in relation to New Zealand.
7 Lynch (2005: 68) provides the following description of a supermax prison: 'inmates are generally subjected to solitary lockdown for approximately 23 hours per day in windowless cells that allow for very little visual stimuli, where possessions are restricted and activities nearly completely eliminated, and where, by design, contact with other human beings is almost non-existent.'
8 In some jurisdictions, such as England, the police may inform teachers and other child welfare professionals. In the USA, under the provisions of Megan's Law, these capabilities tend to be

much wider. Individual states decide what information will be made available and how it should be disseminated. Commonly included information includes the offender's name, picture, address, incarceration date, and nature of crime. The information is often displayed on free public websites, but can be published in newspapers, distributed in pamphlets, or through various other means.

9 On the decline of the Finnish prison population, see Lappi-Seppälä (2000).

10 Immigration has been at such a level that one in ten Swedes have now been born outside Sweden (Rooth and Ekberg, 2003).

11 In contrast, Fleisher (1967: 170) wrote that in Sweden, 'the appreciation of restraint, a certain aloofness, and the disapproval of displays of emotion play a vital part in forming the general outlook toward violence.'

References

Dates given in square brackets are those of first publication.

Balfour, Jabez, (1901), *My Prison Life*, London: Chapman and Hall.

Beck, Ulrich, (1992), *Risk Society,* London: Sage.

Berner, Hagbart E., (1900), *Norway: Official Publication of the Paris Exhibition 1900*, Kristiania: Aktie-bogtrykkeriet.

Braithwaite, John, (1989), *Crime, Shame and Reintegration*, Cambridge: Cambridge University Press.

Brodie, Allan, Jane Croom and James Davies, (1999), *The Prison Experience*, Swindon: English Heritage.

Cavadino, Michael and James Dignan, (2002), *The Penal System: An Introduction*, London: Sage.

Dickens, Charles, (1846), 'Letter', *The Daily News*, 23 February 1846.

Domanick, Joe, (2004), *Cruel Justice: Three Strikes and the Politics of Crime in America's Golden State*, Berkeley: University of California Press.

Du Cane, Edmund, (1875), 'Address on the repression of crime', *Transactions of the National Association for the Promotion of Social Science*: 271–308, London: Longmans Green.

Elias, Norbert, (2000 [1939]), *The Civilizing Process*, rev. edn. Oxford: Blackwell. [*On the Process of Civilisation*, Collected Works, Vol. 3, Dublin: UCD Press, forthcoming].

Elias, Norbert, (1996 [1989]), *The Germans*, Cambridge: Polity Press. [*Studies on the Germans*, Collected Works, Vol. 11, Dublin: UCD Press, forthcoming].

Elias, Norbert and John Scotson, (2008 [1965]), *The Established and Outsiders*, Collected Works, Vol. 4, Dublin: UCD Press.

Evans, Robin, (1982), *The Fabrication of Virtue: English Prison Architecture, 1750–1840*, Cambridge: Cambridge University Press.

Fleisher, Frederic, (1967), *The New Sweden*, New York: David McKay.

Fox, Lionel, (1952), *The English Prison and Borstal Systems: An Account of the English Prison and Borstal Systems After the Criminal Justice Act 1948, with a Historical Introduction and an Examination of the Principles of Imprisonments as a Legal Punishment*, London: Routledge & Kegan Paul.

Fukuyama, Francis, (1995), *Trust: The Social Virtues and the Creation of Prosperity*, New York: Free Press.

Garland, David, (1990), *Punishment and Modern Society: A Study in Social Theory*, Oxford: Oxford University Press.

Garland, David, (2001), *The Culture of Control*, New York: Oxford University Press.

Garside, Richard, (2006), *Right for the Wrong Reasons: Making Sense of Criminal Justice Failure*, London: Crime and Society Foundation.

Gatrell, Vic, (1994), *The Hanging Tree: Execution and the English People, 1770–1868*, Oxford: Oxford University Press.

Giddens, Anthony, (1991), *Modernity and Self-Identity*, Cambridge: Polity Press.

Girling, Evi, Ian Loader and Richard Sparks, (1998), 'A telling tale: A case of vigilantism and its aftermath in an English town', *British Journal of Sociology*, 49, 3: 474–90.

Glover, Elizabeth, (1956), *Probation and Re-education*, London: Routledge & Kegan Paul.

Griffiths, Arthur, (1875), *Memorials of Millbank, and Chapters in Prison History*, London: Chapman & Hall.

Hagelund, Anniken, (2003), 'A matter of decency? The Progress Party in Norwegian immigration politics', *Journal of Ethnic and Migration Studies*, 29, 1: 47–65.

Hough, Mike, (1996), 'People talking about punishment', *Howard Journal of Criminal Justice*, 35, 3: 191–213.

Johnston, Les, (1996), 'What is vigilantism?', *British Journal of Criminology*, 36, 2: 220–36.

Lappi-Seppälä, Tapio, (2000), 'The fall of the Finnish prison population', *Scandinavian Journal of Criminology and Crime Prevention*, 1, 1: 27–40.

Loader, Ian, (2006), 'Fall of the "platonic guardians" : Liberalism, criminology and political responses to crime in England and Wales', *British Journal of Criminology*, 46, 4: 561–86.

Lynch, Mona, (2005), 'Supermax meets death row: Legal struggles around the new punitiveness in the US', in John Pratt, David Brown, Mark Brown, Simon Hallsworth and Wayne Morrison, (eds), *The New Punitiveness: Trends, Theories, Perspectives*, Cullompton: Willan: 66–84.

Mennell, Stephen, (1990), 'Decivilizing processes: Theoretical significance and some lines of research', *International Sociology*, 5, 2: 205–13.

Mennell, Stephen, (2007), *The American Civilizing Process*, Cambridge: Polity.

Pratt, John, (2002), *Punishment and Civilization: Penal Tolerance and Intolerance in Modern Society*, London: Sage.

Pratt, John, (2008), 'Scandinavian Exceptionalism in an Era of Penal Excess, Part I: the nature and roots of Scandinavian Exceptionalism', *British Journal of Criminology* 48, 2: 119–37.

Pratt, John and Marie Clark, (2005), 'Penal populism in New Zealand', *Punishment & Society*, 7, 3: 303–22.

Putnam, Robert, (2000), *Bowling Alone: The Collapse and Revival of American Community*, New York: Simon and Schuster.

Rooth, Dan-Olof and Jan Ekberg, (2003), 'Unemployment and Earnings for Second Generation Immigrants in Sweden: Ethnic Background and Parent Composition', *Population Economics*, 16, 4): 787–814.

Ruggles-Brise, Evelyn, (1985 [1921]), *The English Prison System*, New York: Garland.

Ruck, Sydney Kenneth, (ed), (1951), *Paterson on Prisons*, London: F. Muller.

Spierenburg, Pieter, (1984), *The Spectacle of Suffering*, Cambridge: Cambridge University Press.

Taylor, Richard S., (1960), 'The Habitual Criminal', *British Journal of Criminology*, 1, 1: 21–36.

Thackeray, William M., (1901–3 [1840]), 'Going to see a man hanged', Fraser's Magazine 20: 150–58.

Tham, Henrik, (2001), 'Law and order as a leftist project? The case of Sweden', *Punishment and Society*, 3, 3: 409–26.

Thomas, James E., (1972), *The English Prison Officer*, London: Routledge & Kegan Paul.

Tonry, Michael, (2004), *Punishment and Politics: Evidence and Emulation in English Crime Control Policy*, Cullompton: Willan.

Waller, Irvin and Janet Chan, (1974), 'Prison use: a Canadian and international comparison', *Criminal Law Quarterly*, 17, 1: 47–71.

Wicker, Tom, (1975), 'Sweden: Almost the best of everything', *New York Times*, 28 September: 10.

Zimring, Franklin, (1996), 'Populism, democratic government, and the decline of expert authority: some reflections on "Three Strikes" in California', *Pacific Law Journal*, 28, 1: 243–56.

Official Publications

Home Office, (1959), *Penal Practice in a Changing Society*, Cmnd 645, London: HMSO.

Home Office, (2002), *Justice for All*, Cmnd 5563, London: HMSO.

Official Report, [British] *House of Commons (Hansard)* (5th Series, 1909–81), London: HMSO.

Report of the Director of Penal Services, (1957), Melbourne: Victoria V. and P (1958–9) 2.

John Pratt

Report of the Director of Penal Services (1961), Melbourne: Victoria V and P (1963–4) 2.
Report of the Commissioners of Prisons for the year 1951, (1952), London: HMSO, Cmd. 8692.

Newspapers

The Daily Telegraph (London)
The Dominion Post (Wellington)
The Guardian (London)
The New York Times
The Times (London)
The Observer (London)
The Weekly Telegraph (London)

Internet Sources

'Sensible Sentencing Rally for Safe NZ', www.nzcpr.com/forum/viewtopic.php?f=3&t=562&st=0&sk=t&sd=a. Accessed 4 June 2011.
World Prison Brief, International Centre for Prison Studies, Kings College, London University, www.kcl.ac.uk/depsta/law/research/icps/worldbrief. Accessed 4 June 2011.

Meetings: the frontline of civilization*

Wilbert van Vree

Abstract: The *meetingization of society* as a central aspect of civilizing processes is the theme of this article. This term refers to a long-term social process: as larger numbers of people become mutually dependent over larger areas and/or differences in power decrease between people, an increased number of problems needs to be solved through talking and decision-making in meetings which require an ever-increasingly precise, more equal and more embracing regulation of impulses and short-lived affects. This 'compulsion to meet' is less well developed when the networks of mutual dependence are smaller and less stable, and/or the balances of power are more unequal.

Transformations of the ways in which people behave in meetings are important aspects of the formalization and informalization processes that have been so central to research in the figurational tradition. In the past, people participating in meetings in societies characterized by large internal power differences greatly feared each other's emotions and were unable to trust each other to control themselves and keep polite manners when social tensions increased – for instance, because of differences of opinion about their common future. During the most recent phase of social development, the challenge of ambitious people is to regulate the necessary meetings not so much by the second nature of rigid rules and stately customs but more by what Cas Wouters has called a 'third nature' of conscious considerations of efficiency, effectiveness and pleasure. Those who are more skilled at this gain a social advantage.

Meetings, manners and civilization

Meetings are not covered in manners books, the literary genre that Elias used in *The Civilizing Process* to trace the changes in the behaviour of the worldly

*This article elaborates on my book *Meeting, Manners and Civilization: The Development of Modern Meeting Behaviour* (1999) and my article 'The development of meeting behaviour in modern organizations and the rise of an upper class of professional chairpersons' in van Iterson, A. et al. (eds), (2002), *The Civilized Organization: Norbert Elias and the Future of Organization Studies*, Amsterdam: John Benjamin.

elite of Western Europe. Manners books mainly concern what Elias terms 'outward bodily propriety': forms of behaviour that had until then been studied only as psychological or biological phenomena.[1] Tracing the development of eating from the manners books, Elias proposed that this development was to a certain degree a *pars pro toto* of a general behavioural change. Different aspects of human behaviour are inseparable from each other: 'We may call particular drives by different names according to their different directions and functions. We may speak of hunger and the need to spit, of the sexual drive and of aggressive impulses, but in life these different drives are no more separable than the heart from the stomach or the blood in the brain from the blood in the genitalia.' (Elias, 2000 [1939]: 161). An entire complex of many aspects of behaviour has been altered in a similar way and in the same direction; people have forced each other to behave in a more 'civilized' manner. This is evident in the development of meeting behaviour.

Meeting in the specialized, modern sense of *gathering together in order to talk and come to decisions about the common future* appears to be a most appropriate theme.[2] This behaviour has become an increasingly important means of social integration. As a means of bonding and distinction for the elite, the stylization of meeting behaviour has replaced the stylization of eating and drinking.

The development of society in the last millennium in Europe (and other places) is coupled with a slow and non-linear increase in the number of all kinds of meetings and levels of meeting, and with the development of a continually broader network of meetings, in which manners and habits pass from above to below and in an increasing degree from below to above. As the differences in meeting behaviour between social groups diminished, the variations and nuances in meetings increased. I call this long-term process the *meetingization of society*.

In the last two or three centuries the 'most powerful on earth' have gradually changed from being warriors, courtiers and entrepreneurs to being professional meeting-holders and chairpersons. This is significantly illustrated by the derivation of titles given to functions fulfilled in meetings, such as president, vice-president, chairman, general secretary, presiding officer and congressman.

In parliamentary-industrial societies, power, status and property are to an unprecedented degree largely distributed in and through meetings. The upper classes have not become more clearly distinguished in anything than they have in their meeting behaviour. The everyday work of politicians, civil servants and managers is dominated almost entirely by discussing, deliberating, negotiating, and deciding in groups. If they are not actually participating in meetings, they are preparing the meetings or processing the results of them. They live under relatively extreme meeting pressure.

'Civilizing' indicates the course of psychological processes in a certain direction. Characteristic of the West European civilizing process of the last millennium is that more and more people have become dependent upon each other because of the division of tasks and the monopolization of organized violence, and have been forced to focus upon increasingly longer, more permanent and more specialized chains of actions and, while practising them, take the actions and intentions of an ever increasing number of others into account. As Elias explains,

> Through the interdependence of larger groups of people and the exclusion of physical violence from them, a social apparatus is established in which the constraints between people are lastingly transformed into self-constraints. These self-constraints, a function of the perpetual hindsight and foresight instilled in the individual from childhood in accordance with his integration in extensive chains of action, have partly taken the form of self-control and partly [the form] of automatic habit. They tend to a more even moderation, a more continuous restraint, a more exact control of drives and affects in accordance with the more differentiated pattern of social interweaving. (Elias, 2000 [1939]: 375)

In explaining the civilizing of behaviour Elias has pointed to the extension, the condensing and the differentiating of networks of interdependencies and the monopolizing of organized violence. This can be seen quite directly in the development of meetings if one asks who, and in what manner, have mutually decided about whom.

The restraint of physical violence, at least local and temporary, was the *conditio sine qua non* of meetings. The long-term development of meetings coincides with the organization of violence within basic entities, 'tribes', villages, towns, nation-states, confederations – that is, within the increasingly large and more stable 'survival units' which are in fact 'meeting units'. The process by which survival units grow and become more specialized can be more accurately studied by considering village councils, war councils, court councils, estates assemblies, parliaments and other central meetings, in which the actions of an increasing number of people need to be coordinated. Those meetings may be considered as frontlines of civilization.

The collective mind of organizations

Studying meetings leads right to the dynamics of organizations and, consequently, to what should be a main territory of the sociology of organizations. Most contemporary students of meetings consider them as activities to create consciousness and the conscience of an organization. Meetings are 'the talk which realizes organizations' (Bargiela-Chiappini and Harris, 1997: 29). They are 'that very social action through which institutions produce and reproduce themselves' (Boden, 1994: 81). John E. Tropman, who studied meeting behaviour in the USA for many years and wrote several meeting manuals, sees an organization as a dynamic decision matrix: innumerable decisions about the common future being made every day, most of them in all kinds of (electronic) meetings. He concludes that 'the output of meetings is a decision stream that runs the company and that produces, finally, organizational success or failure' (Tropman, 2003: 164).

The anthropologist Helen B. Schwartzman looks to meetings from a different perspective. In her book *The Meeting: Gatherings in Organizations and*

Communities (1989) she juxtaposes her research at an American mental health organization with anthropological research in non-Western societies to examine the significance of meetings in American society. By comparing the forms and functions of meetings in a variety of cultures, she develops a view of meetings contrary to the common assumption, at least in the Western world, that meetings are a tool for making decisions, solving problems, and resolving conflicts. Meetings are important in American culture 'because they generate the *appearance* that reason and logical processes are guiding discussions and decisions, whereas they facilitate ... relationship negotiations, struggle, and commentary' (Schwartzman, 1989: 42). She points out that decisions, problems and conflicts are tools for creating more meetings, while organizations and communities need meetings to present the organization as an entity to their members. Through back-and-forth talk, as well as the exchange that occurs in pre-meeting and post-meeting interaction, participants negotiate who they are, both as individuals and as a group.

Schwartzman based her view of meetings mainly on Emile Durkheim's study *The Elementary Forms of the Religious Life*. The general conclusion of this study is that 'religious representations are collective representations which express collective realities; the rites are a manner of acting which take rise in the midst of the assembled groups and which are destined to excite, maintain or recreate certain mental states in these groups' (Durkheim, 1965 [1915]: 22). The source of religion and morality is in the 'collective mind of society' and not inherent in the 'isolated minds of individuals'. In shaping this collective mind meetings are of the utmost importance:

> There can be no society which does not feel the need of upholding and reaffirming at regular intervals the collective sentiments and the collective ideas which make its unity and its personality. Now this moral remaking cannot be achieved except by the means of reunions, assemblies and meetings where individuals, being closely united to one another, reaffirm in common their common sentiments. (Durkheim, 1965 [1915]: 475)

Both apparently completely different approaches of meetings have a short-term, rather static, perspective in common. From a more distanced, long-term perspective they complement each other well. The first, most popular, approach of meetings does not render sufficient account of unintended consequences. Outcomes of intended actions are not (or not limited to) the results originally intended by a particular action. An earlier, more dynamic and more-encompassing version of the same idea was formulated by Norbert Elias – a fundamental, sociological notion that the interweaving of decisions, plans and intended actions of people (as individuals, organizations or groups) constitutes and drives more embracing, unintended, social processes:

> from the interweaving of countless individual interests and intentions – whether tending in the same direction or in divergent and hostile directions – something comes into being that was planned and intended by none of these individuals, yet has emerged nevertheless from their intentions and actions. And really this is the whole

secret of social figurations, their compelling dynamics, their structural regularities, their process character and their development; this is the *secret* of sociogenesis and of relational dynamics. (Elias, 2000 [1939]: 312; my italics)

Johan Goudsblom called this passage 'paradigmatic'; 'the 'secret' alluded to belongs to the category of what Thomas Kuhn would call the 'fundamental problems' (Goudsblom, 1977: 148). The paradigmatic meaning of the passage just quoted will increase if it is explicitly added that society's development in the direction of increasingly larger networks of interdependence has been coupled with the development of meeting behaviour, the activity through which people more consciously make communal aims and plans.

Schwarzman's approach partly clarifies the functions and impact of meetings for people, but it does not fit the fact that the meetingization of society (an unintended process itself and as such an outcome of the blind dynamics of people intertwining in their deeds and aims) 'gradually leads towards greater scope for planned intervention into both the social and individual structures – intervention based on a growing knowledge of the unplanned dynamics of these structures' (Elias, 2000 [1939]: 367). Meetings in modern societies differ from the predominantly religious meetings of less developed societies like those studied by Durkheim. For the most part, meetings are now held in order to facilitate talk about mutual plans and relationships.

The development of meeting behaviour is a process in which people constrain each other towards control of their mutual relations and thus also of themselves, by orientation to ever-longer, more permanent, and more differentiated chains of action. Thus, the development of meeting activities is a manifestation of the 'rationalization' of human behaviour. In this context, moreover, the minutes of meetings, especially the most central ones, become an extremely strategic research field for those who want to sharpen the picture of long-term changes in the relationship between social ideals and social facts, between language and social reality. In what words and terms did successive generations of dominant groups depict society? What societal changes and goals did they aim at? What, in fact, happened to their plans? From this long-term perspective, what does the meeting behaviour and language of the present upper classes look like?

The sociogenesis of meeting behaviour

Discussions, decisions, negotiations, and deliberations in groups are barely researched as forms of behaviour that change along with the changes in the balance of power between people. Frequently, implicitly or otherwise, people assume that present-day meeting manners were always as they are now. An image of how meeting regimes and behaviours have developed is lacking. Yet many codes and manners we employ in meetings today have developed as standardized solutions of regularly recurring problems. In a long-term collective learning process, some of these solutions were handed on, almost unchanged, from generation to generation, while others disappeared or were changed together with the functions they had for the group, nation, class, gender or any other social grouping employing them. We may speak of 'functional continuity' in the first case and of 'functional change in structural continuity' in the second case. These formulations are borrowed from biology. One of Darwin's first critics, George Mivart, asked how natural selection can explain the incipient stages of complex structures, like wings or eyes, which can only be used in much more elaborate form. Stephen Jay Gould put the problem as follows: 'if complexity precludes sudden origin, and the dilemma of incipient stages forbid gradual developments in functional continuity, then how can we ever get from here to here?' After all, it is impossible to fly with two percent of a wing. According to Gould, Darwin worked out an adequate and interesting resolution. He suggested that 'if incipient stages originally performed a different function suited to their small size and minimal development, natural selection might superintend their increase as adaptations for this original role until they reached a stage suitable for their current use' (Gould, 1991: 143). This conversion from one function to another is referred to as 'functional change in structural continuity'.

The development of meeting behaviour can be explained with the help of these original biological notions. An example of 'functional continuity' is the development of the agenda. Composing, in advance, a relatively fixed list of items for a meeting probably originated in ancient Greek city councils, passed on to the meetings of the Roman empire and medieval church, developed further in the court society, found its way to estates parliaments and spread to ever more sectors of society. During this journey the agenda requirements were gradually modified up to the present day, when listing the items of a meeting has to conform to new standards involving the avoidance of boring repetition and even the generation of a certain pleasurable tension (akin to that which Elias and Dunning (2008 [1986]) see as being involved in sports and other leisure pursuits).

Other manners and procedures developed as a result of functional change in structural continuity. Many of them, such as opening and closing ceremonies, largely functioned as a means of power and distinction for social upper classes, and were altered in a more practical sense when constraints on the upper classes and pressure from lower classes increased. Another striking example is the development of the chairman's gavel. This attribute, used to open the meeting, close a debate, restore order or confirm a decision, descends from a fighting axe with two sharp blades, which was used in folk meetings to execute lawbreakers and chop off limbs or pieces of cloth from those who violated meeting rules and broke the holy peace of a meeting. The sharp axe has gradually become a blunt gavel, while its functions for the conductor of the meeting and for the assembled group changed in a particular direction. This instance of functional change in structural continuity is to be regarded as a metaphor for what happened to the dominant ways in which people hold their meetings. In the long run the standard meeting behaviour of the most powerful groups has become more 'polite' and 'civilized': more peaceful, more differentiated, more regular, more balanced, more informal and smoother.

Phases in the meetingization of European societies

In the long-term, unplanned or blind process of civilizing meeting behaviour in Europe (and other parts of the world), several phases can be discerned.

We do not know much with any certainty about meeting behaviour in the earliest stages of human development. Nevertheless, it is possible to form a plausible idea of the meeting regimes of prehistoric societies by 'reasoning back' on the basis of archaeological and anthropological material and empirically tested regularities in the dynamics of meeting. So it is possible to say that meeting regimes in small, pre-agrarian, relatively egalitarian societies of gatherers and hunters probably had the characteristics of a 'campfire democracy'.[3] People usually met around a fire, eating, drinking, chatting, singing, making music, dancing, doing some manual work, resolving conflicts and planning common actions. Between these activities there were no sharp boundaries. As we have seen before this view matches with Durkheim's observation of the way people of 'primitive' societies hold their meetings.

Although the meeting regime was to a great extent dominated by adult men, the other group members, women and children, could also exert important influence on the course and outcome of the decision-making process. The relatively large predominance of men was based on their greater physical strength and their arms monopoly. In fact, excluding hunting, the use of weapons was rare. As long as the number of people in relation to the available open land remained small, and groups could avoid each other, aggression remained limited to skirmishes. Presumably, based on the assumption of a monopoly of arms by men, women had played at least an equally important role in the plans of action.

Features of subsequent stages in the development of meeting behaviour in European societies when they developed into agrarian and industrial ones are sketched in the following diagram:

Features of societal stages	Features of dominant meeting standards	Features of corresponding self-regulation
Agrarian Small, vulnerable, unstable, territorial monopolies of organized violence	Incidental, martial, masculine, coarsely regulated, ritualistic, sectional	Less embracing, unsteady, rather undifferentiated, hardly predictable, enforced
Industrializing Larger, less vulnerable more stable, territorial monopolies of organized violence	Regular, more peaceful, elite, more regulated, solemn, fairly particularistic	More embracing, steadier, more differentiated, more predictable, stiff
(Post)industrial Further development in direction of more effective, transnational monopolizing of organized violence	Further development in direction of continuous, generally peaceful, common, increasingly varied, more informal, global	Further development in direction of all-embracing, steady, highly differentiated, generally predictable, smoother
processes continue	processes continue	processes continue

Meeting behaviour in agrarian societies: militarization and demilitarization

The common structural characteristic of agrarian societies, the dominance of warriors, manifested itself in the development and spreading of formal, martial rules of meetings and manners. This development was initially due to the 'spiral of wars' by which larger numbers of people were compelled to act as one body. Waging war demanded, from the able-bodied men in particular, activities such as training boys for defence, the selection of leaders, the discussion and announcement of the strategy to be followed, the court-martialling and punishing of warriors, deliberations about surrender or truce, and the division of seized goods and conquered land. For this purpose warriors issued commands and orders that they sanctioned by harsh physical punishment. Due to permanent warfare or threats of war, the martial meeting rules acted as an example for others.

Threats of war, and waging war itself, forced people to organize themselves into units of offence and defence led by warriors who could protect them against the organized violence of other warriors. Through pressure from above, by imitation, and resulting from habit, the meeting manners of warrior councils spread and participation in meetings became strongly dependent upon military power and military considerations. In such a way, women, children, and often non-able-bodied men were excluded from the central meetings of survival units and from many other meetings. In Europe until long after the Middle Ages, unrelenting rules forbidding women to take part in meetings of courts of justice, guilds, churches, and towns, remained in force.

The trend in the direction of the militarization of meetings was coupled with opposition from the non-military population. This opposition worked in the direction of a further differentiation of manners in meetings. The importance of warrior councils as a general model for meetings decreased as these non-military groups rose in power. The functions of meetings expanded from those concerned with the administration of the law, preparations for war, and the establishment of peace, to controlling taxation, water boards, trade, industry, social services, and many other activities and problems stemming from the extension and differentiation of the chains of actions. As long as the monopolies of violence remained vulnerable and unstable, holding meetings remained limited and they only came to seem to some degree natural within the small upper layers of society. As long as many people were strongly inclined to settle a dispute or difference of opinion by coming to blows or by armed combat, the necessity for holding a meeting was relatively limited, and meetings retained a highly ritualistic character.

Compared with later developments, there was little discussion and argumentation. Corresponding to the relatively short and little differentiated series of transactions, the high level of danger, and the large divisions in power in the society dominated by warriors and priests, the tendency to solve problems by discussion and agreement was, in general, relatively weak. Ecclesiastical meetings mainly consisted of praying and performing religious rituals. For the most part, many secular meetings consisted of swearing oaths, reciting incantations, and indulging in bouts of eating and drinking. Activities used as a means to obtain decisive answers to the question of how to proceed were: trials employing bodily injury; man-to-man fights where men cursed, wounded, or killed each other; dreams; loud screaming; collective hymn singing; communal catcalling; spontaneous flashes of the imagination; and other highly affective behaviour. Agreements were frequently undocumented, but orally endorsed by sworn oaths, meals, and prayers.

It was only during the process of state formation, when organized violence was monopolized over extensive areas and a small number of monopolies came to dominate the rest, that more groups and layers of the population came to participate in meetings and sanctioned rules of conduct were created. The emerging meeting regimes of new, dominant groups presumed and demanded greater and more differentiated self-restraint. While previous meeting regulations contained numerous stipulations referring to disruptions to order, such as fighting, shouting, drunken talk, drawing knives, throwing glasses, and bearing arms, the new meeting rules were more concerned with regulating verbal battles, and made greater demands upon an individual's capacity for thinking and upon his (or, occasionally, her) 'conscience'. Although everyday social intercourse was still far from peaceful, the more violent aspects of society were excluded from the prescribed meeting behaviour, more than they were in the previous period. The meeting rules were not formulated as worldly wisdom or practical requirements for social behaviour, but rather as ethical norms or laws of God, and learnt as 'semi-automatic functioning impulses of conscience'.

As conflicts and tensions between states, and between classes and groups within states lessened, conditions became more favourable for the processes of individual learning about how to hold and attend meetings. The rules became more self-evident. This development accelerated during the process of industrialization and the formation of nation states, when more people were forced to consider the results of centrally held verbal struggles and the decisions prescribing the do's and don'ts to which they could be forced to comply by the use of organized violence. One of the resulting developments was the gradual standardization of manners in meetings or the diminishing of differences in the ways of meeting between groups within nation states. As more layers of the population, by means of their chosen representatives, took part in the struggle for the control and the use of the organized violence, the central meetings were precisely those places where different meeting manners melded together to become new standards of meeting behaviour.

Meeting behaviour in industrial societies

During the process of industrialization in the last few centuries, many societies have developed into differentiated, multi-layered, meeting units which, in turn, are constituents of continental and global units.[4] The number of meetings and meeting levels in the areas of politics, economics, culture, and almost everything else, has increased enormously. More than ever before, opportunities for social success are dependent upon an individual's competence and experience in talking and decision-making concerning lengthy and differentiated chains of actions. The upper level of industrialized society was, and increasingly is, shaped in and by meetings that require a relatively large, precise, constant and flexible self-regulation of expressions of affects and emotions.

The development of meetings during the process of industrialization was maintained by the need to solve the complex problems of co-ordination which arose during the unprecedentedly powerful, extensive and intensive economic growth,[5] and the accompanying processes of the division of tasks, urbanization and organization of people into larger and closer political, economic, and cultural units, in which the power differences became smaller and smaller or, at least, became less pronounced. Likewise, forces against these developments constantly manifested themselves. At their gravest, these took the form of revolts, authoritarian intervention, and wars; less serious forms were laments that meetings were dreadful, boring, and time-consuming. Having to meet has become the fate of civilized people. It is the price that has to be paid for greater security and a more prosperous standard of living.

Two stages can be distinguished in the development of meetings, during the beginnings and then the spread of industrialisation; they are the sign of two consecutive, dominant trends. From the latter half of the eighteenth century to the middle of the twentieth century, there has been a dominant trend which could be designated as the *parliamentarization* of meetings. The trend that later became more prominent could be designated as the *professionalization* of meetings.

Parliamentarization

Elias concluded in *The Civilizing Process* that the courtization of the warriors was a 'key event' in the West European process of civilization: 'Not only in the Western civilizing process, but as far as we see within every major civilizing process, one of the most decisive transitions is that of *warriors to courtiers*'. (Elias, 2000 [1939]: 389). Elaborating upon this, it can be said that a subsequent decisive event in this process of civilization was 'the parliamentarization of the courtiers' (Van Vree and Bos, 1989). Initially, in the parliaments, which took over the co-ordinating tasks from the royal courts, many courtiers were given a seat next to people originating from common stock. The more peaceful, more differentiated, and more businesslike etiquettes which developed in parliaments functioned as examples; a function similar to that of court manners in the previous social stage.

The parliamentarization of the competitive struggle between people within states developed under conditions precipitated by an increasingly faster growth in trade, in lines of transport and communication, and in industry. In the competitive struggle between states, success and failure became more dependent on the resources and support that governments had to demand from commerce and industry. While the production process, involving the increasing use of fossil fuels, became more extensive, more complex and more vulnerable, and more and more people became dependent upon each other as producers and consumers, so too did opportunities arise which made possible a continuous parliamentarization of the social competition within states.

In all European and in many other countries, discussing and deciding about the monopolies of physical force and taxation sooner or later became more public and also centred in elected national parliaments. The continuous competitive struggle between states forced groups within these states to close ranks and take each other into consideration to a greater extent. While increasingly more people became more strongly tied to individual states with the introduction of national duties, such as military service, tax obligations, compulsory education and obligations to social security, and national systems developed for the registration of the population, jurisdiction, the police, education, social and medical care and social security, the competitive struggle for power, possession, and status within states acquired more the character of a regulated battle of words or a parliamentary struggle.

This parliamentarization of the population occurred in waves. With every change in the composition and the position of power of the national parliaments, the rules were altered, adjusted or newly stipulated in the regulation codes. These regulations acted as an object for study for juridical specialists and served as models for the legal regulation of meetings and meeting practices within companies and corporations, societies, associations and other social organizations, with whose help, large groups of outsiders were integrated into society. During the extension of voting rights, a rapidly growing number of manuals appeared for establishing, managing, and running the meetings of associations and companies.

The rise of an upper class of professional chairmen and the professionalization of meeting behaviour

Since the 1930s in the Unites States, and since the Second World War in Western Europe, a trend in meeting behaviour towards professionalisation has become more prominent. This trend became dominant with the integration of national states into continental and worldwide meeting units, with the acceleration of the division of functions, with the enlargement of the scale of institutions, and with functional democratization. Particularly in professional life, more people were more frequently obliged to hold discussions with each other – to negotiate the implementation, division and payment of functions, and to reach agreement on the acquisition, management and spending of capital. In everyday social intercourse, meetings acquired a central position. As far as meeting behaviour was concerned, competence and knowledge became essential ingredients for a successful social career.

Anyone who wishes to rise in present-day society has to climb the meeting ladder. Every rung upwards carries with it the consequences of holding discussions with others and making common decisions more frequently and more regularly, about lengthier, more enduring and more differentiated chains of actions. Little or no participation in meetings is characteristic of an outsider position in society (see Elias and Scotson, 2008 [1965]).

Learning how to participate in meetings has become an important part of the rearing and education of the young. Anyone who wants to participate in society with some degree of success needs to know and be able to apply elementary meeting rules, and to have mastered the type of language spoken in meetings. Pressure increased in meetings for people to take more into account the wishes and feelings of more people, and more aspects of their own personality. Central to this trend was the obligation to refer to oneself and others in a businesslike manner. Self-aggrandising comments became less acceptable. With this, it was quite apparent that there had been increases in the social pressure during meetings to suppress megalomaniac fantasies, and to speak about people in a more distanced manner. In meetings, mutual fear between representatives of different classes and groups diminished. Meeting manners in general became more easy and informal.

In his study *Work and Authority in Industry*, which appeared for the first time in the 1950s, Reinhard Bendix commented that with the spread of meeting activities in companies, an upper layer of 'moderate businessmen' had emerged; 'even-tempered when others rage, brave when others fear, calm when others are excited, self-controlled when others indulge' (Bendix, 1974 [1956]: 332). In his explanation of the changes which had occurred in the attitudes, performance, and ideas of managers of American companies since the 1930s, Bendix focused attention upon a notable correspondence with the process of courtization of warriors as it was outlined by Elias:[6]

> I suggest that the changeover from the idealization of the 'strenuous life' to the idealization of 'human relations' may be an adaptation of a similar kind.[7] The manners commended by the personnel experts of modern American industry certainly facilitate the co-operation which management requires, much as the commendation of polite manners facilitated peace at the Royal Court. . . . The calm eyes which never stray from the other's gaze, the easy control in which laughter is natural but never forced, the attentive and receptive manner, the well-rounded, good-fellowship, the ability to elicit participation and to accomplish change without upsetting relationships, may be so many devices for personal advancement when the man is on his way up. (Bendix, 1974 [1956]: 335)

The ability and the attitude, which, according to Bendix, are characteristic of 'moderate businessmen' or managers, developed during the mainly unplanned spread of meeting activities and negotiations in, and between, complex company organizations; through those people from the less powerful levels of the population – including women – who came to take part in meetings. Demands for such behaviour can be found over and over again in meeting manuals; the following quotes are illustrations of this:

> Your physical listening manner should be animated and expressive. Listeners as well as speakers can be animated. Animation should show in your face, in your eyes, and in your physical bearing. . . . Sloughing in a chair, leaning on elbows, supporting chin on hand, or playing with a pencil are not the habits of a good listener. (Zelko, 1969 [1957]: 137–8)

> If you start out by calling the other person 'foolish', 'ignorant', or 'utterly lacking in common sense', you are insulting him, and he is likely to send back an equally strong reply. Moreover, you are attacking the man rather than his point; this is one of the best ways to destroy good human relations. . . . As you take up someone else's point, do it in a pleasant manner; try to avoid such words as 'disagree' in stating your own position. (Zelko, 1969 [1957]: 135)

The social significance of the forms of conduct that were developed in company meetings and other work organizations has increased even more with the extension of the international market, the growth of world trade and capital exchanges, and the expansion of companies.

As the number and levels of meetings within and between states spread enormously, a new upper layer formed, consisting of managers who delegated, co-ordinated, and controlled functions by means of meetings in which they were more often *primi inter pares* than they were commanders or directors. One of the first modern meeting manuals noticed:

> We have come face to face with the fact that the work scene is a part of the total social and democratic environment of a democracy, no less important as a medium for the discussion process than the legislative hall or the club meeting. . . . Since the work environment strikes so close to the well-being of all of us, we might examine more fully the part that discussion plays in the business world of today. (Zelko, 1969 [1957]: 7)

In all Western industrialized countries, company managers have begun to allocate more and more time for meetings.[8] The higher the individual is in the hierarchy, the more the number of meetings. Bargiela-Chiappini and Harris, who wrote a comparative study about meetings in a large Italian–British telephone company, concluded that meetings were the essence of managerial practice and the corporate communication process. They noted that

> a link could be established between the consistency in underestimating time spent on meetings and the implicit and explicit expressions of scepticism or boredom *vis-à-vis* this practice registered during our company visits. This consideration may become an important one when trying to understand the role played by meetings in situations of strategic and/or cultural change, where high levels of uncertainty are counterbalanced by an increase in the number of meetings at all company levels in order to maintain a semblance of *status quo*. (Bargiela-Chiappini and Harris, 1997: 30)

It is possible to go a step further in one's explanation of the reason why meetings have become a grind and are often associated with boredom and dullness. In present-day organizations, meetings often seem to have similar functions to that which etiquette had in the French court society, as described by Norbert Elias. Courtiers gathered in set places and at set times to perform specific acts according to exact rules. They bitterly complained about these useless rituals, but went through them again and again. The court etiquette endured as a 'ghostly *perpetuum mobile*' (2006 [1969]: 95) because of the current power relationships between the most important social groupings. The slightest modification of a ritual might have been interpreted by a group or faction as an attempt to upset the shaky social power balance. In the same way contemporary organization men seem to be socially fated to meet and to meet again with the same colleagues at set places and set times to perform similar acts every time.

Conferences of various kinds have become important meeting places in work organizations. In large organizations, personnel are also 'assessed' regarding their behaviour during meetings. Individuals may, as a result of their performances within meetings, be seen in a favourable light, and thus enjoy greater chances of promotion and rising within the hierarchy. In view of this, it is somewhat surprising that professionals, in depicting organizations, for the most part usually disregard meetings. To obtain a practically more adequate representation of an organization, it is insufficient to only look at the hierarchical relationships between individuals.

These are just some examples of relevant matters that come up when one puts meetings and meeting behaviour in the centre of organization studies. Organization is normally treated as a thing, but in fact, it is a social activity and process. Anyone who thinks of 'organizing' instead of 'organization' soon enough comes across meetings. Thus, studying meetings and meeting behaviour is a strategic means of approaching the dynamics of organization. Studying the complicated regimes of meetings in which, and by which, an organization is continually shaped would be more important. How have these networks been structured, layered, and subdivided? In which direction have they developed and how did the accompanying meeting manners and the meeting behaviour change at different levels? How did meeting activities change when an organization grew or shrank; if the external market became more dynamic and more complex, or even more stable and simpler? Oddly enough, so far, little use has been made of the possibility of studying and enlightening organizations by answering such questions.

Informalization of meeting behaviour

Parliamentary[9] procedure and motions should be avoided in reaching decisions in most conferences. Parliamentary procedure is the most formal method a group can use, and conference process is based primarily on informal methods. Some informal conference processes do involve controls, but not in the rigorous and exacting sense that prevails under parliamentary procedure. . . . members should feel free to speak up and make contributions at any time, without recognition by the chair or first indicating their desire to speak. (Zelko, 1969 [1957]: 162–3)

After the establishment of the norms and rules of meeting procedures in the social habitus of people, and with the further reduction in the risks of being conquered and humiliated, a more differentiated regulation of behaviour and emotions became possible and necessary. As is evident from meeting manuals, the dominant meeting manners have been further developed in parliamentary – industrial countries in the last fifty years. Attention has shifted from general deliberative assemblies to more differentiated, especially professional and business meetings; from formal rules to informal codes; from debating to discussing; from majority decisions to consensus; from the attitude of parties, administration and opposition to the behaviour of individual meeting participants; and from a chairman's function to the duties of ordinary meeting participants.

This shift reflects a more-embracing process of informalization of manners, as characterized by Cas Wouters: as power relationships became less unequal, people began to be less threatened by those feelings and behaviours, which had been loaded with anxiety and shame in earlier stages of social and psychological development in relation to tensions between social groups, classes, and sects (Wouters, 1990). The controlled expression of feelings of anger, disappointment and aggression were acceptable to a certain degree in meetings on the basis of an increase in the reciprocally anticipated self-control. Meeting manuals reflect these changes clearly, as in the following example:

> Meeting leaders and participants must bear in mind that encouraging the expression of feelings will free the flow of thoughts – and suppressing or ignoring them will filter, distort, or block thoughts. Our feelings come from basic human needs that, though now and then openly discussed, are infrequently served in meetings – or anywhere else in organizations, for that matter. (Dunsing, 1978: 41)

Recent trends

The latest development of meetings in public and private life was able to take place under the condition of a relatively high level of violence control within and between national states and of a resulting, corresponding level of mutually expected self-control. The common regulation of social changes has developed in the direction of an increasingly wider continuum of variants of meetings. The further development of this variation seems to be dependent upon a continuing pacification in the struggle for power, prestige, and wealth and the development of meeting regimes and meeting behaviour at continental and global levels.

Parliamentarization and professionalization of meetings have been continued in many parts of the world in the last twenty years, albeit not at the same pace and in the same degree. With the extension of the European unity we see processes of parliamentarization, with difficulty, in all post-communist countries, while such processes in the Middle East have been slowed down rather than advanced by an ingenuous 'democratic offensive' led by the USA. As with every long-term process, one sees periods of stagnation and even regression followed by periods of slow and accelerated continuation.

National meetings have lost significance with respect to more-embracing meetings such as those of the European Council of Ministers and the Security Council of the United Nations. The growing significance of continental and global negotiation-like meetings is closely related to the strongly increased social interdependencies in the military, economic, and ecological areas. The globalization of the economy and the risk of large-scale wars and ecological disasters forces individual states to discuss closer co-operation and implementation of policy. The biggest tensions and problems of today seem hardly solvable without more representative and more adequately functioning assemblies at higher levels of integration. The latest financial crisis and ecological threats make that quite clear. However the meetingization of the global society often proceeds slowly, with setbacks and temporary stagnations.

The recent spurts in the globalization of the economy and political integration are accompanied by the scaling up of public and private organizations, by mergers and takeovers of companies in the world of insurance and banking, car making, the press and publishing trades, accountancy and consultancy, and almost any other line of business or branch of trade and services. The emergence of bigger companies requires new facilities and organizational structures, involving a marked increase in conferences, conventions and congresses to talk and decide about the common future. The coming together of people from societies with various traditions has made them more conscious of their mutual identities, similarities and differences in thinking and acting. During meetings they are forced to take each other into consideration to a greater extent, to assimilate with each other and to soften and narrow (national) differences in standards of behaviour. Traditional differences and sharp contrasts are being transformed into cultural variations and local colour.

Conferences, congresses and assemblies of companies and clubs pre-eminently offer opportunities for people of different countries to get to know each other. Etiquette and manners in meetings are stricter and more compelling than those on tourist spots. Meetings require more self-discipline. Words and gestures require more precise attention, while the need for mutual understanding and consideration is bigger. That is exactly why meetings strongly promote the development of common etiquettes and languages. They are the trailblazers of contemporary, continental and global, integration processes.

Getting together for consultations has become easier in many cases. Furthermore, it has become possible 'to meet at a distance' via telephone connections, computer networks, and video-conferences, by means of which people in various places in the world take part in front of a camera and video screen, and enter into consultations with each other. These types of meetings appear to have developed rapidly because, particularly for multinationals whose managers almost live in aeroplanes, meeting through a video screen can demonstrably lead to lower costs and higher productivity. The use of such techniques makes consultations and negotiations within companies, and between representatives of companies, states, and other organizations, simpler; so much that it can be expected that in the future they will be further extended. Nevertheless, in their study, *Managing Language: The Discourse of Corporate Meetings*, Francesca Bargiela-Chiappini and Sandra J. Harris point to research which suggests that video-conferencing has not lessened the importance of meetings in organizations, including companies in their various forms. 'Whether two-party or multi-party, internal or cross-organizational, intra-cultural or cross-cultural, face-to-face meetings continue to provide a forum where participants can arguably expect total commitment to the interaction, . . . [a] maximum degree of urgency exerted by the parties and no technical problems . . . as an excuse' (Bargiela-Chiappini and Harris, 1997: 6).

Electronic meetings are just another way of talking and deciding in groups about the common future. They have become serious alternatives for face-to-face-meetings even if meetings involving corporeal co-presence continue to be important.

Conclusions

The latest acceleration of the professionalization of meetings in parliamentary–industrial societies occurred together with the privatization of public organizations and the erosion of national power in the Western world.[10] In large parts of the industrial and post-industrial world, the power balance between private companies and national states has shifted in favour of the companies. As a result, business-like meeting manners have been rapidly developed and widely spread in the last two decades, while the significance of the meeting ideals and manners developed in and spread from national parliaments, political councils, committees and associations has decreased. The older, parliamentary, democratic habitus has come to be at odds with the demands of efficiency and the differences in function, position, and expertise required for the face-to-face and digital meetings that have widely spread in work organizations in the last fifty years. This development has created two related problems in parliamentary–industrial societies.

While parliamentary manners are still for many people the most dominant guidelines for meetings, professional life increasingly requires a different habitus, less democratic and making greater demands on one's own initiative and feeling of responsibility. More varied types of meetings have been developed for every sort of problem. On the one hand, the emphasis lies on the exchange of information, exploration or discussion; on the other it lies on brainstorming, advising or deciding. The older, predominantly political-parliamentary ways of meeting have often proved to be inadequate; they are too little differentiated, geared to debates between parties, to the use of the majority rule and other democratic conditions which do not fit work relations very well. Compared with parliamentary-like meetings, company-like meetings demand more knowledge and abilities, more team spirit, more mutually anticipated self-control and flexibility. These are qualities that advance the opportunity for social success in terms of income, power, and prestige. On the other hand, the deep-rooted parliamentary meeting codes and manners during gatherings in work organizations can be disadvantageous in the context of more severe economic competition on a global scale, if only because the parliamentary – democratic way takes relatively more time and money.

The same trend creates another problem, which Judith Brett put forward, elaborating on my study (Van Vree, 1999) about the development of modern meeting behaviour. With the waning of the parliamentarization of associational life, parliaments – the product of an earlier civilizational wave – 'are left exposed to the criticism of citizens who now do their day to day and community politics in quite different ways. Where once parliament led the way, establishing procedures and protocols which became the model for other assemblies, parliament is now being left behind, its rigid adversarial procedures deployed by our rigidly disciplined parties no longer according with the community's experience of the processes necessary for good decision making' (Brett, 2002: 156).

These problems are reasons for doing more systematic research into the development of meeting regimes – meeting relations and behaviour – in connection with more-embracing social processes. Besides, this study might improve our knowledge of people and societies and anticipate further misjudgements like those made at the attempts of the governments of some parliamentary–industrial states to democratize military–agrarian societies in Asia[11] and at the integration of new generations and newcomers from military–agrarian societies into parliamentary–industrial societies.

Summary

Societies without meetings in which a common future was discussed and decided have never existed as far as I know. However, the way people hold meetings is variable and continually changing. The theme of this paper has been the *meetingization of society* as a central aspect of civilizing processes. This term refers to a long-term social process, the gist of which is: as larger numbers of people become mutually dependent over larger areas and/or differences in power between people decrease, an increased number of problems needs to be solved through talking and decision-making in meetings which require an ever increasing precise, more equal and more embracing regulation of impulses and short-lived affects; this 'compulsion to meet' is less well developed when the networks of mutual dependence are smaller and less stable, and/or the balances of power are more unequal.[12]

Transformations of meeting behaviour of the kind mentioned above can be further explained as aspects of formalization and informalization processes (Wouters, 2007). My research shows that, in societies characterized by large, internal power differences and great fears for each others' emotions, people could not trust each other as meeting participants to control themselves and keep polite manners when social tensions increased – for instance, because of differences of opinion about the common future. In order to decrease these risks, meeting-people decked their gatherings out with ceremonies, formalities and rituals. The dominant – stipulating – meeting manners slowly formalized, became a 'second nature' for many people and were obviously passed on to new generations. Such processes of formalization are characteristic of the military–agrarian phase of social development.

When in the next, parliamentary–industrial phase the differences in power and status between people decreased, together with the direct threat of war, the trend of formalization switched in the opposite direction. As fears of overt physical violence, humiliation and feelings of inferiority in everyday life decreased and the mutual anticipated self-control increased, the dominant meeting manners became smoother, easier, and more flexible.

After the establishment of the parliamentary norms and rules in the social habitus of people, and with the further reduction in the risks of being conquered and humiliated, the number of meetings and meeting levels in the areas of politics, economics, culture, and almost everything else increased enormously. A more differentiated regulation of behaviour and emotions became possible and necessary. Attending meetings lost much of its exclusiveness and some formal meeting manners, which primarily developed as a means of power and distinction for the social upper crust, lost significance. Instead, meetings were making greater demands on one's own initiative and feeling of responsibility.

During this most recent phase of social development, the challenge of ambitious people is to regulate the necessary meetings, not so much by the second nature of rigid rules and stately customs but more by a 'third nature' of conscious considerations of efficiency, effectiveness and pleasure. Deciding if a meeting is necessary or the most effective thing to do or not, choosing the most efficient or appropriate (electronic) form, inviting the right people and the right number of people, tuning procedures in to the current goal of the meeting, choosing the right location, appropriate light, fitting attire and food, using informal but direct manners during meetings, moderate expression of emotions – these are ingredients of a new third nature of meetings, which groups of people are developing today. Those who are better at this have social advantage.

It is to be expected that when, in the long run, social differentiation and integration continue and increasingly larger groups of people become more interdependent, people will develop more-embracing meeting regimes and more civilized meeting behaviour. However, these are not linear processes, but characterized by accelerations, stagnations and reversals. The degree to which these processes will be accompanied by the use of – new forms of – organized violence, is greatly conditional upon the speed, scale and impact of the development of meeting behaviour. And the other way around: one of the most important conditions for a better control of organized violence and the increase in safety, welfare, and quality of life is the further civilization of people's meeting manners – manners that make it possible to focus more adequately on increasingly more complicated and more embracing human figurations and prevent needless sorrow and suffering.

Notes

1 Emile Durkheim's first lines of *Les Régles de la Méthode Sociologique* (1895) were that 'each individual drinks, sleeps, eats and thinks, and it is to society's interest that these functions be exercised in an orderly manner'. He commented further that these facts should not be considered as 'social facts', because in that case sociology would have no exclusive scientific territory for itself, because this would be confused with that of biology and psychology.

2 This meaning of the word 'meeting' has become the dominant one during a long historical process that I have described at length in *Meeting, Manners and Civilization* (1999: 11–19).

3 These ideas are mainly based on Ronald Glassman's work *Democracy and Despotism in Primitive Societies*. His 'ideal type' description of the 'campfire democracy' corresponds mainly to the image of those political processes in societies of hunters and gatherers (Johnson and Earle, 1987; Woodburn, 1980; Silberbauer, 1982; Leacock and Lee, 1982).

4 In *Meeting, Manners and Civilization*, I outlined extensively the development of meeting behaviour during the industrialization and the emergence of inter-state organizations, with the help of European and North American meeting manuals. These books provide a continuous series of detailed information about the problems, ideals, precepts, prohibitions, and customs of meetings. They are a rich source of information about changes in the behaviour and self-control of people at the latest stage of society when meeting, with the increase in mutual dependency and the decrease in power differences, became a central and everyday behaviour. This literature particularly illustrates how, when, and which meeting manners were more widely adopted, or became lost when they were no longer necessary to accentuate or maintain differences in rank (Van Vree, 1999: 256–311).

5 For the distinction between extensive and intensive growth, see chapters 4 and 5 (by Eric Jones), in Goudsblom, Jones and Mennell, 1996: 63–99.

6 This is not so surprising: Bendix and Elias were acquainted with each other – see Bendix's foreword to Elias's *What is Sociology?* (1978).

7 The allusions are to Theodore Roosevelt's celebrated address 'The Strenuous Life' (1900) and to the American 'Human Relations' school of industrial relations centred on Elton Mayo.

8 I reported at length about the time company managers in Western countries spend on meetings in my article 'The development of meeting behaviour in modern organizations and the rise of an upper class of professional chairpersons' (Van Vree, 2002).

9 The word 'parliamentary' is here being used in the American sense pertaining to formal rules of procedure – standing orders and so forth – rather than in the European sense of pertaining to a legislative assembly as an organ of government.

10 The financial crisis might be the beginning of a period of stagnation or regression of these processes. On the other hand, the climate crisis and other global problems might promote integration and meetingization processes on a global scale.

11 See for instance Wittes (2008) and Zakaria (2008).

12 Changes of meeting standards and behaviour are being studied and explained as aspects of social differentiation and integration processes – main social processes that can increase and decrease (Elias, 2009 [1977]).

References

Dates given in square brackets are those of first publication.

Bargiela-Chiappini, Francesca and Sandra J. Harris, (1997), *Managing Language: The Discourse of Corporate Meetings*. Amsterdam/Philadelphia: John Benjamin's Publishing Co.

Bendix, Reinhard, (1974 [1956]), *Work and Authority in Industry*. Berkeley, CA: University of California Press.

Boden, Deirdre, (1994), *The Business of Talk: Organizations in Actions*. Cambridge: Polity Press.

Brett, Judith, (2002), 'Meetings, parliaments and civil society', *Papers on Parliament* (Canberra), 38: 43–160.

Durkheim, Emile, (1966 [1895]), *The Rules of Sociological Method*. New York: The Free Press.

Durkheim, Emile, (1965 [1915]), *The Elementary Forms of the Religious Life*. New York: The Free Press.

Dunsing, Richard J., (1978), *You and I have simply to stop meeting this way*. New York: Amacom.

Elias, Norbert, (1978), *What is Sociology?* London: Hutchinson. [Collected Works, Vol. 5, Dublin: UCD Press, forthcoming].

Elias, Norbert, (2000 [1939]), *The Civilizing Process: Sociogenetic and Psychogenetic Investigations*, rev. edn., *On the Process of Civilization*, Oxford: Blackwell. [Collected Works, *On the Process of Civilisation*, vol. 3, forthcoming].

Elias, Norbert, (2006 [1969]), *The Court Society*, Collected Works, vol. 2, Dublin: UCD Press.

Elias, Norbert, (2009 [1977]), 'Towards a Theory of Social Processes', in *Essays III: On Sociology and the Humanities*. Collected Works, Vol. 16, Dublin: UCD: 9–39.

Elias, Norbert and John L. Scotson, (2008 [1965]), *The Established and the Outsiders*, Collected Works, Vol. 4, Dublin: UCD.

Elias, Norbert and Eric Dunning, (2008 [1986]), *Quest for Excitement: Sport and Leisure in the Civilising Process*, Collected Works, Vol. 7, Dublin: UCD.

Glassman, Ronald M., (1986), *Democracy and Despotism in Primitive Societies*, 2 vols, New York: Millwood.

Goudsblom, Johan, (1977), *Sociology in the Balance*. Oxford: Blackwell.

Goudsblom, Johan, (1992), *Fire and Civilization*. London: Allen Lane.

Goudsblom, Johan, (1996), 'The formation of military–agrarian regimes', in Johan Goudsblom, Eric Jones and Stephen Mennell, (eds), *The Course of Human History: Economic Growth, Social Process, and Civilization,* Armonk, NY: M. E. Sharpe, pp. 49–62.

Goudsblom, Johan, Eric Jones and Stephen Mennell, (1996), *The Course of Human History: Economic Growth, Social Process, and Civilization*. Armonk, NY: M. E. Sharpe.

Gould, Stephen Jay, (1991), *Bully for Brontosaurus*, Harmondsworth: Penguin.

Johnson, Allen W. and Timothy Earle, (1987), *The Evolution of Human Societies*. Stanford, CA: Stanford University Press.

Leacock, Eleanor and Richard Lee, (1982), 'Introduction', *Politics and History in Band Societies*. New York: Cambridge University Press.

Roosevelt, Theodore, (1900) *The Strenuous Life: Essays and Addresses*. New York: Century.

Schwartzman, Helen B., (1989), *The Meeting: Gatherings in Organizations and Communities*. New York: Plenum Press.

Silberbauer, George, (1982), 'Political process in G/wi bands', in Eleanor Leacock and Richard Lee, (eds), *Politics and History in Band Societies*. New York: Cambridge University Press.

Tropman, John E., (2003), *Making Meetings Work*. London: Sage.

van Vree, Wilbert and Gerard Bos, (1989), 'Vergaderen, verhoofsing en parlementarisering', *Amsterdams Sociologisch Tijdschrift*, 16, 3: 52–75.

van Vree, Wilbert, (1999), *Meetings Manners and Civilization: The Development of Modern Meeting Behaviour,* London: University of Leicester Press.

van Vree, Wilbert, (2002), 'The development of meeting behaviour in modern organizations and the rise of an upper class of professional chairpersons', in Ad van Iterson, Willem Mastenbroek, Timothy Newton and Dennis Smith, *The Civilized Organization: Norbert Elias and the Future of Organization Studies*. Amsterdam: John Benjamin.

Wittes, Tamara Cofman, (2008), *Freedom's Unsteady March: America's Role in Building Arab Democracy*, Washington, DC: The Brookings Institution.

Woodburn, James, (1980), 'Hunters and gatherers today and reconstruction of the past', in Ernest Gellner, (ed), *Soviet and Western Anthropology*, London: Gerald Duckworth: 95–117.

Wouters, Cas, (1990), *Van minnen en sterven*. Amsterdam: Bert Bakker.

Wouters, Cas, (2007), *Informalization: Manners and Emotions since 1890*. London: Sage.

Zakaria, Fareed, (2008), *The Post-American World*. New York, W.W. Norton.

Zelko, Harold P., (1969 [1957]), *The Business Conference: Leadership and Participation*. New York: McGraw-Hill Book Company.

Notes on contributors

Nina Baur is Professor of Methods of Social Research at the Department of Sociology at the Technical University Berlin. She is Secretary of ISA RC 33 (Logic and Methodology in Sociology), Vice-President of the Users' Advisory Board of GESIS and Co-operating Editor of the journal *Historical Social Research* (HSR). Her research fields are process sociology, mixed methods research and methods of historical sociology.

Stefanie Ernst holds a professorship in Sociology at the department of socio-economics at the university of Hamburg, with the focus on work, organization and gender. Since 2006 she has been the managing editor of the journal *Sozialwissenschaften und Berufspraxis* (Social Sciences and Professional Practice). She finished her studies in sociology, historical sciences and social anthropology in Marburg and Münster (Germany) as a Master of Arts in 1992 and as a Doctor of Philosophy in Sociology in Hamburg (Germany) in 1998. She has numerous publications and lectures on the topics of sociology of work, organization, gender and equality, quality development, social research methods and figurational sociology.

Norman Gabriel is a lecturer in Early Childhood Studies at the University of Plymouth with research interests in the sociology of early childhood and the relation between sociology and developmental psychology. He also teaches Masters courses in the sociology department at the University of Copenhagen: Norbert Elias and process sociology: a sociological approach for the twenty-first century – and towards a sociology of early childhood. He is currently researching historical changes in parent–child relationships and the role of affective bonding in young children's development.

Richard Kilminster is Honorary Research Fellow in Sociology at the University of Leeds, where he taught until 2010. He gained his PhD at Leeds under Zygmunt Bauman in 1976, having previously studied sociology as an undergraduate at the University of Essex and as graduate student at the University of Leicester, where he was taught by Norbert Elias. In the 1980s he worked with Elias at the University of Bielefeld and in Amsterdam and edited his last major work, *The Symbol Theory*, published posthumously in 1991. He is author of *Praxis and Method: A Sociological Dialogue with Lukács, Gramsci and the Early Frankfurt School* (1979), *The Sociological Revolution: From the*

Enlightenment to the Global Age (1998) and *Norbert Elias: Post-philosophical Sociology* (2007) and numerous articles on sociological theory. He is chair of the Editorial Advisory Board for the *Collected Works of Norbert Elias*, has edited volume 1, *The Early Writings* (2006) and co-edited (with Stephen Mennell) three further volumes (14–16) of *Essays* (2008–09) all with UCD Press, Dublin. He is currently working on a new edition of *The Symbol Theory* for that series (Vol. 13, 2011) and researching the role of psychoanalytic schools in the formation of sociology.

Andrew Linklater is Woodrow Wilson Professor of International Politics at Aberystwyth University. He has published extensively on normative and critical theories of international relations. His current research, which focuses on harm in world politics, builds bridges between process sociology and International Relations. *The Problem of Harm in World Politics: Theoretical Investigations*, the first of three volumes on that subject, was published by Cambridge University Press in 2011.

Katie Liston holds a PhD in sociology from University College Dublin and has worked in the Irish and UK universities sector since 1999. She is currently a lecturer in the social sciences of sport and much of her research draws on the figurational sociological tradition. Together with Stephen Mennell, she edits *Figurations*, the newsletter for the Elias Foundation.

Steven Loyal is a Senior Lecturer in the School of Sociology, University College Dublin. His research interests include the sociology of migration, class and social stratification, and sociological theory. He has previously written on the work of Anthony Giddens, Pierre Bourdieu and Norbert Elias. His most recent book, *Understanding Immigration in Ireland: State, Capital and Labour in a Global Age,* is published by Manchester University Press.

Stephen Mennell is Professor Emeritus of Sociology at University College Dublin, from which he retired in 2009. He read economics at Cambridge (1963–66), and then spent the year 1966–67 in the old Department of Social Relations at Harvard, before teaching at the University of Exeter (1967–90) and at Monash University, Australia (1990–93). His books include *All Manners of Food: Eating and Taste in England and France from the Middle Ages to the Present* (1985), *Norbert Elias: Civilization and the Human Self-Image* (1989, paperback) *Norbert Elias: An Introduction* (1992, 1998), and *The American Civilizing Process* (2007). He holds the degrees of Doctor in de Sociale Wetenschappen (Amsterdam) and Doctor of Letters (Cambridge). He is a member of the board of the Norbert Elias Foundation, Amsterdam, of the Royal Netherlands Academy of Arts and Sciences, and of the Royal Irish Academy.

John Pratt is Professor of Criminology and The Royal Society of New Zealand James Cook Research Fellow in Social Science. He is also a Fellow at the Straus Institute for Advanced Studies of Law and Justice, New York University. His interests are in the history and sociology of punishment. His publications include *Punishment and Civilization* (2002) and *Penal Populism* (2007). He is currently writing a book explaining why Anglophone and Scandinavian penal systems are so different.

Stephen Quilley, technically a sociologist, has too great an interest in biology, human ecology and problems of 'deep time' to make conversation with conventional sociologists straightforward. With a research programme grounded in Eliasian sociology and a focus on long-term processes of social-ecological development, his research interests are varied, including urban regeneration and political economy, ecological economics, sustainability and social innovation. Having studied Social and Political Science (Cambridge University) and Russian and East European Studies (Birmingham), Quilley did his doctoral research on the political economy of urban regeneration (Manchester). After lecturing in sociology at University College Dublin, in 2006 he took up a position in environmental politics at Keele University.

Robert van Krieken is currently Professor of Sociology at University College Dublin, will be returning to the University of Sydney shortly. He is also a Vice-President of the International Sociological Association, as well as being on the editorial boards of *Law & Social Inquiry* and *Childhood*, and a European Science Foundation reviewer. He is the author of *Children and the State* (1991), *Norbert Elias* (1998), the lead author of the best-selling Australian sociology textbook, *Sociology* (2010), and a co-author of *Celebrity and the Law* (2010). His current research interests include sociological studies of law, social theory, the sociology of post-separation parenthood and childhood, globalization and deglobaliza-tion, multiculturalism and national identity, civilizing and decivilizing proc-esses, and the sociology of 'celebrity society'.

Wilbert van Vree is director of his own consultancy for improving meeting cultures and skills in organizations. He was formerly a lecturer in sociology at the University of Amsterdam. Among other publications he wrote *Meetings, Manners and Civilization: The Development of Modern Meeting Behaviour*, which won the Norbert Elias Prize in 2001.

Cas Wouters is a sociologist who has studied twentieth-century social and psychic processes, focusing on the regimes of manners and emotions in relationships between classes, sexes, and generations, and interpreted as a process of informalization. These studies resulted in numerous articles and books. Two recent books resulted from a study of changes in German, Dutch, English and American manners books: *Sex and Manners: Female Emancipation in the West 1890–2000* (Sage, 2004) and *Informalization: Manners and Emotions since 1890* (Sage, 2007).

Index